ISBN 0-8373-5307-6
7 COLLEGE LEVEL EXAMINATION SERIES/CLEP

 *New* **RUDMAN'S QUESTIONS AND ANSWERS ON THE...**

College-Level Examination Program Subject Test In...

COLLEGE ALGEBRA - TRIGONOMETRY

Test Preparation Study Guide

Questions and Answers

D1208370

NATIONAL LEARNING CORPORATION

PASSBOOK®

NOTICE

This book is *SOLELY* intended for, is sold *ONLY* to, and its use is *RESTRICTED* to *individual*, bona fide applicants or candidates who qualify by virtue of having seriously filed applications for appropriate license, certificate, professional and/or promotional advancement, higher school matriculation, scholarship, or other legitimate requirements of educational and/or governmental authorities.

This book is *NOT* intended for use, class instruction, tutoring, training, duplication, copying, reprinting, excerption, or adaptation, etc., by:

(1) Other Publishers

(2) Proprietors and/or Instructors of "Coaching" and/or Preparatory Courses

(3) Personnel and/or Training Divisions of commercial, industrial, and governmental organizations

(4) Schools, colleges, or universities and/or their departments and staffs, including teachers and other personnel

(5) Testing Agencies or Bureaus

(6) Study groups which seek by the purchase of a single volume to copy and/or duplicate and/or adapt this material for use by the group as a whole without having purchased individual volumes for each of the members of the group

(7) Et al.

Such persons would be in violation of appropriate Federal and State statutes.

PROVISION OF LICENSING AGREEMENTS. — Recognized educational commercial, industrial, and governmental institutions and organizations, and others legitimately engaged in educational pursuits, including training, testing, and measurement activities, may address a request for a licensing agreement to the copyright owners, who will determine whether, and under what conditions, including fees and charges, the materials in this book may be used by them. In other words, a licensing facility *exists* for the legitimate use of the material in this book on other than an individual basis. However, it is asseverated and affirmed here that the materials in this book *CANNOT* be used without the receipt of the express permission of such a licensing agreement from the Publishers.

NATIONAL LEARNING CORPORATION
212 Michael Drive
Syosset, New York 11791

Inquiries re licensing agreements should be addressed to:
The President
National Learning Corporation
212 Michael Drive
Syosset, New York 11791

PASSBOOK SERIES®

THE *PASSBOOK SERIES®* has been created to prepare applicants and candidates for the ultimate academic battlefield – the examination room.

At some time in our lives, each and every one of us may be required to take an examination – for validation, matriculation, admission, qualification, registration, certification, or licensure.

Based on the assumption that every applicant or candidate has met the basic formal educational standards, has taken the required number of courses, and read the necessary texts, the *PASSBOOK SERIES®* furnishes the one special preparation which may assure passing with confidence, instead of failing with insecurity. Examination questions – together with answers – are furnished as the basic vehicle for study so that the mysteries of the examination and its compounding difficulties may be eliminated or diminished by a sure method.

This book is meant to help you pass your examination provided that you qualify and are serious in your objective.

The entire field is reviewed through the huge store of content information which is succinctly presented through a provocative and challenging approach – the question-and-answer method.

A climate of success is established by furnishing the correct answers at the end of each test.

You soon learn to recognize types of questions, forms of questions, and patterns of questioning. You may even begin to anticipate expected outcomes.

You perceive that many questions are repeated or adapted so that you can gain acute insights, which may enable you to score many sure points.

You learn how to confront new questions, or types of questions, and to attack them confidently and work out the correct answers.

You note objectives and emphases, and recognize pitfalls and dangers, so that you may make positive educational adjustments.

Moreover, you are kept fully informed in relation to new concepts, methods, practices, and directions in the field.

You discover that you are actually taking the examination all the time: you are preparing for the examination by "taking" an examination, not by reading extraneous and/or supererogatory textbooks.

In short, this PASSBOOK®, used directedly, should be an important factor in helping you to pass your test.

NONTRADITIONAL EDUCATION

Students returning to school as adults bring more varied experience to their studies than do the teenagers who begin college shortly after graduating from high school. As a result, there are numerous programs for students with nontraditional learning curves. Hundreds of colleges and universities grant degrees to people who cannot attend classes at a regular campus or have already learned what the college is supposed to teach.

You can earn nontraditional education credits in many ways:

- Passing standardized exams
- Demonstrating knowledge gained through experience
- Completing campus-based coursework, and
- Taking courses off campus

Some methods of assessing learning for credit are objective, such as standardized tests. Others are more subjective, such as a review of life experiences.

With some help from four hypothetical characters – Alice, Vin, Lynette, and Jorge – this article describes nontraditional ways of earning educational credit. It begins by describing programs in which you can earn a high school diploma without spending 4 years in a classroom. The college picture is more complicated, so it is presented in two parts: one on gaining credit for what you know through course work or experience, and a second on college degree programs. The final section lists resources for locating more information.

Earning High School Credit

People who were prevented from finishing high school as teenagers have several options if they want to do so as adults. Some major cities have back-to-school programs that allow adults to attend high school classes with current students. But the more practical alternatives for most adults are to take the General Educational Development (GED) tests or to earn a high school diploma by demonstrating their skills or taking correspondence classes.

Of course, these options do not match the experience of staying in high school and graduating with one's friends. But they are viable alternatives for adult learners committed to meeting and, often, continuing their educational goals.

GED Program

Alice quit high school her sophomore year and took a job to help support herself, her younger brother, and their newly widowed mother. Now an adult, she wants to earn her high school diploma – and then go on to college. Because her job as head cook and her family responsibilities keep her busy during the day, she plans to get a high school equivalency diploma. She will study for, and take, the GED tests. Every year, about half a million adults earn their high school credentials this way. A GED diploma is accepted in lieu of a high school one by more than 90 percent of employers, colleges, and universities, so it is a good choice for someone like Alice.

The GED testing program is sponsored by the American Council on Education and State and local education departments. It consists of examinations in five subject areas: Writing, science, mathematics, social studies, and literature and the arts. The tests also measure skills such as analytical ability, problem solving, reading comprehension, and ability to understand and apply information. Most of the questions are multiple choice; the writing test includes an essay section on a topic of general interest.

Eligibility rules for taking the exams vary, but some states require that you must be at least 18. Tests are given in English, Spanish, and French. In addition to standard print, versions in large print, Braille, and audiocassette are also available. Total time allotted for the tests is 7 1/2 hours.

The GED tests are not easy. About one-fourth of those who complete the exams every year do not pass. Passing scores are established by administering the tests to a sample of graduating high school seniors. The minimum standard score is set so that about one-third of graduating seniors would not pass the tests if they took them.

Because of the difficulty of the tests, people need to prepare themselves to take them. Often, they start by taking the Official GED Practice Tests, usually available through a local adult education center. Centers are listed in your phone book's blue pages under "Adult Education," "Continuing Education," or "GED." Adult education centers also have information about GED preparation classes and self-study materials. Classes are generally arranged to accommodate adults' work schedules. National Learning Corporation publishes several study guides that aim to thoroughly prepare test-takers for the GED.

School districts, colleges, adult education centers, and community organizations have information about GED testing schedules and practice tests. For more information, contact them, your nearest GED testing center, or:

GED Testing Service
One Dupont Circle, NW, Suite 250
Washington, DC 20036-1163
1(800) 62-MY GED (626-9433)
(202) 939-9490

Skills Demonstration

Adults who have acquired high school level skills through experience might be eligible for the National External Diploma Program. This alternative to the GED does not involve any direct instruction. Instead, adults seeking a high school diploma must demonstrate mastery of 65 competencies in 8 general areas: Communication; computation; occupational preparedness; and self, social, consumer, scientific, and technological awareness.

Mastery is shown through the completion of the tasks. For example, a participant could prove competency in computation by measuring a room for carpeting, figuring out the amount of carpet needed, and computing the cost.

Before being accepted for the program, adults undergo an evaluation. Tests taken at one of the program's offices measure reading, writing, and mathematics abilities. A take-home segment includes a self-assessment of current skills, an individual skill evaluation, and an occupational interest and aptitude test.

Adults accepted for the program have weekly meetings with an assessor. At the meeting, the assessor reviews the participant's work from the previous week. If the task has not been completed properly, the assessor explains the mistake. Participants continue to correct their errors until they master each competency. A high school diploma is awarded upon proven mastery of all 65 competencies.

Fourteen States and the District of Columbia now offer the External Diploma Program. For more information, contact:

External Diploma Program
One Dupont Circle, NW, Suite 250
Washington, DC 20036-1193
(202) 939-9475

Correspondence and Distance Study

Vin dropped out of high school during his junior year because his family's frequent moves made it difficult for him to continue his studies. He promised himself at the time he dropped out that he would someday finish the courses needed for his diploma. For people like Vin, who prefer to earn a traditional diploma in a nontraditional way, there are about a dozen accredited courses of study for earning a high school diploma by correspondence, or distance study. The programs are either privately run, affiliated with a university, or administered by a State education department.

Distance study diploma programs have no residency requirements, allowing students to continue their studies from almost any location. Depending on the course of study, students need not be enrolled full time and usually have more flexible schedules for finishing their work. Selection of courses ranges from vo-tech to college prep, and some programs place different emphasis on the types of diplomas offered. University affiliated schools, for example, allow qualified students to take college courses along with their high school ones. Students can then apply the college credits toward a degree at that university or transfer them to another institution.

Taking courses by distance study is often more challenging and time consuming than attending classes, especially for adults who have other obligations. Success depends on each student's motivation. Students usually do reading assignments on their own. Written exercises, which they complete and send to an instructor for grading, supplement their reading material.

A list of some accredited high schools that offer diplomas by distance study is available free from the Distance Education and Training Council, formerly known as the National Home Study Council. Request the "DETC Directory of Accredited Institutions" from:

The Distance Education and Training Council
1601 18th Street, NW.
Washington, DC 20009-2529
(202) 234-5100

Some publications profiling nontraditional college programs include addresses and descriptions of several high school correspondence ones. See the Resources section at the end of this article for more information.

Getting College Credit For What You Know

Adults can receive college credit for prior coursework, by passing examinations, and documenting experiential learning. With help from a college advisor, nontraditional students should assess their skills, establish their educational goals, and determine the number of college credits they might be eligible for.

Even before you meet with a college advisor, you should collect all your school and training records. Then, make a list of all knowledge and abilities acquired through experience, no matter how irrelevant they seem to your chosen field. Next, determine your educational goals: What specific field do you wish to study? What kind of a degree do you want? Finally, determine how your past work fits into the field of study. Later on, you will evaluate educational programs to find one that's right for you.

People who have complex educational or experiential learning histories might want to have their learning evaluated by the Regents Credit Bank. The Credit Bank, operated by Regents College of the University of the State of New York, allows people to consolidate credits earned through college, experience, or other methods. Special assessments are available for Regents College enrollees whose knowledge in a specific field cannot be adequately evaluated by standardized exams. For more information, contact the Regents Credit Bank at:

Regents College
7 Columbia Circle
Albany, NY 12203-5159
(518) 464-8500

Credit For Prior College Coursework

When Lynette was in college during the 1970s, she attended several different schools and took a variety of courses. She did well in some classes and poorly in others. Now that she is a successful business owner and has more focus, Lynette thinks she should forget about her previous coursework and start from scratch. Instead, she should start from where she is.

Lynette should have all her transcripts sent to the colleges or universities of her choice and let an admissions officer determine which classes are applicable toward a degree. A few credits here and there may not seem like much, but they add up. Even if the subjects do not seem relevant to any major, they might be counted as elective credits toward a degree. And comparing the cost of transcripts with the cost of college courses, it makes sense to spend a few dollars per transcript for a chance to save hundreds, and perhaps thousands, of dollars in books and tuition.

Rules for transferring credits apply to all prior coursework at accredited colleges and universities, whether done on campus or off. Courses completed off campus, often called extended learning, include those available to students through independent study and correspondence. Many schools have extended learning programs; Brigham Young University, for example, offers more than 300 courses through its Department of Independent Study. One type of extended learning is distance learning, a form of correspondence study by technological means such as television, video and audio, CD-ROM, electronic mail, and computer tutorials. See the Resources section at the end of this article for more information about publications available from the National University Continuing Education Association.

Any previously earned college credits should be considered for transfer, no matter what the subject or the grade received. Many schools do not accept the transfer of courses graded below a C or ones taken more than a designated number of years ago. Some colleges and universities also have limits on the number of credits that can be transferred and applied toward a degree. But not all do. For example, Thomas Edison State College, New Jersey's State college for adults, accepts the transfer of all 120 hours of credit required for a baccalaureate degree – provided all the credits are transferred from regionally accredited schools, no more than 80 are at the junior college level, and the student's grades overall and in the field of study average out to C.

To assign credit for prior coursework, most schools require original transcripts. This means you must complete a form or send a written, signed request to have your transcripts released directly to a college or university. Once you have chosen the schools you want to apply to, contact the schools you attended before. Find out how much each transcript costs, and ask them to send your transcripts to the ones you are applying to. Write a letter that includes your name (and names used during attendance, if different) and dates of attendance, along with the names and addresses of the schools to which your transcripts should be sent. Include payment and mail to the registrar at the schools you have attended. The registrar's office will process your request and send an official transcript of your coursework to the colleges or universities you have designated.

Credit For Noncollege Courses

Colleges and universities are not the only ones that offer classes. Volunteer organizations and employers often provide formal training worth college credit. The American Council on Education has two programs that assess thousands of specific courses and make recommendations on the amount of college credit they are worth. Colleges and universities accept the recommendations or use them as guidelines.

One program evaluates educational courses sponsored by government agencies, business and industry, labor unions, and professional and voluntary organizations. It is the Program on Noncollegiate Sponsored Instruction (PONSI). Some of the training seminars Alice has participated in covered topics such as food preparation, kitchen safety, and nutrition. Although she has not yet earned her GED, Alice can earn college credit because of her completion of these formal job-training seminars. The number of credits each seminar is worth does not hinge on Alice's current eligibility for college enrollment.

The other program evaluates courses offered by the Army, Navy, Air Force, Marines, Coast Guard, and Department of Defense. It is the Military Evaluations Program. Jorge has never attended college, but the engineering technology classes he completed as part of his military training are worth college credit. And as an Army veteran, Jorge is eligible for a service that takes the evaluations one step further. The Army/American Council on Education Registry Transcript System (AARTS) will provide Jorge with an individualized transcript of American Council on Education credit recommendations for all courses he completed, the military occupational specialties (MOS's) he held, and examinations he passed while in the Army. All Army and National Guard enlisted personnel and veterans who enlisted after October 1981 are eligible for the transcript. Similar services are being considered by the Navy and Marine Corps.

To obtain a free transcript, see your Army Education Center for a 5454R transcript request form. Include your name, Social Security number, basic active service date, and complete address where you want the transcript sent. Mail your request to:

AARTS Operations Center
415 McPherson Ave.
Fort Leavenworth, KS 66027-1373

Recommendations for PONSI are published in *The National Guide to Educational Credit for Training Programs;* military program recommendations are in *The Guide to the Evaluation of Educational Experiences in the Armed Forces.* See the Resources section at the end of this article for more information about these publications.

Former military personnel who took a foreign language course through the Defense Language Institute may request course transcripts by sending their name, Social Security number, course title, duration of the course, and graduation date to:

Commandant, Defense Language Institute
Attn: ATFL-DAA-AR
Transcripts
Presidio of Monterey
Monterey, CA 93944-5006

Not all of Jorge's and Alice's courses have been assessed by the American Council on Education. Training courses that have no Council credit recommendation should still be assessed by an advisor at the schools they want to attend. Course descriptions, class notes, test scores, and other documentation may be helpful for comparing training courses to their college equivalents. An oral examination or other demonstration of competency might also be required.

There is no guarantee you will receive all the credits you are seeking – but you certainly won't if you make no attempt.

Credit By Examination

Standardized tests are the best-known method of receiving college credit without taking courses. These exams are often taken by high school students seeking advanced placement for college, but they are also available to adult learners. Testing programs and colleges and universities offer exams in a number of subjects. Two U.S. Government institutes have foreign language exams for employees that also may be worth college credit.

It is important to understand that receiving a passing score on these exams does not mean you get college credit automatically. Each school determines which test results it will accept, minimum scores required, how scores are converted for credit, and the amount of credit, if any, to be assigned. Most colleges and universities accept the American Council on Education credit recommendations, published every other year in the 250-page *Guide to Educational Credit by Examination.* For more information, contact:

The American Council on Education
Credit by Examination Program
One Dupont Circle, Suite 250
Washington, DC 20036-1193
(202) 939-9434

Testing programs:

You might know some of the five national testing programs by their acronyms or initials: CLEP, ACT PEP: RCE, DANTES, AP, and NOCTI. (The meanings of these initialisms are explained below.) There is some overlap among programs; for example, four of them have introductory accounting exams. Since you will not be awarded credit more than once for a specific subject, you should carefully evaluate each program for the subject exams you wish to take. And before taking an exam, make sure you will be awarded credit by the college or university you plan to attend.

CLEP (College-Level Examination Program), administered by the College Board, is the most widely accepted of the national testing programs; more than 2,800 accredited schools award credit for passing exam scores. Each test covers material taught in basic undergraduate courses. There are five general exams – English composition, humanities, college mathematics, natural sciences, and social sciences and history – and many subject exams. Most exams are entirely multiple-choice, but English composition exams may include an essay section. For more information, contact:

CLEP
P.O. Box 6600
Princeton, NJ 08541-6600
(609) 771-7865

ACT PEP: RCE (American College Testing Proficiency Exam Program: Regents College Examinations) tests are given in 38 subjects within arts and sciences, business, education, and nursing. Each exam is recommended for either lower- or upper-level credit. Exams contain either objective or extended response questions, and are graded according to a standard score, letter grade, or pass/fail. Fees vary, depending on the subject and type of exam. For more information or to request free study guides, contact:

ACT PEP: Regents College Examinations
P.O. Box 4014
Iowa City, IA 52243
(319) 337-1387
(New York State residents must contact Regents College directly.)

DANTES (Defense Activity for Nontraditional Education Support) standardized tests are developed by the Educational Testing Service for the Department of Defense. Originally administered only to military personnel, the exams have been available to the public since 1983. About 50 subject tests cover business, mathematics, social science, physical science, humanities, foreign languages, and applied technology. Most of the tests consist entirely of multiple-choice questions. Schools determine their own administering fees and testing schedules. For more information or to request free study sheets, contact:

DANTES Program Office
Mail Stop 31-X
Educational Testing Service
Princeton, NJ 08541
1(800) 257-9484

The AP (Advanced Placement) Program is a cooperative effort between secondary schools and colleges and universities. AP exams are developed each year by committees of college and high school faculty appointed by the College Board and assisted by consultants from the Educational Testing Service. Subjects include arts and languages, natural sciences, computer science, social sciences, history, and mathematics. Most tests are 2 or 3 hours long and include both multiple-choice and essay questions. AP courses are available to help students prepare for exams, which are offered in the spring. For more information about the Advanced Placement Program, contact:

Advanced Placement Services
P.O. Box 6671
Princeton, NJ 08541-6671
(609) 771-7300

NOCTI (National Occupational Competency Testing Institute) assessments are designed for people like Alice, who have vocational-technical skills that cannot be evaluated by other tests. NOCTI assesses competency at two levels: Student/job ready and teacher/experienced worker. Standardized evaluations are available for occupations such as auto-body repair, electronics, mechanical drafting, quantity food preparation, and upholstering. The tests consist of multiple-choice questions and a performance component. Other services include workshops, customized assessments, and pre-testing. For more information, contact:

NOCTI
500 N. Bronson Ave.
Ferris State University
Big Rapids, MI 49307
(616) 796-4699

Colleges and universities:

Many colleges and universities have credit-by-exam programs, through which students earn credit by passing a comprehensive exam for a course offered by the institution. Among the most widely recognized are the programs at Ohio University, the University of North Carolina, Thomas Edison State College, and New York University.

Ohio University offers about 150 examinations for credit. In addition, you may sometimes arrange to take special examinations in non-laboratory courses offered at Ohio University. To take a test for credit, you must enroll in the course. If you plan to transfer the credit earned, you also need written permission from an official at your school. Books and study materials are available, for a cost, through the university. Exams must be taken within 6 months of the enrollment date; most last 3 hours. You may arrange to take the exam off campus if you do not live near the university.

Ohio University is on the quarter-hour system; most courses are worth 4 quarter hours, the equivalent of 3 semester hours. For more information, contact:

Independent Study
Tupper Hall 302
Ohio University
Athens, OH 45701-2979
1(800) 444-2910
(614) 593-2910

The University of North Carolina offers a credit-by-examination option for 140 independent study (correspondence) courses in foreign languages, humanities, social sciences, mathematics, business administration, education, electrical and computer engineering, health administration, and natural sciences. To take an exam, you must request and receive approval from both the course instructor and the independent studies department. Exams must be taken within six months of enrollment, and you may register for no more than two at a time. If you are not near the University's Chapel Hill campus, you may take your exam under supervision at an accredited college, university, community college, or technical institute. For more information, contact:

Independent Studies
CB #1020, The Friday Center
UNC-Chapel Hill
Chapel Hill, NC 27599-1020
1(800) 862-5669 / (919) 962-1134

The Thomas Edison College Examination Program offers more than 50 exams in liberal arts, business, and professional areas. Thomas Edison State College administers tests twice a month in Trenton, New Jersey; however, students may arrange to take their tests with a proctor at any accredited American college or university or U.S. military base. Most of the tests are multiple choice; some also include short answer or essay questions. Time limits range from 90 minutes to 4 hours, depending on the exam. For more information, contact:

Thomas Edison State College
TECEP, Office of Testing and Assessment
101 W. State Street
Trenton, NJ 08608-1176
(609) 633-2844

New York University's Foreign Language Program offers proficiency exams in more than 40 languages, from Albanian to Yiddish. Two exams are available in each language: The 12-point test is equivalent to 4 undergraduate semesters, and the 16-point exam may lead to upper level credit. The tests are given at the university's Foreign Language Department throughout the year.

Proof of foreign language proficiency does not guarantee college credit. Some colleges and universities accept transcripts only for languages commonly taught, such as French and Spanish. Nontraditional programs are more likely than traditional ones to grant credit for proficiency in other languages.

For an informational brochure and registration form for NYU's foreign language proficiency exams, contact:

New York University
Foreign Language Department
48 Cooper Square, Room 107
New York, NY 10003
(212) 998-7030

Government institutes:

The Defense Language Institute and Foreign Service Institute administer foreign language proficiency exams for personnel stationed abroad. Usually, the tests are given at the end of intensive language courses or upon completion of service overseas. But some people – like Jorge, who knows Spanish – speak another language fluently and may be allowed to take a proficiency exam in that language before completing their tour of duty. Contact one of the offices listed below to obtain transcripts of those scores. Proof of proficiency does not guarantee college credit, however, as discussed above.

To request score reports from the Defense Language Institute for Defense Language Proficiency Tests, send your name, Social Security number, language for which you were tested, and, most importantly, when and where you took the exam to:

Commandant, Defense Language Institute
Attn: ATFL-ES-T
DLPT Score Report Request
Presidio of Monterey
Monterey, CA 93944-5006

To request transcripts of scores for Foreign Service Institute exams, send your name, Social Security number, language for which you were tested, and dates or year of exams to:

Foreign Service Institute
Arlington Hall
4020 Arlington Boulevard
Rosslyn, VA 22204-1500
Attn: Testing Office (Send your request to the attention of the testing office of the foreign language in which you were tested)

Credit For Experience

Experiential learning credit may be given for knowledge gained through job responsibilities, personal hobbies, volunteer opportunities, homemaking, and other experiences. Colleges and universities base credit awards on the knowledge you have attained, not for the experience alone. In addition, the knowledge must be college level; not just any learning will do. Throwing horseshoes as a hobby is not likely to be worth college credit. But if you've done research on how and where the sport originated, visited blacksmiths, organized tournaments, and written a column for a trade journal – well, that's a horseshoe of a different color.

Adults attempting to get credit for their experience should be forewarned: Having your experience evaluated for college credit is time-consuming, tedious work – not an easy shortcut for people who want quick-fix college credits. And not all experience, no matter how valuable, is the equivalent of college courses.

Requesting college credit for your experiential learning can be tricky. You should get assistance from a credit evaluations officer at the school you plan to attend, but you should also have a general idea of what your knowledge is worth. A common method for converting knowledge into credit is to use a college catalog. Find course titles and descriptions that match what you have learned through experience, and request the number of credits offered for those courses.

Once you know what credit to ask for, you must usually present your case in writing to officials at the college you plan to attend. The most common form of presenting experiential learning for credit is the portfolio. A portfolio is a written record of your knowledge along with a request for equivalent college credit. It includes an identification and description of the knowledge for which you are requesting credit, an explanatory essay of how the knowledge was gained and how it fits into your educational plans, documentation that you have acquired such knowledge, and a request for college credit. Required elements of a portfolio vary by schools but generally follow those guidelines.

In identifying knowledge you have gained, be specific about exactly what you have learned. For example, it is not enough for Lynette to say she runs a business. She must identify the knowledge she has gained from running it, such as personnel management, tax law, marketing strategy, and inventory review. She must also include brief descriptions about her knowledge of each to support her claims of having those skills.

The essay gives you a chance to relay something about who you are. It should address your educational goals, include relevant autobiographical details, and be well organized, neat, and convey confidence. In his essay, Jorge might first state his goal of becoming an engineer. Then he would explain why he joined the Army, where he got hands-on training and experience in developing and servicing electronic equipment.

This, he would say, led to his hobby of creating remote-controlled model cars, of which he has built 20. His conclusion would highlight his accomplishments and tie them to his desire to become an electronic engineer.

Documentation is evidence that you've learned what you claim to have learned. You can show proof of knowledge in a variety of ways, including audio or video recordings, letters from current or former employers describing your specific duties and job performance, blueprints, photographs or artwork, and transcripts of certifying exams for professional licenses and certification – such as Alice's certification from the American Culinary Federation. Although documentation can take many forms, written proof alone is not always enough. If it is impossible to document your knowledge in writing, find out if your experiential learning can be assessed through supplemental oral exams by a faculty expert.

Earning a College Degree

Nontraditional students often have work, family, and financial obligations that prevent them from quitting their jobs to attend school full time. Can they still meet their educational goals? Yes.

More than 150 accredited colleges and universities have nontraditional bachelor's degree programs that require students to spend little or no time on campus; over 300 others have nontraditional campus-based degree programs. Some of those schools, as well as most junior and community colleges, offer associate's degrees nontraditionally. Each school with a nontraditional course of study determines its own rules for awarding credit for prior coursework, exams, or experience, as discussed previously. Most have charges on top of tuition for providing these special services.

Several publications profile nontraditional degree programs; see the Resources section at the end of this article for more information. To determine which school best fits your academic profile and educational goals, first list your criteria. Then, evaluate nontraditional programs based on their accreditation, features, residency requirements, and expenses. Once you have chosen several schools to explore further, write to them for more information. Detailed explanations of school policies should help you decide which ones you want to apply to.

Get beyond the printed word – especially the glowing words each school writes about itself. Check out the schools you are considering with higher education authorities, alumni, employers, family members, and friends. If possible, visit the campus to talk to students and instructors and sit in on a few classes, even if you will be completing most or all of your work off campus. Ask school officials questions about such things as enrollment numbers, graduation rate, faculty qualifications, and confusing details about the application process or academic policies. After you have thoroughly investigated each prospective college or university, you can make an informed decision about which is right for you.

Accreditation

Accreditation is a process colleges and universities submit to voluntarily for getting their credentials. An accredited school has been investigated and visited by teams of observers and has periodic inspections by a private accrediting agency. The initial review can take two years or more.

Regional agencies accredit entire schools, and professional agencies accredit either specialized schools or departments within schools. Although there are no national accrediting standards, not just any accreditation will do. Countless "accreditation associations" have been invented by schools, many of which have no academic programs and sell phony degrees, to accredit themselves. But 6 regional and about 80 professional accrediting associations in the United States are recognized by the U.S. Department of Education or the Commission on Recognition of Postsecondary Accreditation. When checking accreditation, these are the names to look for. For more information about accreditation and accrediting agencies, contact:

Institutional Participation Oversight Service Accreditation and State Liaison Division
U.S. Department of Education
ROB 3, Room 3915
600 Independence Ave., SW
Washington, DC 20202-5244
(202) 708-7417

Because accreditation is not mandatory, lack of accreditation does not necessarily mean a school or program is bad. Some schools choose not to apply for accreditation, are in the process of applying, or have educational methods too unconventional for an accrediting association's standards. For the nontraditional student, however, earning a degree from a college or university with recognized accreditation is an especially important consideration. Although nontraditional education is becoming more widely accepted, it is not yet mainstream. Employers skeptical of a degree earned in a nontraditional manner are likely to be even less accepting of one from an unaccredited school.

Program Features
Because nontraditional students have diverse educational objectives, nontraditional schools are diverse in what they offer. Some programs are geared toward helping students organize their scattered educational credits to get a degree as quickly as possible. Others cater to those who may have specific credits or experience but need assistance in completing requirements. Whatever your educational profile, you should look for a program that works with you in obtaining your educational goals.

A few nontraditional programs have special admissions policies for adult learners like Alice, who plan to earn their GEDs but want to enroll in college in the meantime. Other features of nontraditional programs include individualized learning agreements, intensive academic counseling, cooperative learning and internship placement, and waiver of some prerequisites or other requirements – as well as college credit for prior coursework, examinations, and experiential learning, all discussed previously.

Lynette, whose primary goal is to finish her degree, wants to earn maximum credits for her business experience. She will look for programs that do not limit the number of credits awarded for equivalency exams and experiential learning. And since well-documented proof of knowledge is essential for earning experiential learning credits, Lynette should make sure the program she chooses provides assistance to students submitting a portfolio.

Jorge, on the other hand, has more credits than he needs in certain areas and is willing to forego some. To become an engineer, he must have a bachelor's degree; but because he is accustomed to hands-on learning, Jorge is interested in getting experience as he gains more technical skills. He will concentrate on finding schools with strong cooperative education, supervised fieldwork, or internship programs.

Residency Requirements

Programs are sometimes deemed nontraditional because of their residency requirements. Many people think of residency for colleges and universities in terms of tuition, with in-state students paying less than out-of-state ones. Residency also may refer to where a student lives, either on or off campus, while attending school.

But in nontraditional education, residency usually refers to how much time students must spend on campus, regardless of whether they attend classes there. In some nontraditional programs, students need not ever step foot on campus. Others require only a very short residency, such as one day or a few weeks. Many schools have standard residency requirements of several semesters but schedule classes for evenings or weekends to accommodate working adults.

Lynette, who previously took courses by independent study, prefers to earn credits by distance study. She will focus on schools that have no residency requirement. Several colleges and universities have nonresident degree completion programs for adults with some college credit. Under the direction of a faculty advisor, students devise a plan for earning their remaining credits. Methods for earning credits include independent study, distance learning, seminars, supervised fieldwork, and group study at arranged sites. Students may have to earn a certain number of credits through the degree-granting institution. But many programs allow students to take courses at accredited schools of their choice for transfer toward their degree.

Alice wants to attend lectures but has an unpredictable schedule. Her best course of action will be to seek out short residency programs that require students to attend seminars once or twice a semester. She can take courses that are televised and videotape them to watch when her schedule permits, with the seminars helping to ensure that she properly completes her coursework. Many colleges and universities with short residency requirements also permit students to earn some credits elsewhere, by whatever means the student chooses.

Some fields of study require classroom instruction. As Jorge will discover, few colleges and universities allow students to earn a bachelor's degree in engineering entirely through independent study. Nontraditional residency programs are designed to accommodate adults' daytime work schedules. Jorge should look for programs offering evening, weekend, summer, and accelerated courses.

Tuition and Other Expenses

The final decisions about which schools Alice, Jorge, and Lynette attend may hinge in large part on a single issue: Cost. And rising tuition is only part of the equation. Beginning with application fees and continuing through graduation fees, college expenses add up.

Traditional and nontraditional students have some expenses in common, such as the cost of books and other materials. Tuition might even be the same for some courses, especially for colleges and universities offering standard ones at unusual times. But for nontraditional programs, students may also pay fees for services such as credit or transcript review, evaluation, advisement, and portfolio assessment.

Students are also responsible for postage and handling or setup expenses for independent study courses, as well as for all examination and transcript fees for transferring credits. Usually, the more nontraditional the program, the more detailed the fees. Some schools charge a yearly enrollment fee rather than tuition for degree completion candidates who want their files to remain active.

Although tuition and fees might seem expensive, most educators tell you not to let money come between you and your educational goals. Talk to someone in the financial aid department of the school you plan to attend or check your library for publications about financial aid sources. The U.S. Department of Education publishes a guide to Federal aid programs such as Pell Grants, student loans, and work-study. To order the free 74-page booklet, *The Student Guide: Financial Aid from the U.S. Department of Education,* contact:

Federal Student Aid Information Center
P.O. Box 84
Washington, DC 20044
1 (800) 4FED-AID (433-3243)

Resources

Information on how to earn a high school diploma or college degree without following the usual routes is available from several organizations and in numerous publications. Information on nontraditional graduate degree programs, available for master's through doctoral level, though not discussed in this article, can usually be obtained from the same resources that detail bachelor's degree programs.

National Learning Corporation publishes study guides for all of these exams, for both general examinations and tests in specific subject areas. To order study guides, or to browse their catalog featuring more than 5,000 titles, visit NLC online at www.passbooks.com, or contact them by phone at (800) 632-8888.

Organizations

Adult learners should always contact their local school system, community college, or university to learn about programs that are readily available. The following national organizations can also supply information:

American Council on Education
One Dupont Circle
Washington, DC 20036-1193
(202) 939-9300

Within the American Council on Education, the Center for Adult Learning and Educational Credentials administers the National External Diploma Program, the GED Program, the Program on Noncollegiate Sponsored Instruction, the Credit by Examination Program, and the Military Evaluations Program.

College-Level Examination Program (CLEP)

1. WHAT IS CLEP?

CLEP stands for the College-Level Examination Program, sponsored by the College Board. It is a national program of credit-by-examination that offers you the opportunity to obtain recognition for college-level achievement. No matter when, where, or how you have learned – by means of formal or informal study – you can take CLEP tests. If the results are acceptable to your college, you can receive credit.

You may not realize it, but you probably know more than your academic record reveals. Each day you, like most people, have an opportunity to learn. In private industry and business, as well as at all levels of government, learning opportunities continually occur. If you read widely or intensively in a particular field, think about what you read, discuss it with your family and friends, you are learning. Or you may be learning on a more formal basis by taking a correspondence course, a television or radio course, a course recorded on tape or cassettes, a course assembled into programmed tests, or a course taught in your community adult school or high school.

No matter how, where, or when you gained your knowledge, you may have the opportunity to receive academic credit for your achievement that can be counted toward an undergraduate degree. The College-Level Examination Program (CLEP) enables colleges to evaluate your achievement and give you credit. A wide range of college-level examinations are offered by CLEP to anyone who wishes to take them. Scores on the tests are reported to you and, if you wish, to a college, employer, or individual.

2. WHAT ARE THE PURPOSES OF THE COLLEGE-LEVEL EXAMINATION PROGRAM?

The basic purpose of the College-Level Examination Program is to enable individuals who have acquired their education in nontraditional ways to demonstrate their academic achievement. It is also intended for use by those in higher education, business, industry, government, and other fields who need a reliable method of assessing a person's educational level.

Recognizing that the real issue is not how a person has acquired his education but what education he has, the College Level Examination Program has been designed to serve a variety of purposes. The basic purpose, as listed above, is to enable those who have reached the college level of education in nontraditional ways to assess the level of their achievement and to use the test results in seeking college credit or placement.

In addition, scores on the tests can be used to validate educational experience obtained at a nonaccredited institution or through noncredit college courses.

Some colleges and universities may use the tests to measure the level of educational achievement of their students, and for various institutional research purposes.

Other colleges and universities may wish to use the tests in the admission, placement, and guidance of students who wish to transfer from one institution to another.

Businesses, industries, governmental agencies, and professional groups now accept the results of these tests as a basis for advancement, eligibility for further training, or professional or semi-professional certification.

Many people are interested in the examination simply to assess their own educational progress and attainment.

The college, university, business, industry, or government agency that adopts the tests in the College-Level Examination Program makes its own decision about how it will use and interpret the test scores. The College Board will provide the tests, score them, and report the results either to the individuals who took the tests or the college or agency that administered them. It does NOT, and cannot, award college credit, certify college equivalency, or make recommendations regarding the standards these institutions should establish for the use of the test results.

Therefore, if you are taking the tests to secure credit from an institution, you should FIRST ascertain whether the college or agency involved will accept the scores. Each institution determines which CLEP tests it will accept for credit and the amount of credit it will award. If you want to take tests for college credit, first call, write, or visit the college you wish to attend to inquire about its policy on CLEP scores, as well as its other admission requirements.

The services of the program are also available to people who have been requested to take the tests by an employer, a professional licensing agency, a certifying agency, or by other groups that recognize college equivalency on the basis of satisfactory CLEP scores. You may, of course, take the tests SOLELY for your own information. If you do, your scores will be reported only to you.

While neither CLEP nor the College Board can evaluate previous credentials or award college credit, you will receive, with your scores, basic information to help you interpret your performance on the tests you have taken.

3. WHAT ARE THE COLLEGE-LEVEL EXAMINATIONS?

In order to meet different kinds of curricular organization and testing needs at colleges and universities, the College-Level Examination Program offers 35 different subject tests falling under five separate general categories: Composition and Literature, Foreign Languages, History and Social Sciences, Science and Mathematics, and Business.

4. WHAT ARE THE SUBJECT EXAMINATIONS?

The 35 CLEP tests offered by the College Board are listed below:

COMPOSITION AND LITERATURE:
- American Literature
- Analyzing and Interpreting Literature
- English Composition
- English Composition with Essay
- English Literature
- Freshman College Composition
- Humanities

FOREIGN LANGUAGES
- French
- German
- Spanish

HISTORY AND SOCIAL SCIENCES
- American Government
- Introduction to Educational Psychology
- History of the United States I: Early Colonization to 1877
- History of the United States II: 1865 to the Present
- Human Growth and Development
- Principles of Macroeconomics
- Principles of Microeconomics
- Introductory Psychology
- Social Sciences and History
- Introductory Sociology
- Western Civilization I: Ancient Near East to 1648
- Western Civilization II: 1648 to the Present

SCIENCE AND MATHEMATICS
- College Algebra
- College Algebra-Trigonometry
- Biology
- Calculus
- Chemistry
- College Mathematics
- Natural Sciences
- Trigonometry
- Precalculus (*available 2006)

BUSINESS
- Principles of Accounting
- Introductory Business Law
- Information Systems and Computer Applications
- Principles of Management
- Principles of Marketing

CLEP Examinations cover material taught in courses that most students take as requirements in the first two years of college. A college usually grants the same amount of credit to students earning satisfactory scores on the CLEP examination as it grants to students successfully completing the equivalent course.

Many examinations are designed to correspond to one-semester courses; some, however, correspond to full-year or two-year courses.

Each exam is 90 minutes long and, except for English Composition with Essay, is made up primarily of multiple-choice questions. Some tests have several other types of questions besides multiple choice. To see a more detailed description of a particular CLEP exam, visit www.collegeboard.com/clep.

The English Composition with Essay exam is the only exam that includes a required essay. This essay is scored by college English faculty designated by CLEP and does not require an additional fee. However, other Composition and Literature tests offer optional essays, which some college and universities require and some do not. These essays are graded by faculty at the individual institutions that require them and require an additional $10 fee. Contact the particular institution to ask about essay requirements, and check with your test center for further details.

All 35 CLEP examinations are administered on computer. If you are unfamiliar with taking a test on a computer, consult the CLEP Sampler online at www.collegeboard.com/clep. The Sampler contains the same tutorials as the actual exams and helps familiarize you with navigation and how to answer different types of questions.

Points are not deducted for wrong or skipped answers – you receive one point for every correct answer. Therefore it is best that an answer is supplied for each exam question, whether it is a guess or not. The number of correct answers is then converted to a formula score. This formula, or "scaled," score is determined by a statistical process called *equating*, which adjusts for slight differences in difficulty between test forms and ensures that your score does not depend on the specific test form you took or how well others did on the same form. The scaled scores range from 20 to 80 – this is the number that will appear on your score report.

To ensure that you complete all questions in the time allotted, you would probably be wise to skip the more difficult or perplexing questions and return to them later. Although the multiple-choice items in these tests are carefully designed so as not to be tricky, misleading, or ambiguous, on the other hand, they are not all direct questions of factual information. They attempt, in their way, to elicit a response that indicates your knowledge or lack of knowledge of the material in question or your ability or inability to use or interpret a fact or idea. Thus, you should concentrate on answering the questions as they appear to be without attempting to out-guess the testmakers.

5. WHAT ARE THE FEES?

The fee for all CLEP examinations is $55. Optional essays required by some institutions are an additional $10.

6. WHEN ARE THE TESTS GIVEN?

CLEP tests are administered year-round. Consult the CLEP website (www.collegeboard.com/clep) and individual test centers for specific information.

7. WHERE ARE THE TESTS GIVEN?

More than 1,300 test centers are located on college and university campuses throughout the country, and additional centers are being established to meet increased needs. Any accredited collegiate institution with an explicit and publicly available policy of credit by examination can become a CLEP test center. To obtain a list of these centers, visit the CLEP website at www.collegeboard.com/clep.

8. HOW DO I REGISTER FOR THE COLLEGE-LEVEL EXAMINATION PROGRAM?

Contact an individual test center for information regarding registration, scheduling and fees. Registration/admission forms can also be obtained on the CLEP website.

9. MAY I REPEAT THE COLLEGE-LEVEL EXAMINATIONS?

You may repeat any examination providing at least six months have passed since you were last administered this test. If you repeat a test within a period of time less than six months, your scores will be cancelled and your fees forfeited. To repeat a test, check the appropriate space on the registration form.

10. WHEN MAY I EXPECT MY SCORE REPORTS?

With the exception of the English Composition with Essay exam, you should receive your score report instantly once the test is complete.

11. HOW SHOULD I PREPARE FOR THE COLLEGE-LEVEL EXAMINATIONS?

This book has been specifically designed to prepare candidates for these examinations. It will help you to consider, study, and review important content, principles, practices, procedures, problems, and techniques in the form of varied and concrete applications.

12. QUESTIONS AND ANSWERS APPEARING IN THIS PUBLICATION

The College-Level Examinations are offered by the College Board. Since copies of past examinations have not been made available, we have used equivalent materials, including questions and answers, which are highly recommended by us as an appropriate means of preparing for these examinations.

If you need additional information about CLEP Examinations, visit www.collegeboard.com/clep.

THE COLLEGE-LEVEL EXAMINATION PROGRAM

How The Program Works

CLEP examinations are administered at many colleges and universities across the country, and most institutions award college credit to those who do well on them. The examinations provide people who have acquired knowledge outside the usual educational settings the opportunity to show that they have learned college-level material without taking certain college courses.

The CLEP examinations cover material that is taught in introductory-level courses at many colleges and universities. Faculties at individual colleges review the tests to ensure that they cover the important material taught in their courses. Colleges differ in the examinations they accept; some colleges accept only two or three of the examinations while others accept nearly all of them.

Although CLEP is sponsored by the College Board and the examinations are scored by Educational Testing Service (ETS), neither of these organizations can award college credit. Only accredited colleges may grant credit toward a degree. When you take a CLEP examination, you may request that a copy of your score report be sent to the college you are attending or plan to attend. After evaluating your scores, the college will decide whether or not to award you credit for a certain course or courses, or to exempt you from them. If the college gives you credit, it will record the number of credits on your permanent record, thereby indicating that you have completed work equivalent to a course in that subject. If the college decides to grant exemption without giving you credit for a course, you will be permitted to omit a course that would normally be required of you and to take a course of your choice instead.

What the Examinations Are Like

The examinations consist mostly of multiple-choice questions to be answered within a 90-minute time limit. Additional information about each CLEP examination is given in the examination guide and on the CLEP website.

Where To Take the Examinations

CLEP examinations are administered throughout the year at the test centers of approximately 1,300 colleges and universities. On the CLEP website, you will find a list of institutions that award credit for satisfactory scores on CLEP examinations. Some colleges administer CLEP examinations to their own students only. Other institutions administer the tests to anyone who registers to take them. If your college does not administer the tests, contact the test centers in your area for information about its testing schedule.

Once you have been tested, your score report will be available instantly. CLEP scores are kept on file at ETS for 20 years; and during this period, for a small fee, you may have your transcript sent to another college or to anyone else you specify. (Your scores will never be sent to anyone without your approval.)

APPROACHING A COLLEGE ABOUT CLEP

The following sections provide a step-by-step approach to learning about the CLEP policy at a particular college or university. The person or office that can best assist students desiring CLEP credit may have a different title at each institution, but the following guidelines will lead you to information about CLEP at any institution.

Adults returning to college often benefit from special assistance when they approach a college. Opportunities for adults to return to formal learning in the classroom are now widespread, and colleges and universities have worked hard to make this a smooth process for older students. Many colleges have established special service offices that are staffed with trained professionals who understand the kinds of problems facing adults returning to college. If you think you might benefit from such assistance, be sure to find out whether these services are available at your college.

How to Apply for College Credit

STEP 1. Obtain the General Information Catalog and a copy of the CLEP policy from the colleges you are considering. If you have not yet applied for admission, ask for an admissions application form too.

Information about admissions and CLEP policies can be obtained by contacting college admissions offices or finding admissions information on the school websites. Tell the admissions officer that you are a prospective student and that you are interested in applying for admission and CLEP credit. Ask for a copy of the publication in which the college's complete CLEP policy is explained. Also get the name and the telephone number of the person to contact in case you have further questions about CLEP.

At this step, you may wish to obtain information from external degree colleges. Many adults find that such colleges suit their needs exceptionally well.

STEP 2. If you have not already been admitted to the college you are considering, look at its admission requirements for undergraduate students to see if you can qualify.

This is an important step because if you can't get into college, you can't get college credit for CLEP. Nearly all colleges require students to be admitted and to enroll in one or more courses before granting the students CLEP credit.

Virtually all public community colleges and a number of four-year state colleges have open admission policies for in-state students. This usually means that they admit anyone who has graduated from high school or has earned a high school equivalency diploma.

If you think you do not meet the admission requirements, contact the admissions office for an interview with a counselor. Colleges do sometimes make exceptions, particularly for adult applicants. State why you want the interview and ask what documents you should bring with you or send in advance. (These materials may include a high school transcript, transcript of previous college work, completed application for admission, etc.) Make an extra effort to have all the information requested in time for the interview.

During the interview, relax and be yourself. Be prepared to state honestly why you think you are ready and able to do college work. If you have already taken CLEP examinations and scored high enough to earn credit, you have shown that you are able to do college work. Mention this achievement to the admissions counselor because it may increase your chances of being accepted. If you have not taken a CLEP examination, you can still improve your chances of being accepted by describing how your job training or independent study has helped prepare you for college-level work. Tell the counselor what you have learned from your work and personal experiences.

STEP 3. Evaluate the college's CLEP policy.

Typically, a college lists all its academic policies, including CLEP policies, in its general catalog. You will probably find the CLEP policy statement under a heading such as Credit-by-Examination, Advanced Standing, Advanced Placement, or External Degree Program. These sections can usually be found in the front of the catalog.

Many colleges publish their credit-by-examination policies in a separate brochure, which is distributed through the campus testing office, counseling center, admissions office, or registrar's office. If you find a very general policy statement in the college catalog, seek clarification from one of these offices.

Review the material in the section of this guide entitled Questions to Ask About a College's CLEP Policy. Use these guidelines to evaluate the college's CLEP policy. If you have not yet taken a CLEP examination, this evaluation will help you decide which examinations to take and whether or not to take the free-response or essay portion. Because individual colleges have different CLEP policies, a review of several policies may help you decide which college to attend.

STEP 4. If you have not yet applied for admission, do so early.

Most colleges expect you to apply for admission several months before you enroll, and it is essential that you meet the published application deadlines. It takes time to process your application for admission; and if you have yet to take a CLEP examination, it will be some time before the college receives and reviews your score report. You will probably want to take some, if not all, of the CLEP examinations you are interested in before you enroll so you know which courses you need not register for. In fact, some colleges require that all CLEP scores be submitted before a student registers.

Complete all forms and include all documents requested with your application(s) for admission. Normally, an admissions decision cannot be reached until all documents have been submitted and evaluated. Unless told to do so, do not send your CLEP scores until you have been officially admitted.

STEP 5. Arrange to take CLEP examination(s) or to submit your CLEP score(s).

You may want to wait to take your CLEP examinations until you know definitely which college you will be attending. Then you can make sure you are taking tests your college will accept for credit. You will also be able to request that your scores be sent to the college, free of charge, when you take the tests.

If you have already taken CLEP examinations, but did not have a copy of your score report sent to your college, you may request the College Board to send an official transcript at any time for a small fee. Use the Transcript Request Form that was sent to you with your score report. If you do not have the form, you may find it online at www.collegeboard.com/clep.

Your CLEP scores will be evaluated, probably by someone in the admissions office, and sent to the registrar's office to be posted on your permanent record once you are enrolled. Procedures vary from college to college, but the process usually begins in the admissions office.

STEP 6. Ask to receive a written notice of the credit you receive for your CLEP score(s).

A written notice may save you problems later, when you submit your degree plan or file for graduation. In the event that there is a question about whether or not you earned CLEP credit, you will have an official record of what credit was awarded. You may also need this verification of course credit if you go for academic counseling before the credit is posted on your permanent record.

STEP 7. Before you register for courses, seek academic counseling.

A discussion with your academic advisor can prevent you from taking unnecessary courses and can tell you specifically what your CLEP credit will mean to you. This step may be accomplished at the time you enroll. Most colleges have orientation sessions for new students prior to each enrollment period. During orientation, students are usually assigned an academic advisor who then gives them individual help in developing long-range plans and a course schedule for the next semester. In conjunction with this counseling, you may be asked to take some additional tests so that you can be placed at the proper course level.

External Degree Programs

If you have acquired a considerable amount of college-level knowledge through job experience, reading, or noncredit courses, if you have accumulated college credits at a variety of colleges over a period of years, or if you prefer studying on your own rather than in a classroom setting, you may want to investigate the possibility of enrolling in an external degree program. Many colleges offer external degree programs that allow you to earn a degree by passing examinations (including CLEP), transferring credit from other colleges, and demonstrating in other ways that you have satisfied the educational requirements. No classroom attendance is required, and the programs are open to out-of-state candidates as well as residents. Thomas A. Edison State College in New Jersey and Charter Oaks College in Connecticut are fully accredited independent state colleges; the New York program is part of the state university system and is also fully accredited. If you are interested in exploring an external degree, you can write for more information to:

Charter Oak College
The Exchange, Suite 171
270 Farmington Avenue
Farmington, CT 06032-1909

Regents External Degree Program
Cultural Education Center
Empire State Plaza
Albany, New York 12230

Thomas A. Edison State College
101 West State Street
Trenton, New Jersey 08608

Many other colleges also have external degree or weekend programs. While they often require that a number of courses be taken on campus, the external degree programs tend to be more flexible in transferring credit, granting credit-by-examination, and allowing independent study than other traditional programs. When applying to a college, you may wish to ask whether it has an external degree or weekend program.

Questions to Ask About a College's CLEP Policy

Before taking CLEP examinations for the purpose of earning college credit, try to find the answers to these questions:

1. Which CLEP examinations are accepted by this college?

A college may accept some CLEP examinations for credit and not others - possibly not the one you are considering. The English faculty may decide to grant college English credit based on the CLEP English Composition examination, but not on the Freshman College Composition examination. Or, the mathematics faculty may decide to grant credit based on the College Mathematics to non-mathematics majors only, requiring majors to take an examination in algebra, trigonometry, or calculus to earn credit. For these reasons, it is important that you know the specific CLEP tests for which you can receive credit.

2. Does the college require the optional free-response (essay) section as well as the objective portion of the CLEP examination you are considering?

Knowing the answer to this question ahead of time will permit you to schedule the optional essay examination when you register to take your CLEP examination.

3. Is credit granted for specific courses? If so, which ones?

You are likely to find that credit will be granted for specific courses and the course titles will be designated in the college's CLEP policy. It is not necessary, however, that credit be granted for a specific course in order for you to benefit from your CLEP credit. For instance, at many liberal arts colleges, all students must take certain types of courses; these courses may be labeled the core curriculum, general education requirements, distribution requirements, or liberal arts requirements. The requirements are often expressed in terms of credit hours. For example, all students may be required to take at least six hours of humanities, six hours of English, three hours of mathematics, six hours of natural science, and six hours of social science, with no particular courses in these disciplines specified. In these instances, CLEP credit may be given as 6 hrs. English credit or 3 hrs. Math credit without specifying for which English or mathematics courses credit has been awarded. In order to avoid possible disappointment, you should know before taking a CLEP examination what type of credit you can receive and whether you will only be exempted from a required course but receive no credit.

4. How much credit is granted for each examination you are considering, and does the college place a limit on the total amount of CLEP credit you can earn toward your degree?

Not all colleges that grant CLEP credit award the same amount for individual tests. Furthermore, some colleges place a limit on the total amount of credit you can earn through CLEP or other examinations. Other colleges may grant you exemption but no credit toward your degree. Knowing several colleges' policies concerning these issues may help you decide which college you will attend. If you think you are capable of passing a number of CLEP examinations, you may want to attend a college that will allow you to earn credit for all or most of them. For example, the state external degree programs grant credit for most CLEP examinations (and other tests as well).

5. What is the required score for earning CLEP credit for each test you are considering?

Most colleges publish the required scores or percentile ranks for earning CLEP credit in their general catalog or in a brochure. The required score may vary from test to test, so find out the required score for each test you are considering.

6. What is the college's policy regarding prior course work in the subject in which you are considering taking a CLEP test?

Some colleges will not grant credit for a CLEP test if the student has already attempted a college-level course closely aligned with that test. For example, if you successfully completed English 101 or a comparable course on another campus, you will probably not be permitted to receive CLEP credit in that subject, too. Some colleges will not permit you to earn CLEP credit for a course that you failed.

7. Does the college make additional stipulations before credit will be granted?

It is common practice for colleges to award CLEP credit only to their enrolled students. There are other stipulations, however, that vary from college to college. For example, does the college require you to formally apply for or accept CLEP credit by completing and signing a form? Or does the college require you to validate your CLEP score by successfully completing a more advanced course in the subject? Answers to these and other questions will help to smooth the process of earning college credit through CLEP.

The above questions and the discussions that follow them indicate some of the ways in which colleges' CLEP policies can vary. Find out as much as possible about the CLEP policies at the colleges you are interested in so you can choose a college with a policy that is compatible with your educational goals. Once you have selected the college you will attend, you can find out which CLEP examinations your college recognizes and the requirements for earning CLEP credit.

DECIDING WHICH EXAMINATIONS TO TAKE

If You're Taking the Examinations for College Credit or Career Advancement:

Most people who take CLEP examinations do so in order to earn credit for college courses. Others take the examinations in order to qualify for job promotions or for professional certification or licensing. It is vital to most candidates who are taking the tests for any of these reasons that they be well prepared for the tests they are taking so that they can advance as rapidly as possible toward their educational or career goals.

It is usually advisable that those who have limited knowledge in the subjects covered by the tests they are considering enroll in the college courses in which that material is taught. Those who are uncertain about whether or not they know enough about a subject to do well on a particular CLEP test will find the following guidelines helpful.

There is no way to predict if you will pass a particular CLEP examination, but answers to the questions under the seven headings below should give you an indication of whether or not you are likely to succeed.

1. Test Descriptions

Read the description of the test provided. Are you familiar with most of the topics and terminology in the outline?

2. Textbooks

Examine the suggested textbooks and other resource materials following the test descriptions in this guide. Have you recently read one or more of these books, or have you read similar college-level books on this subject? If you have not, read through one or more of the textbooks listed, or through the textbook used for this course at your college. Are you familiar with most of the topics and terminology in the book?

3. Sample Questions

The sample questions provided are intended to be typical of the content and difficulty of the questions on the test. Although they are not an exact miniature of the test, the proportion of the sample questions you can answer correctly should be a rough estimate of the proportion of questions you will be able to answer correctly on the test.

Answer as many of the sample questions for this test as you can. Check your answers against the correct answers. Did you answer more than half the questions correctly?

Because of variations in course content at different institutions, and because questions on CLEP tests vary from easy to difficult - with most being of moderate difficulty - the average student who passes a course in a subject can usually answer correctly about half the questions on the corresponding CLEP examination. Most colleges set their passing scores near this level, but some set them higher. If your college has set its required score above the level required by most colleges, you may need to answer a larger proportion of questions on the test correctly.

4. Previous Study

Have you taken noncredit courses in this subject offered by an adult school or a private school, through correspondence, or in connection with your job? Did you do exceptionally well in this subject in high school, or did you take an honors course in this subject?

5. Experience

Have you learned or used the knowledge or skills included in this test in your job or life experience? For example, if you lived in a Spanish-speaking country and spoke the language for a year or more, you might consider taking the Spanish examination. Or, if you have worked at a job in which you used accounting and finance skills, Principles of Accounting would be a likely test for you to take. Or, if you have read a considerable amount of literature and attended many art exhibits, concerts, and plays, you might expect to do well on the Humanities exam.

6. Other Examinations

Have you done well on other standardized tests in subjects related to the one you want to take? For example, did you score well above average on a portion of a college entrance examination covering similar skills, or did you obtain an exceptionally high score on a high school equivalency test or a licensing examination in this subject? Although such tests do not cover exactly the same material as the CLEP examinations and may be easier, persons who do well on these tests often do well on CLEP examinations, too.

7. Advice

Has a college counselor, professor, or some other professional person familiar with your ability advised you to take a CLEP examination?

If your answer was yes to questions under several of the above headings, you probably have a good chance of passing the CLEP examination you are considering. It is unlikely that you would have acquired sufficient background from experience alone. Learning gained through reading and study is essential, and you will probably find some additional study helpful before taking a CLEP examination.

If You're Taking the Examinations to Prepare for College

Many people entering college, particularly adults returning to college after several years away from formal education, are uncertain about their ability to compete with other college students. They wonder whether they have sufficient background for college study, and those who have been away from formal study for some time wonder whether they have forgotten how to study, how to take tests, and how to write papers. Such people may wish to improve their test-taking and study skills prior to enrolling in courses.

One way to assess your ability to perform at the college level and to improve your test-taking and study skills at the same time is to prepare for and take one or more CLEP examinations. You need not be enrolled in a college to take a CLEP examination, and you may have your scores sent only to yourself and later request that a transcript be sent to a college if you then decide to apply for credit. By reviewing the test descriptions and sample questions, you may find one or several subject areas in which you think you have substantial knowledge. Select one examination, or more if you like, and carefully read at least one of the textbooks listed in the bibliography for the test. By doing this, you will get a better idea of how much you know of what is usually taught in a college-level course in that subject. Study as much material as you can, until you think you have a good grasp of the subject matter. Then take the test at a college in your area. It will be several weeks before you receive your results, and you may wish to begin reviewing for another test in the meantime.

To find out if you are eligible for credit for your CLEP score, you must compare your score with the score required by the college you plan to attend. If you are not yet sure which college you will attend, or whether you will enroll in college at all, you should begin to follow the steps outlined. It is best that you do this before taking a CLEP test, but if you are taking the test only for the experience and to familiarize yourself with college-level material and requirements, you might take the test before you approach a college. Even if the college you decide to attend does not accept the test you took, the experience of taking such a test will enable you to meet with greater confidence the requirements of courses you will take.

You will find information about how to interpret your scores in WHAT YOUR SCORES MEAN, which you will receive with your score report, and which can also be found online at the CLEP website. Many colleges follow the recommendations of the American Council on Education (ACE) for setting their required scores, so you can use this information as a guide in determining how well you did. The ACE recommendations are included in the booklet.

If you do not do well enough on the test to earn college credit, don't be discouraged. Usually, it is the best college students who are exempted from courses or receive credit-by-examination. The fact that you cannot get credit for your score means that you should probably enroll in a college course to learn the material. However, if your score was close to the required score, or if you feel you could do better on a second try or after some additional study, you may retake the test after six months. Do not take it sooner or your score will not be reported and your fee will be forfeited.

If you do earn the score required to earn credit, you will have demonstrated that you already have some college-level knowledge. You will also have a better idea whether you should take additional CLEP examinations. And, what is most important, you can enroll in college with confidence, knowing that you do have the ability to succeed.

PREPARING TO TAKE CLEP EXAMINATIONS

Having made the decision to take one or more CLEP examinations, most people then want to know if it is worthwhile to prepare for them - how much, how long, when, and how should they go about it? The precise answers to these questions vary greatly from individual to individual. However, most candidates find that some type of test preparation is helpful.

Most people who take CLEP examinations do so to show that they have already learned the important material that is taught in a college course. Many of them need only a quick review to assure themselves that they have not forgotten some of what they once studied, and to fill in some of the gaps in their knowledge of the subject. Others feel that they need a thorough review and spend several weeks studying for a test. A few wish to take a CLEP examination as a kind of final examination for independent study of a subject instead of the college course. This last group requires significantly more study than those who only need to review, and they may need some guidance from professors of the subjects they are studying.

The key to how you prepare for CLEP examinations often lies in locating those skills and areas of prior learning in which you are strong and deciding where to focus your energies. Some people may know a great deal about a certain subject area, but may not test well. These individuals would probably be just as concerned about strengthening their test-taking skills as they are about studying for a specific test. Many mental and physical skills are used in preparing for a test. It is important not only to review or study for the examinations, but to make certain that you are alert, relatively free of anxiety, and aware of how to approach standardized tests. Suggestions on developing test-taking skills and preparing psychologically and physically for a test are given. The following section suggests ways of assessing your knowledge of the content of a test and then reviewing and studying the material.

Using This Study Guide

Begin by carefully reading the test description and outline of knowledge and skills required for the examination, if given. As you read through the topics listed there, ask yourself how much you know about each one. Also note the terms, names, and symbols that are mentioned, and ask yourself whether you are familiar with them. This will give you a quick overview of how much you know about the subject. If you are familiar with nearly all the material, you will probably need a minimum of review; however, if less than half of it is familiar, you will probably require substantial study to do well on the test.

If, after reviewing the test description, you find that you need extensive review, delay answering the sample question until you have done some reading in the subject. If you complete them before reviewing the material, you will probably look for the answers as you study, and then they will not be a good assessment of your ability at a later date.

If you think you are familiar with most of the test material, try to answer the sample questions.

Apply the test-taking strategies given. Keeping within the time limit suggested will give you a rough idea of how quickly you should work in order to complete the actual test.

Check your answers against the answer key. If you answered nearly all the questions correctly, you probably do not need to study the subject extensively. If you got about half the questions correct, you ought o review at least one textbook or other suggested materials on the subject. If you answered less than half the questions correctly, you will probably benefit from more extensive reading in the subject and thorough study of one or more textbooks. The textbooks listed are used at many colleges but they are not the only good texts. You will find helpful almost any standard text available to you., such as the textbook used at your college, or earlier editions of texts listed. For some examinations, topic outlines and textbooks may not be available. Take the sample tests in this book and check your answers at the end of each test. Check wrong answers.

Suggestions for Studying

The following suggestions have been gathered from people who have prepared for CLEP examinations or other college-level tests.

1. Define your goals and locate study materials

First, determine your study goals. Set aside a block of time to review the material provided in this book, and then decide which test(s) you will take. Using the suggestions, locate suitable resource materials. If a preparation course is offered by an adult school or college in your area, you might find it helpful to enroll.

2. Find a good place to study

To determine what kind of place you need for studying, ask yourself questions such as: Do I need a quiet place? Does the telephone distract me? Do objects I see in this place remind me of things I should do? Is it too warm? Is it well lit? Am I too comfortable here? Do I have space to spread out my materials? You may find the library more conducive to studying than your home. If you decide to study at home, you might prevent interruptions by other household members by putting a sign on the door of your study room to indicate when you will be available.

3. Schedule time to study

To help you determine where studying best fits into your schedule, try this exercise: Make a list of your daily activities (for example, sleeping, working, and eating) and estimate how many hours per day you spend on each activity. Now, rate all the activities on your list in order of their importance and evaluate your use of time. Often people are astonished at how an average day appears from this perspective. They may discover that they were unaware how large portions of time are spent, or they learn their time can be scheduled in alternative ways. For example, they can remove the least important activities from their day and devote that time to studying or another important activity.

4. Establish a study routine and a set of goals

In order to study effectively, you should establish specific goals and a schedule for accomplishing them. Some people find it helpful to write out a weekly schedule and cross out each study period when it is completed. Others maintain their concentration better by writing down the time when they expect to complete a study task. Most people find short periods of intense study more productive than long stretches of time. For example, they may follow a regular schedule of several 20- or 30-minute study periods with short breaks between them. Some people like to allow themselves rewards as they complete each study goal. It is not essential that you accomplish every goal exactly within your schedule; the point is to be committed to your task.

5. Learn how to take an active role in studying.

If you have not done much studying for some time, you may find it difficult to concentrate at first. Try a method of studying, such as the one outlined below, that will help you concentrate on and remember what you read.

a. First, read the chapter summary and the introduction. Then you will know what to look for in your reading.

b. Next, convert the section or paragraph headlines into questions. For example, if you are reading a section entitled, The Causes of the American Revolution, ask yourself: *What were the causes of the American Revolution?* Compose the answer as you read the paragraph. Reading and answering questions aloud will help you understand and remember the material.

c. Take notes on key ideas or concepts as you read. Writing will also help you fix concepts more firmly in your mind. Underlining key ideas or writing notes in your book can be helpful and will be useful for review. Underline only important points. If you underline more than a third of each paragraph, you are probably underlining too much.

d. If there are questions or problems at the end of a chapter, answer or solve them on paper as if you were asked to do them for homework. Mathematics textbooks (and some other books) sometimes include answers to some or all of the exercises. If you have such a book, write your answers before looking at the ones given. When problem-solving is involved, work enough problems to master the required methods and concepts. If you have difficulty with problems, review any sample problems or explanations in the chapter.

e. To retain knowledge, most people have to review the material periodically. If you are preparing for a test over an extended period of time, review key concepts and notes each week or so. Do not wait for weeks to review the material or you will need to relearn much of it.

Psychological and Physical Preparation

Most people feel at least some nervousness before taking a test. Adults who are returning to college may not have taken a test in many years or they may have had little experience with standardized tests. Some younger students, as well, are uncomfortable with testing situations. People who received their education in countries outside the United States may find that many tests given in this country are quite different from the ones they are accustomed to taking.

Not only might candidates find the types of tests and the kinds of questions on them unfamiliar, but other aspects of the testing environment may be strange as well. The physical and mental stress that results from meeting this new experience can hinder a candidate's ability to demonstrate his or her true degree of knowledge in the subject area being tested. For this reason, it is important to go to the test center well prepared, both mentally and physically, for taking the test. You may find the following suggestions helpful.

1. Familiarize yourself, as much as possible, with the test and the test situation before the day of the examination. It will be helpful for you to know ahead of time:

a. How much time will be allowed for the test and whether there are timed subsections.

b. What types of questions and directions appear on the examination.

c. How your test score will be computed.

d. How to properly answer the questions on the computer (See the CLEP Sample on the CLEP website)

e. In which building and room the examination will be administered. If you don't know where the building is, locate it or get directions ahead of time.

f. The time of the test administration. You might wish to confirm this information a day or two before the examination and find out what time the building and room will be open so that you can plan to arrive early.

g. Where to park your car or, if you wish to take public transportation, which bus or train to take and the location of the nearest stop.

h. Whether smoking will be permitted during the test.

i. Whether there will be a break between examinations (if you will be taking more than one on the same day), and whether there is a place nearby where you can get something to eat or drink.

2. Go to the test situation relaxed and alert. In order to prepare for the test:

a. Get a good night's sleep. Last minute cramming, particularly late the night before, is usually counterproductive.

b. Eat normally. It is usually not wise to skip breakfast or lunch on the day of the test or to eat a big meal just before the test.

c. Avoid tranquilizers and stimulants. If you follow the other directions in this book, you won't need artificial aids. It's better to be a little tense than to be drowsy, but stimulants such as coffee and cola can make you nervous and interfere with your concentration.

d. Don't drink a lot of liquids before the test. Having to leave the room during the test will disturb your concentration and take valuable time away from the test.

e. If you are inclined to be nervous or tense, learn some relaxation exercises and use them before and perhaps during the test.

3. Arrive for the test early and prepared. Be sure to:

a. Arrive early enough so that you can find a parking place, locate the test center, and get settled comfortably before testing begins. Allow some extra time in case you are delayed unexpectedly.

b. Take the following with you:

- Your completed Registration/Admission Form
- Two forms of identification – one being a government-issued photo ID with signature, such as a driver's license or passport
- Non-mechanical pencil
- A watch so that you can time your progress (digital watches are prohibited)
- Your glasses if you need them for reading or seeing the chalkboard or wall clock

c. Leave all books, papers, and notes outside the test center. You will not be permitted to use your own scratch paper; it will be provided. Also prohibited are calculators, cell phones, beepers, pagers, photo/copy devices, radios, headphones, food, beverages, and several other items.

d. Be prepared for any temperature in the testing room. Wear layers of clothing that can be removed if the room is too hot but will keep you warm if it is too cold.

4. When you enter the test room:

a. Sit in a seat that provides a maximum of comfort and freedom from distraction.

b. Read directions carefully, and listen to all instructions given by the test administrator. If you don't understand the directions, ask for help before test timing begins. If you must ask a question after the test has begun, raise your hand and a proctor will assist you. The proctor can answer certain kinds of questions but cannot help you with the test.

c. Know your rights as a test taker. You can expect to be given the full working time allowed for the test(s) and a reasonably quiet and comfortable place in which to work. If a poor test situation is preventing you from doing your best, ask if the situation can be remedied. If bad test conditions cannot be remedied, ask the person in charge to report the problem in the Irregularity Report that will be sent to ETS with the answer sheets. You may also wish to contact CLEP. Describe the exact circumstances as completely as you can. Be sure to include the test date and name(s) of the test(s) you took. ETS will investigate the problem to make sure it does not happen again, and, if the problem is serious enough, may arrange for you to retake the test without charge.

TAKING THE EXAMINATIONS

A person may know a great deal about the subject being tested, but not do as well as he or she is capable of on the test. Knowing how to approach a test is an important part of the testing process. While a command of test-taking skills cannot substitute for knowledge of the subject matter, it can be a significant factor in successful testing.

Test-taking skills enable a person to use all available information to earn a score that truly reflects his or her ability. There are different strategies for approaching different kinds of test questions. For example, free-response questions require a very different tack than do multiple-choice questions. Other factors, such as how the test will be graded, may also influence your approach to the test and your use of test time. Thus, your preparation for a test should include finding out all you can about the test so that you can use the most effective test-taking strategies.

Before taking a test, you should know approximately how many questions are on the test, how much time you will be allowed, how the test will be scored or graded, what types of questions and directions are on the test, and how you will be required to record your answers.

<u>Taking Multiple-Choice Tests</u>

1. Listen carefully to the instructions given by the test administrator and read carefully all directions before you begin to answer the questions.

2. Note the time that the test administrator starts timing the test. As you proceed, make sure that you are not working too slowly. You should have answered at least half the questions in a section when half the time for that section has passed. If you have not reached that point in the section, speed up your pace on the remaining questions.

3. Before answering a question, read the entire question, including all the answer choices. Don't think that because the first or second answer choice looks good to you, it isn't necessary to read the remaining options. Instructions usually tell you to select the best answer. Sometimes one answer choice is partially correct, but another option is better; therefore, it is usually a good idea to read all the answers before you choose one.

4. Read and consider every question. Questions that look complicated at first glance may not actually be so difficult once you have read them carefully.

5. Do not puzzle too long over any one question. If you don't know the answer after you've considered it briefly, go on to the next question. Make sure you return to the question later.

6. Make sure you record your response properly.

7. In trying to determine the correct answer, you may find it helpful to cross out those options that you know are incorrect, and to make marks next to those you think might be correct. If you decide to skip the question and come back to it later, you will save yourself the time of reconsidering all the options.

8. Watch for the following key words in test questions:

all	generally	never	perhaps
always	however	none	rarely
but	may	not	seldom
except	must	often	sometimes
every	necessary	only	usually

When a question or answer option contains words such as always, every, only, never, and none, there can be no exceptions to the answer you choose. Use of words such as often, rarely, sometimes, and generally indicates that there may be some exceptions to the answer.

9. Do not waste your time looking for clues to right answers based on flaws in question wording or patterns in correct answers. Professionals at the College Board and ETS put

a great deal of effort into developing valid, reliable, fair tests. CLEP test development committees are composed of college faculty who are experts in the subject covered by the test and are appointed by the College Board to write test questions and to scrutinize each question that is included on a CLEP test. Committee members make every effort to ensure that the questions are not ambiguous, that they have only one correct answer, and that they cover college-level topics. These committees do not intentionally include trick questions. If you think a question is flawed, ask the test administrator to report it, or contact CLEP immediately.

Taking Free-Response or Essay Tests

If your college requires the optional free-response or essay portion of a CLEP Composition and Literature exams, you should do some additional preparation for your CLEP test. Taking an essay test is very different from taking a multiple-choice test, so you will need to use some other strategies.

The essay written as part of the English Composition and Essay exam is graded by English professors from a variety of colleges and universities. A process called holistic scoring is used to rate your writing ability.

The optional free-response essays, on the other hand, are graded by the faculty of the college you designate as a score recipient. Guidelines and criteria for grading essays are not specified by the College Board or ETS. You may find it helpful, therefore, to talk with someone at your college to find out what criteria will be used to determine whether you will get credit. If the test requires essay responses, ask how much emphasis will be placed on your writing ability and your ability to organize your thoughts as opposed to your knowledge of subject matter. Find out how much weight will be given to your multiple-choice test score in comparison with your free-response grade in determining whether you will get credit. This will give you an idea where you should expend the greatest effort in preparing for and taking the test.

Here are some strategies you will find useful in taking any essay test:

1. Before you begin to write, read all questions carefully and take a few minutes to jot down some ideas you might include in each answer.

2. If you are given a choice of questions to answer, choose the questions you think you can answer most clearly and knowledgeably.

3. Determine in what order you will answer the questions. Answer those you find the easiest first so that any extra time can be spent on the more difficult questions.

4. When you know which questions you will answer and in what order, determine how much testing time remains and estimate how many minutes you will devote to each question. Unless suggested times are given for the questions or one question appears to require more or less time than the others, allot an equal amount of time to each question.

5. Before answering each question, indicate the number of the question as it is given in the test book. You need not copy the entire question from the question sheet, but it will be helpful to you and to the person grading your test if you indicate briefly the topic you are addressing – particularly if you are not answering the questions in the order in which they appear on the test.

6. Before answering each question, read it again carefully to make sure you are interpreting it correctly. Underline key words, such as those listed below, that often appear in free-response questions. Be sure you know the exact meaning of these words before taking the test.

analyze	demonstrate	enumerate	list
apply	derive	explain	outline
assess	describe	generalize	prove
compare	determine	illustrate	rank
contrast	discuss	interpret	show
define	distinguish	justify	summarize

If a question asks you to outline, define, or summarize, do not write a detailed explanation; if a question asks you to analyze, explain, illustrate, interpret, or show, you must do more than briefly describe the topic.

_____

For a current listing of CLEP Colleges

where you can get credit and be tested, write:

CLEP, P.O. Box 6600, Princeton, NJ 08541-6600

Or e-mail: clep@ets.org, or call: (609) 771-7865

College Algebra-Trigonometry

DESCRIPTION OF THE TEST

The College Algebra-Trigonometry examination covers material that is usually taught in a one-semester course that includes both algebra and trigonometry. Such a course is usually taken by students who have studied algebra and geometry in high school, but need additional study of precalculus mathematics before enrolling in calculus and other advanced courses at the college level.

The College Algebra-Trigonometry examination requires all of the knowledge and skills required by the separate examinations in College Algebra and Trigonometry (see pages 1-2 and 1-2). The combined examination consists of two separately timed 45-minute sections, each containing approximately 40 multiple-choice questions. One section is devoted exclusively to College Algebra; the other to Trigonometry. The test places little emphasis on arithmetic calculations, and the use of calculators is not permitted during the examination.

Separate scores are not reported for College Algebra and Trigonometry. Candidates wishing to earn credit for both of these courses by examination should take the separate examinations in these subjects.

SAMPLE QUESTIONS

Sample questions for the College Algebra portion of this examination can be found on pages 2-6; sample questions for the Trigonometry portion are given on pages 2-6.

STUDY RESOURCES

The textbooks and supplementary reference material suggested for the College Algebra and Trigonometry examinations (see pages 6 and 6) can also be used to prepare for the College Algebra-Trigonometry examination. However, the textbooks listed below are typical of those used in a one-semester course that covers both algebra and trigonometry. These books assume a basic knowledge of algebra and geometry, and provide less explanation of fundamental topics than do the textbooks suggested for the College Algebra and Trigonometry examinations.

Textbooks

Barnett, Raymond A., COLLEGE ALGEBRA WITH TRIGONOMETRY, 4th ed. New York: McGraw-Hill Book Co., 1989.

Beckenbach, Edwin F. et al., MODERN COLLEGE ALGEBRA AND TRIGONOMETRY, 5th ed. Belmont, CA: Wadsworth Publishing Co., 1986.

Christy, Dennis T., ESSENTIALS OF PRECALCULUS MATHEMATICS, 4th ed. New York: W.C. Brown, 1988.

Foerster, Paul, ALGEBRA AND TRIGONOMETRY, 2nd ed. Reading, MA: Addison-Wesley Publishing Co., Inc., 1984.

Goodman, A.W., A SHORT COURSE IN ALGEBRA AND TRIGONOMETRY (illus.), New York: Ardsley House Publishers, 1985.

Keedy, Mervin L. and Marvin L. Bittinger, ALGEBRA AND TRIGONOMETRY: A FUNCTIONS APPROACH, 4th ed. Reading, MA: Addison-Wesley Publishing Co., Inc., 1986.

Lial, Margaret L. and Charles D. Miller, ALGEBRA AND TRIGONOMETRY, 4th ed. Glenview, IL: Scott, Foresman and Co., 1986.

Munem, M.A., and J.P. Yizze, PRECALCULUS: FUNCTION AND GRAPHS, 5th ed. New York: Worth Publishing Inc., 1989.

Swokowski, Earl W., FUNCTIONS AND GRAPHS, 4th ed. Boston: Prindle, Weber, and Schmidt, 1984.

Supplementary Reference Material

Larson, Loren C., ALGEBRA AND TRIGONOMETRY REFRESHER FOR CALCULUS STUDENTS, New York: W.H. Freeman and Co., 1979.

———

College Algebra

DESCRIPTION OF THE TEST

The College Algebra examination covers the material that is usually taught in a one-semester college course in algebra. Nearly half of the test is made up of routine problems requiring basic algebraic skills; the remainder involves solving nonroutine problems in which candidates must demonstrate their understanding of concepts. The test includes questions on basic algebraic operations; linear and quadratic equations, inequalities, and graphs; algebraic, exponential, and logarithmic functions; theory of equations; and miscellaneous other topics. It is assumed that the candidate is familiar with currently taught algebraic vocabulary, symbols, and notation. The test places little emphasis on arithmetic calculations, and the use of calculators and other computing devices is not permitted during the examination.

The examination consists of approximately 80 multiple-choice questions to be answered in two separately timed 45-minute sections.

KNOWLEDGE AND SKILLS REQUIRED

The subject matter covered by the College Algebra examination is distributed approximately as follows:

Approximate Percent of Examination	
25%	Basic algebraic operations
	Combining algebraic expressions
	Factoring
	Simplifying algebraic fractions
	Operating with powers and roots
10%	Linear equations and inequalities and their graphs
10%	Quadratic equations and inequalities and their graphs
20%	Algebraic, exponential, and logarithmic functions
	Domain
	Range
	Composition
	Inverse of functions
10%	Theory of equations
25%	Miscellaneous topics
	Sets
	The real number system
	Complex numbers
	Systems of equations
	Sequences and series
	Matrix addition and multiplication
	Evaluation of determinants
	Mathematical induction

Within the subject-matter content described above, questions on the test require candidates to demonstrate the abilities given below in the approximate proportions indicated.

- Solving routine, straightforward problems (about 50 percent of the examination)

- Solving nonroutine problems requiring an understanding of concepts and the application of skills and concepts (about 50 percent of the examination)

SAMPLE QUESTIONS

The 25 questions given here are similar to questions on the College Algebra examination, but do not actually appear on the examination.
Before attempting to answer the sample questions, read all the information about the College Algebra examination given above.
Try to answer correctly as many questions as possible within 30 minutes. Then compare your answers with the correct answers on the last page.

Directions: Solve the following problems. Do not spend too much time on any one problem.
Note: i will be used to denote $\sqrt{-1}$.

1. If R = {1,2}, S = {2,3,4}, and T = {2,4}, then (R∪S)∩T is   1.___
     A. {2}   B. {4}   C. {2,4}
     D. {1,2,3,4}   E. the empty set

2. Which of the lines in the figure shown at the right is the graph of x = 3?   2.___
     A. m
     B. n
     C. p
     D. q
     E. r

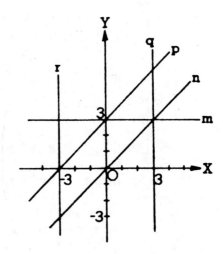

3. If f(x) = 2x - 1, then f(3x) =   3.___
     A. 3x - 1   B. 6x - 1   C. 6x - 3
     D. $6x^2 - 1$ E. $6x^2 - 3x$

4. If $x + 2 = y$, what is the value of $|x - y| + |y - x|$?
    A. -4
    B. 0
    C. 2
    D. 4
    E. It cannot be determined from the information given.

4.___

5. If $i^2 = -1$, which of the following is an expression for $\sqrt{-49} - \sqrt{-25}$ in the form $a + bi$, where a and b are real numbers?
    A. $0 + (\sqrt{24})i$ B. $0 + (\sqrt{74})i$ C. $0 + 24i$
    D. $0 + 2i$ E. $2 + 0i$

5.___

6. Where defined, $(x^a)^a =$
    A. $x^{\frac{a}{2}}$ B. x^{a^2} C. x^{a+2} D. x^{2a} E. $2x^a$

6.___

7. Which of the shaded regions below represents the graph of $\{(x,y) \mid x \geqq 2 \text{ and } y \leqq 0\}$?

7.___

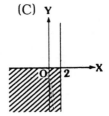

8. Where defined, $\dfrac{x^3 - 1}{x-1} =$
    A. $x + 1$ B. $x^2 + 1$ C. $x^2 - x + 1$
    D. $x^2 - x - 1$ E. $x^2 + x + 1$

8.___

9. Where defined, $\dfrac{x - \dfrac{4y^2}{9x}}{\dfrac{3x}{2} + y} =$

9.___

    A. $\dfrac{9x(3x - 2y)}{2y(3x + 2y)}$ B. $\dfrac{2(3x + 2y)^2}{9(3x - 2y)}$ C. $\dfrac{3x + 2y}{9}$

    D. $\dfrac{2(3x - 2y)}{9x}$ E. $\dfrac{(3x - 2)(3x + 2y)^2}{18x}$

3

10. For what real numbers x is $y = 2^{-x}$ a negative number?   10.____
   A. All real x   B. x > 0 only   C. $x \geqq 0$ only
   D. x < 0 only   E. No real x

11. If $\log_x 16 = 8$, then x =   11.____

   A. $\dfrac{1}{2}$ B. $\dfrac{1}{\sqrt{2}}$ C. $\sqrt{2}$ D. 2   E. $2\sqrt{2}$

12. The set of all real numbers that satisfy the inequality   12.____
   $|x - 2| \leqq 5$ is
   A. $\{x: -5 \leqq x \leqq 5\}$ B. $\{x: -3 \leqq x \leqq 7\}$
   C. $\{x: -7 \leqq x \leqq 3\}$ D. $\{x: x < -5\}$
   E. $\{x: x < -7 \text{ or } x > 3\}$

13. If $f(x) = 2x + 1$ and $g(x) = 3x - 1$, then $f(g(x)) =$ 13.____
   A. 6x - 1   B. 6x + 2   C. x - 2
   D. 5x   E. $6x^2 + x - 1$

14. If the remainder is 7 when $x^3 + kx^2 - 3x - 15$ is divided   14.____
   by x - 2, then k =
   A. 5   B. 6   C. 7   D. 9   E. 11

15. The set of all values of b for which the equation   15.____
   $4x^2 + bx + 1 = 0$ has one or two real roots is defined by
   A. b > 4   B. b < 4
   C. $b \geqq 4$ or $b \leqq -4$ D. b > 4 or b < -4
   E. $b \geqq 1$ or $b \leqq -1$

16. Given the two complex numbers, Z = p + qi and $\overline{Z} = p - qi$,   16.____
   where p and q are real numbers.
   Which of the following statements involving Z and $\overline{Z}$ must
   be true?
   A. $Z = -\overline{Z}$ B. $(\overline{Z})^2$ is a real number
   C. $Z \cdot \overline{Z}$ is a real number   D. $(\overline{Z})^2 = Z^2$
   E. $Z^2 = -(\overline{Z})^2$

17. $\dfrac{(n + 1)!}{n!} - n =$ 17.____

   A. 0   B. 1   C. n   D. n + 1   E. n!

18. In how many points do the graphs of $x^2 + y^2 = 9$ and   18.____
   $x^2 = 8y$ intersect?
   A. One   B. Two   C. Three
   D. Four   E. More than four

19. $\dfrac{1 + 2i}{1 - 2i} =$ 19.____

   A. $\dfrac{4 - 3i}{-3}$ B. $\dfrac{-3 + 4i}{5}$ C. 1   D. $\dfrac{3 - 4i}{5}$ E. $\dfrac{4 - 3i}{3}$

4

20.   2x + y − z = 3
         x + 3y − 2z = 7
         3x − y + 4z = 11
    What is the value of z in the solution set of the system
    of equations above?

    A. $-\dfrac{11}{3}$ B. $-\dfrac{3}{2}$ C. 1   D. 2   E. 3

20.___

21. Which quadrants of the plane contain points of the graph
    of 2x − y > 4?
    A. First, second, and third *only*
    B. First, second, and fourth *only*
    C. First, third, and fourth *only*
    D. Second, third, and fourth *only*
    E. First, second, third, and fourth

21.___

22. The figure shown at the right is the
    graph of y = f(x).
    Which of the following is the graph
    of y = |f(x)|?

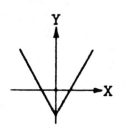

22.___

(A) 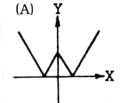   (B) 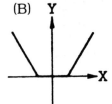   (C)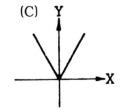

(D) 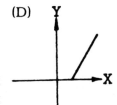   (E)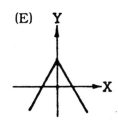

23. If $\begin{vmatrix} 2 & 0 & 1 \\ 4 & x & 5 \\ 3 & 4 & -2 \end{vmatrix} = -10$, then x =

    A. −2   B. −1   C. 0   D. 3   E. 30

23.___

5

24. If x, 3x + 2, and 8x + 3 are the first three terms of an   24. ___
    arithmetic progression, then x =

    A. -1   B. $-\dfrac{1}{5}$ C. 0   D. $\dfrac{1}{3}$ E. 3

25. What is the middle term in the expansion of $(x - \dfrac{1}{x})^6$?   25. ___

    A. $20x^3$ B. $\dfrac{20}{x^3}$ C. $-15x^2$ D. -15   E. -20

STUDY RESOURCES

    The list below contains a number of textbooks that are typical
of those widely used in algebra courses at the college level. All
the books cover the major topics in the outline given on page 1, but
their approaches to certain topics and the emphases given to them
may differ. To prepare for the College Algebra examination, a
candidate is advised to study one or more of these or other similar
books.

Textbooks

Barnett, Raymond A., and Michael R. Ziegler, COLLEGE ALGEBRA, 4th ed.
    New York: McGraw-Hill Book Co., 1989.

Beckenbach, Edwin et al., MODERN COLLEGE ALGEBRA AND TRIGONOMETRY,
    5th ed. Belmont, CA: Wadsworth Publishing Co., 1986.

Keedy, M.L. and M.L. Bittinger, COLLEGE ALGEBRA: A FUNCTIONS
    APPROACH, 4th ed. Reading, MA: Addison-Wesley Publishing Co.,
    Inc., 1986.

Leithold, Louis, COLLEGE ALGEBRA, 2nd ed. New York: Macmillan
    Publishing Co., Inc., 1989.

Munem, Mustafa et al., COLLEGE ALGEBRA, 2nd ed. New York: Worth
    Publishers, Inc., 1979. [Study Guide included.]

Swokowski, Earl W., FUNDAMENTALS OF COLLEGE ALGEBRA, 7th ed. Boston:
    Prindle, Weber, and Schmidt, 1989.

KEY (CORRECT ANSWERS)

1. C	6. B	11. C	16. C	21. C
2. D	7. D	12. B	17. B	22. A
3. B	8. E	13. A	18. B	23. A
4. D	9. D	14. A	19. B	24. D
5. D	10. E	15. C	20. E	25. E

Trigonometry

DESCRIPTION OF THE TEST

The Trigonometry examination covers material that is usually taught in a one-semester college course in trigonometry with primary emphasis on analytical trigonometry. Nearly half of the test is made up of routine problems requiring basic trigonometric skills; the remainder involves solving nonroutine problems in which candidates must demonstrate their understanding of concepts. The test includes questions on trigonometric functions and their relationships, evaluation of trigonometric functions of positive and negative angles, trigonometric equations and inequalities, graphs of trigonometric functions, trigonometry of the triangle, and miscellaneous other topics. It is assumed that the candidate is familiar with currently taught trigonometric vocabulary and notation and with both radian and degree measure. The test places little emphasis on arithmetic calculations, and the use of calculators and other computing devices is not permitted during the examination.

The examination consists of approximately 80 multiple-choice questions to be answered in two separately timed 45-minute sections.

KNOWLEDGE AND SKILLS REQUIRED

The following subject matter is included on the Trigonometry examination:

Approximate Percent of Examination

30% Trigonometric functions and their relationships
    Cofunction relationships
    Reciprocal relationships
    Pythagorean relationships such as $\sin^2\theta + \cos^2\theta = 1$
    Functions of two angles such as $\sin(\alpha+\beta)$
    Functions of double angles such as $\cos 2\theta$
    Functions of half angles such as $\sin \frac{\theta}{2}$
    Identities

20% Evaluation of trigonometric functions of angles with terminal sides in the various quadrants or on the axes, including positive and negative angles greater than 360° (or 2π radians)

10% Trigonometric equations and inequalities

10% Graphs of trigonometric functions

10% Trigonometry of the triangle including the law of sines and the law of cosines

20% Miscellaneous
    Inverse functions (arc sin, arc cos, arc tan)
    Trigonometric form (polar form) of complex numbers including DeMoivre's theorem

Within the subject-matter content described above, questions on the test require candidates to demonstrate the abilities given below in the approximate proportions indicated.

- Solving routine problems involving basic trigonometric skills (about 60 percent of the examination)

- Solving nonroutine problems requiring an understanding of concepts and the application of skills and concepts (about 40 percent of the examination)

SAMPLE QUESTIONS

The 25 questions given here are similar to questions on the Trigonometry examination, but they do not actually appear on the examination.

Before attempting to answer the sample questions, read all the information about the Trigonometry examination given above.

Try to answer correctly as many questions as possible within 30 minutes. Then compare your answers with the correct answers on the last page.

Directions: Solve the following problems. Do not spend too much time on any one problem.
Note: On this test the inverse function of a trigonometric function f(x) may be expressed as either $f^{-1}(x)$ or arc f(x).

1. $\cos 60° \sin 30° =$ 1.____

   A. $\frac{1}{4}$ B. $\frac{1}{2}$ C. $\frac{3}{4}$ D. 1   E. 2

2. If $0 < x < \pi$ and $\tan x = 1$, then $x =$ 2.____

   A. $\frac{\pi}{6}$ B. $\frac{\pi}{4}$ C. $\frac{\pi}{2}$ D. $\frac{2\pi}{3}$ E. $\frac{3\pi}{4}$

3. A circular gear turns 60 degrees per hour.   3.____
   Through how many radians does it turn in 12 hours?

   A. $\frac{4}{\pi}$ B. $\frac{36}{\pi}$ C. 4π D. 12π E. 36π

4. If x is the measure of an acute angle such that $\tan x = \frac{k}{3}$,   4.____
   then $\sin x =$

   A. $\frac{k}{3 + k}$ B. $\frac{3}{\sqrt{9 - k^2}}$ C. $\frac{k}{\sqrt{9 - k^2}}$ D. $\frac{3}{\sqrt{9 + k^2}}$ E. $\frac{k}{\sqrt{9 + k^2}}$

2

5. cos 240° =
    A. -sin 240°   B. -cos 60°   C. sin(-240°)
    D. sin 150°   E. cos 60°

5.___

6. In right triangle RST in the figure shown

    at the right, RS is 9 and $\tan\theta = \frac{3}{4}$.

    What is the area of $\triangle$RST?
    A. 18
    B. 27
    C. 36
    D. 54
    E. 108

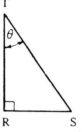

Figure 1

6.___

7. If θ is an angle in standard position such that the terminal ray of θ passes through the point (12,-5), then $\sin\theta$ =

    A. $-\frac{12}{13}$ B. $-\frac{5}{13}$ C. $-\frac{5}{17}$ D. $\frac{5}{17}$ E. $\frac{12}{13}$

7.___

8.

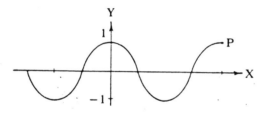

Figure 2

On the portion of the graph of $y = \cos \frac{2}{3}x$ in the figure above, what is the x-coordinate of point P if the y-coordinate is 1?

    A. $\frac{2\pi}{3}$ B. 2π C. 3π D. 4π E. 6π

8.___

9. If sin x = 2cos x, what is tan x?

    A. $\frac{1}{2}$

    B. $\frac{\sqrt{2}}{2}$

    C. $\sqrt{2}$
    D. 2
    E. It cannot be determined from the information given

9.___

10. If $\sin\theta$ = 0.8, then cos 2θ =
    A. -0.36   B. -0.28   C. -0.20   D. 0.20   E. 0.36

10.___

11. $\cos[\sin^{-1}(-\frac{1}{2})] =$

    A. $-\frac{\pi}{6}$ B. $\frac{\pi}{3}$ C. $\frac{1}{2}$ D. $\frac{\sqrt{3}}{2}$ E. $2\sqrt{3}$

    11.____

12. Wherever defined, $\frac{\csc x}{\sec x} =$

    A. $1 - \cos^2 x$ B. $\cos x$ C. $\cot x$
    D. $\sin x$ E. $\tan x$

    12.____

13. For $0 \leqq x \leqq 2\pi$, $\sin x > \cos x$ if and only if

    A. $0 < x < \frac{\pi}{4}$ B. $\frac{\pi}{6} < x < \frac{\pi}{2}$ C. $0 < x \leqq \frac{}{2}$

    D. $\frac{\pi}{4} \leqq x < \frac{\pi}{2}$ E. $\frac{\pi}{4} < x < \frac{5\pi}{4}$

    13.____

14. $(\cos\theta \, \tan\theta)^2 =$
    A. 0 B. 1 C. $\cot^2\theta$
    D. $\sin^2\theta$ E. $\cos^2\theta\csc^2\theta$

    14.____

15. How many values of t are there between 0° and 360°, inclusive, for which $\cos t = 0$?
    A. None   B. One   C. Two   D. Three   E. Four

    15.____

16. $\sin(\arc\tan 1) =$

    A. 0 B. $\frac{1}{2}$ C. $\frac{\sqrt{2}}{2}$ D. $\frac{\sqrt{3}}{2}$ E. 1

    16.____

17. Which of the following equations has the graph shown in the figure at the right?
y =
    A. $\sin \frac{x}{2} + 1$

    B. $\sin 2x$

    C. $2\sin \frac{x}{2}$

    D. $2\sin x$

    E. $2\sin 2x$

    17.____

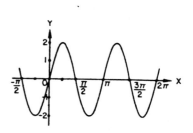

Figure 3

18. If $0 < y < x < \frac{\pi}{2}$, which of the following are TRUE?

    I. $\sin y < \sin x$ II. $\cos y < \cos x$
    III. $\tan y < \tan x$

    The CORRECT answer is:
    A. None   B. I, II   C. I, III
    D. II, III   E. I, II, III

    18.____

19. What is the solution set of $\cos^2 x + 2\cos x = 0$, where $-\frac{\pi}{2} \le x \le \frac{\pi}{2}$?

    A. $\{-\frac{\pi}{2},\frac{\pi}{2}\}$ B. $\{-\frac{\pi}{2},\pi\}$ C. $\{-\pi,\pi\}$

    D. $\{-\pi,0,\pi\}$ E. The empty set

                                                          19.___

20. Where defined, $\dfrac{\sin x}{-1 + \sec x} + \dfrac{\sin x}{1 + \sec x} =$ 20.___

    A. $-2\cot x$ B. $-2\tan x$ C. $2\cot x$

    D. $2\tan x$ E. $\tan 2x$

21. In the figure at the right, if $\triangle BCD$ is equilateral, what is the length of side AC in $\triangle ABC$?   21.___

Figure 4

    A. $\sqrt{5}$

    B. $\sqrt{7}$

    C. $2\sqrt{2}$

    D. 3

    E. It cannot be determined from the information given

22. What are the real numbers x for which $\sin(-x) = \sin x$?   22.___

    A. No number

    B. Zero

    C. All integral multiples of π

    D. All integral multiples of $\frac{\pi}{2}$

    E. All numbers

23. Using DeMoivre's theorem, $[4\cos \frac{\pi}{3} + i\sin \frac{\pi}{3})]^3$ can be expressed as   23.___

    A. -64 B. $-64i$ C. $12 + 12i$

    D. $12 - 12i$ E. $-12 - 12i$

24. Which of the following could represent the graph of $y = 3\sin 2x$?   24.___

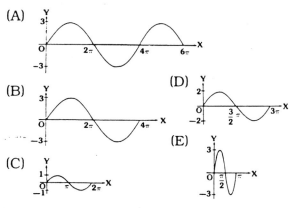

5

25. If $0 \leq \theta \leq \frac{\pi}{2}$ and $\frac{2\tan\theta}{1 - \tan^2\theta} = \cot\theta$, then $\theta =$ 25.___

   A. $\frac{\pi}{2}$ B. $\frac{\pi}{3}$ C. $\frac{\pi}{4}$ D. $\frac{\pi}{6}$ E. 0

STUDY RESOURCES

The list below contains a number of textbooks that are typical of those widely used in trigonometry courses at the college level. All the books cover the major topics in the outline on page 1, but the approaches to certain topics may differ. To prepare for the Trigonometry examination, a candidate is advised to study one or more of these or other similar books. The supplementary reference, by Farley et al., is a paperback designed for self-study.

Textbooks

Barnett, Raymond A., COLLEGE ALGEBRA WITH TRIGONOMETRY, 4th ed. New York: McGraw-Hill Book Co., 1989.

Keedy, M.L. and M.L. Bittinger, TRIGONOMETRY: TRIANGLES AND FUNCTIONS, 4th ed. Reading, MA: Addison-Wesley Publishing Co., Inc., 1986.

Swokowski, Earl W., FUNDAMENTALS OF TRIGONOMETRY, 7th ed. Boston: Prindle, Weber, and Schmidt, 1989.

Supplementary Reference Material

Farley, Reuben W. et al., TRIGONOMETRY: A UNITIZED APPROACH. Englewood Cliffs, NJ: Prentice-Hall, Inc., 1975.

———

KEY (CORRECT ANSWERS)

1. A		11. D	
2. B		12. C	
3. C		13. E	
4. E		14. D	
5. B		15. C	
6. D		16. C	
7. B		17. E	
8. C		18. C	
9. D		19. A	
10. B		20. C	

                21. B
                22. C
                23. A
                24. E
                25. D

———

HOW TO TAKE A TEST

You have studied long, hard and conscientiously.

With your official admission card in hand, and your heart pounding, you have been admitted to the examination room.

You note that there are several hundred other applicants in the examination room waiting to take the same test.

They all appear to be equally well prepared.

You know that nothing but your best effort will suffice. The "moment of truth" is at hand: you now have to demonstrate objectively, in writing, your knowledge of content and your understanding of subject matter.

You are fighting the most important battle of your life—to pass and/or score high on an examination which will determine your career and provide the economic basis for your livelihood.

What extra, special things should you know and should you do in taking the examination?

BEFORE THE TEST

YOUR PHYSICAL CONDITION IS IMPORTANT

      If you are not well, you can't do your best work on tests. If you are half asleep, you can't do your best either. Here are some tips:

1) Get about the same amount of sleep you usually get. Don't stay up all night before the test, either partying or worrying—DON'T DO IT!
2) If you wear glasses, be sure to wear them when you go to take the test. This goes for hearing aids, too.
3) If you have any physical problems that may keep you from doing your best, be sure to tell the person giving the test. If you are sick or in poor health, you really cannot do your best on any test. You can always come back and take the test some other time.

AT THE TEST

EXAMINATION TECHNIQUES

1) Read the general instructions carefully. These are usually printed on the first page of the exam booklet. As a rule, these instructions refer to the timing of the examination; the fact that you should not start work until the signal and must stop work at a signal, etc. If there are any *special* instructions, such as a choice of questions to be answered, make sure that you note this instruction carefully.

2) When you are ready to start work on the examination, that is as soon as the signal has been given, read the instructions to each question booklet, underline any key words or phrases, such as *least, best, outline, describe* and the like. In this way you will tend to answer as requested rather than discover on reviewing your paper that you *listed without describing*, that you selected the *worst* choice rather than the *best* choice, etc.

3) If the examination is of the objective or multiple-choice type – that is, each question will also give a series of possible answers: A, B, C or D, and you are called upon to select the best answer and write the letter next to that answer on your answer paper – it is advisable to start answering each question in turn. There may be anywhere from 50 to 100 such questions in the three or four hours allotted and you can see how much time would be taken if you read through all the questions before beginning to answer any. Furthermore, if you come across a question or group of questions which you know would be difficult to answer, it would undoubtedly affect your handling of all the other questions.

4) If the examination is of the essay type and contains but a few questions, it is a moot point as to whether you should read all the questions before starting to answer any one. Of course, if you are given a choice – say five out of seven and the like – then it is essential to read all the questions so you can eliminate the two which are most difficult. If, however, you are asked to answer all the questions, there may be danger in trying to answer the easiest one first because you may find that you will spend too much time on it. The best technique is to answer the first question, then proceed to the second, etc.

5) Time your answers. Before the exam begins, write down the time it started, then add the time allowed for the examination and write down the time it must be completed, then divide the time available somewhat as follows:
   - If 3-1/2 hours are allowed, that would be 210 minutes. If you have 80 objective-type questions, that would be an average of 2-1/2 minutes per question. Allow yourself no more than 2 minutes per question, or a total of 160 minutes, which will permit about 50 minutes to review.
   - If for the time allotment of 210 minutes there are 7 essay questions to answer, that would average about 30 minutes a question. Give yourself only 25 minutes per question so that you have about 35 minutes to review.

6) The most important instruction is to *read each question* and make sure you know what is wanted. The second most important instruction is to *time yourself properly* so that you answer every question. The third most important instruction is to *answer every question*. Guess if you have to but include something for each question. Remember that you will receive no credit for a blank and will probably receive some credit if you write something in answer to an essay question. If you guess a letter – say "B" for a multiple-choice question – you may have guessed right. If you leave a blank as an answer to a multiple-choice question, the examiners may respect your

feelings but it will not add a point to your score. Some exams may penalize you for wrong answers, so in such cases *only*, you may not want to guess unless you have some basis for your answer.

7) Suggestions
   a. Objective-type questions
      1. Examine the question booklet for proper sequence of pages and questions
      2. Read all instructions carefully
      3. Skip any question which seems too difficult; return to it after all other questions have been answered
      4. Apportion your time properly; do not spend too much time on any single question or group of questions
      5. Note and underline key words – *all, most, fewest, least, best, worst, same, opposite,* etc.
      6. Pay particular attention to negatives
      7. Note unusual option, e.g., unduly long, short, complex, different or similar in content to the body of the question
      8. Observe the use of "hedging" words – *probably, may, most likely,* etc.
      9. Make sure that your answer is put next to the same number as the question
      10. Do not second-guess unless you have good reason to believe the second answer is definitely more correct
      11. Cross out original answer if you decide another answer is more accurate; do not erase until you are ready to hand your paper in
      12. Answer all questions; guess unless instructed otherwise
      13. Leave time for review

   b. Essay questions
      1. Read each question carefully
      2. Determine exactly what is wanted. Underline key words or phrases.
      3. Decide on outline or paragraph answer
      4. Include many different points and elements unless asked to develop any one or two points or elements
      5. Show impartiality by giving pros and cons unless directed to select one side only
      6. Make and write down any assumptions you find necessary to answer the questions
      7. Watch your English, grammar, punctuation and choice of words
      8. Time your answers; don't crowd material

8) Answering the essay question

Most essay questions can be answered by framing the specific response around several key words or ideas. Here are a few such key words or ideas:

M's: manpower, materials, methods, money, management
P's: purpose, program, policy, plan, procedure, practice, problems, pitfalls, personnel, public relations

a. Six basic steps in handling problems:
   1. Preliminary plan and background development
   2. Collect information, data and facts
   3. Analyze and interpret information, data and facts
   4. Analyze and develop solutions as well as make recommendations
   5. Prepare report and sell recommendations
   6. Install recommendations and follow up effectiveness

b. Pitfalls to avoid
   1. *Taking things for granted* – A statement of the situation does not necessarily imply that each of the elements is necessarily true; for example, a complaint may be invalid and biased so that all that can be taken for granted is that a complaint has been registered
   2. *Considering only one side of a situation* – Wherever possible, indicate several alternatives and then point out the reasons you selected the best one
   3. *Failing to indicate follow up* – Whenever your answer indicates action on your part, make certain that you will take proper follow-up action to see how successful your recommendations, procedures or actions turn out to be
   4. *Taking too long in answering any single question* – Remember to time your answers properly

EXAMINATION SECTION

EXAMINATION SECTION

DIRECTIONS: Each question or incomplete statement is followed by
              several suggested answers or completions. Select the
              one that BEST answers the question or completes the
              statement. *PRINT THE LETTER OF THE CORRECT ANSWER IN
              THE SPACE AT THE RIGHT.*

1. If the projections of the legs of a right triangle on the   1.___
    hypotenuse are in the ratio of 1:2, then the ratio of the
    smaller leg to the larger leg is
        A. 1:2   B. 1:3   C. 1:$\sqrt{2}$ D. 1:$\sqrt{3}$

2. Which one of the following is equivalent to $\tan \frac{\theta}{2}$ +   2.___
    $\cot \frac{\theta}{2}$?

        A. 2 sin θ   B. 2 sec θ   C. 2 csc θ   D. 2 cos θ

3. In triangle ACD, angle D is a right angle and B is a   3.___
    point on AD between A and D.
    If angle CBD is represented by x, angle CAD by y, AB by d,
    and CD by h, then which one of the following is equal to
    h?

        A. $\dfrac{d}{\cot y - \cot x}$ B. $\dfrac{d}{\cot x - \cot y}$

        C. $\dfrac{d}{\tan x - \tan y}$ D. $\dfrac{d}{\cot x + \cot y}$

4. Among the following, the one that is the polar graph of   4.___
    r = 2 cos θ is a
        A. straight line through (2,0°)
        B. circle centered at (1,0°) with radius = 1
        C. straight line through the pole
        D. circle centered at the pole, with radius = 1

5. If the bisector of the right angle of a certain right   5.___
    triangle divides the hypotenuse into segments in the
    ratio 3:5, then the ratio of the longer segment of the
    hypotenuse to the longer leg of the triangle is
        A. $\sqrt{34}$:8
        B. $\sqrt{17}$:2
        C. 3:5
        D. not determinable from the given data

6. In triangle ABC, C = 90°, BC = 3, AC = 4; point D lies on $\overline{AB}$. Angle DCB = 30°; the length of CD is

A. $\dfrac{5}{4 - \sqrt{3}}$ B. $\dfrac{24}{3 + 4\sqrt{3}}$ C. $\dfrac{24}{4 + 3\sqrt{3}}$ D. $\dfrac{3\sqrt{3}}{2}$

6.___

7. If the sides of a triangle are 3, 4, and x, which one of the following will represent only those values of x for which the triangle will be acute?

A. $1 < x < \sqrt{7}$ B. $1 < x < 5$
C. $\sqrt{7} < x < 5$ D. $\sqrt{7} < x < 7$

7.___

8. The number of elements in the solution set of sin x + cos 2x = 1, if the domain of x is $0 \leq x < 2\pi$, is

A. 2   B. 3   C. 4   D. 5

8.___

9. All of the points which are both on the line 3x + 5y = 15 and equidistant from the coordinate axes lie in quadrant(s)

A. I *only*   B. I and II *only*
C. I, II, III *only*   D. I, II, III, IV

9.___

10. Which one of the following is an element of the solution set of 2 sin^{2}x - 3 sin x - 2 = 0 if $0 \leq x \leq 2$?

A. $\dfrac{2}{3}$ B. $\dfrac{5}{6}$ C. $\dfrac{7}{6}$ D. none of these

10.___

11. If the greatest common factor of two numbers x and y is c, c being composite, and X is the set of prime factors of x, while Y is the set of prime factors of y, then the set of prime factors of c is

A. equal to X $\cup$ Y
B. a proper subset of X $\cup$ Y
C. equal to X $\cap$ Y
D. a proper subset of X $\cap$ Y

11.___

12. In making up a blend containing 45% cotton, 35% dacron, and 20% wool, the formula needed to determine the weight C of cotton needed to mix with D pounds of dacron and W pounds of wool is

A. $C = \dfrac{.45(W+D)}{.55}$ B. $C = \dfrac{.55(W+D)}{.45}$

C. $C = \dfrac{.35D+.20W}{.45}$ D. $C = .45(.35D+.20W)$

12.___

13. A piece of wire 6¼ yards long is to be cut into two pieces such that the longer piece is one and one-half as long as the shorter piece.
The length, in inches, of the SHORTER piece must be

A. 90   B. 100   C. 135   D. 150

13.___

14. The number of cc of water that must be added to 75 cc of a 60% solution of alcohol and water to change it to a 50% solution is CLOSEST to

A. 10   B. 15   C. 20   D. 30

14.___

15. A rectangular picture measuring x inches by y inches is   15.____
    surrounded by a frame of uniform width z inches.
    The number of square inches in the area of the frame is
    A. $2xz + 2yz + 4z^2$ B. $xy + 2xz + 2yz + 4z^2$
    C. $2xz + 2yz + 2z^2$ D. $2xy + 2xz + 2yz$

16. When $x^3 + 4x^2 + 3x - 10$ is divided by x-2, the remainder   16.____
    is
    A. 20   B. 8   C. -8   D. -10

17. Which one of the following subsets of the set of integers   17.____
    is closed under addition and multiplication?
    A. {0,1,2,3}   B. {0,1,2}   C. {0,1}   D. {0}

18. The total number of subsets of set {a,b,c} is   18.____
    A. 6   B. 7   C. 3   D. 8

19. A small hose can fill a tank with water in two hours   19.____
    while a larger hose can fill the same tank in one hour.
    The number of minutes it will take for the tank to be
    filled if both hoses are used at the same time is
    A. 30   B. 40   C. 45   D. 90

20. The volume of an average atom is about 10^{-23} cubic   20.____
    centimeters. The volume of one gene in a human body is
    about 10^{-17} cubic centimeters.
    Using these figures, we can conclude that the ratio of
    the volume of a gene to that of an atom is about
    A. 60 to 1   B. 1 to 10^6 C. 10^{-6} to 1   D. 10^6 to 1

21. The solution set of the equation $\dfrac{x}{x-3} - \dfrac{1}{x+2} = \dfrac{15}{x^2-x-6}$ is   21.____

    A. ∅   B. {3,-4}   C. {3}   D. {-4}

22. If the graphs of y = 2 log x and y = log 2x are drawn   22.____
    on the same set of axes, these graphs will
    A. not intersect
    B. intersect at one point only
    C. intersect at two points only
    D. coincide

23. A gear with 48 teeth drives a 64 tooth idler gear which,   23.____
    in turn, is engaged to a gear with 32 teeth.
    If the first gear rotates at 1200 rpm, then the last gear
    rotates, in rpm, at
    A. 800   B. 900   C. 1600   D. 1800

24. The power used in an electric circuit is proportional to   24.____
    the square of the current flow.
    If the power used in a circuit is 630 watts when the
    current is 3 amperes, then the power in watts when the
    current is 4 amperes will be

    A. $354\frac{3}{8}$ B. $472\frac{1}{2}$ C. 840   D. 1120

25. The intensity of illumination, I, on the page of a book varies inversely as the square of the distance, d, between the book and the source of light.
    If I = 6 when d = 4, then the value of I when d = 8 is
    A. 24   B. 8   C. 4.5   C. 1.5

26. Find the solution set of cos 2A + 3 cos A = -2 where 0° ≤ A ≤ 360°.
    A. {0°,60°,300°}   B. {60°,180°,300°}
    C. {120°,180°,240°}   D. {0°,120°,240°}

27. The algebraic statement $x^2 + y^2 = (x+y)^2$ is
    A. true for all values of x and y
    B. never true
    C. true only if x and/or y equals zero
    D. true only if x equals y

28. If the formula $a = \dfrac{V-v}{t}$ is solved for v, the expression equivalent to v is
    A. at - V   B. V - at   C. $-\dfrac{at}{V}$ D. $\dfrac{V}{at}$

29. If $\log_4 y = 3$, then y is equal to
    A. 81   B. 64   C. 12   D. 7

30. The distance between the two parallel lines 3x - 4y = 7 and 9x - 12y = 5 is
    A. 1/3   B. 16/15   C. 7/5   D. 26/15

KEY (CORRECT ANSWERS)

1. C	11. C	21. D
2. C	12. A	22. B
3. A	13. A	23. D
4. B	14. B	24. D
5. A	15. A	25. D
6. B	16. A	26. C
7. C	17. D	27. C
8. C	18. D	28. B
9. B	19. B	29. B
10. D	20. D	30. B

5

SOLUTIONS TO PROBLEMS

1.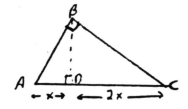

The altitude BD is the geometric mean of AD and DC. So, BD = $x\sqrt{2}$. Using the Pythagorean Theorem twice, we get AB = $x\sqrt{3}$ and BC = $x\sqrt{6}$. Now, AB/BC = $x\sqrt{3}/x\sqrt{6}$, which reduces to $1:\sqrt{2}$. (Ans. C)

2. $\tan\frac{\theta}{2} + \cot\frac{\theta}{2} = \dfrac{\sin\frac{\theta}{2}}{\cos\frac{\theta}{2}} + \dfrac{\cos\frac{\theta}{2}}{\sin\frac{\theta}{2}} = \dfrac{1}{(\cos\frac{\theta}{2})(\sin\frac{\theta}{2})} = \dfrac{1}{\sqrt{\frac{1+\cos\theta}{2}}\sqrt{\frac{1-\cos\theta}{2}}}$

$= \dfrac{2}{\sin\theta} = 2\csc\theta$. (Ans. C)

3.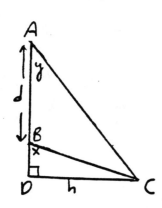

$\tan x = \dfrac{h}{BD}$ or BD = h cot x

tan y = h/(d+h cot x)
d tan y + h(tan y cot x) = h
h = d tan y/(1-tan y cot x) =
d/(cot y - cot x).
(Ans. A)

4. The graph of any equation in the form r = 2a cos θ is a circle centered at (a,0). Since a = 1 in this example, the graph is a circle centered at $(1,0)$ with radius = 1. (Ans. B)

5.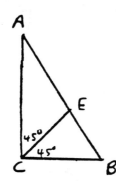

Let EB = 3, AE = 5. Using the Law of sines for triangles ACB and EAC and letting ∠B = k°, AB/sin 90° = AC/sin k° and AE/sin 45° = AC/sin ∠AEC. Now, ∠AEC = (45+k)° and by solving the two equations involving AC and k, we get k = 59.036° and AC = 6.86. Finally, AE/AC = 5/6.86 = .7289, which is $\sqrt{34}/8$. (Ans. A)

6.

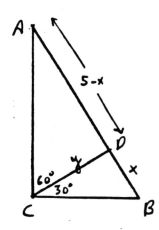

$\angle ACB = 90°$, $AB^2 = 3^2+4^2$, so $AB = 5$.
$\tan \angle B = \frac{4}{3}$, thus $\angle B = 53°$. Now,

$\angle A = 37°$. Using Law of Sines,

$\frac{\sin 53°}{y} = \frac{\sin 60°}{x}$ and $\frac{\sin 47°}{y} =$

$\frac{\sin 60°}{5-x}$. Solving these two

equations, $CD = y = \frac{24}{3+4\sqrt{3}}$. (Ans.

7. Case 1: The angle opposite x is largest (if x = largest side).
Call this $\angle A$. By the Law of Cosines, $x^2 = 3^2 + 4^2 - (2)(3)(4) \cos \angle A$, which becomes $\frac{x^2-25}{-24} = \cos \angle A$.

In order for $\angle A$ to be acute, $\frac{x^2-25}{-24} > 0$. Solving, $x < 5$.

Case 2: The angle opposite 4 is largest (x is not the largest side). Call this $\angle B$. $4^2 = 3^2 + x^2 - (2)(3)(x) \cos \angle B$.

$16 = 9 + x^2 - 6x \cos \angle B$, which becomes $\frac{7-x^2}{-6x} = \cos \angle B$.

Now, for $\angle B$ to be acute, we must have $\frac{7-x^2}{-6x} > 0$.

Solving, $x > \sqrt{7}$. Thus, $\sqrt{7} < x < 5$. (Ans. C)

8. $\sin x + \cos 2x = 1$ can be written as $\sin x - 2 \sin^2 x + 1 = 1$, which is $\sin x(1-2 \sin x) = 0$. Solving, $\sin x = 0$ gives $0, \pi$. Solving $1 - 2 \sin x = 0$ gives $\pi/6$, $5\pi/6$. Thus, there are four answers. (Ans. C)

9. The two points which are equidistant from both the coordinate axes and which lie on the line $3x + 5y = 15$ are found by identifying the intersection of $3x + 5y = 15$ with both $y = x$

and $y = -x$. Thus, the two points are $(\frac{15}{8}, \frac{15}{8})$ and $(- \frac{15}{2}, \frac{15}{2})$.

These points are in quadrants I and II, respectively.
(Ans. B)

10. Factor as $(2 \sin x+1)(\sin x-2) = 0$. Then, $\sin x = -\frac{1}{2}$ and $\sin x = 2$. From $\sin x = -\frac{1}{2}$, we get $x = 210°$ or $7\pi/6$ radians Since $7\pi/6 \approx 3.67$, none of the first three selections is correct. Note that $\sin x = 2$ has no solution. (Ans. D)

11. Let $c = p_1 \cdot p_2 \cdot p_3$, where p_1, p_2, p_3 are primes. Then, $x = (p_1 \cdot p_2 \cdot p_3)$(other primes) and $y = (p_1 \cdot p_2 \cdot p_3)$(other primes different than those contained in x).
Now, $X \cap Y = \{p_1, p_2, p_3\} = \{$prime factors of $c\}$. (Ans. C)

12. Since D = .35(Total Wt) and W = .20(Total Wt), D + W = .55(Total Wt)
     or Total Wt = (D+W)/.55. Now, C = .45(Total Wt), which by
     substitution becomes C = .45(D+W)/.55.   (Ans. A)

13. Use x for the shorter piece, 1.5x for the longer piece.
     x + 1.5x = 6.25. x = 2.5 yds. = 90 in.
     Note the correction in the wording. (Ans. A)

14. Let x be required number. The original amount of water =
     (.40)(75) = 30 cc. The new solution will have (30+x) cc of
     water and (75+x) cc of alcohol and water. Then, we have
     (30+x)/(75+x) = 50% = .50. Solving, x = 15.   (Ans. B)

15. 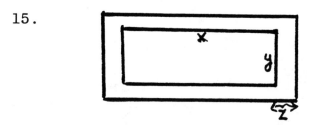   Area of frame = area of larger
                             rectangle - area of smaller
                             rectangle = $(x+2z)(y+2z) - xy$
                             $= 2xz + 2yz + 4z^2$.   (Ans. A)

16. The remainder is the value of $x^3 + 4x^2 + 3x - 10$ when x = 2.
     Thus, $2^3 + 4(2^2) + 3(2) - 10 = 20$.   (Ans. A)

17. Only {0} is closed under addition and multiplication
     {0,1,2,3} and {0,1,2} are open under both operations, and
     {0,1} is open under addition.   (Ans. D)

18. If a set has n elements, 2^n = number of subsets.
     Here, n = 3, so 2^3 = 8.   (Ans. D)

19. Let x = required time operating together (in minutes)

     $\frac{x}{120}$ + $\frac{x}{60}$ = 1, which yields x = 40. Note that $\frac{x}{120}$ represents

     the fraction of the tank that will be filled by the small
     hose.   (Ans. B)

20. $10^{-17}/10^{-23} = 10^6$ or 10^6 to 1.   (Ans. D)

21. Multiplying the equation by (x-3)(x+2): x(x+2) - (x-3) = 15.
     Then, $x^2 + 2x - x + 3 = 15$, whereby (x+4)(x-3) = 0, leading
     to x = -4 and x = 3. However, a value of x = 3 causes two
     denominators to be zero, and so must be rejected. Only x = -4
     can be accepted.   (Ans. D)

22. To find out if there is any intersection, set 2 Log x = Log 2x.
     Since 2 Log x = Log x^2, we get x^2 = 2x. This statement leads
     to x = 0 and x = 2. However, x = 0 is rejected since Log 0
     does not exist. Thus, only x = 2 is a point of intersection.
     (Ans. B)

23. Let x = speed of 64 tooth idler. By inverse proportion,
$\frac{1200}{x} = \frac{64}{48}$ and x = 900. Likewise, if y = speed of last gear,
$\frac{900}{y} = \frac{32}{64}$. y = 1800 rpm. (Ans. D)

24. $P = KC^2$ where P = power, C = current. $630 = (K)(3^2)$ and
K = 70. Now, $P = 70C^2$. When C = 4, $P = (70)(4^2) = 1120$.
(Ans. D)

25. $I = \frac{k}{d^2}$, k a constant. $6 = \frac{k}{16}$, so k = 96.
Now, $I = \frac{96}{d^2}$. If d = 8, $I = \frac{96}{64} = 1.5$. (Ans. D)

26. Since $\cos 2A = 2\cos^2 A - 1$, the given equation becomes:
$2\cos^2 A - 1 + 3\cos A = -2$, which will transform to:
$2\cos^2 A + 3\cos A + 1 = 0$ or $(2\cos A + 1)(\cos A + 1) = 0$.
From $2\cos A + 1 = 0$, $A = 120°, 240°$ and from $\cos A + 1 = 0$, $A = 180°$.
Final answer is $\{120°, 180°, 240°\}$. (Ans. C)

27. Since $(x+y)^2 = x^2 + 2xy + y^2$, this expression can $= x^2 + y^2$ only
if $2xy = 0$. This means either x or y or both x,y = 0. (Ans. C)

28. $a = \frac{V-v}{t}$ implies at = V-v. Then, v = V - at. (Ans. B)

29. $\text{Log}_4 y = 3$ means $y = 4^3 = 64$. (Ans. B)

30. Transforming both equations to slope-intercept form, $y = \frac{3}{4}x - \frac{7}{4}$
and $y = \frac{3}{4}x - \frac{5}{12}$. The equation of any line perpendicular to
these two lines has the form $y = -\frac{4}{3}x + k$, k a constant.
Let k = 0. Then, $y = -\frac{4}{3}x$ intersects $y = \frac{3}{4}x - \frac{7}{4}$ and
$y = \frac{3}{4}x - \frac{5}{12}$ at $(\frac{21}{25}, -\frac{112}{100})$ and $(\frac{1}{5}, -\frac{4}{15})$. Converting to
decimals, we get (.84, -1.12) and (-.2, -.27). Distance between
these points $= \sqrt{(.84-.2)^2 + (-1.12+.27)^2} = 1.064 \approx \frac{16}{15}$. (Ans. B)

EXAMINATION SECTION

TEST 1

DIRECTIONS: Each question or incomplete statement is followed by several suggested answers or completions. Select the one that BEST answers the question or completes the statement. *PRINT THE LETTER OF THE CORRECT ANSWER IN THE SPACE AT THE RIGHT.*

1. If $x = 2$ and $y = 5$, which of the following is TRUE?   1.___
    A. $x + y > 8$ B. $x + y < 8$
    C. $x + y \neq 7$ D. $x + y = 3$

2. The expression $(3a - 7b)^2$ equals   2.___
    A. $9a^2 - 42ab + 49b^2$ B. $9a^2 - 42ab - 49b^2$
    C. $9a^2 - 49b^2$ D. $9a^2 - 21ab + 49b^2$

3. The three children in the Brown family were born in   3.___
    consecutive years. The sum of their ages is now 24 years.
    Which of the following equations expresses the above?
    A. $n + (n+1) = n + 2$ B. $n + (n+2) + (n+4) = 24$
    C. $n(n+1)(n+2) = 24$ D. $n + (n+1) + (n+2) = 24$

4. *Twice the sum of the numbers x and y added to three times*   4.___
    their product would be written as
    A. $2xy + 3(x+y)$ B. $2(x+y) + 3xy$
    C. $5x + 5y$ D. $2x + y + 3xy$

5. The symbol $\{1,2,3\}$ represents   5.___
    A. an infinite set   B. a finite set
    C. a cardinal number   D. the number three

6. The product of 4^6 times 4^{-2} equals   6.___
    A. 4^{-8} B. 4^{-4} C. 4^4 D. 16^4

7. The expression $(27a^3b^9)^{\frac{1}{3}}$ equals   7.___
    A. $3ab^3$ B. $9ab^3$ C. $9ab^6$ D. $3a^9b^{27}$

8. The value of $|-3|$ is   8.___
    A. less than -3 B. -3 C. 0 D. 3

9. If John can shovel the snow from a drive in 20 minutes   9.___
    and Bob can shovel it in 30 minutes, how long will it take
    them working together? ____ minutes.
    A. 6 B. 10 C. 12 D. 50

10. Three times a positive real number is less than 3.   10.___
    The solution set is
    A. $\{1\}$ B. $\{3\}$
    C. $\{1,2,3\}$ D. $\{x$ such that $0 < x < 1\}$

11. The graph of the relation $y = 3 + 2x - x^2$ 11.___
is shown at the right.
Which one of the following statements
about the graph is NOT true? The

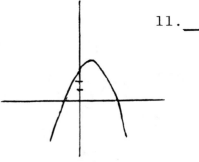

   A. x-intercepts are -1 and +3
   B. point (1,4) is called a maximum point
   C. curve is called a hyperbola
   D. y-intercept is +3

12. The expression $\dfrac{3}{\sqrt{2}+\sqrt{5}}$ may be written with a rational   12.___

denominator by multiplying
   A. *both* numerator and denominator by $\sqrt{10}$
   B. *only* the denominator by $\sqrt{2} - \sqrt{5}$
   C. *both* numerator and denominator by the expression
      $\sqrt{2} + \sqrt{5}$
   D. *both* numerator and denominator by the expression
      $\sqrt{2} - \sqrt{5}$

13. At a constant temperature, the volume of a gas is   13.___
inversely proportional to the pressure.
If the pressure is multiplied by 3 while the temperature
is unchanged, then the volume is ___ by 3.
   A. decreased   B. divided   C. increased D. multiplied

14. Which of the following is an arithmetic progression?   14.___
   A. 4, 7, 10, 13,...   B. 4, 7, 8, 11,...
   C. 4, 8, 16, 32,...   D. 4, 5, 7, 10,...

15. What is the resulting equation when the value of x in   15.___
the linear equation below is substituted in the quadratic
equation below?
     $x^2 + 2y^2 = 10$
     $x + y \quad = 3$

   A. $3 - y + 2y^2 = 10$ B. $(3+y)^2 + 2y^2 = 10$
   C. $(3-y)^2 + 2y^2 = 10$ D. $(3-y+2y)^2 = 10$

16. One factor of $12x^2 + 7x - 10$ is   16.___
   A. 4x + 5   B. 4x - 5   C. 3x - 5   D. 3x + 2

17. If $S = \pi r^2 + 2\pi rh$, then h equals   17.___

   A. $\dfrac{S + \pi r^2}{2\pi r}$ B. $\dfrac{S - \pi r^2}{2\pi r}$ C. $S - \dfrac{r}{2}$ D. $S - \pi r^2 - 2\pi r$

18. The equation $3x^2 - 75x = 0$ has   18.___
   A. only one solution, 25
   B. two solutions, 0 and 5
   C. two solutions, 0 and 25
   D. three solutions, 0, +5, and -5

19. If $2x + 3 > x - 1$, then   19.___
   A. x > -4   B. x > -2   C. x > 2   D. x > 4

20. The graphs whose equations are $x^2 + y^2 = 4$
and $x - y + 6 = 0$ are shown at the right.
What is the common solution of the two
equations?

20.____

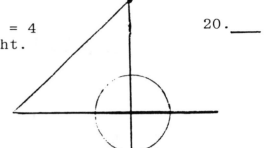

   A. (-6,0) and (0,6)
   B. (0,0)
   C. (2,0), (0,2), and (0,-2)
   D. There is none

21. What are the factors of $8x^3 + 27y^3$?   21.____
   A. $(2x+3y)(4x^2+6xy+9y^2)$ B. $(2x+3y)(2x^2-xy+3y^2)$
   C. $(2x+3y)(4x^2-6xy+9y^2)$ D. $(2x+3y)(4x^2-12xy+9y^2)$

22. Which of the following facts would be applied in solving   22.____
the equation $(x-a)(x-b)(x-c) = 0$?
   A. Both sides of an equation may be divided by any
      number except zero.
   B. The product of two or more factors is zero only if
      one or more factors is equal to zero.
   C. Both sides of an equation may be multiplied by any
      number.
   D. If equals are subtracted from equals, the results
      are equal.

23. If log 3.62 is given as .5587 and log 3.63 as .5599, what   23.____
is the APPROXIMATE value of log 3.626?
   A. .5580   B. .5592   C. .5594   D. .5595

24. The fraction $\dfrac{x + 2i}{x - 3i}$ can be simplified by multiplying   24.____

both numerator and denominator by
   A. $x - 3i$ B. $x + 3$ C. $x + 3i$ D. $x + i$

25. The roots of $2x^2 - 5x - 1 = 0$ are   25.____

   A. $\dfrac{5 \pm \sqrt{33}}{4}$ B. $\dfrac{5 \pm \sqrt{17}}{4}$ C. $\dfrac{-5 \pm \sqrt{33}}{44}$ D. $\dfrac{-2 \pm \sqrt{33}}{4}$

KEY (CORRECT ANSWERS)

1. B		11. C	
2. A		12. D	
3. D		13. B	
4. B		14. A	
5. B		15. C	
6. C		16. A	
7. A		17. B	
8. D		18. C	
9. C		19. A	
10. D		20. D	

21. C
22. B
23. C
24. C
25. A

SOLUTIONS TO PROBLEMS

1. If $x = 2$ and $y = 5$, then $x + y = 7 < 8$

2. $(3a-7b)^2 = 9a^2 - 21ab - 21ab + 49b^2 = 9a^2 - 42ab + 49b^2$

3. If n = age of youngest child, the other two children's ages are $n+1$ and $n+2$. Then, $n + (n+1) + (n+2) = 24$

4. Twice the sum of x and y is written as $2(x+y)$. Three times the product of x and y is written as $3xy$. The sum of these two expressions is $2(x+y) + 3xy$

5. $\{1,2,3\}$ is a finite set of three elements.

6. $4^6 \cdot 4^{-2} = 4^4$

7. $(27a^3b^9)^{\frac{1}{3}} = \sqrt[3]{27a^3b^9} = 3ab^3$

8. $|-3| = 3$. The symbol $|-3|$ means the absolute (positive) value of -3

9. Let x = time in minutes working together. Then, $\frac{x}{20} + \frac{x}{30} = 1$ Multiplying the equation by 60, $3x + 2x = 60$. Solving, $x = 12$

10. If three times a positive real number is less than 3, then the actual number is less than 1. Thus, $0 < x < 1$

11. The curve associated with $y = 3 + 2x - x^2$ is called a parabola

12. $\frac{3}{\sqrt{2} + \sqrt{5}}$ will have a rational denominator if both numerator and denominator are multiplied by $\sqrt{2} - \sqrt{5}$ to become $\frac{3(\sqrt{2}-\sqrt{5})}{-3}$

13. Since volume is inversely proportional to pressure, we can write $PV = K$, K a constant. If P is multiplied by 3, then V must be divided by 3. (Temperature is constant)

14. 4, 7, 10, 13, ... is an arithmetic progression since there is a constant difference between consecutive terms

15. Since $x + y = 3$, $x = 3 - y$. Then, $x^2 + 2y^2 = 10$ becomes $(3-y)^2 + 2y^2 = 10$

16. $12x^2 + 7x - 10$ factors as $(4x+5)(3x-2)$

17. $S = \pi r^2 + 2\pi rh$. Then, $S - \pi r^2 = 2\pi rh$. Finally, $h = (S-\pi r^2)/2\pi r$

18. $3x^2 - 75x = 0$. Then, $3x(x-25) = 0$. Then the two solutions are $x = 0$ and $x = 25$

19. $2x + 3 > x - 1$. Adding $-x - 3$ to each side, $x > -4$

20. There is no common solution for $x^2 + y^2 = 4$ and $x - y + 6 = 0$

21. $8x^3 + 27y^3 = (2x+3y)(4x^2-6xy+9y^2)$. The general factoring of $A^3 + B^3$ is $(A+B)(A^2-AB+B^2)$. Here $A = 2x$, $B = 3y$

22. If $(x-a)(x-b)(x-c) = 0$, then one or more factors must equal zero, so that $x - a = 0$ or $x - b = 0$ or $x - c = 0$

23. Log $3.626 \approx$ Log $3.62 + .6($Log $3.63 -$ Log $3.62) \approx$ $.5587 + .6(.5599 - .5587) = .55942 \approx .5594$
    This is called linear interpolation.

24. To simplify $\frac{x+2i}{x-3i}$, multiply numerator and denominator by $x+3i$.
    This will yield $(x^2+5ix-6)/(x^2+9)$

25. $2x^2 - 5x - 1 = 0$. Then, $x = (5\pm\sqrt{25-4(2)(-1)})/4 = (5\pm\sqrt{33})/4$

TEST 2

DIRECTIONS: Each question or incomplete statement is followed by several suggested answers or completions. Select the one that BEST answers the question or completes the statement. *PRINT THE LETTER OF THE CORRECT ANSWER IN THE SPACE AT THE RIGHT.*

1. If $x + 2 = \sqrt{x^2 + 6}$, then x equals   1.____
   A. $-2\frac{1}{2}$ B. $-\frac{1}{2}$ C. $+\frac{1}{2}$ D. $+2\frac{1}{2}$

2. The sum of $|-4| + |+2|$ equals   2.____
   A. -6 B. -2 C. $+2$ D. $+6$

3. The expression $x + 7 = 7 + x$ illustrates the ____ property.   3.____
   A. commutative   B. transitive
   C. distributive   D. associative

4. In the system of real numbers, zero is called the   4.____
   A. additive inverse   B. multiplicative identity
   C. reciprocal   D. additive identity

5. The slope of the line at the right is   5.____
   A. $\frac{1}{4}$
   B. $\frac{1}{2}$
   C. 2
   D. 4

6. If $A = \{1,2,3,4\}$ and $B = \{1,3\}$, then   6.____
   A. $A \subset B$ B. $B \subset A$
   C. $A = B$ D. B is the complement of A

7. A geometric progression is one in which every term after   7.____
   the first is formed by
   A. adding all the terms preceding it
   B. subtracting a fixed number from the preceding term
   C. adding a fixed number to the preceding term
   D. multiplying the preceding term by a fixed number

8. Which one of the following points does NOT lie on the   8.____
   curve whose equation is $y = 2x^2 + x - 3$?
   A. $(0,3)$ B. $(0,-3)$ C. $(1,0)$ D. $(-1,-2)$

9. The expression $\dfrac{\frac{1}{a} + \frac{1}{b}}{\frac{2}{ab}}$ equals   9.____

   A. $\frac{a}{2} + b$ B. $a + b$ C. $\frac{a + b}{2}$ D. $2(a+b)$

10. How many permutations of 3 letters each may be made with   10.____
    the letters a, b, c, d?
    A. 3   B. 4   C. 6   D. 24

11. If $\frac{x}{y} = 5$, what is the value of $\frac{x - 4y}{y}$?   11.___

    A. 5 - 4y   B. y   C. 1   D. -1

12. An example of the associative property is   12.___
    A. $(xy)z = x(yz)$ B. $a + b = b + a$
    C. $ab = ba$ D. $x(a+b) = xa + xb$

13. In the process of solving $\sqrt{2x} - 1 = \sqrt{2x - 7}$, we get which   13.___
of the following?
    A. $2x + 1 = 2x - 7$
    B. $2x - 2\sqrt{2x} + 1 = 2x - 7$
    C. $4x^2 - 4x + 1 = 4x^2 - 28x + 49$
    D. $2x - 1 = 2x - 7$

14. The graph at the right includes all the   14.___
points outside but not on the circle.
This is the graph of
    A. $x^2 + y^2 > 4$
    B. $x^2 + y^2 < 4$
    C. $x^2 + y^2 \geq 4$
    D. $x^2 + y^2 \leq 4$

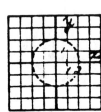

15. What is the range if the domain of the relationship   15.___
$y = |x|$ is $\{-3, -2, -1, 0, 1, 2, 3\}$?
    A. $\{-3, -2, -1, 0, 1, 2, 3\}$
    B. {all real numbers less than 3}
    C. $\{0, 1, 2, 3\}$
    D. null set

16. The product of $(a+bi)(2a-3bi)$ equals   16.___
    A. $2a^2 + 3b^2 - abi$ B. $2a^2 + 3b^2 + abi$
    C. $2a^2 - 3b^2 - abi$ D. $2a^2 - 3b^2 + abi$

17. $\frac{6 \pm \sqrt{36 - 24}}{4}$ can be expressed as   17.___

    A. $\frac{3 \pm \sqrt{12}}{2}$ B. $\frac{3}{2} \pm \sqrt{3}$ C. $\frac{3 \pm 2\sqrt{3}}{2}$ D. $\frac{3 \pm \sqrt{3}}{2}$

18. The roots of $ax^2 + bx + c = 0$ are NOT real if   18.___
    A. c is negative   B. $b^2 - 4ac >$ zero
    C. $b^2 = 4ac$ D. $b^2 - 4ac <$ zero

19. The sum of $\frac{x + 1}{x - 2} + \frac{x + 2}{2 - x}$ equals   19.___

    A. $\frac{1}{x - 2}$ B. $\frac{1}{2 - x}$ C. $\frac{2x + 3}{x - 2}$ D. $\frac{x - 3}{(x - 2)^2}$

20. The graph at the right consisting only   20.___
of four points is the graph of $y = 2x$
where the domain of x is
    A. x real and $-1 \leq x \leq 2$
    B. $\{-2,0,2,4\}$
    C. $\{-1,0,1,2\}$
    D. x rational and $-1 \leq x \leq 2$

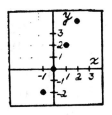

21. Which of the following represents the value of y in the   21.___
    system of equations below?

    $$2x - y + 3z = 8$$
    $$x + y + z = 2$$
    $$3x + 2y + z = 5$$

    A.
    $$\frac{\begin{vmatrix} 2 & -1 & 3 \\ 1 & 1 & 1 \\ 3 & 2 & 1 \end{vmatrix}}{\begin{vmatrix} 2 & 8 & 3 \\ 1 & 2 & 1 \\ 3 & 5 & 1 \end{vmatrix}}$$

    B.
    $$\frac{\begin{vmatrix} 2 & 8 & 3 \\ 1 & 2 & 1 \\ 3 & 5 & 1 \end{vmatrix}}{\begin{vmatrix} 2 & -1 & 3 \\ 1 & 1 & 1 \\ 3 & 2 & 1 \end{vmatrix}}$$

    C.
    $$\begin{vmatrix} 2 & 8 & 3 \\ 1 & 2 & 1 \\ 3 & 5 & 1 \end{vmatrix}$$

    D.
    $$\begin{vmatrix} 2 & -1 & 3 \\ 1 & 1 & 1 \\ 3 & 2 & 1 \end{vmatrix} - \begin{vmatrix} 2 & 8 & 3 \\ 1 & 2 & 1 \\ 3 & 5 & 1 \end{vmatrix}$$

22. If x pencils cost m cents, the formula for the cost c   22.___
    of y pencils is

    A. $c = \frac{my}{x}$ B. $c = \frac{mx}{y}$ C. $c = mxy$ D. $c = \frac{m}{x} + y$

23. Use the factor theorem to determine which of the following 23.___
    is a factor of $x^3 - 5x^2 - 2x + 4$.
    A. $x + 2$ B. $x - 2$ C. $x - 1$ D. $x + 1$

24. The trigonometric ratio cosine of   24.___
    angle 0 is defined as

    A. $\frac{y}{r}$

    B. $\frac{x}{r}$

    C. $\frac{y}{x}$

    D. $\frac{r}{y}$

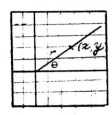

25. If $S = \{1,2,3\}$ and $T = \{3,4,5\}$, then   25.___
    A. $5 \in S$ B. $S \cup T = 3$ C. $5 \in T$ D. $S \cup T = T$

KEY (CORRECT ANSWERS)

1. C	11. C
2. D	12. A
3. A	13. B
4. D	14. A
5. B	15. C
6. B	16. A
7. D	17. D
8. A	18. D
9. C	19. B
10. D	20. C

21. B
22. A
23. D
24. B
25. C

SOLUTIONS TO PROBLEMS

1. $x + 2 = \sqrt{x^2+6}$. Squaring both sides, $x^2 + 4x + 4 = x^2 + 6$. Then, $4x = 2$, so $x = \frac{1}{2}$

2. $|-4| + |+2| = 4 + 2 = 6$

3. $x + 7 = 7 + x$ illustrates the commutative property of addition.

4. Zero is considered the additive identity since $n+0 = n$ for any real number n

5. Slope $= \frac{2-0}{4-0} = \frac{1}{2}$

6. If $A = \{1,2,3,4\}$ and $B = \{1,3\}$, then B is a subset of A. This is written $B \subset A$

7. In a geometric progression, each term (except the 1st) is a constant multiplier of the previous term. Example: 3, 12, 48, 192,.

8. The point (0,3) does NOT lie on the curve with equation $y = 2x^2 + x - 3$ since $3 \neq 2(0) + 0 - 3$

9. $(\frac{1}{a} + \frac{1}{b})/\frac{2}{ab} = \frac{b+a}{ab} \cdot \frac{ab}{2} = \frac{b+a}{2} = \frac{a+b}{2}$

10. The number of permutations using 3 letters out of 4 is $(4)(3)(2) = 24$

11. $\frac{x}{y} = 5$, then $x = 5y$. Thus, $(x-4y)/y = (5y-4y)/y = 1$

12. $(xy)(z) = (x)(yz)$ illustrates the associative property of multiplication.

13. $\sqrt{2x} - 1 = \sqrt{2x-7}$. In squaring both sides, we get: $2x - 2\sqrt{2x} + 1 = 2x - 7$. The solution is $x = 8$

14. $x^2 + y^2 > 4$ describes all points outside the circle with center at (0,0) and a radius of 2

15. If $y = |x|$ and $x = -3, -2, -1, 0, 1, 2, 3$, then the corresponding y values are 3, 2, 1, 0, 1, 2, 3. The range is $\{0,1,2,3\}$

16. $(a+bi)(2a-3bi) = 2a^2 - 3abi + 2abi - 3b^2i^2 = 2a^2 - abi + 3b^2$

17. $(6\pm\sqrt{36-24})/4 = (6\pm2\sqrt{3})/4 = (3\pm\sqrt{3})/2$
    Note: $\sqrt{12} = \sqrt{4}\sqrt{3} = 2\sqrt{3}$

18. If $b^2 - 4ac < 0$, then the roots of $ax^2 + bx + c = 0$ are not real. They are complex roots.

19. $\frac{x+1}{x-2} + \frac{x+2}{2-x} = \frac{x+1}{x-2} + \frac{-x-2}{x-2} = \frac{-1}{x-2} = \frac{1}{2-x}$

20. In the graph, the x values are -1, 0, 1, and 2

21. For the system $2x - y + 3z = 8$, $x + y + z = 2$, $3x + 2y + z = 5$, the determinants for the value of y is given by:

    $$\frac{\begin{vmatrix} 2 & 8 & 3 \\ 1 & 2 & 1 \\ 3 & 5 & 1 \end{vmatrix}}{\begin{vmatrix} 2 & -1 & 3 \\ 1 & 1 & 1 \\ 3 & 2 & 1 \end{vmatrix}}$$

    which equals $\frac{7}{-7} = -1$

22. $\frac{x}{m} = \frac{y}{c}$. Then, $xc = my$. Finally, $c = \frac{my}{x}$

23. Since -1 makes the expression $x^3 - 5x^2 - 2x + 4$ equal to 0, $x+1$ must be a factor of $x^3 - 5x^2 - 2x + 4$. Actually, $x^3 - 5x^2 - 2x + 4 = (x+1)(x^2-6x+4)$

24. Cosineθ = adjacent side/hypotenuse = $\frac{x}{r}$, where $r = \sqrt{x^2+y^2}$

25. Given $S = \{1,2,3\}$ and $T = \{3,4,5\}$, $5\varepsilon T$ is a correct statement.

EXAMINATION SECTION

TEST 1

DIRECTIONS: Each question or incomplete statement is followed by several suggested answers or completions. Select the one that BEST answers the question or completes the statement. *PRINT THE LETTER OF THE CORRECT ANSWER IN THE SPACE AT THE RIGHT.*

1. $\log(x^2-y^2)$ is equal to which one of the following? 1.___
   A. $2 \log x - 2 \log y$
   B. $\log (x+y) + \log (x-y)$
   C. $2 \log (x-y)$
   D. None of the above

2. If $\log x \geq \log 2 + \frac{1}{2} \log x$, then   2.___
   A. $x \geq 2$ B. $x \leq 2$ C. $x \leq 4$ D. $x \geq 4$

3. The graph of $y > x$ has points in quadrant(s)   3.___
   A. I *only*   B. I and II *only*
   C. I, II, and III *only*   D. I and III *only*

4. If $3x + 5 > x$ and n is a negative integer, an equivalent   4.___
   sentence is
   A. $n(3x+5) > nx$ B. $3x + 5 + n < n + x$

   C. $n - (3x+5) > n - x$ D. $\dfrac{3x + 5}{n} < \dfrac{x}{n}$

5. The statement that is mathematically CORRECT is   5.___
   A. $\sin 2x = 2 \sin x \cos x$ for all values of x
   B. $x^0 = 1$ for all values of x
   C. $\sqrt{x^2} = x$ for all values of x

   D. $\dfrac{x^2-1}{x-1} = x + 1$ for all values of x

6. If n is an integer, then $\left(-\dfrac{1}{\sqrt{-1}}\right)^{4n+5}$ is equal to   6.___

   A. 1   B. -1   C. i   D. -i

7. If $x + y = 2xy$, then $\dfrac{1}{x} + \dfrac{1}{y}$ equals   7.___

   A. 1   B. 2
   C. 3   D. none of the above

8. Two roots of the equation $x^3 + cx + d = 0$ are -1 and -2.   8.___
   The third root is
   A. 1   B. -3   C. 3   D. -7

9. A train makes a trip between two towns at the rate of
   a miles per hour and makes the return trip on the same
   track at the rate of b miles per hour.
   The AVERAGE rate for the round trip is

   A. $\dfrac{2ab}{a+b}$ B. $\dfrac{a+b}{2}$ C. $\sqrt{ab}$ D. $\dfrac{2(a+b)}{ab}$

   9.___

10. An automobile radiator contains 15 quarts of a 20% solution
    of antifreeze.
    How many quarts of the solution should be drained from the
    radiator and replaced with an equal amount of pure anti-
    freeze to raise the concentration to 50%?

    A. $4\frac{1}{2}$ B. $4\frac{3}{8}$ C. $5\frac{5}{8}$ D. $7\frac{1}{2}$

    10.___

11. If f(x) and g(x) are two functions defined by $f(x) = 2x+1$
    and $g(x) = x^2-2$, then g[f(x)] is
    A. $x^2 + 2x - 1$ B. $4x^2 + 4x - 1$
    C. $2x^2 - 3$ D. $4x^2 + 4x + 1$

    11.___

12. If $\log 4x^5 - \log x^4 + \log 5 = 4$, the value of x is

    A. $\dfrac{1}{5}$ B. 5   C. 50   D. 500

    12.___

13. The parabola whose equation is $(y-1)^2 = 4(x+2)$ has
    A. its vertex at (2,-1)
    B. its focus at (2,1)
    C. a directrix whose equation is x = -3
    D. a relative minimum point

    13.___

14. The equation $x^9 + 16x^3 + 64 = 0$ has ___ positive root(s),
    ___ negative root(s), and ___ imaginary roots.
    A. 2; 1; 6   B. 1; 0; 8   C. 0; 1; 8   D. 8; 1; 0

    14.___

15. The coefficient of the fifth term of the expansion of
    $(x+1)^8$ is equal to
    A. 28   B. 56   C. $8C4$ D. $8C5$

    15.___

16. One of the cube roots of -8i is
    A. $-2i$ B. $\sqrt{3} + i$ C. $\sqrt{3} - i$ D. $-\sqrt{3} + i$

    16.___

17. $\dfrac{x}{x^2-1} > 0$ if and only if

    A. $x > 1$ or $-1 < x < 0$ B. $x > 1$
    C. $|x| > 1$ D. $|x| < 1$

    17.___

18. The domain of $f(x) = \dfrac{1}{\sqrt{9-x^2}}$, if f(x) is real, is

    A. $x < 3$ B. $|x| < 3$
    C. $|x| < 3$ D. $|x| > 3$

    18.___

19. The value of $(1+i)^4$ is
    A. $-4 + 8i$ B. $4 - 8i$ C. -4 D. 4

    19.___

20. The sum of the reciprocals of the roots of the equation
$ax^2 + bx + c = 0$ will be

    A. $-\dfrac{a}{b}$ B. $-\dfrac{b}{a}$ C. $-\dfrac{b}{c}$ D. $-\dfrac{c}{b}$

20.____

———

KEY (CORRECT ANSWERS)

1. B	11. B
2. A	12. D
3. C	13. C
4. D	14. C
5. A	15. C
6. C	16. C
7. B	17. A
8. C	18. B
9. A	19. C
10. C	20. C

———

SOLUTIONS TO PROBLEMS

1. Log (x^2-y^2) = Log $[(x+y)(x-y)]$ = Log $(x+y)$ + Log $(x-y)$. (Ans. B)

2. Log 2 + $\frac{1}{2}$ Log x = Log $2x^{\frac{1}{2}}$. Now, since Log x $\geq$ Log $2x^{\frac{1}{2}}$, x $\geq 2x^{\frac{1}{2}}$. This becomes $x^2 \geq 2x$, which is solved as $x \geq 2$. (Ans. A)

3. 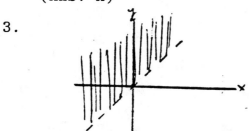 The dotted line represents y = x. The shaded area represents y > x and it occupies parts of quadrants I, III, and all of quadrant II. (Ans. C)

4. If 3x + 5 > x and n < 0, then $\frac{3x+5}{n} < \frac{x}{n}$, since dividing by a negative number reverses the inequality. (Ans. D)

5. $x^0 = 1$ is NOT true if x = 0, since 0^0 is undefined. $\sqrt{x^2} = x$ only if $x \geq 0$, and $\sqrt{x^2} = -x$ if x is negative. $\frac{x^2-1}{x-1}$ is undefined if x = 1. However, sin 2x = 2 sin x cos x for all x. (Ans. A)

6. $\frac{1}{-\sqrt{-1}} = \frac{1}{-i} = \frac{1}{-i} \cdot \frac{i}{i} = \frac{i}{-i^2} = i$. Now, i runs in cycles of 4 as: i, $i^2 = -1$, $i^3 = -i$, $i^4 = 1$. If n is integral, then 4n+5, when divided by 4, leaves a remainder of 1. This corresponds to i. (Ans. C)

7. $\frac{1}{x} + \frac{1}{y} = \frac{y+x}{xy} = \frac{2xy}{xy} = 2$.   (Ans. B)

8. Since -1 is a root, $(-1)^3 + c(-1) + d = 0$. Also, since -2 is a root, $(-2)^3 + c(-2) + d = 0$. Solving, c = -7, d = -6. Now, $x^3 - 7x - 6 = (x+1)(x+2)(x-3)$; thus 3 is the last root. (Ans. C)

9. Let x = distance each way. Time for first trip = $\frac{x}{a}$. Time for second trip = $\frac{x}{b}$. Average rate = total distance $\div$ total time = 2x $\div$ $(\frac{x}{a} + \frac{x}{b})$ = 2x $\div$ ([ax+bx]/ab) = 2ab/(a+b).   (Ans. A)

10. Let x = amount of solution drained. At this point, there are 15-x quarts of the solution and 3-.20x quarts of antifreeze (recognize that for every quart of solution drained, only one-fifth of a quart of antifreeze is drained).
Now add the x quarts of antifreeze, so that the solution again becomes 15 quarts and the amount of antifreeze = 3-.20x + x. Finally, 3-.20x + x = .50(15), whereby x = 5$\frac{5}{8}$.   (Ans. C)

11. $g[f(x)] = g(2x+1) = (2x+1)^2 - 2 = 4x^2 + 4x + 1 - 2 = 4x^2 + 4x - 1$.
(Ans. B)

12. Log $4x^5$ = Log 4 + 5 Log x and Log x^4 = 4 Log x.
Thus, Log 4 + 5 Log x - 4 Log x + Log 5 = 4.
Log x + Log 4 + Log 5 = 4, Log 20x = 4.
This implies 10^4 = 20x, x = 500.   (Ans. D)

13. The parabola $(y-k)^2 = 4p(x-h)$ has a vertex at (h,k), directrix is x = h-p and focus of (h+p,k). For the equation $(y-1)^2 = 4(x+2)$, the vertex is (-2,1), directrix is the equation x = -3, and focus is (-1,1).   (Ans. C)

14. Since all signs of the terms are positive, there can be no positive roots. Only choice C could be correct. (Ans. C)

15. Fifth coeff. = $\frac{8 \cdot 7 \cdot 6 \cdot 5}{1 \cdot 2 \cdot 3 \cdot 4}$ = 8 C 4.   (Ans. C)

16. $(-8i)^{\frac{1}{3}} = [8(\cos 270° + i \sin 270°)]^{\frac{1}{3}} = 2(\cos 90° + i \sin 90°)$, $2(\cos 210° + i \sin 210°)$, and $2(\cos 330° + i \sin 330°)$.
This leads to the three roots: 2i, $-\sqrt{3}-i$, and $\sqrt{3}-i$.
(Ans. C)

17. Case 1: Both x > 0 and x^2-1 > 0, satisfied by x > 1.
Case 2: Both x < 0 and x^2-1 < 0, satisfied by -1 < x < 0.
(Ans. A)

18. $\sqrt{9-x^2}$ > 0, in order for f(x) to be real.
Thus, $9-x^2$ >0, solved by -3 < x < 3 or $|x|$ < 3.
(Ans. B)

19. $(1+i)^4 = 1 + 4i + 6i^2 + 4i^3 + i^4 = 1 + 4i - 6 - 4i + 1 = -4$.
(Ans. C)

20. Let R_1, R_2 be the roots. Then, $\frac{1}{R_1} + \frac{1}{R_2} = \frac{R_2+R_1}{R_1 R_2} = \frac{-\frac{b}{a}}{\frac{c}{a}} = -\frac{b}{c}$

(Ans. C)

TEST 2

DIRECTIONS: Each question or incomplete statement is followed by several suggested answers or completions. Select the one that BEST answers the question or completes the statement. *PRINT THE LETTER OF THE CORRECT ANSWER IN THE SPACE AT THE RIGHT.*

1. Log 4 ÷ log ¼ is equal to
   A. -1   B. 0   C. 2 log 2   D. log 2

   1.___

2. $(16)^{(-2)^{-2}}$ has the SAME value as

   A. $\frac{1}{16^4}$ B. $\frac{1}{2}$ C. 2   D. 16^4

   2.___

3. Given the equation in determinant form $\begin{vmatrix} 2x & 1 \\ x & x \end{vmatrix} = 3$, the equation is satisfied for ____ values of x.
   A. two real   B. two imaginary
   C. no   D. all real

   3.___

4. A purse contains one penny, one nickel, one dime, one quarter, and one half-dollar.
   How many different sums of money can be formed using one or more of these coins?
   A. 5   B. 16   C. 31   D. 32

   4.___

5. The solution set of the equation $x^3 - 5x + 6 = 2x^2$ is
   A. {-1,2,-3}   B. {1,-2,-3}   C. {-1,1,-6}   D. {1,-2,3}

   5.___

6. The graph of $x^2 - 4y^2 = 0$ is a(n)
   A. hyperbola   B. parabola
   C. ellipse   D. pair of straight lines

   6.___

7. The time required for one oscillation of a pendulum is given by the formula $t = 2\pi\sqrt{\frac{L}{G}}$, where L is the length and

   G is a constant.
   In order to DOUBLE the time for one oscillation, the length of the pendulum should be
   A. halved   B. doubled
   C. squared   D. quadrupled

   7.___

8. The infinite repeating decimal $2.\overline{52}$ is equal to

   A. $2\frac{13}{25}$ B. $2\frac{14}{33}$ C. $2\frac{50}{99}$ D. $2\frac{52}{99}$

   8.___

9. The distance travelled by a falling body is given by the formula $S = 16t^2$, where S is the distance, in feet, and t is the time in seconds.
   During the fifth second, a falling body will travel ____ feet.
   A. 80   B. 144   C. 256   D. 400

   9.___

10. If $g = \dfrac{K}{d^2}$, then d varies   10.___

     A. *directly* as the square root of g
     B. *inversely* as the square of g
     C. *inversely* as the square root of g
     D. *directly* as the square of g

11. The set of values satisfying the inequality $\left|\dfrac{5-x}{3}\right| < 2$ is   11.___
     A. 1 < x < 11   B. -1 < x < 11
     C. x < -1 or x > 11   D. x < 1 or x > 11

12. If $\log_{10}(x^2-x-2) = 1$, then x is equal to   12.___

     A. 4 or -3   B. -1 or 2   C. -4 or 3   D. 1 or -2

13. If the discriminant of the equation $ax^2 + 2bx + c = 0$ is   13.___
equal to zero, then it is ALWAYS true that
     A. a,b,c form an arithmetic progression
     B. a,b, and c form a geometric progression
     C. b is always negative
     D. a and c are equal

14. If the square of a two digit number is DECREASED by the   14.___
square of the number formed by reversing the digits, then
the result is NOT ALWAYS divisible by
     A. 9   B. the product of the digits
     C. the sum of the digits   D. the difference of the digits

15. Fifteen girls left a mixed group of boys and girls. There   15.___
remained two boys for each girl. After this, 45 boys leave
the group, and there were 5 girls for each boy.
The number of girls in the ORIGINAL group must have been
     A. 29   B. 40   C. 43   D. 50

16. The repeating decimal $0.\overline{247}$ may be represented by   16.___
     A. $\dfrac{2470}{9999}$ B. $\dfrac{247247}{1,000,000}$ C. $\dfrac{247}{999}$ D. $\dfrac{247}{1000}$

17. Let x represent a positive real number. Consider the   17.___
following statements:
     I. $\sqrt{-x} = -\sqrt{x}$ II. $\sqrt[3]{-x} = -\sqrt[3]{x}$

     The CORRECT answer is:
     A. I and II are *false*
     B. I is *false* and II is *true*
     C. I is *true* and II is *false*
     D. I and II are *true*

18. If a and b are real numbers, then $\sqrt{a}\sqrt{b}$ is NOT equal to   18.___
$\sqrt{ab}$ when
     A. a > 0 and b > 0   B. a > 0 and b < 0
     C. a < 0 and b = 0   D. a < 0 and b < 0

19. If $x^7 - 7x - 56$ is divided by x-2, the remainder is   19.___
    A. 28   B. 58   C. 86   D. -170

20. Which of the following equations has 0 and 1+i as   20.___
    elements in its solution set?
    A. $x^2 - 2x + 2 = 0$ B. $x^3 - 2x^2 + 2x = 0$
    C. $x^2 + 2x - 2 = 0$ D. $x^3 + 2x^2 - 2x = 0$

———

KEY (CORRECT ANSWERS)

1. A		11. B
2. C		12. A
3. A		13. B
4. C		14. B
5. D		15. B
6. A		16. C
7. D		17. B
8. D		18. D
9. B		19. B
10. C		20. B

———

SOLUTIONS TO PROBLEMS

1. Log $4 \div$ Log $\frac{1}{4}$ = Log $4 \div$ [Log 1 - Log 4], and since Log $1 = 0$, the result is Log $4 \div$ -Log $4 = -1$.　(Ans. A)

2. $(-2)^{-2} = \dfrac{1}{(-2)^2} = \dfrac{1}{4}$. Thus, $(16)^{(-2)^{-2}} = (16)^{\frac{1}{4}} = 2$.　(Ans. C)

3. The value of the determinant $\begin{vmatrix} 2x & 1 \\ x & x \end{vmatrix}$ is $2x^2 - x$.
Now, if $2x^2 - x = 3$, x can be -1 or $1\frac{1}{2}$, which are 2 real values.
(Ans. A)

4. The number of different sums of money = $_5C_1 + {}_5C_2 + {}_5C_3 + {}_5C_4 + {}_5C_5 = 5 + 10 + 10 + 5 + 1 = 31$. Then, symbol $_nC_x$ means the number of combinations of n items taken x at a time.
(Ans. C)

5. The expression $x^3 - 2x^2 - 5x + 6$ factors into $(x-1)(x+2)(x-3)$. Setting this product = to 0 gives roots of $1, -2,$ and 3.
(Ans. D)

6. Any equation which can be written as $\dfrac{x^2}{a^2} - \dfrac{y^2}{b^2} = 1$ is a

hyperbola. (a and b are constants.) Now, $x^2 - 4y^2 = 0$ can

be written as $\dfrac{x^2}{4} - \dfrac{y^2}{1} = 0$, so that $a = 2$ and $b = 1$.　(Ans. A)

7. Given $t = 2\pi\sqrt{\dfrac{L}{G}}$, in order to double the t value, the length L

should be quadrupled. When L is replaced by 4L, the right side

of the equation becomes $2\pi\dfrac{\sqrt{4L}}{G} = 4\pi\dfrac{\sqrt{L}}{G}$. This is double the

original t value.　(Ans. D)

8. Let $N = .\overline{52}$. Then, $100N = 52.\overline{52}$ and by subtraction $99N = 52$.

Thus, $N = \dfrac{52}{99}$, and so $2.\overline{52} = 2\dfrac{52}{99}$.　(Ans. D)

9. The distance traveled in 5 seconds = $16(5^2) = 400$ ft.
The distance traveled in 4 seconds = $16(4^2) = 256$ ft.
Thus, the distance traveled ONLY during the fifth second = $400 - 256 = 144$ ft.　(Ans. B)

10. From $g = \dfrac{K}{d^2}$, we can get $d = \sqrt{\dfrac{K}{g}} = K'/\sqrt{g}$, where $K' = \sqrt{K}$

(K, K' are constants.) This means that d varies inversely as the square root of g.　(Ans. C)

11. Rewrite as $-2 < \frac{5-x}{3} < 2$, and the solution becomes $-1 < x < 11$

    (Ans. B)

12. $\text{Log}_{10}(x^2-x-2) = 1$ implies $x^2 - x - 2 = 10$ or $(x-4)(x+3) = 0$.
    Solving, $x = 4$ or $x = -3$.   (Ans. A)

13. Discriminant $= b^2 - 4ac$ in the equation $ax^2 + bx + c = 0$.
    Here, the discriminant $= 4b^2 - 4ac$. If this expression equals
    0, $b^2 - ac = 0$. Thus, $b^2 = ac$ and so a,b,c form a geometric

    progression, since $\frac{c}{b} = \frac{b}{a}$.   (Ans. B)

14. Let $10t+u$ be the original number. Then, $(10t+u)^2 - (10u+t)^2$
    $= 99t^2 - 99u^2$, which is NOT necessarily divisible by the
    product of the digits, tu. Note that $99t^2 - 99u^2 = 99(t+u)(t-u)$
    so that the quantities mentioned in selections A, B, and C
    are factors (can be divided into) of $99t^2 - 99u^2$.   (Ans. B)

15. Let $x =$ original number of girls. When 15 girls left, $x-15$
    was the number of girls left, and $2(x-15) =$ the number of
    boys. When 45 boys then left, $2(x-15) - 45 = 2x - 75 =$
    number of boys remaining. Since there were now five times
    as many girls as boys, we have $x-15 = 5(2x-75)$. Solving,
    $x = 40$.   (Ans. B)

16. Let $N = .\overline{247}$. Then, $1000N = 247.\overline{247}$. By subtraction,
    $999N = 247$ and so $N = 247/999$.   (Ans. C)

17. As a numerical example, $\sqrt{-4} = 2i \neq -\sqrt{4}$, but $\sqrt[3]{-27} = -3 = -\sqrt[3]{27}$.
    (Ans. B)

18. $\sqrt{a} \cdot \sqrt{b} \neq \sqrt{ab}$ when both a and b are negative.
    Example: $\sqrt{-9} \cdot \sqrt{-25} = (3i)(5i) = 15i^2 = -15 \neq \sqrt{(-9)(-25)} =$
    $\sqrt{225} = 15$.   (Ans. D)

19. By the Remainder Theorem, the remainder is the value of
    $x^7 - 7x - 56$ when x is replaced by 2. This value is
    $2^7 - 7(2) - 56 = 58$.   (Ans. B)

20. Since $1+i$ is one of the roots, $1-i$ must also be a root.
    Now, if 0, $1+i$, and $1-i$ are the roots, then the equation
    with these roots can be written: $x(x-[1+i])(x-[1-i]) = 0$.
    This becomes $x^3 - 2x^2 + 2x = 0$.   (Ans. B)

TEST 3

DIRECTIONS: Each question or incomplete statement is followed by several suggested answers or completions. Select the one that BEST answers the question or completes the statement. *PRINT THE LETTER OF THE CORRECT ANSWER IN THE SPACE AT THE RIGHT.*

1. The solution set for $x^2 - 2x - 3 < 0$ is   1.____
   A. $\{x \mid x < -1\}$ B. $\{x \mid x > 3\}$
   C. $\{x \mid -1 < x < 3\}$ D. $\{x \mid x < -1 \text{ or } x > 3\}$

2. If $\left| \dfrac{3(3x-5)}{2} \right| = 15$, then the solution set for x is   2.____

   A. $\{5\}$ B. $\{5,-5\}$ C. $\{-5,\frac{5}{3}\}$ D. $\{5,-\frac{5}{3}\}$

3. The graph of $\{(x,y) \mid ax^2+by^2 = c\}$, where a, b, and c are   3.____
   real numbers, CANNOT be a(n)
   A. circle   B. parabola   C. ellipse   D. hyperbola

4. An equation of the locus of a point whose distance from   4.____
   the origin is twice its distance from the point (3,0) is
   A. $x^2 + y^2 + 8x + 12 = 0$ B. $x^2 + y^2 - 8x + 12 = 0$
   C. $x^2 + y^2 + 12x + 18 = 0$ D. $x^2 + y^2 - 12x + 18 = 0$

5. Which of the following expressions is equal to $\log_2 10$?   5.____
   A. $\dfrac{1}{\log_{10} 2}$ B. $\dfrac{10}{\log_{10} 2}$ C. $1 - \log_{10} 2$ D. $- \log_{10} 2$

6. Consider the four relations: 5.____
   I. $\{(x,y) \mid x+y = 6\}$ II. $\{(x,y) \mid x+y^2 = 6\}$
   III. $\{(x,y) \mid x^2+y = 6\}$ IV. $\{(x,y) \mid x^2 + y^2 = 6\}$

   Of the four relations, those which are also functions are
   A. I, II   B. I, III   C. I, IV   D. II, III

7. If A represents the set of algebraic numbers and R   7.____
   represents the set of real numbers, then a number which
   belongs to $A \cap R$ is
   A. e   B. π C. i   D. $\sqrt{5}$

8. Let us define a*b to mean $\dfrac{a-2b}{3}$ where a and b represent   8.____
   integers.
   If a = 15, b = 6, and c = 3, then a*(b*c) equals
   A. 5   B. 0   C. $-\dfrac{5}{3}$ D. -2

9. The equations of two lines are, respectively, $a_1x + b_1y = c_1$ and $a_2x + b_2y = c_2$. The two lines are parallel IF and ONLY IF

   A. $a_1b_2 - a_2b_1 \neq 0$ and $c_1b_2 - c_2b_1 \neq 0$
   B. $a_1b_2 - a_2b_1 \neq 0$ and $c_1b_2 - c_2b_1 = 0$
   C. $a_1b_2 - a_2b_1 = 0$ and $c_1b_2 - c_2b_1 \neq 0$
   D. $a_1b_2 - a_2b_1 = 0$ and $c_1b_2 - c_2b_1 = 0$

   9.___

10. Let r_1 and r_2 be the roots of the equation $x^2 - bx + c = 0$.

    If r_1^2 and r_2^2 are the roots of equation $x^2 - dx + e = 0$,

    then d equals
    A. $b^2 + c^2$ B. $b^2 + 2c$ C. $b^2 - 2c$ D. b^2

    10.___

11. A trip from A to B was made at a speed of r km/hr. The return trip from B to A along the same route was made at a speed of 3r km/hr.
    The average speed, in km/hr, for the entire trip was

    A. $\frac{5}{4}$ r   B. $\frac{3}{2}$ r   C. 2r   D. $\frac{5}{2}$ r

    11.___

12. In calculating an average, English and Social Studies are weighted at 3 each, Mathematics is weighted at 2, and Music is weighted at 1.
    If a student receives a grade of 82 in English, 85 in Mathematics, and 91 in Music, what grade MUST he achieve in Social Studies to attain an average of 85?
    A. 82   B. 84   C. 86   D. 87

    12.___

13. The roots of the quadratic equation $4 = \frac{2}{x^2} + \frac{7}{x}$ are

    A. imaginary
    B. real, unequal, and rational
    C. real, unequal, and irrational
    D. real, equal, and rational

    13.___

14. The arithmetic mean of two numbers is 17, and their geometric mean is 15.
    A quadratic equation of which the numbers are roots is
    A. $x^2 + 34x - 225 = 0$ B. $x^2 + 17x - 15 = 0$
    C. $x^2 - 34x + 225 = 0$ D. $x^2 - 17x + 15 = 0$

    14.___

15. If $3x^4 - 3$ is factored completely, then the result is
    A. $3(x^2-1)(x^2+1)$ B. $3(x+1)(x+1)(x-1)(x-1)$
    C. $(3x+3)(x-1)(x^2+1)$ D. $3(x^2+1)(x+1)(x-1)$

    15.___

16. If $S = \frac{1}{2}m(a+b)$, then a solution for b would be

    A. $b = \frac{2S-2a}{m}$ B. $b = \frac{2m}{S} - a$ C. $b = \frac{2S-am}{m}$ D. $b = 2S-am$

    16.___

17. The solution set of $x^2 = 2$ is NOT the empty set if the
    domain of x is either the
    A. real numbers or the rational numbers
    B. real numbers or the complex numbers
    C. irrational numbers or the rational numbers
    D. irrational numbers or the imaginary numbers

17.___

18. H varies directly as x and inversely as d^2.
    If H = 20 when x = 2 and d = 3, find H when x = 4 and
    d = 6.
    A. 10   B. 20   C. 40   D. 90

18.___

19. Two of the roots of $x^3 + px + q = 0$ are 2 and 3.
    The third root is
    A. 5   B. -5   C. 6   D. -6

19.___

20. If $\log_{10}12 = a$ and $\log_{10}2 = b$, then $\log_{10}60$ equals

    A. a-b+1   B. 5a   C. 4a + 6b   D. $\dfrac{10a}{b}$

20.___

KEY (CORRECT ANSWERS)

1. C		11. B	
2. D		12. C	
3. B		13. B	
4. B		14. C	
5. A		15. D	
6. B		16. C	
7. D		17. B	
8. A		18. A	
9. C		19. B	
10. C		20. A	

SOLUTIONS TO PROBLEMS

1. $x^2 - 2x - 3 = (x-3)(x+1) < 0$
   Case 1: $x - 3 < 0$ and $x + 1 > 0$, which implies $-1 < x < 3$
   Case 2: $x - 3 > 0$ and $x + 1 < 0$, which is impossible
   Final answer: $-1 < x < 3$.
   (Ans. C)

2. Case 1: $3(3x-5)/2 = 15$, which yields $x = 5$
   Case 2: $3(3x-5)/2 = -15$, from which $x = -\frac{5}{3}$.

   Answer: $\{5, -\frac{5}{3}\}$
   (Ans. D)

3. In the equation of a parabola, one variable is quadratic and the other variable must be linear. (Ans. B)

4. Let (x,y) be a general point. Then, $\sqrt{x^2+y^2} = 2\sqrt{(x-3)^2+y^2}$, which reduces to $x^2 + y^2 - 8x + 12 = 0$. (Ans. B)

5. Let $x = \log_2 10$. Then, $2^x = 10$, from which $x \log_{10} 2 = \log_{10} 10$ or $x \log_{10} 2 = 1$. Thus, $x = \frac{1}{\log_{10} 2}$. (Ans. A)

6. To be a function, each value of x must correspond to exactly one y. Only equations I and III are functions. (Ans. B)

7. Only $\sqrt{5} = 5^{\frac{1}{2}}$ is algebraic. Both e and π are transcendental. i is imaginary. (Ans. D)

8. $b*c = (b-2c)/3 = [6-2(3)]/3 = 0$. Now, $a*0 = [a-2(0)]/3 = (15-0)/3 = 5$. (Ans. A)

9. Slope of the first line $= -\frac{a_1}{b_1}$. Slope of the second line $= -\frac{a_2}{b_2}$.
   In order for the two lines to be parallel, $-\frac{a_1}{b_1} = -\frac{a_2}{b_2}$, which implies $a_1 b_2 - a_2 b_1 = 0$. Since the y intercepts must be different, $\frac{c_1}{b_1} \neq \frac{c_2}{b_2}$. This means $c_1 b_2 - c_2 b_1 \neq 0$.
   (Ans. C)

10. Since R_1, R_2 are roots of $x^2 - bx + c = 0$, we know that $R_1 + R_2 = b$ and $(R_1)(R_2) = c$. Likewise, we have R_1^2, R_2^2 are roots of $x^2 - dx + e = 0$; thus, $R_1^2 + R_2^2 = d$ and $(R_1^2)(R_2^2) = e$.
    Now, $R_1^2 + 2R_1 R_2 + R_2^2 = (R_1+R_2)^2 = b^2$, and since $2R_1 R_2 = 2c$, we have $R_1^2 + 2C + R_2^2 = b^2$ or $R_1^2 + R_2^2 = b^2 - 2c$. This means $d = b^2 - 2c$. (Ans. C)

11. Average speed = total distance/total time = $(x+x)/(\frac{x}{r} + \frac{x}{3r})$ = $2x/\frac{4x}{3r} = \frac{3}{2}r$. Here, x = distance from A to B. (Ans. B)

12. Let x = required score. Then, $\frac{(82)(3)+(x)(3)+(85)(2)+(91)(1)}{9}$ = 85. Solving, x = 86. (Ans. C)

13. Convert the equation to $4x^2 - 7x - 2 = 0$, which becomes $(4x+1)(x-2) = 0$. The answers, 2 and $-\frac{1}{4}$, are real, unequal, and rational. (Ans. B)

14. Let x = 1st number, y = 2nd number. Then, $\frac{x+y}{2}$ = 17 and xy = 225.

By substitution of y = 34-x from the first equation into the second equation, x(34-x) = 225. This becomes $x^2 - 34x + 225 = 0$. (Ans. C)

15. $3x^4 - 3 = 3(x^4-1) = 3(x^2+1)(x+1)(x-1)$. (Ans. D)

16. Dividing both sides by $\frac{1}{2}m$, $\frac{2S}{m}$ = a+b, so b = $\frac{2S}{m}$ - a or, equivalently, b = $\frac{2S-am}{m}$. (Ans. C)

17. $x^2 = 2$ has roots $\pm\sqrt{2}$, provided the domain of x will include irrational numbers. (Ans. B)

18. H = $\frac{Kx}{d^2}$, where K is a constant. When H = 20, x = 2, d = 3, so K = (20)(9)/2 = 90. Thus, we can write $H = 90x/d^2$. Now, H = (90)(4)/36 = 10. (Ans. A)

19. Since 2,3 are roots, x-2, x-3 are factors. Also, by the substitution of 2,3 for x, we get 8 + 2p + q = 0 and 27 + 3p + q = 0 Solving, p = -19, q = 30. The equation becomes $x^3 - 19x + 30 = 0$. Let R = third root. Then, $(x-2)(x-3)(x-R) = x^3 - 19x + 30$. Thus, R = -5. (Ans. B)

20. $Log_{10}60 = Log_{10}[(12)(10)\div2] = Log_{10}12 + Log_{10}10 - Log_{10}2$ = a + 1 - b or a - b + 1. (Ans. A)

TEST 4

DIRECTIONS: Each question or incomplete statement is followed by several suggested answers or completions. Select the one that BEST answers the question or completes the statement. *PRINT THE LETTER OF THE CORRECT ANSWER IN THE SPACE AT THE RIGHT.*

1. The sum of the integers from 1 to 100, inclusive, is
   A. 5049   B. 5050   C. 5051   D. 5055

   1.___

2. If $\sqrt{x+5} = 3$, then $(x+5)^2$ equals
   A. 9   B. 81   C. 3   D. 4

   2.___

3. The solution set of $|5-2x| < 9$ is
   A. $\{x \mid x < -2\}$ B. $\{x \mid x > -2\}$
   C. $\{x \mid -2 < x < 7\}$ D. $\{x \mid x < -2 \text{ or } x > 7\}$

   3.___

4. The solution set of the equation $\log x^2 = (\log x)^2$ is
   A. $\{0,2\}$
   B. $\{1,100\}$
   C. $\{$all real values of $x\}$
   D. $\{$all real values of $x > 0\}$

   4.___

5. Simplify the following expression $\dfrac{(n+k+1)!}{(n+k-1)!}$.

   A. $(n+k+1)(n+k)!$
   B. -1
   C. $(n+k+1)(n+k)$
   D. The expression cannot be simplified

   5.___

6. The circle whose equation is $4x^2 + 4y^2 - 8x + 24y + 4 = 0$ has a radius whose length is
   A. 6   B. $\sqrt{6}$ C. 3   D. 9

   6.___

7. If one root of a quadratic equation is $3+i$, then which of the following is a possible equation?
   A. $x^2 + 6x - 8 = 0$ B. $x^2 - 6x + 8 = 0$
   C. $x^2 + 6x - 10 = 0$ D. $x^2 - 6x + 10 = 0$

   7.___

8. The graph of the equation $y = \dfrac{8}{x}$ is
   A. two straight lines   B. an ellipse
   C. a straight line   D. a hyperbola

   8.___

9. How much pure hydrochloric acid should be added to 80 oz. of a 20% solution of hydrochloric acid to produce a solution which is 36% acid?
   A. 10 oz.   B. 20 oz.   C. 26.4 oz.   D. 30 oz.

   9.___

10. If f and g are functions such that $f(x) = 3x+2$ and $f(g(x)) = x$, then $g(x) =$ 10.___

    A. $\dfrac{x-2}{3}$ B. $2x+3$ C. $-3x+2$ D. $\dfrac{x-3}{2}$

11. The lines whose equations are $2x + 3y = 7$ and $3x - 4y = -15$ intersect at the point P.   11.___
    What is the distance from P to the origin?

    A. $\dfrac{\sqrt{34}}{3}$ B. $\dfrac{\sqrt{85}}{4}$ C. $\sqrt{8}$ D. $\sqrt{10}$

12. The coefficient of the third term of the expansion of   12.___

    $(2x + \dfrac{1}{\sqrt{3x}})^6$ is

    A. $\dfrac{16}{3}$ B. 10 C. 15 D. 80

13. The infinite repeating decimal $0.\overline{04}$ (where 4 is repeated)   13.___
    is equal to

    A. $\dfrac{2}{45}$ B. $\dfrac{1}{25}$ C. $\dfrac{11}{225}$ D. $\dfrac{11}{250}$

14. Some properties that hold for equalities of real numbers   14.___
    are the
    I. reflexive property
    II. symmetric property
    III. transitive property

    Which of these properties hold true for the relation
    greater than applied to real numbers?
    A. III *only*   B. I, II, III
    C. II, III   D. I, III

15. The fraction $\dfrac{2}{1+2\sqrt{3}}$ is equivalent to   15.___

    A. $\dfrac{4\sqrt{3}+2}{13}$ B. $\dfrac{4\sqrt{3}-2}{11}$ C. $\dfrac{4\sqrt{3}+1}{13}$ D. $\dfrac{4\sqrt{3}-1}{11}$

16. If c represents a real number and $c \neq 0$, then the sum of   16.___
    the additive and multiplicative inverses of c is
    A. -1 B. $1-c$ C. $\dfrac{(1+c)(1-c)}{c}$ D. $-\dfrac{1+c^2}{c}$

17. If A is the set of odd integers between 0 and 10 and B   17.___
    is a subset of integers such that $B = \{x \mid 1 < x < 6\}$,
    then the set $A \cap B$ is
    A. $\{3,5\}$ B. $\{1,3,5\}$
    C. $\{1,3,5,7,9\}$ D. $\{1,2,3,4,5,7,9\}$

18. The sum of two numbers a and b is equal to their product.   18.___
An equation which expresses this fact is:

A. $b = \dfrac{a-1}{a}$ B. $b = \dfrac{a}{a-1}$ C. $b = \dfrac{a+1}{a}$ D. $b = \dfrac{a}{a+1}$

19. When $x^3 + 4x^2 + 3x - 10$ is divided by x-1, the remainder   19.___
is
   A. -18   B. -9   C. -10   D. -2

20. If the roots of $x^2 + bx + c = 0$ are the negatives of the   20.___
roots of $x^2 + 3x + 2 = 0$, then
   A. b = 3 and c = 2   B. b = 3 and c = -2
   C. b = -3 and c = 2   D. b = -3 and c = -2

———

KEY (CORRECT ANSWERS)

1. B	11. D
2. B	12. D
3. C	13. A
4. B	14. A
5. C	15. B
6. C	16. C
7. D	17. A
8. D	18. B
9. B	19. D
10. A	20. C

———

SOLUTIONS TO PROBLEMS

1. Sum = $\frac{n}{2}$(a+L), n = number of numbers, a = first number, L = last number in an arithmetic progression. Thus, Sum = $\frac{100}{2}$(1+100) = 5050. (Ans. B)

2. $\sqrt{x+5}$ = 3 means x = 4. Then, $(4+5)^2$ = 81. (Ans. B)

3. $|5-2x|$ < 9 means −9 < 5−2x < 9, which implies −2 < x < 7. (Ans. C)

4. Log x^2 = 2Log x. Now, 2Log x = $(\text{Log } x)^2$. Factoring, we get Log x(2−Log x) = 0. If Log x = 0, x = 1. If 2 − Log x = 0, then x = 100. The solution set is {1,100}. (Ans. B)

5. $\frac{(n+k+1)!}{(n+k-1)!} = \frac{(n+k+1)(n+k)(n+k-1)(\ldots)(1)}{(n+k-1)(n+k-2)(\ldots)(1)} = $ (n+k+1)(n+k)

   (Ans. C)

6. Transform the equation by first dividing by 4 to get $x^2 - 2x + y^2 + 6y = -1$. Then, $(x^2-2x+1)+(y^2+6y+9) = -1+1+9$ or $(x-1)^2+(y+3)^2 = 3^2$. The radius = 3. (Ans. C)

7. The other root must be 3−i. The sum of the roots is 6 and the product of the roots is 10. The equation must be $x^2 - 6x + 10 = 0$. (Ans. D)

8. y = $\frac{8}{x}$ becomes xy = 8. Any equation of the form xy = k, with k a constant, is a hyperbola. (Ans. D)

9. Let x = amount of acid added. Originally, there was (80)(.20) = 16 oz. of acid. Now, 16+x = .36(80+x). x = 20 oz. (Ans. B)

10. 3[g(x)] + 2 = x. Thus, g(x) = $\frac{x-2}{3}$. (Ans. A)

11. Solving 2x + 3y = 7 and 3x − 4y = −15, x = −1, y = 3. The point (−1,3) is $\sqrt{(-1)^2+(3)^2} = \sqrt{10}$ from the origin. (Ans. D)

12. Third term = $\frac{6\cdot5}{1\cdot2}$ $(2x)^4(\frac{1}{\sqrt{3x}})^2$ = $80x^4$, so the coefficient is 80. (Ans. D)

13. Let N = $.0\overline{4}$, so that 10N = $.\overline{4}$. Now, by subtraction, 9N = .4 and N = $\frac{4}{90}$ or $\frac{2}{45}$. (Ans. A)

14. Only the transitive property holds, i.e.: if $x > y$ and $y > w$, then $x > w$.   (Ans. A)

15. $\dfrac{2}{1+2\sqrt{3}} \quad \dfrac{1-2\sqrt{3}}{1-2\sqrt{3}} = \dfrac{2-4\sqrt{3}}{1-12} = \dfrac{4\sqrt{3}-2}{11}$.   (Ans. B)

16. The additive inverse of c is $-c$, and the multiplicative inverse of c is $\dfrac{1}{c}$.   Now, $-c + \dfrac{1}{c} = \dfrac{-c^2+1}{c} = \dfrac{(1+c)(1-c)}{c}$ (Ans. C)

17. $A = \{1,3,5,7,9\}$, $B = \{2,3,4,5\}$, then $A \wedge B = \{3,5\}$.   (Ans. A)

18. Since $a + b = ab$ from the given information, $a = ab-b$ or $a = b(a-1)$, which becomes $b = \dfrac{a}{a-1}$.   (Ans. B)

19. By the Remainder Theorem, when $P(x)$ is divided by $x-R$, the remainder is $P(R)$. In this example, the remainder is $P(1) = 1^3 + 4(1)^2 + 3(1) - 10 = -2$.   (Ans. D)

20. The roots of $x^2 + 3x + 2 = 0$ are $-1,-2$. The negatives of these roots are $1,2$.

Sum of roots $= -\dfrac{b}{1} = 3$, so $b = -3$. Product of roots $= \dfrac{c}{1} = 2$, so $c = 2$.   (Ans. C)

EXAMINATION SECTION

TEST 1

DIRECTIONS: Each question or incomplete statement is followed by several suggested answers or completions. Select the one that BEST answers the question or completes the statement. *PRINT THE LETTER OF THE CORRECT ANSWER IN THE SPACE AT THE RIGHT.*

1. If $2x + 1 = 7$, then $x =$ 1.____

    A. $\frac{1}{4}$ B. $\frac{1}{3}$ C. 3   D. 4   E. 11

2. The statement, *A certain number f increased by twice another number n is equal to 30,* can be written   2.____
    A. $f + 2n = 30$ B. $f + 2f = 30$ C. $2f + n = 30$
    D. $2f + 2n = 30$ E. $2nf = 30$

3. $(-5) - (-9) =$ 3.____
    A. -14 B. -4 C. 4   D. 14   E. 45

4. If $x = y = z = 1$, then $\frac{x-y}{x+z} =$ 4.____

    A. -2 B. -1 C. 0   D. $\frac{1}{2}$ E. 1

5. $-2x + 5x - 9x =$ 5.____
    A. $-16x$ B. $-14x$ C. $-11x$ D. $-6x$ E. $-2x$

6. If n is an even number, what is the next larger even number?   6.____
    A. $n-2$ B. $n-1$ C. $n+1$ D. $n+2$ E. $2n$

7. What is the coefficient of y in the expression $2y^5 + 6y^4 - 4y^2 - 5y + 1$?   7.____
    A. -5 B. -1 C. 1   D. 2   E. 3

8. If $A = LW$ and if $A = 12$ and $L = 3$, then $W =$ 8.____

    A. $\frac{3}{4}$ B. 3   C. 4   D. 12   E. 36

9. $\frac{x^7}{x^3} =$ 9.____

    A. $x^{3 \cdot 5}$ B. x^4 C. x^{10} D. x^{21} E. 3.5

10. Which of these is equivalent to $x(x+a) - a(x-a)$?   10.____
    A. $(x+a)(x-a)^2$ B. $(x+a)^2(x-a)$ C. $(x+a)^3$
    D. $(x+a)^2$ E. x^2+a^2

11. $-11x^2y + 5x^2y =$ 11.___
    A. -6 B. $-6x^2y$ C. $-6x^4y^2$
    D. $16x^2y$ E. $16x^4y^2$

12. If $x = -2$, then $5x^3 =$ 12.___
    A. $1,000$ B. 40 C. 30 D. -40 E. $-1,000$

13. $\dfrac{5}{x} - \dfrac{3}{2x} =$ 13.___
    A. $-\dfrac{2}{x}$ B. $\dfrac{2}{2x}$ C. $\dfrac{7}{2x}$ D. $7x$ E. 7

14. $\dfrac{7x^6}{42x^2} =$ 14.___
    A. $\dfrac{x^6}{6x^2}$ B. $6x^4$ C. $\dfrac{x^4}{6}$ D. $6x^3$ E. $\dfrac{x^3}{6}$

15. $\dfrac{20x^3y^3}{7} \div \dfrac{35x^3}{4y^3} =$ 15.___
    A. $\dfrac{16x^6}{49}$ B. $\dfrac{16y^6}{49}$ C. $25x^6$ D. $25y^6$ E. $\dfrac{16}{49x^3y^3}$

16. $(r+5)(r-3) =$ 16.___
    A. r^2-15 B. $r^2-2r-15$ C. r^2-2r-8
    D. r^2+2r-8 E. $r^2+2r-15$

17. $5y^3(2y+4xy) =$ 17.___
    A. $10y^3 + 20xy^3$ B. $2y^4 + 4xy^4$ C. $10y^4 + 4xy^4$
    D. $10y^4 + 20xy^4$ E. $10y^4 + 10xy^4$

18. $3(2-3a) - (5-a) =$ 18.___
    A. $1 - 10a$ B. $1 - 8a$ C. $1 - 4a$
    D. $11 - 8a$ E. $11 - 10a$

19. If $3x - 7 = x$, then $x =$ 19.___
    A. 4 B. 3.5 C. 1 D. -3.5 E. -4

20. Every fifth degree polynomial with real coefficients   20.___
must have _____ real root(s).
    A. 0   B. at least 1   C. at least 2
    D. 3   E. 5

21. If $\dfrac{a}{c^2} = 5$, $c^2 = 2ax$, then $x =$ 21.___
    A. $\dfrac{1}{10}$ B. $\dfrac{1}{5}$ C. $\dfrac{2}{5}$ D. $\dfrac{5}{2}$ E. 10

22. If $px^3 + qx - 2 = 0$ when $x = -1$, what is the value of   22.___
$px^3 + qx - 2$ when $x = 1$?
    A. -4 B. -2 C. 0 D. 2 E. 4

23. If $\log x = \log 1 + \log 2 + \log 3 + \log 4 + \log 5$, then   23.___
$x =$
    A. 6 B. 15 C. 36 D. 55 E. 120

24. If $\begin{cases} y - x^2 - 5 = 0 \\ y - x = 7 \end{cases}$, then x =   24.___

    A. −1 or 2   B. −2 or 2   C. −3 or 4
    D. $-\sqrt{5}$ or $\sqrt{5}$ E. $-\sqrt{2}$ or $\sqrt{2}$

25. Which of these is the graph of the set of points (x,y)   25.___
    in the plane for which the y-coordinate of each point
    is one *less* than twice the x-coordinate?

A.
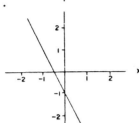
B.
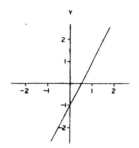
C.
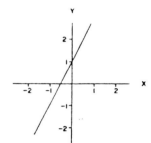

D.
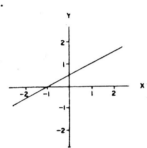
E.
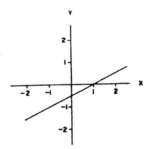

KEY (CORRECT ANSWERS)

1. C		11. B	
2. A		12. D	
3. C		13. C	
4. C		14. C	
5. D		15. B	
6. D		16. E	
7. A		17. D	
8. C		18. B	
9. B		19. B	
10. E		20. B	

             21. A
             22. A
             23. E
             24. A
             25. B

SOLUTIONS TO PROBLEMS

1. Given $2x+1 = 7$, subtract 1 from both sides to get $2x = 6$. Solving, $x = 3$

2. f increased by twice n equals 30: $f + 2n = 30$

3. $(-5) - (-9) = -5 + 9 = 4$

4. $(x-y)/(x+z) = (1-1)/(1+1) = 0$

5. $-2x + 5x - 9x = -6x$

6. The next largest even number is $n+2$, when n is even

7. For the term $-5y$, -5 is the coefficient

8. $12 = 3W$, then $W = 4$

9. $x^7/x^3 = x^4$. When dividing with like bases, subtract the exponents.

10. $x(x+a) - a(x-a) = x^2 + ax - ax + a^2 = x^2 + a^2$

11. $-11x^2y + 5x^2y = -6x^2y$

12. $5x^3 = 5(-2)^3 = 5(-8) = -40$

13. $\dfrac{5}{x} - \dfrac{3}{2x} = \dfrac{10-3}{2x} = \dfrac{7}{2x}$

14. $\dfrac{7x^6}{42x^2} = \dfrac{x^4}{6}$

15. $(20x^3y^3/7)(4y^3/35x^3) = (4y^3/7)^2 = 16y^6/49$

16. $(r+5)(r-3) = r^2 - 3r + 5r - 15 = r^2 + 2r - 15$

17. $5y^3(2y+4xy) = 10y^4 + 20xy^4$

18. $3(2-3a) - (5-a) = 6 - 9a - 5 + a = 1 - 8a$

19. $3x - 7 = x$. Subtract 3x from each side to get $-7 = -2x$. Solving, $x = 3.5$

20. A polynomial of 5th degree needs to have at least 1 real root. Note that if any of the roots are complex, they always appear as paired conjugates in the form $a+bi$ and $a-bi$.

21. $c^2 = 2ax$, so $x = c^2/2a$. Since $a/c^2 = 5$, $a/2c^2 = 2\frac{1}{2} = \dfrac{5}{2}$

Finally, $x = c^2/2a = 1 \div (2a/c^2) = 1 \div [4(a/2c^2)] =$

$1 \div [(4)(\dfrac{5}{2})] = \dfrac{1}{10}$

22. $p(-1)^3 + q(-1) - 2 = 0$ becomes $- p - q - 2 = 0$, or $p + q = -2$.
Then, $p(1)^3 + q(1) - 2 = p + q - 2 = - 2 - 2 = -4$

23. Log x = Log 1 + Log 2 + Log 3 + Log 4 + Log 5 = Log(1·2·3·4·5)
= Log 120. So, $x = 120$.

24. Since $y = x+7$, $x + 7 - x^2 - 5 = 0$ simplifies to $x^2 - x - 2 = 0$.
Factoring, $(x-2)(x+1) = 0$, so $x = 2$ or $x = -1$

25. For $y = 2x-1$, the intercepts are $(0,-1)$ and $(\frac{1}{2},0)$.
Choice B is then the appropriate graph.

———

TEST 2

DIRECTIONS: Each question or incomplete statement is followed by several suggested answers or completions. Select the one that BEST answers the question or completes the statement. *PRINT THE LETTER OF THE CORRECT ANSWER IN THE SPACE AT THE RIGHT.*

1. $x^2 - 4x - 12 =$ 1.___
   A. $(x-6)(x+2)$ B. $(x-3)(x+4)$ C. $(x+3)(x-4)$
   D. $(x+6)(x-2)$ E. $(x-4)(x-3)$

2. $\dfrac{3y^3 - 7y^2 + y}{y} =$ 2.___

   A. $3y^2 - 7y^2 + y$ B. $3y^3 - 7y^2$ C. $3y^2 - 7y$
   D. $3y^2 - 7y + 1$ E. $3y^3 - 7y + 0$

3. $\dfrac{6m^2}{n} \cdot \dfrac{2n}{3m} =$ (reduced completely)   3.___

   A. $\dfrac{12m^2 n}{3mn}$ B. $\dfrac{12m}{3}$ C. $\dfrac{2m^3}{2n^2}$ D. $4m$ E. $6m$

4. If $c - ax = b$, then $x =$ 4.___
   A. abc B. $\dfrac{b+ax}{c}$ C. $\dfrac{c-b}{a}$ D. $\dfrac{1}{a}$ E. $\dfrac{c-a}{b}$

5. $\sqrt{125} - \sqrt{20} =$ 5.___
   A. $5\sqrt{3}$ B. $3\sqrt{5}$ C. $21\sqrt{5}$ D. $\sqrt{105}$ E. 105

6. If $\dfrac{3}{n} - 2 = \dfrac{5}{2n} - \dfrac{3}{2}$, then $n =$ 6.___

   A. -4 B. -3 C. -2 D. -1 E. 1

7. $\sqrt{45x} \cdot \sqrt{3x^3} =$ 7.___
   A. $135x^4$ B. $135x^2$ C. $x^2\sqrt{135}$ D. $3x^2\sqrt{15}$ E. $5x^2\sqrt{3}$

8. What is $\sqrt{126}$ to the nearest tenth?   8.___
   A. 63.0 B. 12.6 C. 11.9 D. 11.2 E. 10.8

9. What is the slope of the line $3x + 2y = 6$?   9.___

   A. $-\dfrac{3}{2}$ B. $-\dfrac{2}{3}$ C. $\dfrac{2}{3}$ D. 2 E. 3

10. If $\begin{array}{l} x + y = 4 \\ x - y = 2 \end{array}$, then $x =$ 10.___

    A. 0 B. 1 C. 2 D. 3 E. 6

11.

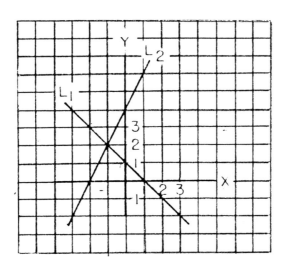

The figure above shows the graphs of two linear equations.
What is the solution of these equations?
   A. (-2,4)   B. (-1,2)   C. (-2,1)   D. (1,4)   E. (1,1)

11.___

12. If $9x - 63 = 18$, then $x =$
   A. -9   B. -5   C. 0   D. 5   E. 9

12.___

13. What is the square root of $16b^8$?
   A. $2b^2$ B. $4b^2$ C. $4b^4$ D. $8b^2$ E. $8b^4$

13.___

14. $2x^2(3x+4xy) =$
   A. $6x^2 + 8x^2y$ B. $3x^3 + 4x^3y$ C. $6x^3 + 4x^3y$
   D. $6x^3 + 8x^3y$ E. $6x^3 + 6x^3y$

14.___

15. Solve $R = \dfrac{K}{\pi d}$ for d. $d =$

   A. $\dfrac{\pi R}{K}$ B. $\dfrac{KR}{\pi}$ C. $\dfrac{\pi K}{R}$ D. $\dfrac{K}{\pi R}$ E. πKR

15.___

16. Two of a student's test marks are 68 and 84. A third
    mark is at least 40.
    What is his LOWEST possible average for the three tests?
   A. 40   B. 58   C. 62   D. 64   E. 76

16.___

17. When factored, $4a^2 + 12ab^2 =$
   A. $4a(a+3b^2)$ B. $4a(a+12b^2)$ C. $4ab(a+3b)$
   D. $4ab(a+12b)$ E. $4a^2(1+3b^2)$

17.___

18. A boy who has q quarters and d dimes buys p pencils at
    5 cents each.
    How many cents does he have left?
   A. $q + d - p$ B. $q + d - 5p$ C. $25q + 2(d-p)$
   D. $25q + 10d - p$ E. $25q + 10d - 5p$

18.___

19. If $x + y = 5$ and $x - y = 3$, then $x =$
   A. 1   B. 2   C. 4   D. 8

19.___

20. If $\frac{9}{n} - \frac{7}{n} = \frac{1}{6}$, then n =   20.____

    A. $\frac{1}{12}$ B. $\frac{1}{3}$ C. 6   D. 12

21. If $k = \frac{3}{5}(n+60)$, which of these gives n in terms of k?   21.____

    A. $\frac{5k}{3} - 60$ B. $\frac{5k}{3} - 12$ C. $\frac{3k}{5} + 60$ D. $\frac{3k}{5} + 12$

22. $8a^2b + 12b^2 =$ 22.____
    A. $4b(2a^2+3b)$ B. $8b(a^2+4b)$
    C. $4b^2(2a^2+3)$ D. $4ab(2a+3b)$

23. If p = 2 and r = -5, then $\frac{p+r}{p} =$ 23.____

    A. -5   B. $\frac{-5}{2}$ C. $\frac{-3}{2}$ D. $\frac{3}{2}$

24. $(m+3n)(2m-n) =$ 24.____
    A. $2m^2 - 3n^2$ B. $2m^2 - 3n^2 + 6$
    C. $2m^2 + 5mn - 3n^2$ D. $m^2 + 6mn - 3n^2$

25. Which of the following is the graph of $2x \leq 6$?   25.____

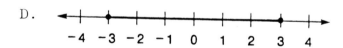

KEY (CORRECT ANSWERS)

1. A	6. E	11. B	16. D	21. A
2. D	7. D	12. E	17. A	22. A
3. D	8. D	13. C	18. E	23. C
4. C	9. A	14. D	19. C	24. C
5. B	10. D	15. D	20. D	25. A

SOLUTIONS TO PROBLEMS

1. $x^2 - 4x - 12$ can be factored as $(x-6)(x+2)$

2. $(3y^3 - 7y^2 + y) \div y = 3y^2 - 7y + 1$

3. $(6m^2/n)(2n/3m) = (12m^2n/3mn) = 4m$

4. $c - ax = b$. Subtract c from both sides to get $-ax = b-c$. Divide by $-a$ to get $x = (b-c)/-a$ or $(c-b)/a$.

5. $\sqrt{125} - \sqrt{20} = \sqrt{25}\sqrt{5} - \sqrt{4}\sqrt{5} = 5\sqrt{5} - 2\sqrt{5} = 3\sqrt{5}$

6. $\frac{3}{n} - 2 = \frac{5}{2n} - \frac{3}{2}$. Multiply every term by $2n$ to get $6 - 4n = 5 - 3n$. Simplifying, $-n = -1$, so $n = 1$.

7. $\sqrt{45x} \cdot \sqrt{3x^3} = \sqrt{135x^4} = x^2\sqrt{9}\sqrt{15} = 3x^2\sqrt{15}$

8. $\sqrt{126} \approx 11.225 \approx 11.2$

9. $3x + 2y = 6$ can be written as $y = -\frac{3}{2}x + 3$. In this form, the slope corresponds to the coefficient of x, which is $-\frac{3}{2}$.

10. Add the given equations to get $2x = 6$. Then, $x = 3$.

11. The solution is the intersection point $(-1,2)$.

12. Add 63 to both sides to get $9x = 81$. Then, $x = 9$.

13. $\sqrt{16b^8} = 4b^4$, since $(4b^4)^2 = 16b^8$

14. $2x^2(3x+4xy) = 6x^3 + 8x^3y$

15. $R = k/(\pi d)$. Then, $\pi Rd = k$, so $d = k/(\pi R)$

16. $(68+84+40) \div 3 = 192 \div 3 = 64$

17. $4a^2 + 12ab^2 = 4a(a+3b^2)$

18. q quarters and d dimes is worth $25q + 10d$ cents. p pencils at 5 cents each cost $5p$ cents. After buying these pencils, he has $25q + 10d - 5p$ cents left.

19. Add the given equations to get $2x = 8$. Then, $x = 4$.

20. $\frac{9}{n} - \frac{7}{n} = \frac{2}{n}$. Now, $\frac{2}{n} = \frac{1}{6}$. Cross-multiply to get $n = 12$.

21. Rewrite as $k = \frac{3}{5}n + 36$. Then, $\frac{3}{5}n = k - 36$. Solving,
    $n = (k-36)/\frac{3}{5} = \frac{5}{3}k - 60$

22. $8a^2b + 12b^2$ can be factored as $4b(2a^2+3b)$

23. $(p+r)/p = (2-5)/2 = -\frac{3}{2}$

24. $(m+3n)(2m-n) = 2m^2 - mn + 6mn - 3n^2 = 2m^2 + 5mn - 3n^2$

25. Given $2x \leq 6$, then $x \leq 3$. The graph corresponding to this inequality would show a dot on 3 and an arrow going to the left, as in choice A.

———

TEST 3

1. Which of these is a factor of $x^2 - 36$?
   A. x-4   B. x-2   C. x+6   D. x+9

   1.____

2. If x is an integer greater than 2, which formula is GREATEST?
   A. $\frac{2}{x}$ B. $\frac{x}{2}$ C. $\frac{2}{x+1}$ D. $\frac{x+1}{2}$

   2.____

3. If $-2x + 5 > -11$, it must be TRUE that
   x > -3   B. x > 8   C. x < 3   D. x < 8

   3.____

4. $\frac{x^{10}}{x^2} =$
   A. 5   B. x^5 C. x^8 D. x^{12}

   4.____

5. Which of the following is a factor of $2x^2 - 4x - 6$?
   A. x+1   B. x+3   C. 2x-1   D. 2x+3

   5.____

6. Consider these two equations:
   2x + y = 5
   2x - y = 7
   At what point will the graphs of these two equations cross each other?
   A. (2,1)   B. (3,-1)   C. (3,0)   D. (3,1)

   6.____

7. $(a-3b)^2 =$
   A. a^2-9b^2
   C. $a^2-3ab-9b^2$
   B. a^2+9b^2
   D. $a^2-6ab+9b^2$

   7.____

8. During a soccer game, José scored 3 more than twice as many points as Carlos scored.
   If Carlos scored c points, which of the following represents the number of points José scored?
   A. 2c+3   B. 3c+2   C. 2(c+3)   D. 3(c+2)

   8.____

9. If $y = x^2 + kx - 5$ and y = 0 when x = 3, then k =
   A. -4   B. $\frac{-4}{3}$ C. $\frac{4}{3}$ D. 4

   9.____

10. Which of these is an equation of the line that passes through the origin and has a slope of 7?
    A. $y = \frac{x}{7}$ B. y = 7x   C. y = x-7   D. y = x+7

    10.____

11. Solve the equation $x^2 + 10x - 24 = 0$ for x.   11.___
   x equals
       A. 12 or x = -2   B. 12 or x = 2   C. 6 or x = -4
       D. 6 or x = 4   E. -12 or x = 2

12. On which of these number lines does the heavy line   12.___
   represent all numbers x such that $-3 \leq x \leq 3$?

13. If $y = \frac{1}{x}$ and x is greater than 0, which of these state-   13.___
   ments is TRUE?
       A. As x increases, y increases.
       B. As x increases, y decreases.
       C. As x decreases, y decreases.
       D. When x is greater than 1, y is greater than 1.
       E. When x is less than 1, y is less than 1.

14. What number MUST be added to $x^2 - 6x + 4$ in order to   14.___
   make it a perfect square?
       A. -4   B. 0   C. 2   D. 5   E. 32

15. For what values of x is $\frac{x}{6} = \frac{1}{2}(x-3) - \frac{x}{3}$ a true statement?   15.___

       A. 0 *only*   B. 3 *only*   C. 0 and 3 *only*
       D. All values   E. No value

16. Solve the formula $E = \frac{ar}{a+r}$ for r. r =   16.___
       A. $\frac{aE}{a-E}$ B. $\frac{aE}{a+E}$ C. aE-a+E   D. aE-a-E   E. $a - \frac{E}{a-E}$

17. If x is greater than 3, which of the following is the   17.___
   SMALLEST?
       A. $\frac{3}{x}$ B. $\frac{3}{x+1}$ C. $\frac{3}{x-1}$ D. $\frac{x}{3}$ E. $\frac{x+1}{3}$

18. 2(x+5) =   18.___
     A. x+10   B. 2x+5   C. 2x+7   D. 2x+10

19. -8 - (-7) =   19.___
     A. -15   B. -1   C. 1   D. 15

20. (x²+x+2) + (2x+2) =   20.___
     A. x²+3x+2   B. x²+3x+4   C. 3x²+2x+4   D. 3x²+3x+2

21. 5 + 3(n+5) - 2n =   21.___
     A. n+10   B. n+20   C. 6n+5   D. 6n+40

22. If k(k-1)(k+2) = 0, then k =   22.___
     A. 0 *only*   B. 1 and -2 *only*
     C. -1 and 2 *only*   D. 0, -1, 2
     E. 0, 1, -2

23. What value of k will make x² - 10x + k a perfect square   23.___
     trinomial?
     A. -25   B. -5   C. 5   D. 25   E. 100

24. If $\frac{x-5}{8x} = \frac{3}{x+5}$, then the solution set for x is   24.___

     A. {1,-5,5}   B. {0,-5,5}   C. {-5,5}
     D. {-25,1}   E. {25,-1}

25.   25.___

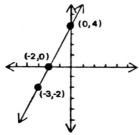

     What equation represents the line above?
     A. y = ½x-2   B. y = ½x+4   C. y = 2x-2
     D. y = 2x+4   E. y = -3x-2

     ———————

KEY (CORRECT ANSWERS)

1. C	6. B	11. E	16. A	21. B
2. D	7. D	12. A	17. B	22. E
3. D	8. A	13. B	18. D	23. D
4. C	9. B	14. D	19. B	24. E
5. A	10. B	15. E	20. B	25. D

———————

SOLUTIONS TO PROBLEMS

1. $x^2 - 36 = (x-6)(x+6)$, so $x+6$ is one of the factors.

2. The value of $x = 2$ will yield the values 1, 1, $\frac{2}{3}$, $\frac{3}{2}$ for choices A, B, C, D, respectively. Choice D is largest.

3. $-2x + 5 > -11$. Subtract 5 from each side to get $-2x > -16$. Now, $x < 8$. Remember to change the order of inequality when dividing or multiplying by a negative number.

4. $x^{10}/x^2 = x^8$. When dividing numbers with like bases, subtract the exponents.

5. $2x^2 - 4x - 6 = 2(x^2-2x-3) = 2(x-3)(x+1)$, so $x+1$ is one of the factors.

6. Add the given equations to get $4x = 12$, so $x = 3$. Substitute $x = 3$ into the 1st equation to get $(2)(3) + y = 5$. Solving, $y = -1$. The point of intersection is $(3,-1)$.

7. $(a-3b)^2 = (a-3b)(a-3b) = a^2 - 3ab - 3ab + 9b^2 = a^2 - 6ab + 9b^2$

8. 3 more than twice c becomes $2c+3$

9. $0 = 3^2 + k(3) - 5$. Simplifying, $0 = 9 + 3k - 5$. Solving, $k = -4/3$

10. A slope of 7 means $y = 7x+k$, k a constant. Since the line passes through $(0,0)$, $0 = 7(0) + k$, so $k = 0$. Thus, $y = 7x$

11. $x^2 + 10x - 24 = 0$ becomes $(x+12)(x-2) = 0$. Thus, $x = -12$ or 2

12. If $-3 \leq x \leq 3$, then graphically a solid line segment should be drawn from -3 to 3. Choice A has the right graph.

13. As x increases, the value of y decreases (for $x>0$). Example: When $x = 5$, $y = \frac{1}{5}$. But when $x = 10$, $y = \frac{1}{10}$

14. $x^2 - 6x + 9$ is a perfect square since it equals $(x-3)^2$. Given $x^2 - 6x + 4$, a 5 must be added.

15. $\frac{x}{6} = \frac{1}{2}(x-3) - \frac{x}{3}$. Multiply every term by 6 to get $x = 3(x-3) - 2x$. Simplifying, $x = 3x - 9 - 2x$. Then, $x = x-9$ and thus no value of x is correct.

16. $E = ar/(a+r)$. Multiply both sides by $a+r$ to get $Ea + Er = ar$. Then, $Ea = ar - Er = r(a-E)$. Then, $r = Ea/(a-E)$ or $aE/(a-E)$.

17. The five choices have values of $\frac{3}{4}$, $\frac{3}{5}$, 1, $\frac{4}{3}$, $\frac{5}{3}$, if x = 4.

Evidently, choice B is the smallest.

18. 2(x+5) = 2x + 10

19. - 8 - (-7) = - 8 + 7 = -1

20. (x^2+x+2) + (2x+2) = x^2 + 3x + 4

21. 5 + 3(n+5) - 2n = 5 + 3n + 15 - 2n = n + 20

22. If k(k-1)(k+2) = 0, then k = 0, k-1 = 0, or k+2 = 0.
The values of k are 0, 1, -2.

23. Let k = 25. Then, x^2 - 10x + 25, which equals $(x-5)^2$, is
a perfect square trinomial.

24. (x-5)/8x = 3/(x+5). Cross-multiply to get x^2 - 25 = 24x.
Then, x^2 - 24x - 25 = 0. Factoring, (x-25)(x+1) = 0.
Solving, x = 25 or x = -1

25. Slope of line is (4-0)/(0-(-2)) = 2. So, y = 2x + k.
Substituting (0,4), 4 = 2(0) + k, so k = 4. Then final
equation is y = 2x + 4

TEST 4

DIRECTIONS: Each question or incomplete statement is followed by several suggested answers or completions. Select the one that BEST answers the question or completes the statement. *PRINT THE LETTER OF THE CORRECT ANSWER IN THE SPACE AT THE RIGHT.*

1. If $2x + y = 7$ and $x - 4y = 4$, then $y =$ 1. ___

    A. $-\dfrac{15}{9}$ B. $-\dfrac{1}{9}$ C. $\dfrac{7}{16}$ D. $\dfrac{11}{9}$ E. 7

2. $\dfrac{1}{y} + \dfrac{2}{3+y} =$ 2. ___

    A. $\dfrac{3}{3+2y}$ B. $\dfrac{3y+3}{3+2y}$ C. $\dfrac{y+1}{y+y^2}$ D. $\dfrac{y+3}{3y+y^2}$ E. $\dfrac{3y+3}{3y+y^2}$

3. For what real numbers x does $3x^2 - x - 4 = 0$?   3. ___

    A. -4 and 3 B. $-\dfrac{4}{3}$ and 1 C. $-\dfrac{2}{3}$ and 2

    C. $\dfrac{2}{3}$ and 2 E. $\dfrac{4}{3}$ and -1

4. If $\dfrac{x}{3} + \dfrac{5}{6} = 2$, then $x =$ 4. ___

    A. -3 B. $\dfrac{6}{5}$ C. $\dfrac{7}{2}$ D. 7 E. $\dfrac{17}{2}$

5. If $f(x) = 2x^3 - 3x^2 - x + 2$, then $f(-1) =$ 5. ___
    A. -4 B. -2 C. 0 D. 2 E. 4

6. If $\dfrac{3}{3k+x} = \dfrac{1}{k+1}$ and $k \neq -1$, then $x =$ 6. ___

    A. $\dfrac{1}{3}$ B. 1 C. 3 D. $3k$ E. $6k+3$

7. The LOWEST common denominator of the fractions   7. ___

    $\dfrac{1}{s^2+s-12}$ and $\dfrac{1}{s^2-5s+6}$ is

    A. $(s-2)(s-3)(s+4)$ B. $(s-2)(s-3)^2(s+4)$
    C. $(s-2)(s+3)(s-4)$ D. $(s-2)(s-3)(s+3)(s-4)$
    E. $(s+2)(s-3)(s+3)(s-4)$

8. Which equation states that the average of the numbers   8.____
   x, y, and z is 4 *more* than z?

   A. $x + y + z = z - 4$ B. $\dfrac{x + y + z}{3} = z - 4$

   C. $\dfrac{x + y + z}{3} = z + 4$ D. $3x + 3y + 3z = z + 4$

9. What is the solution set of the equation $x^2 - 2x = 0$?   9.____
   A. $\{0\}$ B. $\{0,2\}$ C. $\{-2,2\}$ D. $\{-2,0,2\}$

10. Jean, Paul, and Terry shared the driving on a trip.   10.____
    Jean drove 50 miles less than one-third the total
    distance, and Paul drove 40 miles more than one-third
    the total distance.
    If Terry drove the remaining 200 miles, how many miles
    did they drive?
    A. 570   B. 590   C. 610   D. 630

11. A team played 70 games and won 20 more games than it   11.____
    lost.
    If there were no ties, how many games did the team win?
    A. 25   B. 40   C. 45   D. 50

12. To mail some letters, Jane used only 20-cent and   12.____
    25-cent stamps.
    If she used a total of 22 stamps that cost a total of
    $5.00, how many of the stamps were 20-cent stamps?
    A. 5   B. 10   C. 12   D. 15

13. If $6x - 2 = 10x$, then $x =$ 13.____
    A. $\dfrac{-1}{2}$ B. $\dfrac{-1}{8}$ C. $\dfrac{1}{2}$ D. 2

14. The length of a rectangular room is 4 feet greater than   14.____
    its width.
    If the area of the room is 96 square feet, what is the
    width of the room in feet?
    A. $2\sqrt{6}$ B. 6   C. 8   D. $8\sqrt{6}$

15. If $x = \sqrt{b^2-9}$, for which one of the following values of   15.____
    b will x be a *real* number?
    A. -1 B. 0   C. 2   D. 4

16. What is the solution set for the equation $|x| - 2 = 8$?   16.____
    A. $\{10\}$ B. $\{-6,6\}$ C. $\{6,10\}$ D. $\{-10,10\}$

17. If $x = 2$, then $x^0 + x^{-2} =$ 17.____
    A. -4 B. $1\frac{1}{4}$ C. $2\frac{1}{4}$ D. 6

18. If $\log_b 10 = p$ and $\log_b 2 = q$, then $\log_b 20 =$ 18.____

    A. pq B. $p+q$ C. p^q D. q^p E. $2(p+q)$

19. If $x - 7$ is a factor of $x^2 - 3x + p$, what is the value   19.____
    of p?
    A. -28 B. -21 C. -10 D. 21   E. 28

20. $-16^{\frac{1}{2}} + 8^{\frac{2}{3}} =$ 20.____

    A. $-\dfrac{8}{3}$ B. 0   C. $3\dfrac{3}{4}$ D. $4\frac{1}{4}$ E. 8

21. If $f(x) = 2x^4 - 3x^3 - 2x - 4$, then $f(2) =$ 21.____
    A. -10 B. -7 C. -4 D. 0   E. 4

22. The two solutions of the equation $2x^2 - x - 4 = 0$ are   22.____
    A. opposite in sign
    B. both positive and equal
    C. both negative and equal
    D. both positive but unequal
    E. both negative but unequal

23. The equation $ax^2 + bx + c = 0$ has imaginary roots   23.____
    whenever $b^2 - 4ac$ is negative.
    What are ALL the values of c for which $x^2 + 2x + c = 0$
    has imaginary roots?
    A. $c < -1$ B. $c < 1$ C. $c > -1$
    D. $c > 0$ E. $c > 1$

24.   24.____

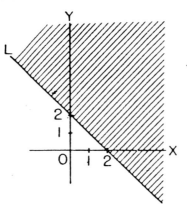

The equation of line L in the figure above is $x + y = 2$.
Which of these conditions is satisfied by *every* point (x,y)
in the shaded region?
    A. $x \geq 2$ B. $y \geq 2$ C. $x + y \geq 2$
    D. $x + y \leq 2$ E. $x \leq y + 2$

25. Which of these is the graph of y = |x|?   25.___

A.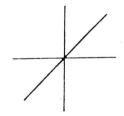

B.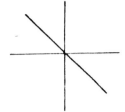

C.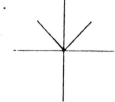

D.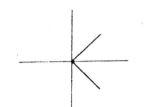

E.

___

KEY (CORRECT ANSWERS)

1. B		11. C	
2. E		12. B	
3. E		13. A	
4. C		14. C	
5. B		15. D	
6. C		16. D	
7. A		17. B	
8. C		18. B	
9. B		19. A	
10. A		20. B	

21. D
22. A
23. E
24. C
25. C

___

SOLUTIONS TO PROBLEMS

1. Double the 2nd equation to get $2x - 8y = 8$. Subtract the 1st equation to get $-9y = 1$. Solving, $y = -1/9$

2. $\dfrac{1}{y} + \dfrac{2}{3+y} = \dfrac{3+y+2y}{y(3+y)} = \dfrac{3y+3}{3y+y^2}$

3. $3x^2 - x - 4 = 0$ can be written as $(3x-4)(x+1) = 0$. Then, $x = \dfrac{4}{3}$ and -1.

4. $\dfrac{x}{3} + \dfrac{5}{6} = 2$. Multiply equation by 6 to get $2x + 5 = 12$. Then, $2x = 7$. Solving, $x = \dfrac{7}{2}$

5. $f(-1) = 2(-1)^3 - 3(-1)^2 - (-1) + 2 = -2 - 3 + 1 + 2 = -2$

6. Cross-multiply to get $3(k+1) = 3k + x$. $3k + 3 = 3k + x$. By inspection, $k = 3$

7. Since $s^2 + s - 12 = (s+4)(s-3)$ and $s^2 - 5s + 6 = (s-3)(s-2)$, the L.C.D. must be $(s+4)(s-3)(s-2)$

8. The average of x, y, z is $(x+y+z)/3$, and since this is 4 more than z, $(x+y+z)/3 = z + 4$

9. $x^2 - 2x = 0$ can be factored as $x(x-2) = 0$. Thus, $x = 0, 2$

10. Let d = total distance. The distances Jean, Paul, and Terry drove were $\frac{1}{3}d - 50$, $\frac{1}{3}d + 40$, and 200, respectively. Now, $\frac{1}{3}d - 50 + \frac{1}{3}d + 40 + 200 = d$. Then, $\frac{2}{3}d + 190 = d$. This reduces to $\frac{1}{3}d = 190$. Solving, d = 570 miles.

11. Let x = games won, x-20 = games lost. Then, $x + x - 20 = 70$. $2x = 90$. Solving, $x = 45$.

12. Let x = number of 20-cent stamps, 22-x = number of 25-cent stamps. Then, $.20x + .25(22-x) = 5.00$. $.20x + 5.50 - .25x = 5.00$. Simplifying, $-.05x = .50$. Solving, $x = 10$

13. $6x - 2 = 10x$. Subtract 6x from both sides to get $-2 = 4x$. Solving, $x = -\dfrac{2}{4} = -\frac{1}{2}$

14. Let w = width, w+4 = length. Then, w(w+4) = 96.
    w^2 + 4w - 96 = 0. Factoring, (w+12)(w-8) = 0.
    Using only the positive w value, w = 8.

15. If b = 4, then x = $\sqrt{4^2-9}$ = $\sqrt{7}$, which is a real number.

16. $|x|$ - 2 = 8 becomes $|x|$ = 10. Thus, x = -10 and 10

17. 2^0 + 2^{-2} = 1 + $\frac{1}{4}$ = $1\frac{1}{4}$

18. $Log_b 20$ = $Log_b(10 \cdot 2)$ = $Log_b 10$ + $Log_b 2$ = p + q

19. x-7 is a factor of x^2 - 3x - 28, which equals (x-7)(x+4).
    Thus, p = -28

20. $-16^{\frac{1}{2}}$ + $8^{\frac{2}{3}}$ = $-\sqrt{16}$ + $(\sqrt[3]{8})^2$ = - 4 + 4 = 0

21. f(2) = $2(2^4)$ - $3(2^3)$ - 2(2) - 4 = 32 - 24 - 4 - 4 = 0

22. The solutions to $2x^2$ - x - 4 = 0 are $(1+\sqrt{33})/4$ and $(1-\sqrt{33})/4$,
    which are approximately 1.69 and -1.19. These solutions
    are opposite in sign.

23. For x^2 + 2x + c = 0 to have imaginary (or complex) roots,
    2^2 - (4)(1)(c) < 0. Then, 4 < 4c. Solving, c > 1.

24. x + y = 2 can be written as y = 2 - x. Since the shaded region
    is above this line, y ≥ 2 - x, which is equivalent to x + y ≥ 2

25. If y = $|x|$, then y = x when x ≥ 0 and y = -x when x < 0.
    The graph shown in choice C fits this description.

EXAMINATION SECTION

DIRECTIONS: Each question or incomplete statement is followed by several suggested answers or completions. Select the one that BEST answers the question or completes the statement. *PRINT THE LETTER OF THE CORRECT ANSWER IN THE SPACE AT THE RIGHT.*

1. On a $10,000 order, a merchant has a choice between three successive discounts of 20%, 20%, and 10%, and three successive discounts of 40%, 5%, and 5%. By choosing the better offer, he can save
   A. $330   B. $345   C. $360   D. $400

   1.___

2. An article was sold for $21.00 more than it cost. If the marked price of this article was 150% of its cost price, and if it was sold at a discount of 30%, then its cost price was
   A. $19.09   B. $70   C. $210   D. $420

   2.___

3. Three purses A, B and C together contain 48 coins. Purse A contains more coins than purse B, and purse B contains more coins than purse C. What is the GREATEST number of coins that purse B can have?
   A. 15   B. 16   C. 23   D. 45

   3.___

4. If the statement $202_b = (13_b) \cdot (13_b)$ is true in a number system whose base is b, and b is a natural number, then b is equal to
   A. 5   B. 6   C. 7   D. 8

   4.___

5. If a * b is defined as a + 2b, where a and b are real numbers, then
   A. the operation * is commutative
   B. the operation * is associative
   C. the operation * has the closure property
   D. a * 1 = a

   5.___

6. If twenty pupils took both English and Mathematics, and if thirteen passed English, fifteen passed Math, and two failed both, how many pupils passed both subjects?
   A. 8   B. 10   C. 13   D. 18

   6.___

7. If x is a real number, the solution set of $\{x \mid -x^2+3x-2<0\}$ may be described in which one of the following ways?
   A. $\{x \mid x<1 \text{ or } x>2\}$ B. $\{x \mid x<-2 \text{ or } x>-1\}$
   C. $\{x \mid -2<x<-1\}$ D. $\{x \mid 1<x<2\}$

   7.___

8. If $x=2 (\cos 315^0 + i \sin 315^0)$ is a root of $x^4+k=0$, then the value of k is
   A. -16   B. -8   C. 8   D. 16

   8.___

9. If a car travels two equal distances with a different speed   9.____
for each distance, then its average speed for the entire
trip is (with consistent units) which one of the following?
    A. The geometric mean of the speeds involved
    B. The arithmetic mean of the speeds involved
    C. The reciprocal of the arithmetic mean of the speeds
       involved
    D. The harmonic mean of the speeds involved

10. If $\log_4 x + \log_4 \frac{1}{3} = -\frac{5}{2}$, then x equals   10.____

    A. $\frac{3}{32}$ B. $\frac{5}{8}$ C. $\frac{3}{4}$ D. 4

11. If r and s are the roots of $x^2-px+q=0$, then r^2+s^2 equals   11.____
    A. p^2+2q B. p^2-2q
    C. p^2+q D. p^2-q

12. The number of terms in the simplified expansion of   12.____
$[(x+2y)^2(x-2y)^2]^3$ is which one of the following?
    A. 6   B. 7   C. 12   D. 13

13. If $0.3^x = 6$, log 2 = .3010 and log 3 = .4771, then the   13.____
value of x to the nearest tenth is
    A. -1.6   B. -1.5   C. -.5   D. -.3

14. The sum of the roots of the equation $|x|^2+|x|-6 =0$ is   14.____
    A. -6   B. -1   C. 0   D. 1

15. If the complex number a + bi is represented by the ordered   15.____
pair (a,b), then the multiplicative inverse of the complex
number (1,-1) may be represented by which one of the
following?
    A. (-1,1)   B. (1,-1)   C. $(\frac{1}{2},\frac{1}{2})$ D. $(\frac{1}{2},-\frac{1}{2})$

16. If the projections of the legs of a right triangle on the   16.____
hypotenuse are in the ratio of 1:2, then the ratio of the
smaller leg to the larger leg is
    A. 1:2   B. 1:3   C. $1:\sqrt{2}$ D. $1:\sqrt{3}$

17. A wheel has a diameter of 25 inches. If the radius of this   17.____
wheel is decreased by a quarter of an inch, then the
number of revolutions it will make in one mile of travel
will be APPROXIMATELY increased by which one of the following?
    A. $\frac{1}{2}\%$ B. 1%   C. 2%   D. 20%

18. C is a point on line segment AB such that AC = 3CB. If   18.____
circles are constructed with AC and CB as diameters, and
a common external tangent to these circles meets AB
produced at D, then BD equals the
    A. diameter of the smaller circle
    B. radius of the smaller circle
    C. radius of the large circle
    D. difference between the two radii

19. If the median, altitude, and angle bisector are drawn   19.____
    from the same vertex of a scalene triangle, then the
    A. altitude always falls between the median and the
       angle bisector
    B. median always falls between the altitude and the
       angle bisector
    C. angle bisector always falls between the median and
       the altitude
    D. order of the three lines has no consistency

20. If medians AD and BE of △ABC intersect in M, if N is the   20.____
    midpoint of AE, then the ratio of the area of △MEN to
    the area of △ABC is
    A. 1:8   B. 1:9   C. 1:12   D. 1:16

21. The number of square inches in the area of a circle   21.____
    inscribed in a triangle whose sides are 10", 24" and 26" is
    A. 9π B. 16π C. 36π D. 64π

22. If the bases of a trapezoid are 8" and 12" and its   22.____
    altitude is 3", then the length of a line segment drawn
    between the non-parallel sides, parallel to the bases,
    at a distance of 2" from the longer base, is
    A. 9"   B. $9\frac{1}{3}$"   C. 10"   D. $10\frac{2}{3}$"

23. If a regular octagon is formed by cutting congruent   23.____
    isosceles right triangles from the corners of a square
    whose side has length of one unit, then the number of
    square units in the area of the octagon is
    A. $\frac{5}{9}$ B. $2(\sqrt{2}-1)$ C. $\frac{7}{9}$ D. $4\sqrt{2}-5$

24. Assume that in a circle whose radius is one foot, a central   24.____
    angle intercepts an arc of 3 inches, then the number of
    radians in the angle is
    A. $\frac{1}{4}$ B. $\frac{1}{3}$ C. 3   D. 4

25. If x and y are real numbers, the area of the region   25.____
    containing the points defined by
    $\{(x,y)|(x^2+4y^2<16)\cap(2y\geq x-2)\cap(x\geq 0)\cap y\leq 0\}$

    A. 1   B. 2   C. 4   D. 6

26. The value of x, such that $\cos^2 x - \sin^2 x - 2\sin x \cos x = 0$ 26.____
    and $0\leq x\leq\frac{\pi}{2}$, is

    A. 0   B. $\frac{\pi}{8}$ C. $\frac{\pi}{4}$ D. $\frac{\pi}{2}$

27. Using principal values only, the value of arc $\tan\frac{1}{2}$ + arc   27.____
    $\tan\frac{1}{3}$ is

    A. $\frac{\pi}{6}$ B. $\frac{\pi}{4}$ C. $\frac{\pi}{3}$ D. $\frac{\pi}{2}$

28. Which one of the following is equivalent to $\tan\frac{\theta}{2} + \cot\frac{\theta}{2}$?

    28. _____

    A. 2 sin θ   B. 2 sec θ
    C. 2 csc θ   D. 2 cos θ

29. In triangle ACD, angle D is a right angle and B is a point on AD between A and D. If angle CBD is represented by x, angle CAD by y, AB by d and CD by h, then which one of the following is equal to h?

    29. _____

    A. $\dfrac{d}{\cot y - \cot x}$

    B. $\dfrac{d}{\cot x - \cot y}$

    C. $\dfrac{d}{\tan x - \tan y}$

    D. $\dfrac{d}{\cot x + \cot y}$

30. Among the following, the one that is the polar graph of r = 2 cosθ is a

    30. _____

    A. straight line through $(2,0^0)$
    B. circle centered at $(1,0^0)$ with radius = 1
    C. straight line through the pole
    D. circle centered at the pole, with radius = 1

31. If a plane parallel to the base of a cone divides the altitude into two segments from vertex to base in the ratio a:b, then which one of the following is the ratio of the volumes of the two parts into which this cone is divided?

    31. _____

    A. $a^3 : b^3$
    B. $a^3 : b(3a^2+3ab+b^2)$
    C. $a^3 : (a+b)^3$
    D. $b^3 : a(a^2+3ab+3b^2)$

32. If the figure formed by an equilateral triangle inscribed in a circle whose radius is r units is revolved through 360^0 about a diameter of the circle which is perpendicular to a side of the Δ, then the difference in volume between the resulting sphere and cone is

    32. _____

    A. $\dfrac{23\pi r^3\sqrt{3}}{24}$

    B. $\dfrac{69\pi r^3}{24}$

    C. $\dfrac{4}{3}\pi r^3 - \dfrac{9\pi r^3\sqrt{3}}{8}$

    D. $\dfrac{23\pi r^3}{24}$

33. If line AB passes through points (6,0) and (2,3), and intersects the Y-axis at point P, then the line which is perpendicular to AB and passes through point P has a slope and Y-intercept respectively equal to

    33. _____

    A. $-\dfrac{3}{4}$ and $4\frac{1}{2}$

    B. $\dfrac{3}{4}$ and $4\frac{1}{2}$

    C. $\dfrac{4}{3}$ and -8

    D. $\dfrac{4}{3}$ and $4\frac{1}{2}$

34. Of the following, the equation of a circle which passes through (2,0) and (6,0) and is tangent to the Y-axis is
    A. $(x-4)^2+(y-\sqrt{12})^2 =4$
    B. $(x-\sqrt{12})^2+(y-3)^2 =8$
    C. $(x-4)^2+(y-\sqrt{12})^2 =16$
    D. $x^2+(y-12)^2 =16$

    34.____

35. Which one of the following lines is NOT an asymptote of the graph of the equation $xy^2-y^2-4x+1=0$?
    A. x=1   B. x=-1   C. y=2   D. y=-2

    35.____

36. The SHORTEST distance from the point (-8,2) to the curve $x^2+y^2-8x-14y+40=0$ is
    A. 5   B. 8   C. 12   D. 13

    36.____

37. The equation of the ellipse, the length of whose minor axis is 8 and whose foci are at the points in which the circle $x^2+y^2=9$ intercepts the x-axis, is which one of the following?
    A. $\dfrac{x^2}{9} + \dfrac{y^2}{16} = 1$ B. $\dfrac{x^2}{16} + \dfrac{y^2}{9} = 1$

    C. $\dfrac{x^2}{16} + \dfrac{y^2}{25} = 1$ D. $\dfrac{x^2}{25} + \dfrac{y^2}{16} = 1$

    37.____

38. The equation of the directrix of the parabola $y^2-4x-6y+9=0$ is
    A. x=-2   B. x=-1   C. x=1   D. x=2

    38.____

39. If a line segment 6" long moves so that its endpoints always lie on each of two fixed perpendicular lines, then the locus of a point 2" from one of its endpoints is a(n)
    A. ellipse   B. hyperbola
    C. parabola   D. straight line

    39.____

40. The MAXIMUM value of sin x + cos x is
    A. $\dfrac{1}{\sqrt{2}}$ B. 1   C. $\sqrt{2}$ D. 2

    40.____

41. If the region bounded by the curve $y=x^3$, the x-axis and the line x=2 is revolved about the x-axis, then the measure of the volume generated is
    A. $\dfrac{32\pi}{5}$ B. $\dfrac{32\pi}{3}$ C. $\dfrac{128\pi}{7}$ D. 4π

    41.____

42. The area of the region bounded by the curve $x^2=8y$ and the line y=2 is
    A. $\dfrac{8}{3}$ B. $\dfrac{16}{3}$ C. $\dfrac{32}{3}$ D. $\dfrac{40}{3}$

    42.____

43. Assuming two points, whose abscissas differ by a non-zero constant k, lie on the curve $y=x^3$, then the SMALLEST possible slope that the line joining these points can have is which one of the following?
    A. $\dfrac{k}{2}$ B. $\dfrac{k}{3}$ C. $\dfrac{k^2}{3}$ D. $\dfrac{k^2}{4}$

    43.____

44. Assume that two automobiles start from point A at the same time and one travels due east at 60 m.p.h. and the other travels due north at 45 m.p.h. How fast (in m.p.h.) is the distance between them increasing 2 hours later?
   A. 25   B. 50   C. 75   D. 150

45. If the median of a set of 45 marks is 82.5, and if the marks 100, 95, 40, and 15 are added to the set, the new median is
   A. 72.5   B. 77.0   C. 80.0   D. 82.5

46. The standard deviation of the set of scores 2,5,8 is equal to the standard deviation of which one of the following sets of scores?
   A. 4,5,6   B. 4,25,64   C. 4,10,16   D. 4,7,10

47. Assume that a jury panel contains 70 names, and among these are the names of Mr. C and Mr. D. If 12 jury men are to be selected by lot, the probability that BOTH Mr. C and Mr. D will be selected is
   A. $\frac{1}{66}$ B. $\frac{22}{805}$ C. $\frac{36}{1225}$ D. $\frac{1}{6}$

48. The odds in favor of getting a seven or an eleven on a single throw of a pair of dice are
   A. 1:9   B. 1:8   C. 2:9   D. 2:7

49. Which one of the following men demonstrated that π is transcendental?
   A. Lindemann   B. Dedekind
   C. Abel   D. Cantor

50. A sextant is MOST closely associated with which one of the following?
   A. Finding the height of a tree
   B. Determining the length of a line segment
   C. Determining the latitude and longitude of a position
   D. Finding the distance to the horizon

KEY (CORRECT ANSWERS)

1. B	11. B	21. B	31. C	41. C
2. D	12. B	22. B	32. D	42. C
3. C	13. B	23. B	33. D	43. D
4. C	14. C	24. A	34. C	44. C
5. C	15. C	25. A	35. B	45. D
6. B	16. C	26. B	36. B	46. D
7. A	17. C	27. B	37. D	47. B
8. D	18. B	28. C	38. B	48. D
9. D	19. C	29. A	39. A	49. A
10. A	20. C	30. B	40. C	50. C

SOLUTIONS TO PROBLEMS

1. Under the 1st option, the merchant would pay ($10,000)(.8)(.8)(.1) = $5,760; but under the 2nd option, he would pay ($10,000)(.6) (.95)(.95) = $5,415. This represents a savings of $345. (Ans. B)

2. Let c = cost. Then, c+21 = selling price and 1.50c = marked price. Since the article was sold at a 30% discount (off the marked price), c+21 = .70(1.50c). Solving, c=$420. (Ans. D)

3. Since A contains more than B, the latter must contain less than half of the 48 coins. Thus, B could contain at most 23 coins. Then A would have 24 and C would have 1 coin. (Ans. C)

4. $202_7=(2)(7^2)+2 = 100$ and $13_7=10$. Now, $202_7 = (13_7)(13_7)$. (Ans. C)

5. a*b = a+2b which is still a real number when a,b are reals. Note a*b ≠ b*a since a+2b ≠ b+2a and that neither the associative property nor the statement a*1 = a hold. (Ans. C)

6. The number who take both subjects = number who pass math + number who pass English + number who fail both - number who pass both. Thus, 20 = 15+13+2- number who pass both. So, 10 passed both. (Ans. B)

7. $-x^2+3x-2<0$ means $x^2-3x+2>0$, which implies $(x-2)(x-1)>0$.
   Case 1: both (x-2) and (x-1)>0, which implies x>2.
   Case 2: both (x-2) and (x-1)<0, which implies x<1.
   The final answer is x>2 or x<1. (Ans. A)

8. $x^4 = [2(\cos 315° + i \sin 315°)]^4 = 2^4(\cos 1260° + i \sin 1260°)$ $= 16[-1+(i)(0)] = -16$. K must then be 16. (Ans. D)

9. Let D = common distance. Let x_1= 1st speed, x_2=2nd speed.
   Average speed = total distance ÷ total time = $(D+D)÷ (\frac{D}{x_1} + \frac{D}{x_2})$
   = $(2x_1x_2)/(x_1+x_2)$. The harmonic mean of 2 numbers x_1, x_2 =
   $1/[(\frac{1}{x_1} + \frac{1}{x_2})÷2]$, which can be shown to be equivalent to
   $(2x_1x_2)/(x_1+x_2)$. (Ans. D)

10. $\text{Log}_4 x + \text{Log}_4\frac{1}{3} = \text{Log}_4\frac{1}{3}x$ by a rule of logs. Now, $\text{Log}_4\frac{1}{3}x = -\frac{5}{2}$
    means $\frac{1}{3}x = 4^{-\frac{5}{2}} = \frac{1}{32}$. Thus, $x = \frac{3}{32}$. (Ans. A)

11. rs=q and r+s=p, since this follows as properties as the roots of a quadratic equation. $(r+s)^2 = r^2+2rs+s^2 = p^2$. Since rs=q, we have $r^2+2q+s^2 = p^2$. Now, r^2+s^2 must be p^2-2q. (Ans. B)

12. $[(x+2y)^2(x-2y)^2]^3 = \{[(x+2y)(x-2y)]^2\}^3 = (x^2-4y^2)^6$.
    This last expression has 7 different terms. (Ans. B)

13. $.3^x = 6$ means $(x)(\log .3) = \text{Log } 6$. Then, $(x)[\text{Log } 3 + \text{Log } .1]$
    $= [\text{Log } 3 + \text{Log } 2]$. $x(.4771-1) = .4771 + .3010$. Solving,
    $x = -1.488$ or approximately -1.5. (Ans. B)

14. If x is positive, this equation reads x^2+x-6 and if x is
    negative, the equation reads x^2-x-6. For x positive, the
    sum of the 2 roots $= -1$ and for x negative, the sum of the
    2 roots $= 1$. Thus, the sum of all 4 roots $= 0$. (Ans. C)

15. $(1.-1)$ means $1-i$. The multiplicative inverse is $\dfrac{1}{1-i}$ which
    $= (\dfrac{1}{1-i})(\dfrac{1+i}{1+i}) = \dfrac{1+i}{2} = \frac{1}{2} + \frac{1}{2}i$. This is represented by $(\frac{1}{2},\frac{1}{2})$.
    (Ans. C)

16.

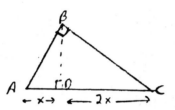

The altitude BD is the geometric
mean of AD and DC. So, BD $= x\sqrt{2}$.
Using the Pythagorean Theorem
twice, we get AB $= x\sqrt{3}$ and
BC $= x\sqrt{6}$. Now, AB/BC $= x\sqrt{3}/x\sqrt{6}$
which reduces to $1:\sqrt{2}$.
(Ans. C)

17. Original circumference $= (3.14)(25) = 78.5"$. The new circum-
    ference $= (3.14)(24.5) = 76.93"$. Since $63360" = 1$ mi., the
    original wheel required 807 revolutions, whereas the new
    wheel will require 824 revolutions (approx.). The increase
    is about 2%. (Ans. C)

18.

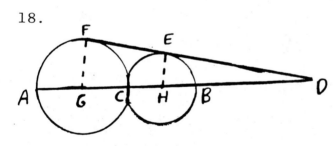

Let G,H be centers of the two
circles. $\angle F, \angle E = 90$, so $\triangle DEH$
is similar to $\triangle DEG$ since $\angle D=\angle D$
and $\angle G=\angle H$. We know EH:FG = 1:3.
Let GC=3x, CH=x, BD=y. Since
DH:DG = 1:3, also $(x+y):(5x+y) =$
1:3. Then, y=x= radius of small
circle. (Ans. B)

19.

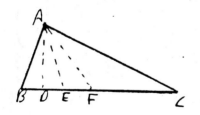

This is just one example showing
that the angle bisector $\overline{AE}$ falls
between the median $\overline{AF}$ and $\overline{AD}$, the
altitude. (Ans. C)

20.

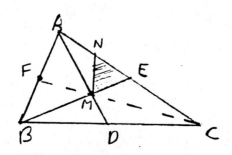

Let $\overline{AD}$, $\overline{CF}$, $\overline{BE}$ = medians. Then,
MF=$\frac{1}{3}$MC so that area of $\triangle AMB = \frac{1}{3}$
area of $\triangle ABC$. Area of $\triangle AMB +$
area of $\triangle AME = \frac{1}{2}$ area of $\triangle ABC$.
Thus, area of $\triangle AME = \frac{1}{6}$ area of
$\triangle ABC$. Since area of $\triangle AMN =$ area
of $\triangle MEN$, then ratio of area of $\triangle MEN$
to area of $\triangle ABC = 1:12$. (Ans. C)

21.

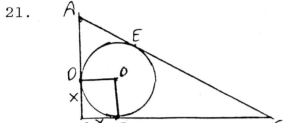

If AB=10, BC=24, AC=26, then ∠B=90⁰
since 10²+24²= 26². Now, DB=BF=x,
since tangents drawn to a circle
from an external point to a circle
are equal. Then AD=10-x=AE.
FC=24-x=EC. Now, AC=26=AE+EC=
10-x+24-x. So, x=4. Also, DOFB
is a square, so DO=4. Area of
circle = 16π. (Ans. B)

22.

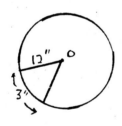

DF:AD = 2:3 = FE:8. Thus, FE = $5\frac{1}{3}$
BG:BC = 1:3 = EG:12. Thus EG=4
Now, FG = FE+EG = $9\frac{1}{3}$. (Ans. B)

23.

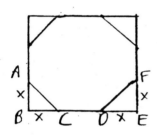

Let x = one leg of right ∆ABC.
Then, DE=EF=x. CD=1-2x=AC. By
Pythagorean Theorem, AC = $x\sqrt{2}$, so
$x\sqrt{2}$ = 1-2x and x = $1-\frac{1}{2}\sqrt{2}$. Area of
any corner = $\frac{1}{2}x^2=\frac{1}{2}(1-\frac{1}{2}\sqrt{2})^2=\frac{3}{4}-\frac{1}{2}\sqrt{2}$.
Thus, area of all 4 corners = $3-2\sqrt{2}$.
Now, area of octagon = $1-(3-2\sqrt{2})$ =
$2\sqrt{2}-2 = 2(\sqrt{2}-1)$. (Ans. B)

24.

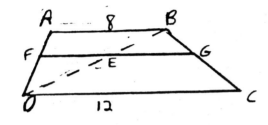

The circumference = (π)(24) which
is equivalent to 2π radians. By
proportion, $\dfrac{3}{x\ \text{radians}} = \dfrac{24\pi}{2\pi}$.
Thus, x=¼ radian. (Ans. A)

25.

$x^2+4y^2=16$ becomes $\dfrac{x^2}{4^2} + \dfrac{y^2}{2^2} < 1$ which

represents the inside of an ellipse
shown here. Shaded area = (½)(1)(2)=1.
(Ans. A)

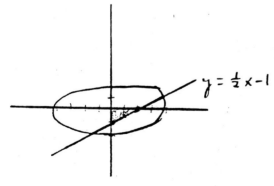

26. cos²x - sin²x -2sin x cos x =0 becomes cos 2x - sin 2x=0, using
    trigonometric identities. Since $\cos\frac{\pi}{4} = \sin\frac{\pi}{4}$, $x=\frac{\pi}{8}$. (Ans. B)

27. Arctan $\frac{1}{2}$=27^0. Arctan $\frac{1}{3}$=18^0. Value of sum = 45^0 = $\frac{\pi}{4}$.
(Ans. B)

28. $\tan\frac{\theta}{2}+\cot\frac{\theta}{2} = \dfrac{\sin\frac{\theta}{2}}{\cos\frac{\theta}{2}} + \dfrac{\cos\frac{\theta}{2}}{\sin\frac{\theta}{2}} = \dfrac{1}{(\cos\frac{\theta}{2})(\sin\frac{\theta}{2})} = \dfrac{1}{\sqrt{\frac{1+\cos\theta}{2}}\sqrt{\frac{1-\cos\theta}{2}}} = \dfrac{2}{\sin\theta} = 2c$
(Ans. C)

29.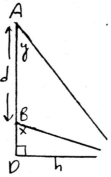

tan x = $\dfrac{h}{BD}$ or BD=hcot x

tan y = h/(d+hcot x)

dtan y + h(tan y cot x) = h
h = dtan y/(1-tan y cot x) =
d/(cot y-cot x)
(Ans. A)

30. The graph of any equation in the form r = 2acosθ is a circle centered at (a,o). Since a=1 in this example, the graph is a circle centered at (1,o^0) with radius = 1.
(Ans. B)

31.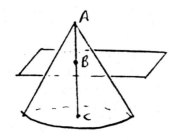

Let AB=a, BC=b, r = radius of circular base of small cone, R = radius of base of large cone. Note a:a+b = r:R
Volume of small cone = $\frac{1}{3}\pi r^2 a$

Volume of large cone = $\frac{1}{3}\pi R^2(a+b)$

Ratio of volumes = $r^2 a/R^2(a+b)$ = $a^3/(a+b)^3$. (Ans. C)

32.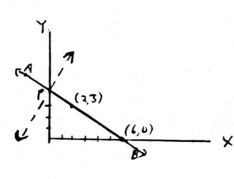

Since ∠ADB=60^0, OB=$\frac{r}{2}$, AB=$\frac{r}{2}\sqrt{3}$,

EB=$\frac{3}{2}$r. Volume of sphere = $\frac{4}{3}\pi r^3$

Volume of cone = $\frac{1}{3}\pi(\frac{r}{2}\sqrt{3})^2(\frac{3}{2}r)$ =

$\frac{3}{8}\pi r^3$

Difference of volumes = $\frac{23}{24}\pi r^3$.

(Ans. D)

33.

The equation of $\vec{AB}$ is y = $-\frac{3}{4}$x + $\frac{9}{2}$

Then, P is located at $(0,\frac{9}{2})$. Now,

slope of dotted line = $\frac{4}{3}$. (Ans. D)

34.

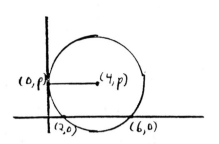

Let point of tangency be $(0,p)$. Since a radius drawn to p must be parallel to the x-axis, the y coordinate of the center is p. Also, the x coordinate is 4 because the center must be equidistant from $(2,0)$ and $(6,0)$. Now, distance from $(0,p)$ to $(4,p)$ = 4 = distance from $(4,p)$ to $(2,0)$ = $\sqrt{p^2+4}$. Solving, $4 = \sqrt{p^2+4}$, $p = \sqrt{12}$. A circle with center at $(4,\sqrt{12})$ and radius of 4 has equation $(x-4)^2+(y-\sqrt{12})^2 = 16$. (Ans. C)

35. $x=-1$ is NOT an asymptote since by substitution $-y^2-y^2+4+1=0$ and $y=\pm\sqrt{2.5}$. For the other choices, an unsolvable equation appears.

36.

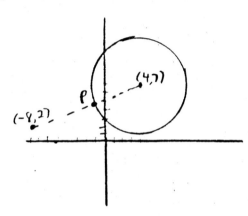

Rewrite $x^2+y^2-8x-14y+40=0$ as $(x-4)^2+(y-7)^2=25$. This is a circle with center at $(4,7)$ and radius = 5. The shortest distance will be the distance from $(-8,2)$ and P. The equation of the dotted line is

$$y=\frac{5}{12}x + \frac{64}{12}$$ and P lies at the

intersection of this dotted line and the circle, which is 5 units from $(4,7)$. Since the distance from $(-8,2)$ to $(4,7)$ is 13, the distance from $(-8,2)$ to P must be 8. (Ans. B)

37.

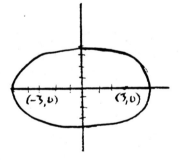

Foci are at $(\pm3,0)$, $a=5$, $b=4$, so the equation is $x^2/25 + y^2/16=1$. Here $a=\frac{1}{2}$ length of major axis and $b = \frac{1}{2}$ length of minor axis. (Ans. D)

38. If the equation of a parabola is given by $(y-k)^2=4p(x-h)$ and the equation of the directrix is $x=h-p$. Transform $y^2-4x-6y+9=0$ to $(y-3)^2=4(x-0)$. Thus, $p=1$, $h=0$. The equation of the directrix is $x=-1$. (Ans. B)

39. By inspection. (Ans. A)

40. Let $Y = \sin x + \cos x$. $dY/dx = \cos x - \sin x$. Setting $dY/dx=0$, $x=45^0$. At that value, $\sin x + \cos x = \frac{1}{\sqrt{2}} + \frac{1}{\sqrt{2}} = \sqrt{2}$. (Ans. C)

41.

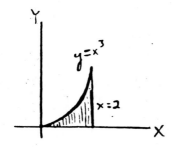

$$\text{Volume} = \int_0^2 \pi(x^3)^2 dx = [\frac{\pi x^7}{7}]_0^2 = \frac{128\pi}{7}$$

(Ans. C)

42.

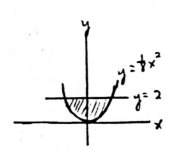

Area of shaded area $= \int_{-4}^4 (2-\frac{1}{8}x^2)dx =$

$[2x-\frac{1}{24}x^3]_{-4}^4 = \frac{32}{3}$. Note that $(-4,2)$

and $(4,2)$ are points of intersection
(Ans. C)

43.

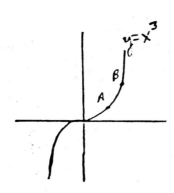

Let points A,B be such that the
difference of their x coordinates is
k. If A is located at (x,x^3), then
B is found at $(x+k, [x+k]^3)$. Slope
of $\overleftrightarrow{AB} = [(x+k)^3-x^3]/[(x+k)-x]$, which
reduces to $3x^2+3xk+k^2$. By
differentiating this expression and
setting $=$ to 0, we get $6x+3k=0$ or
$x=-\frac{1}{2}k$. Replacing x by $-\frac{1}{2}k$ into
$3x^2+3xk+k^2$ yields the value $k^2/4$.
(Ans. D)

44.

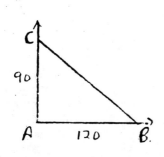

After 2 hours, the autos have
traveled 120 miles and 90 miles,
respectively. To find the rate at
which $\overline{BC}$ is changing, $AB^2+AC^2= BC^2$
can be used. Differentiating with
respect to time, $2(AB)\frac{d(AB)}{dt} +$

$2(AC)\frac{d(AC)}{dt} = 2(BC)\frac{d(BC)}{dt}$. When

AB=120 and AC=90, then BC=150. Now
$(2)(120) \cdot (60)+(2)(90)(45) = (2)(150)$

$\frac{d(BC)}{dt}$. Solving, $\frac{d(BC)}{dt} = 75$.

(Ans. C)

45.   82.5 must be the 23rd score, either counting from the highest
to lowest or lowest to highest scores. By adding 100, 95, 40,
and 15, 82.5 would still be the median since 24 scores lie below
82.5 and 24 scores lie above it. (Ans. D)

46. Standard deviation $= \sqrt{\dfrac{\Sigma(x-\overline{x})^2}{N}}$. For 2,5,8 standard deviation = $\sqrt{6}$ which is exactly the same for the numbers 4,7,10. (Ans. D)

47. The probability that C and D will be chosen 1st and 2nd in either order is $(\frac{2}{70})(\frac{1}{69})$. However, since a total of 12 will be selected, there are $_{12}C_2 = 66$ different combinations of selection numbers for C and D when both are chosen. Final

    probability $= 66(\frac{2}{70})(\frac{1}{69}) = \frac{22}{805}$. (Ans. B)

48. There are a total of 8 combinations which will yield 7 or 11. There are a total of 36 combinations for both dice. Odds = probability of success ÷ probability of failure $= \frac{8}{36} \div \frac{28}{36} = 2:7$.

    (Ans. D)

49. By reference. (Ans. A)

50. A sextant is a navigational instrument, so is best used for determining latitude and longitude. (Ans. C)

———

EXAMINATION SECTION

DIRECTIONS: Each question or incomplete statement is followed by several suggested answers or completions. Select the one that BEST answers the question or completes the statement. *PRINT THE LETTER OF THE CORRECT ANSWER IN THE SPACE AT THE RIGHT.*

1. A rope 10 yards long is divided into 3 lengths so that the shortest is equal to the difference in the lengths of the two others. Then the LONGEST piece is what part of the whole rope?

    A. $\frac{1}{4}$ B. $\frac{1}{2}$ C. $\frac{2}{3}$ D. $\frac{3}{4}$

    1.___

2. Assume that a storekeeper reduces his profit on all merchandise in the store from 40% of the cost to $33\frac{1}{3}$% of the cost. If an article originally sold for $14.70, what would its new selling price be?

    A. $9.80   B. $10.78   C. $11.76   D. $14.00

    2.___

3. Which one of the following need NOT be a property of a group?

    A. The associative law
    B. The principle of closure
    C. The existence of an identity element
    D. The commutative law

    3.___

4. In a certain homeroom class, all the students are studying French or Spanish, or both French and Spanish. Fifteen students are studying French and eighteen students are studying Spanish. However, of these, six students are studying both languages. The number of students in the class is

    A. 24   B. 27   C. 33   D. 39

    4.___

5. Using each vertex of an equilateral triangle of side e as a center, circles of radius $\frac{e}{2}$ are drawn; then the area of the portion of the triangle NOT covered by the circles is

    A. $\dfrac{2e^2\sqrt{3} - \pi e}{4}$ B. $\dfrac{e^2(2\sqrt{3} - \pi)}{8}$

    C. $\dfrac{e^2(\pi - 2\sqrt{3})}{8}$ D. $\dfrac{\pi e - 2e^2\sqrt{3}}{4}$

    5.___

6. All triangles in the set of triangles having a given side and a given angle opposite that side

    A. are congruent
    B. are equivalent
    C. have the same circumscribed circle
    D. have the same inscribed circle

    6.___

7. The quadrilateral formed by two tangents from an external point to a circle and the two radii to the points of contact is a rhombus only if the central angle formed by the two radii is
   A. acute
   B. right
   C. obtuse
   D. the supplement of the angle between the two tangents

7. ____

8. If two circles have radii of 3 and 8, respectively, and the distance between their centers is 13, the length of their common external tangent is
   A. 12   B. $4\sqrt{10}$ C. $\sqrt{194}$ D. 15

8. ____

9. If the sides of a certain triangle are 13, 14, and 15, the radius of the inscribed circle is
   A. 4   B. 13/3   C. 8   D. 26/3

9. ____

10. If the bisector of the right angle of a certain right triangle divides the hypotenuse into segments in the ratio 3:5, then the ratio of the longer segment of the hypotenuse to the longer leg of the triangle is
    A. $\sqrt{34}:8$
    B. $\sqrt{17}:2$
    C. 3:5
    D. not determinable from the given data

10. ____

11. If the radius of a regular dodecagon is 10 inches, its area expressed in square inches is
    A. 120   B. 300   C. 100π D. $300\sqrt{3}$

11. ____

12. If, in acute $\triangle ABC$, altitude CD and angle bisector CF are drawn, then the number of degrees in $\angle DCF$ is
    A. $\dfrac{A - B}{2}$ B. $\left|\dfrac{A - B}{2}\right|$ C. $A - B$ D. $|A - B|$

12. ____

13. The distance between two given points in space whose coordinates are (-2,5,3) and (3,-1,-2) is
    A. $3\sqrt{2}$ B. $5\sqrt{3}$ C. 9   D. $\sqrt{86}$

13. ____

14. If the sides of a triangle are 6", 8", 10", then the total surface of the solid generated by revolving the triangle 360° about the 10" side is
    A. 33.6π B. 67.2π C. 100.8π D. 134.4π

14. ____

15. A right circular cylinder is circumscribed about a sphere. If S represents the surface area of the sphere and T represents the total area of the cylinder, then
    A. $S = \dfrac{2}{3}T$ B. $S > \dfrac{2}{3}T$ C. $S < \dfrac{2}{3}T$ D. $S = T$

15. ____

16. The solution set of $2x^2+7x-4 < 0$ consists of all real values of x, such that
    A. $x>4$ or $x<\frac{1}{2}$
    C. $-4<x<-\frac{1}{2}$
    B. $x<-4$ or $x>\frac{1}{2}$
    D. $-4<x<\frac{1}{2}$

16. ____

17. The repeating decimal, .152525.., is equivalent to which   17.___
one of the following fractions?
    A. $\dfrac{146}{957}$ B. $\dfrac{151}{990}$ C. $\dfrac{6,101}{40,000}$ D. $\dfrac{610,101}{4,000,000}$

18. If $3x^2 - 9x^2 + kx - 12$ is exactly divisible by x-3, then   18.___
it is also exactly divisible by which one of the following?
    A. $3x^2-x+4$ B. $3x^2-4$
    C. $3x^2+4$ D. x-4

19. A, B, and C are the vertices of an equilateral triangle.   19.___
A man traveled along its perimeter with the following
average speeds: from A to B at r feet per minute, from
B to C at s feet per minute, and from C to A at t feet per
minute. His average speed for the entire trip, in feet
per minute, was
    A. $\frac{1}{3}$(r+s+t)   B. $\frac{1}{3}(\frac{1}{r}+\frac{1}{s}+\frac{1}{t})$

    C. $\dfrac{3\ rst}{rs+rt+st}$ D. none of the above

20. Given the three sets of coplanar points represented by   20.___
$3x+4y\leq24$, $x\geq1$ and $y\geq2$, then the area of the polygon
common to the three sets of points is
    A. 2   B. $\dfrac{169}{24}$ C. 14   D. $\dfrac{169}{12}$

21. Other things being equal, the electrical resistance of a   21.___
wire varies directly as its length and inversely as the
square of its diameter. If a wire 400 feet long and 2.5 mm
in diameter has a resistance of 1.1 ohms, then the
resistance of a wire of the same material whose length
is 300 feet and whose diameter is 2 mm. is, to the NEAREST
tenth of an ohm,
    A. .5   B. 1.0
    C. 1.3   D. none of the above

22. The numbers 314 and 1011 are written in two different   22.___
bases. Each number contains the largest digit available
on its base. The sum of these two numbers, if written
in base 3, is
    A. 10112   B. 1211002   C. 20220   D. 1011111

23. Consider the following sets of numbers: positive   23.___
irrational numbers, complex numbers, positive real numbers,
positive rational numbers, positive integers, positive
even integers.
These sets can be arranged in a nest of sets and subsets,
with the exception of one of them. The one which does NOT
fit in such a nest is
    A. positive even integers
    B. complex numbers
    C. positive irrational numbers
    D. positive rational numbers

24. If p, r, s, and t are non-negative real numbers, p, r, and s are in arithmetic progression, and r, s, and t are in geometric progression, which one of the following statements is NOT true?

    A. If $p \neq r$, then $s \neq t$ B. $rt = (2r-p)^2$

    C. $rs = pt$ D. If $p = 0$, $t = 4r$

24.___

25. Of the following, the equation which represents the set of points such that the distance of each from the point $(5,3)$ is twice its distance from the x axis, is

    A. $x^2-3y^2-10x-6y+34=0$ B. $x^2-y^2-10x-6y+34=0$

    C. $x^2-3y^2-34=0$ D. $x^2-3y^2-8x+34=0$

25.___

26. In the hyperbola, $9x^2-y^2-36=0$, the eccentricity is

    A. $2\sqrt{5}$ B. $\sqrt{10}$ C. $2\sqrt{10}$ D. 12

26.___

27. If the vertices of a triangle have the coordinates $(4,2)$, $(-1,2)$, and $(-1,-10)$, the center of the circle which can be circumscribed about this triangle has the coordinates

    A. $(1\frac{1}{2},-4)$ B. $(1\frac{1}{2},8)$

    C. $(-1,-4)$ D. none of the above

27.___

28. The area enclosed by the curve, $25(x-2)^2+4(y+3)^2=400$, is

    A. 6π B. 10π C. 36π D. 40π

28.___

29. Which one of the following statements is TRUE concerning the graph of $xy-2y=x$?

    A. It is continuous.

    B. It is asymptotic only to the line, $x=2$.

    C. It is asymptotic only to the line, $y=1$.

    D. It is asymptotic to both lines, $x=2$ and $y=1$.

29.___

30. The area of a triangle whose vertices have the following sets of coordinates: $(0,-4)$, $(5,3)$, $(8,-2)$ is

    A. $17\frac{1}{2}$ B. 23   C. 46   D. 56

30.___

31. The distance between the two parallel lines $3x-4y=7$ and $9x-12y=5$ is

    A. $\dfrac{1}{3}$ B. $\dfrac{16}{15}$ C. $\dfrac{7}{5}$ D. $\dfrac{26}{15}$

31.___

32. The congruences, $a \equiv p \pmod{3}$ and $a \equiv p^2 \pmod{3}$, imply that

    A. either p or $p-1$ is a multiple of 3

    B. $p-1$ is a multiple of 3

    C. p is a multiple of 3

    D. neither p nor $p-1$ is a multiple of 3

32.___

33. If the greatest common factor of two numbers x and y is c, c being composite, and X is the set of prime factors of x, while Y is the set of prime factors of y, then the set of prime factors of c is

    A. equal to $X \cup Y$

    B. a proper subset of $X \cup Y$

    C. equal to $X \cap Y$

    D. a proper subset of $X \cap Y$

33.___

34. If, in $\triangle ABC$, $\angle A = 30^0$, a=6, b=10, then $\angle C$ is   34.___
    A. acute   B. either acute or right
    C. either acute or obtuse   D. obtuse

35. Of the following, the one which is a cube root of i is   35.___
    A. $+i$ B. $\cos 30^0 + i \sin 30^0$
    C. $\cos 90^0 + i \sin 90^0$ D. $\cos 120^0 + i \sin 120^0$

36. A ship sailing on a 45^0 course from home port, H, and   36.___
5 miles from it sighted a lighthouse, L, directly north
of H and found that L had a bearing of 90^0 from the ship.
The distance, in miles, of L from the ship at that time
was
    A. 3
    B. 5
    C. $5\sqrt{2}$
    D. not determinable from the given data

37. The period of the curve whose equation is $y=\frac{1}{3}(\cos^2 x - \sin^2)$ 37.___
   is
    A. 60^0 B. 180^0 C. 720^0 D. $\frac{1}{3}$

38. The product, $\sin 40^0 \cos 20^0$, can be rewritten as the sum   38.___
of two functions. This sum is
    A. $\frac{\sin 60^0}{2} + \frac{\sin 20^0}{2}$ B. $\frac{\cos 60^0}{2} + \frac{\cos 20^0}{2}$

    C. $\sin 30^0 + \sin 10^0$ D. $\cos 30^0 + \cos 10^0$

39. If x and y are acute angles, tan x=2 and $\tan y=\frac{1}{3}$, which   39.___
one of the following statements is NOT true?
    A. $\tan(x+y) = 2\frac{1}{3}$ B. $x+y$ = arc tan 7

    C. $x-y = \frac{\pi}{4}$ D. $\tan 2y = \frac{3}{4}$

40. The slope of a curve is 4x+5. If the curve passes through   40.___
the point (-1,5), the equation of the curve is
    A. $y = 2x^2+5x+8$ B. $y = 4x^2+5x+3$
    C. $y = 2x^2-5x+8$ D. $y = 2x^2+5x-8$

41. A farmer has a certain length of fencing and wishes to   41.___
enclose a rectangular garden using the side of an adjoining
barn as one side of the rectangle. If the garden is to have
the maximum possible area, its dimensions should have the
ratio of
    A. 1:1   B. 1:2   C. 1:3   D. none of these

42. The limit of $\frac{\sin 3x}{x}$ as x approaches 0 is   42.___

    A. 0   B. $\frac{1}{3}$ C. 1   D. 3

6

43. Given the equation of the ellipse, $x^2+9y^2=37$, find the
equation of the line tangent to the ellipse, at the point
(-1,2).
    A. x+18y-35=0   B. 18x+y+16=0
    C. 18x-y-34=0   D. x-18y+37=0

43.____

44. A conical filter is 2 in. in radius and 6 in. deep.
Liquid passes through the filter at the constant rate of
$\frac{1}{15}$ cu. in./sec. When the depth of the liquid is 3 in.,
then the number of in./sec. at which the surface of the
liquid is falling is

  A. $\frac{1}{15}$ B. $\frac{1}{15\pi}$ C. $\frac{1}{5\pi}$ D. $\frac{1}{81\pi}$

44.____

45. A man in a boat is 3 miles due east of a point, P, which
is on a coastline running due north and south. He wishes
to reach another point, Q, on the coastline and 6 miles
south of P. If he can travel 4 mi./hr. on water and 5 mi./hr.
on land, how many miles south of P should he land in order
to minimize his total travel time?
    A. 2   B. 3   C. 4   D. 5

45.____

46. If the arithmetic mean of 40 marks is 72.5 and if four
additional marks of 55, 65, 85, and 96 are added to the
first 40, the new arithmetic mean is
    A. 72.00   B. 72.50   C. 72.70   D. 72.75

46.____

47. The statistic which is obtained from a set of N numbers,
x_i, (i=1,2...N) by the computation

$$\frac{\sum_{i=1}^{N} x_i}{N}$$

is the set's
    A. median   B. arithmetic mean
    C. mode   D. standard deviation

47.____

48. A hypsometer is an instrument used for measuring which
one of the following?
    A. Heights of objects too far away to be seen with the
       naked eye
    B. Distance across a body of water when the shore
       distance is known
    C. The circumference of a great circle of a sphere
    D. Heights of visible objects when the distance of the
       observer from the foot of the object is known

48.____

49. Which one of the following statements about Eratosthenes
is TRUE?
    A. He invented algebra.
    B. He determined the circumference of the earth.
    C. He was known as the "Father of Geometry".
    D. He developed coordinate geometry.

49.____

50. Galois, through the Theory of Groups, demonstrated that   50.___
    A. the set of complex numbers is not ordered
    B. the fifth Euclidean postulate is independent of
       the others
    C. it is impossible to construct a square equal in area
       to a given circle
    D. the equation of degree 5 cannot be solved by means
       of radicals

_____

KEY (CORRECT ANSWERS)

1. B	11. B	21. C	31. B	41. B
2. D	12. B	22. A	32. A	42. D
3. D	13. D	23. C	33. C	43. D
4. B	14. B	24. C	34. C	44. B
5. B	15. A	25. A	35. B	45. C
6. C	16. D	26. B	36. A	46. D
7. B	17. B	27. A	37. B	47. B
8. A	18. C	28. C	38. A	48. D
9. A	19. C	29. D	39. A	49. B
10. A	20. B	30. B	40. A	50. C

_____

SOLUTIONS TO PROBLEMS

1. Let x = shortest piece, y = 2nd piece, then 10-x-y = longest piece. Now, x=(10-x-y)-y. Thus, x+y=5. Then, 10-x-y must equal 5, and this represents ½ the length of the rope. (Ans. B)

2. Let x = cost. Then, 14.70 =(1.40)(x) and x=10.50. The new selling price is (10.50)(133⅓%) = $14.00. (Ans. D)

3. If a group happens to have the commutative property, it is called Abelian. (Ans. D)

4. 15-6=9 students studying only French, whereas 18-6=12 students studying only Spanish. Total number of students = 9+12+6=27. (Ans. B)

5.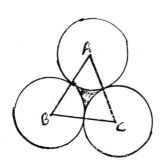

    The radius of each circle is $\frac{e}{2}$ so that the area of each circle is $\frac{\pi e^2}{4}$. The 3 sectors are formed by central angles of 60⁰, so that the area of each sector is $\frac{1}{6}(\frac{\pi e^2}{4})$. Thus, 3 such sectors comprise an area of $\frac{\pi e^2}{8}$ This amount would be subtracted from the area of the equilateral triangle ABC which is $\frac{e^2\sqrt{3}}{4}$. This results in $\frac{e^2\sqrt{3}}{4} - \frac{\pi e^2}{8} = e^2(2\sqrt{3}-\pi)/8$. (Ans. B)

6.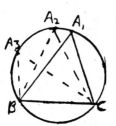

    Since an inscribed angle = ½ the intercepted arc (in degrees), $\triangle A_1BC$, $\triangle A_2BC$, and $\triangle A_3BC$ are just 3 examples where $\angle A = \angle A_1 = \angle A_3$ and all 3 triangl(es) share the same side $\overline{BC}$. (Ans. C)

7.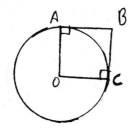

    If 0 is the center, with $\overline{AB}$ and $\overline{BC}$ tangents to the circle, $\angle A=\angle C=90^0$. The only way the quadrilateral can be a rhombus is if all four sides are equal. This would imply that ABCD is a square. Thus, $\angle O=90^0$. (Ans. B)

8.

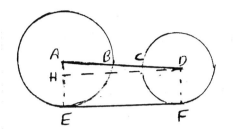

We know that AD=13, AE=8, and DF=3. Since radii must form 90⁰ angles with tangents at contact point, ∠E=∠F=90⁰. Construct $\overline{HD}$ // $\overline{EF}$. Then, HDFE is a rectangle. AH=8-3=5 and $HD^2+5^2=13^2$ since △AHD is a right triangle. Then, HD=12 and so is EF=12. (Ans. A)

9.

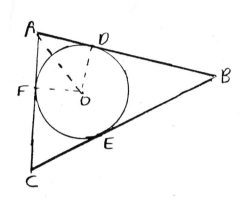

Let AC=13, AB=14, BC=15, ∠D and ∠F=90⁰. If AD=x, DB=14-x=BE. Then, CE=15-(14-x)=1+x=FC. AF=13-(1+x) = 12-x=AD. But, AD also = x. Thus, 12-x=x, so x=6. Now, $15^2=13^2+14^2-(2)(13)(14) \cos ∠FAD$. Then, ∠FAD = 67.38⁰. Since △ AFO, ADO are congruent, ∠OAD=33.69⁰. Finally,

$$\tan 33.69⁰ = \frac{OD}{6}, \text{ and OD=4.}$$
(Ans. A)

10.

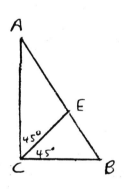

Let EB=3, AE=5. Using the law of sines for △ ACB, EAC and letting ∠B=K⁰, AB/sin 90⁰=AC/sin K⁰ and AE/sin 45⁰=AC/sin ∠AEC. Now, ∠AEC = (45+K)⁰ and by solving the 2 equations involving AC and K, we get K=59.036⁰ and AC=6.86. Finally, AE/AC = 5/6.86 = .7289 which is √34/8. (Ans. A)

11.

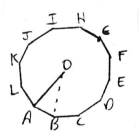

OA=10, OB=10, ∠AOB=30⁰. To find AB, $AB^2=10^2+10^2-(2)(10)(10) \cos 30⁰$, so that AB=5.17. Area of △AOB = $\sqrt{s(s-a)(s-b)(s-c)}$ where s = semi-perimeter. △ Area = $\sqrt{630.3}$ = 25.1. Area of dodecagon = 12(25.1) = 301.27 or approximately 300. (Ans. B)

12.

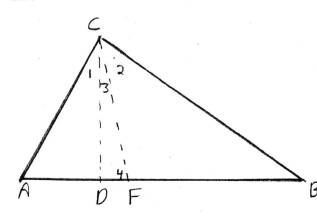

∠4=90⁰-∠3 = ∠A+∠1
∠2=∠1-∠3 = 90⁰-∠B
Adding the middle and third parts of the above 2 equations:
90⁰+∠1 -2·∠3 = 90⁰+∠A+∠1-∠B
-2∠3=∠A-∠B, so that:
$∠3 = (∠B-∠A)/2 = \left|\dfrac{A-B}{2}\right|$

NOTE: If B and A were interchanged, ∠A would be smaller than ∠B, but the answer would remain the same. (Ans. B)

13. The distance from $(-2,5,3)$ to $(3,-1,3)$ is $\sqrt{(-2-3)^2+(5-(-1))^2}$
$=\sqrt{61}$. The distance from $(3,-1,3)$ to $(3,-1,-2)$ is 5. The
required distance between $(-2,5,3)$ and $(3,-1,-2)$ = $\sqrt{61+25}$ = $\sqrt{86}$.
(Ans. D)

14.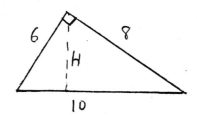

The area of the $\triangle$ is $(\frac{1}{2})(6)(8)=24$.
Thus, H=4.8. Total surface = sum
of 2 cones = $\pi r s_1 + \pi r s_2$
(s_1, s_2= slant heights) = $(\pi)(4.8)(6)$
+ $\pi(4.8)(8)$ = 67.2π
(Ans. B)

15. The surface area of the sphere = $4\pi R^2$ =S, whereas T= surface
area of cylinder = $2\pi R^2 + 2\pi RH$, and since H=2R, T = $2\pi R^2 + 4\pi R^2$ =
$6\pi R^2$. Now, S = $\frac{2}{3}$T. (Ans. A)

16. By factoring, $(2x-1)(x+4)<0$, which is solved by:
Case 1: $2x-1<0$ and $x+4>0$, which implies $-4<x<\frac{1}{2}$
Case 2: $2x-1>0$ and $x+4<0$, which has no answer
Final answer: $-4<x<\frac{1}{2}$
(Ans. D)

17. Let N = .152525..., then 100N = 15.2525... Now, 99N=15.1.
Thus, N = $\frac{151}{990}$. (Ans. B)

18. 3 must be a solution of $3x^3-9x^2+Kx-12=0$ if x-3 is a factor.
$3(3)^3-9(3)^2+k(3)-12=0$. Then, K=4. Since $3x^3-9x^2+4x-12 = (x-3)$
$(3x^2+4)$, then $3x^2+4$ must also divide evenly into $3x^3-9x^2+4x-12$.
(Ans. C)

19. Let d = distance of each side. The times required to travel
from A to B, B to C, and C to A are d/r, d/s, and d/t,
respectively. Average speed = Total distance ÷ Total time =
$3d/(d/r + d/s + d/t) = 3rst/(rs + rt + st)$. (Ans. C)

20.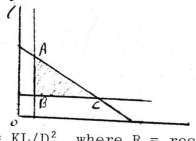

The vertices of A, B, C are $(1,5\frac{1}{4})$,
$(1,2)$, and $(5\frac{1}{3},2)$, respectively.
Area = $(\frac{1}{2})(BC)(AB)$ = $(\frac{1}{2})(4\frac{1}{3})(3\frac{1}{4})$ =
169/24.
(Ans. B)

21. R = KL/D^2, where R = resistance, L = length, D = diameter,
K = constant. 1.1 = (K)(400)/6.25, so that K = .0172.
Now, R = (.0172)(300)/4 = about 1.3. (Ans. C)

22. $314_{\text{base 5}}$ = (3)(25)+(1)(5)+4 = 84

$1011_{\text{base 2}}$ = (1)(8)+(0)(4)+1(2)+1 = 11

The sum = 95 which is $10112_{\text{base 3}}$. (Ans. A)

23. The positive IRRATIONAL numbers don't fit in the nest.
From the smallest to largest set, we have: positive even
integers, positive integers, positive rational numbers,
positive real numbers, complex numbers. (Ans. C)

24. Let p=1, r=3, s=5, t=$\frac{25}{3}$. Then, rs=15 $\neq$ pt = $\frac{25}{3}$.
Algebraically, we must have r = (p+s)/2 and r/s = s/t.
(Ans. C)

25. Let (x,y) be any point of the required equation. The distance
from (x,y) to the x-axis is y. The distance from (x,y) to (5,3)
is $\sqrt{(x-5)^2+(y-3)^2}$. Now, 2y = $\sqrt{x^2-10x+25+y^2-6y+9}$, which
becomes $x^2-3y^2-10x-6y+34=0$. (Ans. A)

26. Rewrite as $\frac{x^2}{4} - \frac{y^2}{36} = 1$, so that a=2, b=6, c=$\sqrt{40}$ or $2\sqrt{10}$
Eccentricity = $\frac{c}{a}$ = $\frac{2\sqrt{10}}{2}$ = $\sqrt{10}$. (Ans. B)

27.
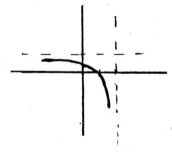
Since this is a right triangle, $\overline{BC}$
would be a diameter of the circle
which would circumscribe the
triangle. The circle's center is
located at the midpoint of $\overline{BC}$ which
is ($\frac{4-1}{2}$, $\frac{2-10}{2}$) = ($1\frac{1}{2}$,-4). (Ans. A)

28. The equation $25(x-2)^2+4(y+3)^2= 400$ is equivalent to $(x-2)^2/16 +$
$(y+3)^2/100= 1$. This represents an ellipse with center at (2,-3),
major axis extends from (2,-13) to (2,7), minor axis extends
from (-2,-3) to (6,-3). Center the ellipse at (0,0) so that
using $\frac{x^2}{16} + \frac{y^2}{100} = 1$ and the fact that Area = $4 \cdot \int_0^4 \sqrt{100-6.25x^2}dx$,
we get Area = 36π. (Ans. C)

29.
xy-2y=x would be asymptotic to x=2
(since 2y-2y $\neq$ 2) and to y=1 (since
x-2 $\neq$ x). (Ans. D)

30.
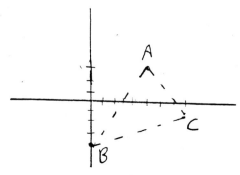
AB = $\sqrt{5^2+ 7^2}$= 8.6
AC = $\sqrt{3^2+ 5^2}$ = 5.8, BC = $\sqrt{2^2+ 8^2}$= 8.2
s = $\frac{1}{2}$(perimeter) = 11.3
Area=$\sqrt{(11.3)(11.3-8.6)(11.3-5.8)(11.3-8}$.
= $\sqrt{520.2}$ = 22.8 or approx. 23
(Ans. B)

31. Transforming both equations to slope-intercept form, $y = \frac{3}{4}x - \frac{7}{4}$ and $y = \frac{3}{4}x - \frac{5}{12}$. The equation of any line perpendicular to these 2 lines has the form $y = -\frac{4}{3}x + K$, K a constant. Let K=0. Then, $y = -\frac{4}{3}x$ intersects $y = \frac{3}{4}x - \frac{7}{4}$ and $y = \frac{3}{4}x - \frac{5}{12}$ at $(\frac{21}{25}, -\frac{112}{100})$ and $(\frac{1}{5}, -\frac{4}{15})$. Converting to decimals, we get $(.84, -1.12)$ and $(.2, -.27)$. Distance between these points $= \sqrt{(.84-.2)^2 + (-1.12+.27)^2}$ $= 1.064 \approx \frac{16}{15}$. (Ans. B)

32. $a \equiv p \bmod 3$ means $\frac{a-p}{3}$ is an integer. $a \equiv p^2 \bmod 3$ means $\frac{a-p^2}{3}$ is also an integer. Since the difference of 2 constants is an integer, this means that $(a-p)/3 - (a-p^2)/3 = (p^2-p)/3 = p(p-1)/3$ is an integer. Thus, either p or p-1 must be a multiple of 3. (Ans. A)

33. Let $c = p_1 \cdot p_2 \cdot p_3$, where p_1, p_2, p_3 are primes. Then, $x = (p_1 \cdot p_2 \cdot p_3)$ (other primes) and $y = (p_1 \cdot p_2 \cdot p_3)$ (other primes different than those contained in x). Now, $X \cap Y = \{p_1, p_2, p_3\} = \{$prime factors of c (Ans. C)

34. By the law of sines, $\frac{6}{\sin 30^0} = \frac{10}{\sin \angle B}$. $\sin \angle B = \frac{5}{6}$ and so $\angle B = 57^0$ or 123^0. Thus, $\angle C = 93^0$ or 27^0. (Ans. C)

35. $\sqrt[3]{i} = (i)^{\frac{1}{3}} = (0+i)^{\frac{1}{3}} = [1(\cos 90^0 + i \sin 90^0)]^{\frac{1}{3}} =$ $1^{\frac{1}{3}}(\cos \frac{90+360n}{3} + i \sin \frac{90+360n}{3})$, which gives 3 roots

Root 1: $\cos 30^0 + i \sin 30^0$
Root 2: $\cos 150^0 + i \sin 150^0$
Root 3: $\cos 270^0 + i \sin 270^0 = -i$
[Thus, BOTH choices A and B are correct.]
(Ans. B)

36.

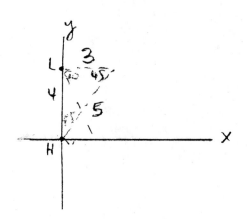

37. $y = \frac{1}{3}(\cos^2 x - \sin^2 x)$ becomes $y = \frac{1}{3}(\cos 2x)$. The period is

$\frac{360}{2} = 180^0$. (Ans. B)

38. $(\sin 40^0)(\cos 20^0) = (.6428)(.9397) = .604$, which equals $\sin 60^0/2 + \sin 20^0/2$. (Ans. A)

39. $\tan (x+y) = (\tan x + \tan y)/[1-\tan x \cdot \tan y]$
In this example, $\tan (x+y) = (2+\frac{1}{3})/(1-2\cdot\frac{1}{3}) = 7$ which is not $2\frac{1}{3}$.
(Ans. A)

40. The general equation: $y = \int 4x+5 = 2x^2+5x+K$ (K is a constant).
Using the point $(-1,5)$, $5 = 2(-1)^2+5(-1)+K$. Thus, K=8. (Ans. A)

41. Let P = given length (a constant). Then, P = L+2W, since one side (a length) is not needed because a barn is positioned there. Area = A = (L)(W) = (P-2W)(W) = $PW-2W^2$. Setting dA/dW = P-4W=0, we get W = $\frac{P}{4}$. Substituting this value in P = L+2W,

L = $\frac{P}{2}$. Then, the ratio of $\frac{P}{4}$ to $\frac{P}{2}$ = 1 to 2. (Ans. B)

42. Using L'Hospital's rule, $\lim_{x\to 0} \frac{\sin 3x}{x} = \lim_{x\to 0} \frac{3\cos 3x}{1} = 3$.

This rule is useful when both lim (numerator) and lim (denominator) = 0. In this case, take the limits of the derivatives of the functions in the numerator and denominator. (Ans. D)

43. Differentiating implicitly, $2x+18y\cdot \frac{dy}{dx} = 0$. Replacing (x,y) by

$(-1,2)$, $-2+(36)(\frac{dy}{dx}) = 0$, and $\frac{dy}{dx} = \frac{1}{18}$. The equation of the

tangent line is $y = \frac{1}{18}x + k$(a constant). Again using

$(-1,2)$, $2 = -\frac{1}{18} + k$, and k = $\frac{37}{18}$. So, $y = \frac{1}{18}x + \frac{37}{18}$

or x - 18y + 37 = 0.

44. $V = \frac{1}{3}\pi R^2 H$. $dV/dt = \frac{\pi}{3}[2R\cdot dR/dt\cdot H + R^2 dH/dt]$

But, H=3, R=1, since $\frac{H}{R} = \frac{6}{2} = 3$ must be constant.

Since H = 3R, $V = \frac{1}{3}\pi R^2(3R) = \pi R^3$.

$dv/dt = 3\pi R^2 \cdot dR/dt$. $\frac{1}{15} = 3\pi(1)^2\cdot dR/dt$, so $dR/dt = \frac{1}{45\pi}$.

Now, to find dH/dt, return to 2nd equation on the 1st line.

$\frac{1}{15} = \frac{\pi}{3}[2\cdot\frac{1}{45\pi}\cdot 3+1^2\cdot dH/dt]$. Thus, dH/dt = $\frac{1}{15\pi}$. (Ans. B)

45.

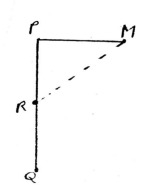

The man is located at M, PM=3, PQ=6. He plans to reach Q by first traveling to R. Let PR=x. Then, MR = $\sqrt{x^2+9}$ and RQ = 6-x. The time required to travel from M to R = $\sqrt{x^2+9}/4$. The required time to go from R to Q = (6-x)/5. Total time T = $\sqrt{x^2+9}/4$ +(6-x)/5.

dT/dx = $\frac{x}{4}(x^2+9)^{-\frac{1}{2}}-\frac{1}{5}$. To find

minimal T, set dT/dx =0. Solving, x=4. (Ans. C)

46. The total sum of all 40 marks = (72.5)(40) = 2900. By adding the 4 new numbers, the new total = 3201. Then 3201÷44 = 72.75. (Ans. D)

47. The arithmetic mean is denoted by the sum of the numbers divided by the number of numbers. (Ans. B)

48. A hypsometer measures the elevation above sea level of an object. (Ans. D)

49. Eratosthenes is also known for a method of determining all the primes within a specific set of natural numbers. (Ans. B)

50. The Galois Theory of Groups proved that 3 problems are unsolvable, using only a straight-edge and compass:
   1. Squaring of the circle
   2. Trisecting an angle
   3. Doubling a cube
(Ans. C)

EXAMINATION SECTION

DIRECTIONS: Each question or incomplete statement is followed by several suggested answers or completions. Select the one that BEST answers the question or completes the statement. *PRINT THE LETTER OF THE CORRECT ANSWER IN THE SPACE AT THE RIGHT.*

1. A refrigerator was originally marked to sell at a profit of $66\frac{2}{3}\%$ of the cost. It was finally sold at a profit of $33\frac{1}{3}\%$ of the cost. What percent discount did the purchaser receive on the marked price?
   A. 15   B. 20   C. 25   D. $33\frac{1}{3}$

   1.___

2. A store offers a discount of 30%. An additional discount, in percent, to make the combined discount equivalent to a single discount of 37% would be
   A. 7   B. 10   C. 23   D. 67

   2.___

3. Given log 2 = 0.3010, log 3 = 0.4771, and log 7 = 0.8451. Using these values, find $\log 46\frac{2}{3}$,

   A. .6690   B. 1.6690   C. 1.6232   D. .6232

   3.___

4. A coin which may fall either heads or tails is tossed 4 times. The probability of getting at least one head is
   A. $\frac{3}{4}$ B. $\frac{13}{16}$ C. $\frac{7}{8}$ D. $\frac{15}{16}$

   4.___

5. $x^2-6x+8>0$ is true for all values of x where
   A. 2<x<4   B. x<2 or x>4
   C. x<4   D. x>2

   5.___

6. The graph of $|x|+|y|= 8$ consists of
   A. one straight line
   B. a pair of straight lines
   C. the sides of a square
   D. a circle

   6.___

7. The expansion of the determinant:
$$\begin{vmatrix} x+a & x+2a & x+3a \\ x+2a & x+3a & x+4a \\ x+3a & x+4a & x+5a \end{vmatrix}$$
   is, when simplified,
   A. equal to 0
   B. a third degree expression in x
   C. a linear expression in x
   D. an expression that contains a, but does not contain x

   7.___

8. The fraction, $\dfrac{6}{x^2-x}$, is equal to the sum of two other fractions whose denominators are x and x-1, respectively, and whose numerators are integers. Of the following, which one is one of the two fractions?

    A. $\dfrac{-6}{x-1}$ B. $\dfrac{-3}{x-1}$ C. $\dfrac{6}{x-1}$ D. $\dfrac{3}{x-1}$

8.___

9. A certain number is represented by $1 + \dfrac{1}{x^2}$, with x a real number. If the sum of this number and its reciprocal is $2\frac{1}{6}$, then x MUST be either

    A. $\sqrt{-3}$ or $-\sqrt{-3}$ B. $\sqrt{3}$ or $-\sqrt{3}$
    C. 2 or -2   D. $\sqrt{2}$ or $-\sqrt{2}$

9.___

10. The solution of the inequality, $4^{2-2x} < 8^{x^2}$ is

    A. $x<-2$ B. $x>\dfrac{2}{3}$
    C. $x>\dfrac{2}{3}$ or $x<-2$ D. $x>\dfrac{2}{3}$ and $x<-2$

10.___

11. If the annual percent increase in population of a given community is known to have been constant, and if the population in 1950 was a, and in 1960 was b, then the expression below that represents the population for 1955 was

    A. $\dfrac{a+b}{2}$ B. $\sqrt{ab}$ C. $\dfrac{2ab}{a+b}$ D. $\dfrac{ab}{a+b}$

11.___

12. The set of values satisfying the inequality, $\left|\dfrac{10-x}{3}\right|<2$, is

    A. $4<x<16$ B. $4>x>-16$
    C. $-4>x>-16$ D. $x<16$

12.___

13. A circle is inscribed in a triangle whose sides are 8.1", 11.3", and 15.8". The lengths of the two segments of the longest side into which it is divided by the point of tangency are represented by r and s, where r is less than s. Which one of the following statements is TRUE?

    A. r:s = 8.1:11.3   B. r = 6.3
    C. r = 7.9   D. none of these

13.___

14. If two unequal circles are tangent externally at point C, and the common external tangent, AB, touches one circle at A and the other at B, then $\angle ACB$

    A. equals $45°$
    B. equals $90°$
    C. equals $160°$
    D. varies with the relative size of the tangents

14.___

15. Consider all triangles ABC lying in a given plane and having base AB, C lying on one side of AB, and $\angle ACB = 40°$. The locus of the intersection of the perpendicular bisectors of AC and BC is

15.___

A. the perpendicular bisector of AB
B. a circle whose diameter is AB
C. a point
D. a straight line parallel to AB

16. AB, AC, and PQR are tangent to a given circle at points 16.___
B, C, and Q, respectively; PQR intersects segment AB in P,
and segment AC in R. If AB = 20, the perimeter of
triangle APR
A. is 36
B. is 40
C. is 44
D. cannot be determined from the given information

17. If a square, a circle, a rhombus having one of its 17.___
diagonals equal to twice the other and a rectangle having
one of its sides equal to four times the other, all have
equal areas, which one has the GREATEST perimeter?
A. The square   B. The circle
C. The rhombus   D. The rectangle

18. If the perimeter of an isosceles triangle is 36 inches and 18.___
the altitude to the base is 6 inches, the length of the
altitude to one of the legs

A. is $4\frac{4}{5}$ inches

B. is 6 inches

C. is $9\frac{3}{5}$ inches

D. cannot be found on the basis of these data

19. In triangle ABC: C = 90^0, BC = 3, AC = 4; point D lies 19.___
on $\overline{AB}$. Angle DCB = 30^0; the length of CD is
A. $\frac{5}{4-\sqrt{3}}$ B. $\frac{24}{3+4\sqrt{3}}$ C. $\frac{24}{4+3\sqrt{3}}$ D. $\frac{3\sqrt{3}}{2}$

20. Which one of the following angles CANNOT be constructed 20.___
with a straight edge and a pair of compasses in a finite
number of steps?
A. 3^0 B. 5^0 C. 9^0 D. 15^0

21. A sheet of paper in the form of a sector of a circle with 21.___
a radius of 12 inches and with a central angle of $5\pi/6$
radians is reshaped into the form of a cone by making its
two straight edges coincide. The volume of this cone,
expressed in cubic inches, is
A. 100π B. $48\pi\sqrt{119}$ C. $\frac{25}{3}\sqrt{119}$ D. none of these

22. The area of a spherical triangle is 10 square feet. If 22.___
the sides of its polar triangle each contain 70 degrees,
then the radius of the sphere, expressed in feet, is
A. $\frac{2\sqrt{3\pi}}{\pi}$ B. $\frac{\sqrt{30}}{\pi}$ C. $\frac{\sqrt{60}}{\pi}$ D. none of these

23. If the radius of a sphere is doubled, the percent increase   23.___
    in volume is
       A. 200   B. 400   C. 700   D. 800

24. If $\tan x = \dfrac{\sin 5^0 + \sin 47^0}{\cos 5^0 - \cos 47^0}$ and x lies between 0^0 and 360^0,   24.___
    then x equals
       A. 21^0 or 201^0 B. 52^0 or 232^0
       C. 69^0 or 111^0 D. 69^0 or 249^0

25. A small plane is headed due north at an air speed of 100   25.___
    miles per hour, but because of the wind, actually travels
    in a direction N 60^0E at a speed of 120 miles per hour.
    What is the speed of the wind in miles per hour?
       A. $15\sqrt{60}$ B. $20\sqrt{11}$ C. $20\sqrt{30}$ D. $20\sqrt{31}$

26. One side of a triangle is equal to 6 inches and the angle   26.___
    opposite this side is 30^0. The radius of the circle
    circumscribing this triangle
       A. cannot be determined from the above data
       B. equals $2\sqrt{3}$ inches
       C. equals 4 inches
       D. equals 6 inches

27. The navigator of a ship observes a light bearing 344^0 and   27.___
    5 miles distant. After a straight run of $12\frac{1}{2}$ minutes at a
    speed of 24 m.p.h., he finds that the light bears 50^0. The
    course of the ship on this run
       A. was 64^0
       B. was 66^0
       C. was 296^0
       D. cannot be found on the basis of these data

28. If A is any angle such that $0^0 < A < 90^0$, then which one of   28.___
    the following statements is true of the four expressions
    labeled a, b, c, and d?
       a. $\tan \frac{1}{2}A$ b. $\dfrac{1-\cos A}{\sin A}$ c. $\dfrac{\sin A}{1+\cos A}$ d. $\dfrac{1+\cos A}{\sin A}$

       A. All have different values.
       B. Two and only two have the same value.
       C. Three and only three have the same value.
       D. All four have the same value.

29. There are four test scores of which three are known to be   29.___
    83, 82, and 72. If, using an assumed arithmetic mean of
    80, the mean deviation of the four scores from the assumed
    mean is -2.25, the fourth score is
       A. the smallest of the four
       B. 74
       C. 76
       D. 79

30. The mean of a set of n numbers is equal to m, and the   30.___
    standard deviation is s. If each number of the set is
    tripled, and then increased by 5, the mean and the standard
    deviation of the new set of numbers are, respectively,

A. m+5, 3s   B. 3m, 9s
C. 3m+5, 3s   D. 3m+5, 3s+5

31. If the circle, $(x-1)^2+(y-3)^2=r^2$, is tangent to the line,   31.____
    5x+12y=60, the value of r is
    A. $\sqrt{10}$ B. $\dfrac{13}{12}$ C. $\dfrac{19}{13}$ D. $\dfrac{60}{13}$

32. In a coordinate system in which the Y axis is inclined   32.____
    60° to the X axis (measured counter-clockwise from the
    positive X axis), the points P(-3,7) and Q(6,-5) are
    given. The distance $\overline{PQ}$ equals
    A. $\sqrt{117}$ B. $\sqrt{189}$ C. 15   D. $\sqrt{333}$

33. The graph of the equation, $r^2 = \dfrac{9}{2-\sin^2\theta}$, is which one of   33.____
    the following?
    A. A circle   B. An hyperbola
    C. An ellipse   D. A parabola

34. If two points, A(1,0) and B(4,0), are plotted on a graph   34.____
    chart, and a point P(x,y) moves in such a way that $\overline{AP}=2(\overline{BP})$,
    the locus of point P is a(n)
    A. straight line   B. circle
    C. parabola   D. hyperbola

35. The intersection of a surface (whose equation is $x^2+y^2-z^2$ 35.____
    =0) and a plane parallel to the z axis is
    A. two intersecting straight lines
    B. a circle
    C. a parabola
    D. an hyperbola

36. The curve whose equation is $y=3x^3-13x^2+19x-5$ has   36.____
    A. two turning points and one inflection point
    B. no turning point and two inflection points
    C. no turning point and one inflection point
    D. no turning point and no inflection point

37. The transcendental number, e, equals   37.____

    A. $\lim_{x\to o} (1+x)^x$ B. $\lim_{x\to o} (\frac{x+1}{x})^{\frac{1}{x}}$

    C. $\lim_{x\to\infty} (1+\frac{1}{x})^x$ D. $\lim_{x\to\infty} (\frac{x+1}{x})^{\frac{1}{x}}$

38. At a price of x dollars each, the manufacturer of an   38.____
    article can sell each month y articles, where y =180-5x.
    If the cost of these articles to the manufacturer was
    600+4y dollars, he would obtain the MAXIMUM profit when
    x is equal to
    A. 15   B. 20   C. 25   D. 30

39. The figure bounded by the curve $y=\sqrt{x}$ and the three lines   39.____
    x=1, x=3, and y=0 is rotated 360^0 about the x axis. The
    volume of the solid thus formed is
    A. 4π B. 8π C. 4   D. 8

40. The volume of a spherical balloon is increasing at the rate of 20 cubic feet per minute. At what rate (in feet per minute) is the radius increasing when the radius is 5 feet?

   A. $\dfrac{1}{5\pi}$ B. $\dfrac{1}{\pi}$ C. π D. 5

40. ___

41. The shape taken by a freely suspended rope held at its ends is a curve called a(n)
   A. parabola   B. hyperbola
   C. cycloid   D. catenary

41. ___

42. When placed at one end of a class 1 lever, a certain object will balance a 4 lb. weight at the other end. However, when the object is placed at the other end of the lever (the fulcrum remaining in the same position), it will balance a weight of 25 lbs. The weight of the object
   A. is 10 lbs.
   B. is 14½ lbs.
   C. is 29 lbs.
   D. cannot be found on the basis of these data

42. ___

43. In the number system with base 5, the value of the repeating decimal, .232323...., expressed as a common fraction is

   A. $\dfrac{44}{344}$ B. $\dfrac{13}{24}$ C. $\dfrac{23}{44}$ D. none of these

43. ___

44. The number 122, base 4, is added to the number 212, base 3. Their sum, when expressed in the base 5, is written
   A. 2,314   B. 334   C. 144   D. 49

44. ___

45. If 13^{62} is multiplied out, the units digit in the final product is
   A. 1   B. 3   C. 7   D. 9

45. ___

46. Given the following three statements:
   a. All A's are B's.
   b. Some C's are B's.
   c. Some D's are not B's.
   Which one of the following conclusions MUST be true?
   A. Some D's are C's.   B. No D's are A's.
   C. Some D's are not A's.   D. Some C's are A's.

46. ___

47. The symbol [x] means the greatest integer less than or equal to x. Consider the two limits:
   a. limit [x] as x→2
   b. limit [x] as x→2.5
   Which of the following statements is TRUE?
   A. Both limits exist.
   B. Limit (a) exists and limit (b) does not exist.
   C. Limit (a) does not exist and limit (b) does exist.
   D. Neither limit exists.

47. ___

48. Each of the following is based mainly on the properties   48.____
of one type of conic sections:
   a. auto headlight
   b. whispering gallery
   c. sound range finding
The conic sections involved are, respectively,
   A. a. parabola, b. ellipse, c. hyperbola
   B. a. parabola, b. hyperbola, c. ellipse
   C. a. ellipse, b. parabola, c. hyperbola
   D. a. parabola, b. ellipse, c. circle

49. The mathematicians MOST closely associated with   49.____
   a. the theory of groups, and
   b. the construction of regular polygons
are, respectively,
   A. Godel and Euler   B. Cantor and Gauss
   C. Galois and Gauss   D. Galois and Newton

50. Which one of the following men is LEAST associated with   50.____
the development of Hyperbolic Geometry?
   A. Gauss   B. Lobachevski
   C. Bolyai   D. Hilbert

KEY (CORRECT ANSWERS)

1. B	11. B	21. C	31. C	41. D
2. B	12. A	22. A	32. C	42. A
3. B	13. B	23. D	33. A	43. B
4. D	14. B	24. D	34. B	44. C
5. B	15. C	25. D	35. D	45. D
6. C	16. B	26. D	36. C	46. C
7. A	17. D	27. C	37. C	47. A
8. C	18. C	28. B	38. B	48. D
9. D	19. B	29. B	39. A	49. C
10. C	20. B	30. C	40. A	50. D

SOLUTIONS TO PROBLEMS

1. Let C = cost. Then $1\frac{2}{3}$C = original marked price. The item was finally sold at $1\frac{1}{3}$C. The percent discount on the marked price is $[(1\frac{2}{3} - 1\frac{1}{3})/1\frac{2}{3}][100]$ = 20%. (Ans. B)

2. Let P = original price. After one discount of 30%, the price is .70P. If the second discount is x%, then the new price is $(\frac{100-x}{100})(.70P)$. Since the combined discount is equivalent to one 37% discount, $(\frac{100-x}{100})(.70P)$ = .63P. Solving, x=10. (Ans. B)

3. $\text{Log } 46\frac{2}{3}$ = $\text{Log } \frac{140}{3}$ = Log 140 - Log 3 = (Log 10 + Log 7 + Log 2) - Log 3 = 1.6690. (Ans. B)

4. Probability (at least one head) = 1 - Probability (no heads) = $1 - (\frac{1}{2})^4 = \frac{15}{16}$. (Ans. D)

5. Factor into (x-4)(x-2)>0.
   Case 1: Both factors are >0, so that x>4.
   Case 2: Both factors are <0, so that x<2.
   Final answer is x<2 or x>4. (Ans. B)

6.

   The vertices are: A:(0,8), B:(8,0), C:(0,-8), and D:(-8,0).
   The graph is actually a combination of 4 segments: x+y=8, y-x=8, x+y=-8, y-x=-8. This represents a square. (Ans. C)

7. This determinant can be reduced to $\begin{vmatrix} 1 & 2 & 3 \\ 2 & 3 & 4 \\ 3 & 4 & 5 \end{vmatrix}$

   The value becomes (1)(3)(5) + (2)(4)(3) + (3)(4)(2) - (3)(3)(3) - (2)(2)(5) - (1)(4)(4) = 0.
   (Ans. A)

8. Writing $\frac{6}{x^2-x} = \frac{-6}{x} + \frac{6}{x-1}$, one of the fractions is $\frac{6}{x-1}$. (Ans. C)

9. The reciprocal of $1 + \dfrac{1}{x^2}$ is $\dfrac{x^2}{x^2+1}$. The sum of these two expressions is $\dfrac{x^4+3x^2+1}{x^2(x^2+1)}$ which is to equal $2\frac{1}{6}$ or $\frac{13}{6}$. This is equivalent to $6x^4+12x^2+6 + 6x^4 = 13x^4+13x^2$. Solving, $x = \pm\sqrt{2}$ and $\pm 3i$. Thus, only choice D is correct, since $\pm 3i$ are imaginary numbers. (Ans. D)

10. $4^{2-2x}<8^{x^2}$ can be rewritten as $2^{4-4x}< 2^{3x^2}$, which becomes $4-4x<3x^2$. Now, $(3x-2)(x+2)>0$, which leads to $x>\frac{2}{3}$ or $x<-2$. (Ans. C)

11. Let K = annual percent increase. Then $a(1 + \dfrac{k}{100})^{10}= b$. Thus, $K = \sqrt[10]{b/a} - 1$. Now, in 1955, the population can be denoted as $a(1+\sqrt[10]{b/a} - 1)^5 = a\cdot\sqrt{b/a} = \sqrt{ab}$. (Ans. B)

12. $\left|\dfrac{10-x}{3}\right| <2$ means $-2 <\dfrac{10-x}{3} < 2$, which is satisfied by $4<x<16$. (Ans. A)

13.

Let BC = 15.8, BE = r, CE = s, and r<s. Now, FC = s, so that AF = 11.3-s = AD. Since AB = 8.1, DB = 8.1 – (11.3-s) = s-3.2. Thus, since BD = BE, s-3.2 = r. However, BE can also be represented by 15.8-s. Then, s = 9.5 and r = 6.3. (Ans. B)

14.

Let D,E be centers of the 2 circles, respectively. Then, C must lie on $\overline{DE}$. Also, $\angle DAB = \angle EBA = 90^0$. $\angle DAC = \angle DCA$ and $\angle EBC = \angle ECB$. Let $\angle DAC = x$; then $\angle CAB = 90-x$. Let $\angle EBC = y$; then $\angle CBA = 90-y$. Now, $\angle ACB = 180-(90-x)-(90-y) = x+y = \angle DCA + \angle ECB$. This implies that $\angle ACB$ must be 90^0 since $\angle ACD + \angle ACB + \angle ECB = 180^0$. (Ans. B)

15. By inspection. (Ans. C)

16.

Perimeter of inscribed $\triangle APR$ would = the lengths of the tangents AB=20 (and so AC=20) = 40. (Ans. B)

17. Let K^2 = area of the square, then each side = K and perimeter = 4K
If K^2 = area of rhombus in which d_1 $2d_1$ are the diagonals, then
$(\frac{1}{2})(d_1)(2d_1) = K^2$. So, d_1=K. To determine one side x, since
the diagonal meet at right angles, $(\frac{1}{2}diagonal\ 1)^2 + (\frac{1}{2}diagonal\ 2)^2$
$=x^2$. Thus, $(\frac{K}{2})^2 + K^2 = x^2$ and $x = \frac{K}{2}\sqrt{5}$. Thus, the perimeter of the
rhombus is $2K\sqrt{5}$.
If K^2 = area of circle = πR^2, $R = K/\sqrt{\pi}$. Circumference = $2\pi(K/\sqrt{\pi})$
$= 2\sqrt{\pi}K$.
If K^2 = area of rectangle = (w)(4w), $w = \frac{K}{2}$ and 4w = 2K

Perimeter = $2(\frac{K}{2}) + 2(2K) = 5K$.

Of the four quantities, 4K, $2K\sqrt{5}$, $2K\sqrt{\pi}$, and 5K, the amount 5K,
which is the perimeter of the rectangle, is greatest. (Ans. D)

18.

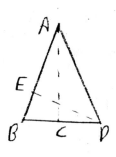

Let AB = AD = x. Then, BD =36-2x
and since BC = CD = 18-x. BC^2+AC^2
$=AB^2$. Thus, $(18-x)^2+6^2=x^2$. Solving
x=10. Then, BC=8, BD=16. Area of
triangle = $(\frac{1}{2})(16)(6) = 48$. Also,
48 = $(\frac{1}{2})(AB)(ED)$. Since AB=10,

ED = $9\frac{3}{5}$. (Ans. C)

19.

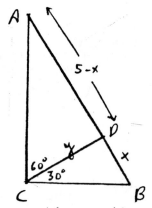

$\angle ACB = 90°$, $AB^2=3^2+4^2$, so AB=5
$\tan\angle B = \frac{4}{3}$, thus $\angle B = 53°$. Now,
$\angle A=37°$. Using Law of Sines, $\frac{\sin 53°}{y}$
$\frac{\sin 30°}{x}$ and $\frac{\sin 47°}{y} = \frac{\sin 60°}{5-x}$.
Solving these 2 equations, CD = y =

$\frac{24}{3+4\sqrt{3}}$. (Ans. B)

20. By inspection. (Ans. B)

21.

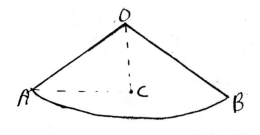

The length of $\overset{\frown}{AB}$ = $(\frac{150}{360})(24\pi) = 10\pi$

inches. This would become the
circumference of the base of the con
The radius would = 5.
Height = OC = $\sqrt{12^2-5^2}$ $=\sqrt{119}$

Volume = $\frac{1}{3}\pi(5)^2 \cdot \sqrt{119} = \frac{25\pi}{3}\sqrt{119}$

(Ans. C)

22. By inspection. (Ans. A)

23. Volume = $\frac{4}{3}\pi R^3$. If 2R replaces R, new volume = $\frac{32}{3}\pi^2 R^3$. $2^3=8$.

The percent increase is 800%. (Ans. D)

24. By substitution, the value of the right side = 2.60487.
    arctan 2.60487 = 69^0 or 249^0. (Ans. D)

25.

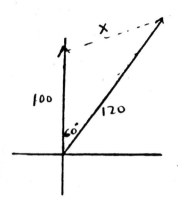

100 and 120 represent the miles
covered in 1 hour. Let x = unknown
distance. Then, x^2=100^2+120^2
-2(100)(120)cos 60^0. Solving,
x = $\sqrt{12400}$ = 20$\sqrt{31}$. (Ans. D)

26.

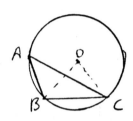

∠A=30^0, BC=6. $\overset{\frown}{BC}$ must =60^0 and
thus ∠BOC=60^0 (0= center of circle).
∠OBC = ∠OCB = 60^0 also. Thus,
OB=6, and △BOC is equilateral.
(Ans. D)

27.

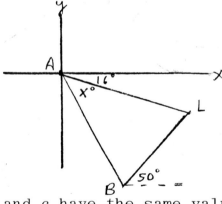

At a speed of 24 m.p.h., the distance
covered in 12.5 minutes is 5 miles.
So, AL = AB = 5. ∠L = 16+50 = 66^0.
To determine x, ∠B must also be 66^0.
Then, x = 180-2(66) = 48^0. The
course of the ship = 360-(48+16)=296^0.
(Ans. C)

28. b and c have the same value. This can be verified by noting that
    (1-cosA)/sinA = sinA/(1+cosA) implies sin^{2}A = 1-cos^{2}A, which
    must be true. b and d would only be equal if A=0 (not allowed).
    Finally, tan½A = $\sqrt{\dfrac{1-\cos A}{1+\cos A}}$ and this value is distinct from the
    other three.
    (Ans. B)

29. The mean deviation is the average of the ABSOLUTE values (positive)
    of the differences between the raw scores and the mean.
    Assumed mean = 80. Mean deviation = -2.25 = 77.75.
     Four scores 83, 82, 72 and x must average 77.75. Fourth score
    is 74. (Ans. B)

30. Each operation on the original numbers will affect the mean of
    those numbers in the same way. However, the standard deviation
    is NOT affected by adding a constant to each number. (Ans. C)

31.

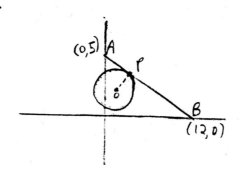

The slope of the line connecting (12,0) and (0,5) is -5/12. If P = point of tangency, the $\overline{OP} \perp \overline{AB}$ and so 12/5 = slope of $\overline{OP}$. O is located at (1,3) and the equation of $\overline{OP}$ is $y = \frac{12}{5}x + \frac{3}{5}$. P will be

thus located at the intersection of $\overline{OP}$ and $\overline{AB}$, which is $(\frac{264}{169}, \frac{735}{169})$.

Note: P NOT DRAWN TO SCALE. Now,

$$OP = \sqrt{(1-\frac{264}{169})^2 + (3-\frac{735}{169})^2} = \frac{247}{169} = \frac{19}{13}.$$

(Ans. C)

32.

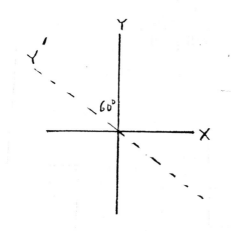

Although the y-axis has been rotated, the distance between 2 given points is unchanged.
Distance = $\sqrt{(6+3)^2+(7+5)^2}$ = 15.
(Ans. C)

33. Using $r^2=x^2+y^2$ and $\frac{y^2}{x^2+y^2} = \sin^2\theta$, the given equation can be changed to: $x^2/\frac{2}{9} + y^2/9 = 1$, and this is a circle with radius 1.
(Ans. A)

34.

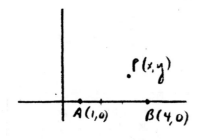

$AP = \sqrt{(x-1)^2+y^2}$, $BP = \sqrt{(x-4)^2+y^2}$

Now, $\sqrt{(x-1)^2+y^2} = 2\sqrt{(x-4)^2+y^2}$

Rewriting, $4 = (x-5)^2+y^2$, which is a circle with center at (5,0) and radius = 2. (Ans. B)

35. The surface $x^2+y^2-z^2 = 0$ is a cone. A plane which intersects this surface at right angles to the base forms an hyperbola.
(Ans. D)

36. 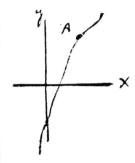 $y = 3x^3-13x^2+19x-5$ has no turning point. The one inflection point is located between $(1,4)$ and $(2,5)$. This will occur where the second derivative changes sign. (Ans. C)

37. $e = \lim_{x\to\infty} (1+\frac{1}{x})^x$. Also, $e = 1 + \frac{1}{1!} + \frac{1}{2!} + \frac{1}{3!} + \dots$ (Ans. C)

38. The sales from all y articles = xy dollars. The cost for all y articles = 600+4y. Profit = xy - (600+4y). Since y = 180-5x, substitution yields: Profit = P = $-5x^2+200x-1320$. To maximize P, set dP/dx = 0. Thus, $-10x+200 = 0$ and x=20. Incidentally, the profit will be $680. (Ans. B)

39. Volume $= \int_1^3 \pi(\sqrt{x})^2 dx = \pi[\frac{x^2}{2}]_1^3 = 4\pi$. (Ans. A)

40. $V = \frac{4}{3}\pi R^3$. $dV/dt = dV/dR \cdot dR/dt$.

$20 = 4\pi R^2 \cdot dR/dt$. When R=5, $20 = 100\pi \cdot dR/dt$. $dR/dt = \frac{1}{5\pi}$. (Ans. A)

41. A catenary is the mathematical curve formed when a freely suspended rope or chain is held by its ends. The equation is $y = K\cos h \frac{x}{K}$ (cos h = hyperbolic cosine). (Ans. D)

42.

x ———————— 4

25 ———————— x

$\frac{x}{4} = \frac{25}{x}$. Thus, $x^2=100$ and x=10. (Ans. A)

43. $.232323\dots$ base 5 $= (\frac{2}{5} + \frac{3}{25} + \frac{2}{125} + \frac{3}{625} + \frac{2}{3125} + \frac{3}{15625} \dots)$ base 10 = $.541632\dots$ which approaches $\frac{13}{24}$. (Ans. B)

44. 122 base 4 $= 26$ base 10. 212 base 3 $= 23$ base 10. Sum = 49 base 10 which is 144 base 5. (Ans. C)

45. $13^1 =13$, $13^2=169$, $13^3=2197$, $13^4=28561$, $13^5=371293$, etc. The last digit is of a cyclic nature and has the pattern 3, 9, 7, 1, 3, 9, 7, 1, etc. for consecutive powers of 13. Now, 13^{62} would end in the same digit as 13^2 which is 9. (Ans. D)

46. Since some D's are not B's and yet all A's must be B's, it follows that some D's are not A's. (Ans. C)

47. Both limits exist and are equal to 2. (Ans. A)

48. Auto headlight's reflection = parabola, whispering gallery = ellipse, sound range finding distance = a constant from a point = circle. (Ans. D)

49. Galois is associated with groups, Gauss with regular polygons. (Ans. C)

50. Hilbert's axioms dealt mainly with Euclidean Geometry. (Ans. D)

EXAMINATION SECTION

DIRECTIONS: Each question or incomplete statement is followed by several suggested answers or completions. Select the one that BEST answers the question or completes the statement. *PRINT THE LETTER OF THE CORRECT ANSWER IN THE SPACE AT THE RIGHT.*

1. To win an election, a candidate needs 3/4 of the votes cast. If after 2/3 of the votes have been counted, a candidate has 5/6 of what he needs, what part of the remaining votes does he still need?

    A. $\dfrac{1}{8}$ B. $\dfrac{1}{4}$ C. $\dfrac{3}{8}$ D. $\dfrac{1}{2}$ 1.____

2. A sells an article for D dollars, less 20% and 10%. B sells the same article for D dollars less 25%. What additional discount should B allow in order to match A's selling price?

    A. 1.8%   B. 2%   C. 4%   D. 5%   2.____

3. A radioactive isotope loses 1/3 of its strength during the first minute of its existence, 1/3 of its remaining strength during the second minute, 1/3 of its remaining strength during the third minute, etc. How long to the nearest minute will it be before the isotope will have lost 87% of its original activity?

    A. 2 minutes   B. 3 minutes   3.____
    C. 4 minutes   D. 5 minutes

4. The sum of the reciprocals of the roots of the equation $X^2+px+q=0$ is

    A. $\dfrac{-p}{q}$ B. $\dfrac{q}{p}$ C. $\dfrac{p}{q}$ D. $\dfrac{-q}{p}$ 4.____

5. If $n \neq 0$, the expression $\sqrt[n]{\dfrac{20}{4^{n+2} + 2^{2n+2}}}$ is equal to

    A. $\frac{1}{4}$ B. $\frac{1}{2}\sqrt[n]{10}$ C. $\frac{1}{4}\sqrt[n]{5}$ D. $\dfrac{4}{n}$ 5.____

6. If log 2 =.301, log 3 =.477, and log 7 =.845, then log 14.4 =

    A. 1.158   B. 1.447   C. 2.158   D. 2.447   6.____

7. If $\dfrac{A}{x^2-1} + \dfrac{B}{x^2+2} = \dfrac{2x^2+3}{(x^2-1)(x^2+2)}$, the value of (A+B) is

    A. -2   B. $\dfrac{2}{3}$ C. $\dfrac{4}{3}$ D. 2   7.____

8. The product of
$(1-\frac{1}{6})(1-\frac{1}{7})(1-\frac{1}{8})\ldots(1-\frac{1}{n+4})(1-\frac{1}{n+5})$ is

    A. $\dfrac{3}{(n+4)(n+5)}$ B. $\dfrac{5}{(n+4)}$

    C. $\dfrac{5}{(n+5)}$ D. ∞

8. ___

9. The 8th term of $(\frac{2a}{3} - \frac{3}{2a})^{12}$ is

    A. $\dfrac{1782}{a^2}$ B. $-1782a^2$ C. $\dfrac{-1782}{a^2}$ D. $1782a^2$

9. ___

10. If $f(x) = \dfrac{x}{x-1}$, then $f(x+1) =$

    A. $\dfrac{1}{f(x)}$ B. $\dfrac{1}{f(x)}+2$ C. $\dfrac{1}{f(x)} + \dfrac{2}{x}$ D. $f(x)+2$

10. ___

11. How many even numbers greater than 40,000 may be formed using the digits, 3,4,5,6, and 9, if each digit must be used exactly once in each number?
    A. 36   B. 48   C. 64   D. 96

11. ___

12. A circle passes through one vertex of an equilateral triangle and is tangent to the opposite side at its mid-point. The ratio of the segments into which the circle divides one of the other sides to which the circle is NOT tangent is
    A. 1:1   B. 2:1   C. 3:1   D. 4:1

12. ___

13. A 25 foot ladder is placed against a vertical wall so that the foot of the ladder is 7 feet from the bottom of the wall. If the top of the ladder slips 4 feet, then how many feet will the foot of the ladder slide?
    A. 4   B. 5   C. 8   D. 9

13. ___

14. A regular octagon is formed by cutting off each corner of a square whose side is 6. The length of one side of the octagon is
    A. 2   B. $2\sqrt{2}$ C. $2\sqrt{2}-2$ D. $6\sqrt{2}-6$

14. ___

15. If the centers of two intersecting circles are 10 inches apart and if the radii of the circles are 6 inches and 10 inches, respectively, then the length of their common chord, in inches, is
    A. $2\sqrt{21}$ B. $6\sqrt{3}$ C. $\frac{6}{5}\sqrt{91}$ D. $2\sqrt{51}$

15. ___

16. Two circles of radii R and r, (R>r), are tangent externally. The length of their common external tangent is
    A. $R + r$ B. $2\sqrt{Rr}$
    C. $\sqrt{2(R^2+r^2)}$ D. $\sqrt{2(R^2-r^2)}$

16. ___

17. ABCD is a rectangle with AB=16 and BC=12. A rhombus is   17.___
    formed by drawing parallel lines inside the rectangle
    from vertices A and C, meeting CD in E and AB in F. The
    length of diagonal EF is
        A. 7.5   B. 11.5   C. 12.5   D. 15

18. In triangle ABC, DE is parallel to BC and FE is parallel   18.___
    to DC. If AF=4, and FD=6, then DB is

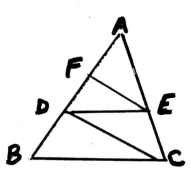

        A. $7\frac{1}{2}$ B. 10   C. 12   D. 15

19. In triangle ABC, CB>AC. Point D is located on CB such   19.___
    that CA = CD, $\angle$CAB = $\angle$ABC equals 30^0. Then, angle BAD is
        A. 15^0 B. 20^0 C. $22\frac{1}{2}^0$ D. 30^0

20. The solution set for $x^2-x-2>0$ may be represented by which   20.___
    one of the following?
        A. $\{x|x>-1\}\cup\{x|x<2\}$
        B. $\{x|x>-1\}\cap\{x|x<2\}$
        C. $\{x|x<-1\}\cup\{x|x>2\}$
        D. $\{x|x<-1\}\cap\{x|x>2\}$

21. The figure below is the graph of which one of the   21.___
    following sentences?

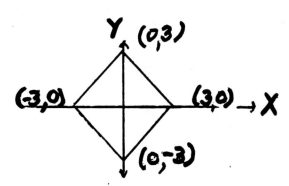

        A. $x^2+y^2= 9$ B. $|x| = 3$ and $|y| = 3$
        C. $|x+y| = 3$ D. $|x| + |y| = 3$

22. If the operation "*" is defined as follows: a*b = 2a+3b,   22.___
    and all other numerical operational rules hold as always,
    then the value of 1 * (3*2) is equal to
        A. 13   B. 22   C. 28   D. 38

4

23. If f = {(1,3), (2,5), (3,5)}, which one of the following
    statements is FALSE?   23. ___
    A. The domain of f is {1,2,3}.
    B. f(f[1]) = 5
    C. f is a function.
    D. The inverse of f is a function.

24. The integers, modulo 7, form a group under "multiplication"   24. ___
    $\otimes$.
    The inverse of 4 $\otimes$ 6 is
    A. 1   B. 3   C. 5   D. 6

25. If X and Y are subsets of the set I, and X^1 and Y^1 are   25. ___
    the complements of X and Y, respectively, with respect
    to I, then the complement of $X \cap Y$ is
    A. $X^1 \cap Y$ B. $X \cup Y^1$
    C. $X^1 \cap Y^1$ D. $X^1 \cup Y^1$

26. An Abelian group is a group whose elements satisfy   26. ___
    A. the commutative law but not the associative law
    B. the associative law but not the commutative law
    C. both the commutative and the associative laws
    D. neither the commutative nor the associative laws

27. The shaded portion below is   27. ___

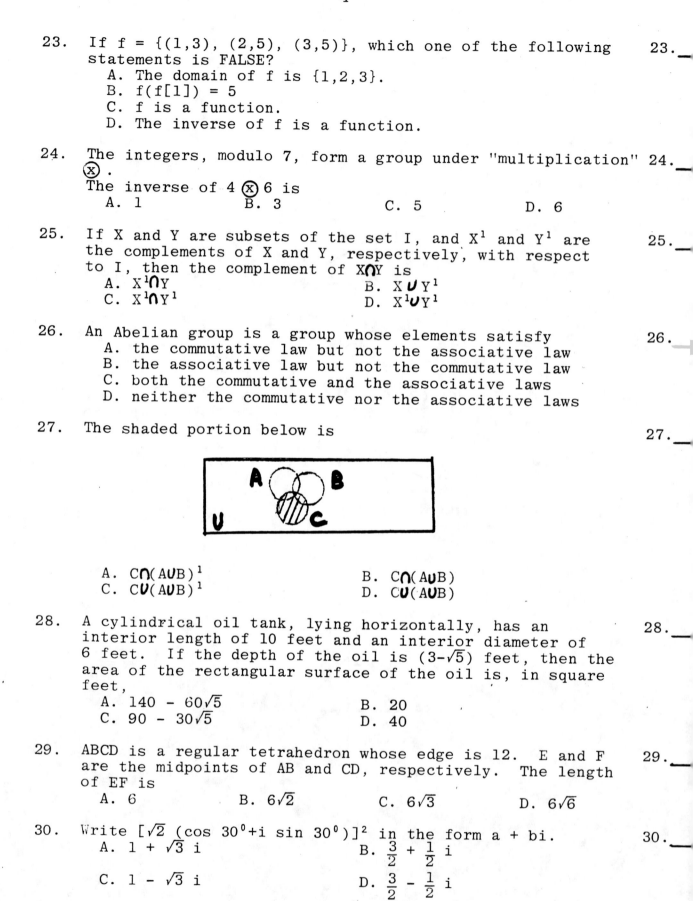

    A. $C \cap (A \cup B)^1$ B. $C \cap (A \cup B)$
    C. $C \cup (A \cup B)^1$ D. $C \cup (A \cup B)$

28. A cylindrical oil tank, lying horizontally, has an   28. ___
    interior length of 10 feet and an interior diameter of
    6 feet. If the depth of the oil is $(3-\sqrt{5})$ feet, then the
    area of the rectangular surface of the oil is, in square
    feet,
    A. $140 - 60\sqrt{5}$ B. 20
    C. $90 - 30\sqrt{5}$ D. 40

29. ABCD is a regular tetrahedron whose edge is 12. E and F   29. ___
    are the midpoints of AB and CD, respectively. The length
    of EF is
    A. 6   B. $6\sqrt{2}$ C. $6\sqrt{3}$ D. $6\sqrt{6}$

30. Write $[\sqrt{2}(\cos 30° + i \sin 30°)]^2$ in the form a + bi.   30. ___
    A. $1 + \sqrt{3}\,i$ B. $\frac{3}{2} + \frac{1}{2}\,i$

    C. $1 - \sqrt{3}\,i$ D. $\frac{3}{2} - \frac{1}{2}\,i$

31. From two ships due east of a lighthouse and in line with   31.___
    its foot, the angles of elevation of the top of the light-
    house are x and y, with x greater than y. The distance
    between the ships is m. The distance from the lighthouse
    to the nearer ship is given by

    A. $\dfrac{m \sin x \cos y}{\sin (x-y)}$ B. $\dfrac{m \sin y}{\sin (x-y)}$

    C. $\dfrac{\cos x \sin y}{m \sin (x-y)}$ D. $m \cot x \sin y$

32. Using principal values only, the value of arc sin $\dfrac{3}{5}$ +   32.___
    arc cos $\dfrac{3}{5}$ is

    A. 0 B. $\dfrac{\pi}{4}$ C. $\dfrac{\pi}{2}$ D. π

33. If $x = \dfrac{\pi}{5}$, the value of $2 \cos \pi \sin (\pi - x) \sin (\dfrac{3}{2}\pi + X)$ is   33.___
    equal to

    A. $\cos\dfrac{2}{5}\pi$ B. $-\cos\dfrac{2}{5}\pi$

    C. $\sin\dfrac{2}{5}\pi$ D. $-\sin\dfrac{2}{5}\pi$

34. Which one of the following is equal to cos 15 ?   34.___

    A. $\tfrac{1}{2}\sqrt{1+\sqrt{3}}$ B. $\tfrac{1}{2}\sqrt{1-\sqrt{3}}$

    C. $\dfrac{\sqrt{3}+1}{2\sqrt{2}}$ D. $\dfrac{\sqrt{3}-1}{2\sqrt{2}}$

35. Tan $\dfrac{A}{2}$ + cot $\dfrac{A}{2}$ is equivalent to   35.___

    A. 2 sin A B. 2 cos A
    C. 2 sec A D. 2 csc A

36. If $\cos 200^{0} = k$, then the value of $\cot 70^{0}$ expressed in   36.___
    terms of k is

    A. $\dfrac{k}{\sqrt{1-k^{2}}}$ B. $\dfrac{k}{\sqrt{1-k^{2}}}$

    C. $\dfrac{\sqrt{1-k^{2}}}{k}$ D. $\dfrac{-\sqrt{1-k^{2}}}{k}$

37. The equations of the asymptotes of 2x+3y+1=xy are   37.___
    A. x-3=0 and y-2=0
    B. x-3=0 and 3y+1=0
    C. 2x+1=0 and y-2=0
    D. 2x+1=0 and 3y+1=0

38. The distance between point A $(1,2,-1)$ and point B $(x,-2,4)$ is $5\sqrt{2}$. Which one of the following pairs represents the possible values of x?
    A. 1 and 2
    B. 1 and -2
    C. 4 and 2
    D. 4 and -2
    38. ___

39. Find the coordinates of the center of a circle whose equation is $x^2+y^2-4x-2y-75=0$.
    A. (4,1)
    B. (1,4)
    C. (2,1)
    D. (1,2)
    39. ___

40. The end-points of a diameter of a circle are $(-6,4)$ and $(8,6)$. If A and B are the y-intercept points of the circle, then the length of AB is
    A. $5\sqrt{2}$
    B. 10
    C. 14
    D. $10\sqrt{2}$
    40. ___

41. The equation $r = \dfrac{3}{1-\cos\theta}$ represents a(n)
    A. circle
    B. ellipse
    C. hyperbola
    D. parabola
    41. ___

42. What is the equation of the perpendicular bisector of the line segment whose end points are $(2,6)$ and $(-4,3)$?
    A. $4x+2y-5=0$
    B. $x-2y+10=0$
    C. $4x-2y+13=0$
    D. $x+2y-8=0$
    42. ___

43. What is the area of the region bounded by the parabola $y = x^2$ and the line $y = 2x+3$?
    A. $\dfrac{37}{6}$
    B. $\dfrac{32}{3}$
    C. $\dfrac{34}{3}$
    D. 9
    43. ___

44. $\int_{2}^{4} \int_{0}^{3} (x^2y+x)\, dx\, dy =$
    A. $9y+2$
    B. $9x+2$
    C. 55
    D. 63
    44. ___

45. Which one of the following is an equation of a line tangent to the curve $y = \dfrac{1}{x}$ at the point $(2,\tfrac{1}{2})$?
    A. $x-4y=0$
    B. $x+4y=4$
    C. $8x+2y=17$
    D. $8x-2y=15$
    45. ___

46. The expression $\sqrt{\dfrac{1-\cos x}{1+\cos x}}$ is NOT differentiable for which one of the following values of x?
    A. $x = \dfrac{\pi}{3}$
    B. $x = \dfrac{\pi}{2}$
    C. $x = \pi$
    D. $x = \dfrac{3\pi}{2}$
    46. ___

47. If $y = x^2-x$, then the derivative of y^2 with respect to x^2 is
    A. $2x-1$
    B. $2x^2-3x+1$
    C. $4x^3-6x^2+2x$
    D. $1 - \dfrac{1}{2x}$
    47. ___

48. The mathematician who demonstrated a relationship among   48.____
    the four numbers e, π, i and -1 was
    A. Fermat   B. Leibniz
    C. Euler   D. Pascal

49. What is the probability of getting 80% or more of the   49.____
    questions correct on a 5 question true-false exam merely
    by guessing?
    A. $\frac{1}{16}$ B. $\frac{5}{32}$ C. $\frac{3}{16}$ D. $\frac{7}{32}$

50. Bag A contains 5 red and 4 black balls. Bag B contains   50.____
    4 red and 6 black balls. If a bag is chosen at random
    and a ball is drawn from this bag, which is the probability
    that it will be black?
    A. $\frac{4}{15}$ B. $\frac{10}{19}$ C. $\frac{47}{90}$ D. $\frac{7}{10}$

KEY (CORRECT ANSWERS)

1. C	11. A	21. D	31. B	41. D
2. C	12. C	22. D	32. C	42. A
3. D	13. C	23. D	33. C	43. B
4. A	14. D	24. C	34. C	44. D
5. A	15. C	25. D	35. D	45. B
6. A	16. C	26. C	36. D	46. C
7. D	17. D	27. A	37. A	47. B
8. C	18. D	28. D	38. D	48. C
9. C	19. A	29. B	39. C	49. C
10. C	20. C	30. A	40. C	50. C

SOLUTIONS TO PROBLEMS

1. Let V = number of votes to be casted. After $\frac{2}{3}$V have been tallied, the candidate has $\frac{5}{6}$ of the $\frac{3}{4}$V he needs to win. $(\frac{5}{6})(\frac{3}{4}V) = \frac{5}{8}V$. From the remaining $\frac{1}{3}V$ votes he needs to be nominated, $\frac{3}{4}V - \frac{5}{8}V = \frac{1}{8}V$ times. Finally, $\frac{1}{8}V/\frac{1}{3}V = \frac{3}{8}$. (Ans. C)

2. Two consecutive discounts of 20% and 10% on D dollars means .90(.800) = .72D is the selling price. If the first discount is 25%, the selling price is then .75D (B's first discount). In order to match .72D as the final selling price, a second discount of x% means (100-x)(.75D) = .72D. Then, x=4%. (Ans. C)

3. Let x = number of minutes required. After x minutes, the isotope will retain $(\frac{2}{3})^x \cdot S$ of its strength, where S = original strength. We seek x such that the retention will be $\frac{13}{100} \cdot S$. Solving, $(\frac{2}{3})^x = \frac{13}{100}$ by Logs yields x=5.03 or about 5 minutes. (Ans. D)

4. Let R_1, R_2 be the two roots. We require $\frac{1}{R_1} + \frac{1}{R_2}$, which equals $(R_2+R_1)/(R_1)(R_2)$ = sum of roots/product of roots = -p/q. (Ans. A)

5. $\sqrt[n]{\frac{20}{4^{n+2}+2^{2n+2}}} = \sqrt[n]{\frac{2^2 \cdot 5}{2^{2n+4}+2^{2n+2}}} = \sqrt[n]{\frac{2^2 \cdot 5}{2^{2n+2}(2^2+1)}}$

    $= \sqrt[n]{\frac{1}{2^{2n}}} = \frac{1}{4}$ (Ans. A)

6. $Log\ 14.4 = Log\ \frac{144}{10} = Log\ 144 - Log\ 10 = Log\ 2^4 + Log\ 3^2 - Log\ 10$
    $= (4)(.301) + (2)(.477) -1 = 1.158$ (Ans. A)

7. $\frac{A}{x^2-1} + \frac{B}{x^2+2} = \frac{A(x^2+2)+B(x^2-1)}{(x^2-1)(x^2+2)}$. Thus, since $Ax^2+Bx^2=2x^2$, A+B=2. (Ans. D)

8. This product can be rewritten as $(\frac{5}{6})(\frac{6}{7})(...)(\frac{n+3}{n+4})(\frac{n+4}{n+5})$.

    Through multiple cancellations, this becomes $\frac{5}{n+5}$. (Ans. C)

9. The eighth term $= -({}_{12}C_7)(\frac{2a}{3})^5(\frac{3}{2a})^7 = (-792)(\frac{9}{4a^2}) = -\frac{1782}{a^2}$.

This procedure is known as the binomial expansion.
(Ans. C)

10. $f(x+1) = \frac{x+1}{x+1-1} = \frac{x+1}{x} = \frac{x-1}{x} + \frac{2}{x} = \frac{1}{f(x)} + \frac{2}{x}$. (Ans. C)

11. If the first digit is 4, then the last digit must be 6 and
there would be ${}_3P_3 = 6$ possibilities. Since 6 and 4 could
be interchanged, there would be 6 possibilities of 6_ _ _ 4.
But, if the first (highest) digit is 5 or 9, then the last
digit could be 4 or 6 and the number of possibilities is
$(2)({}_3P_3)(2) = 24$. Total number of possibilities = 6+6+24=36.
(Ans. A)

12.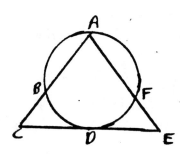

Let x = any side of ΔACE. Then,
CD = ½x, since D is the midpoint
of $\overline{CE}$.
A geometric theorem states that if
a tangent and a secant are both
drawn to a circle from the same
external point, then the tangent
is the geometric mean between the
secant and that portion of the
secant outside the circle.
Let BC=p, AB=x-p.

Then, $\frac{p}{\frac{1}{2}x} = \frac{\frac{1}{2}x}{x}$. Solving, x=4p.

Thus, AB=3p and the ratio is 3p:p
or 3:1. (Ans. C)

13. Using the Pythagorean Theorem, the top of the ladder is
$\sqrt{25^2-7^2} = 24$ feet above the ground. If it slips 4 feet, the
distance from the base of the ladder to the wall is $\sqrt{25^2-20^2} =$
15 feet. Thus, the ladder will have slid 15-7=8 feet. (Ans. C)

14.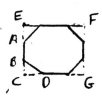

Let C,E,F,G be vertices of the
square. Let BC=CD=EA=x. Then,
BD = $\sqrt{x^2+x^2}$ = x√2. Now, AB = x√2.
Since EC=6=EA+AB+BC = x+x√2+x.
Solving, x=6-3√2. Thus, AB =
(6-3√2)(√2) = 6√2-6. (Ans. D)

15.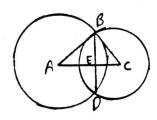

To find ∠A, using ΔABC, $BC^2 = AB^2 + AC^2$
$-2(AB)(AC)\cos\angle A$. $6^2 = 10^2 + 10^2 - (2)(10)$
$(10)\cos\angle A$. Solving, ∠A=34.9°. Now,
in ΔAEB, sin 34.9° = $\frac{BE}{AB}$ = $\frac{BE}{10}$. Thus,
BE=5.72. Since BD=2(BE), BD=11.44,
which is approximately $\frac{6\sqrt{91}}{5}$. (Ans. C)

16.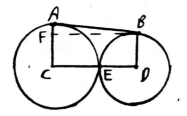

CE=R, ED=r, ∠A=∠B=90⁰, $\overline{BF}$ // $\overline{CD}$.
Since BD=r, CF=r, AF=R-r, let AB=x
$AF^2+FB^2=AB^2$. $(R-r)^2+(R+r)^2=x^2$.
Solving for x, $x=\sqrt{2(R^2+r^2)}$.
NOTE that FB=CD=CE+ED=R+r.
(Ans. C)

17.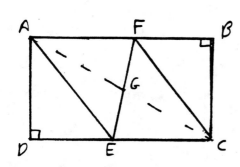

Let FB=x. Then, FC = $\sqrt{x^2+12^2}$ =
$\sqrt{x^2+144}$. AF=16-x, but since AF=FC
16-x = $\sqrt{x^2+144}$. Solving, x=3.5.
Now, each side of rhombus AFCE =12.
Diagonals of a rhombus are perpen-
dicular bisectors of each other, so
∠G=90⁰. $(AC)^2=16^2+12^2$, so AG =20.
Then, AG=10. Using ∆AGE, $10^2+(EG)^2$
=$(12.5)^2$, so EG=7.5. Finally,
EF=2(7.5) =15. (Ans. D)

18. $\frac{AF}{AD} = \frac{AE}{AC} = \frac{AD}{AB}$. Using the first and third ratios and letting
DB=x, $\frac{4}{10} = \frac{10}{10+x}$. Solving, x=15. (Ans. D)

19.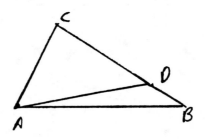

20. $x^2-x-2>0$ becomes (x-2)(x+1)>0.
Case 1: x-2>0 and x+1>0, which yields x>2.
Case 2: x-2<0 and x+1<0, which yields x<-1
Thus, either x>2 or x<-1; ie: {x|x<-1}∪{x|x>2}
(Ans. C)

21. The four sides can be represented by x+y=3, y=x-3, y=-x-3, and
y=x+3. Condensing, this is equivalent to |x|+|y|= 3. (Ans. D)

22. 1*(3*2) = 1*[(2)(3)+(3)(2)]= 1*12 = 2(1)+3(12) =38.
(Ans. D)

23. Inverse of f = {(3,1),(5,2),(5,3)}, which is NOT a function.
(Ans. D)

24. 4 × 6 =24, which is 3(mod 7). The inverse n is such that
3 × n =1. By trying different numbers, we find n=5. (Ans. C)

25.

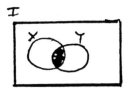

Complement of X∩Y is everything in
I which is NOT shaded = X´∪Y´.
(Ans. D)

26. A group must have the property of associativity. If it is an
Abelian group, the commutativity property must also exist.
(Ans. C)

27.

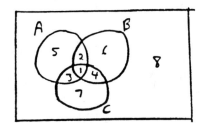

By numbering the regions, we seek
region 7. C = regions 1,3,4,7 and
A∪B = regions 1,2,3,4,5,6. Thus,
(A∪B)´ = regions 7,8. Now,
C∩(A∪B)´ = region 7.
(Ans. A)

28.

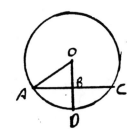

OA=3; since OD=3 and BD=3−√5,
OB=3−(3−√5) =√5
Now, (AB)²+(√5)²=3², and AB=2.
Thus, AC=4 and the area of the
rectangular surface = (10)(4) = 40.
(Ans. D)

29.

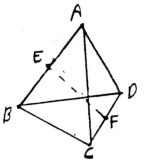

By inspection.

30. $[\sqrt{2}(\cos 30^0 + i \sin 30^0)]^2 = (\sqrt{2})^2[\cos 60^0 + i \sin 60^0]$
$= 2[\frac{1}{2} + i \cdot \frac{\sqrt{3}}{2}] = 1 + \sqrt{3}\, i.$ (Ans. A)

31.

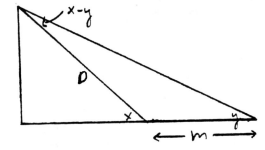

By the Law of sines,

$$\frac{D}{\sin y} = \frac{m}{\sin(x-y)}$$

Solving, $D = \dfrac{m \sin y}{\sin(x-y)}$

(Ans. B)

32.

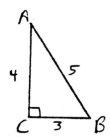

Let ABC be a right triangle with
sides 3,4,5.

Arc sin $\frac{3}{5}$ = ∠A. Arc cos $\frac{3}{5}$ = ∠B.

Thus, Arc sin $\frac{3}{5}$ + Arc cos $\frac{3}{5}$ =

∠A +∠B = 90⁰ or $\frac{\pi}{2}$. (Ans. C)

33. $2 \cdot \cos \pi \cdot \sin(\pi-x) \cdot \sin(\frac{3}{2}\pi+x) =$

$(2)(-1)(\sin x)[(\sin\frac{3}{2}\pi \cos x + \sin x \cos\frac{3}{2}\pi)]$

$= -2\sin x (-\cos x+0) = 2\sin x \cos x = \sin 2x.$

Since $x = \frac{\pi}{5}$, the final answer $= \sin\frac{2}{5}\pi$. (Ans. C)

34. $\cos\frac{1}{2}\theta = \sqrt{(\cos\theta+1)/2}$. So, $\cos 15° = \sqrt{(\cos 30°+1)/2}$

$= \sqrt{(\sqrt{3}/2+1)/2}$, which is equivalent to $(\sqrt{3}+1)/2\sqrt{2}$. (Ans. C)

35. $\text{Tan} \frac{A}{2} = \sqrt{(1-\cos A)/(1+\cos A)}$ and $\cot \frac{A}{2} = \sin A/(1-\cos A)$

$\text{Tan} \frac{A}{2}$ can also be written as $\sin A/(1+\cos A)$.

Now, $\sin A/(1-\cos A) + \sin A/(1+\cos A) = 2\sin A/(1-\cos^2 A)$

$= 2/\sin A = 2\csc A.$ (Ans. D)

36. If $\cos 200°=K$, $\sin 200° = -\sqrt{1-K^2}$ (3rd quadrant angle).

$\text{Cot } 70° = \tan 20° = \tan 200° = \sin 200°/\cos 200° = \frac{-\sqrt{1-k^2}}{K}.$

(Ans. D)

37. If $x=3$, $2x+3y+1=xy$ becomes $6+3y+1=3y$ (no value for y).
If $y=2$, the above equation becomes $2x+6+1=2x$ (no value for x).
(Ans. A)

38. Distance $= \sqrt{(1-x)^2+(2-[-2])^2+(-1-4)^2} = 5\sqrt{2}.$
This reduces to $x^2-2x-8=0$. Solving, $x=4$ and $x=-2$. (Ans. D)

39. Rewrite as $x^2-4x+4+y^2-2y+1 = 75+4+1$, which becomes
$(x-2)^2+(y-1)^2=80$. The center is located at $(2,1)$. (Ans. C)

40.

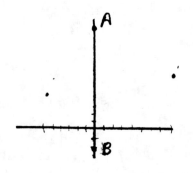

The center of the circle is

$(\frac{-6+8}{2}, \frac{4+6}{2}) = (1,5).$

The radius is of length $\sqrt{(8-1)^2+(6-5)^2}$
$=\sqrt{50}$. Thus, the equation of the
circle can be written as
$(x-1)^2+(y-5)^2=50$. The y-intercepts
would be solutions to $(0-1)^2+(y-5)^2$
$=50$. So, the y-intercepts are 12
and -2. Length of AB=14. (Ans. C)

41. Convert the equation to $r - r\cos\theta = 3$, which becomes $\sqrt{x^2+y^2}-x=3$. This simplifies to $y^2=6x+9$, which is a parabola. (Ans. D)

42.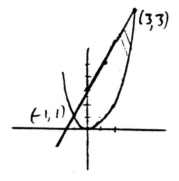

The midpoint of the line segment is $(-1, 4.5)$. Since the slope of this segment is $\frac{1}{2}$, the slope of the perpendicular bisector is -2. The equation of the perpendicular bisector is $y-4.5 = -2(x+1)$, which becomes $4x+2y-5=0$. (Ans. A)

43.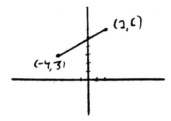

Area of shaded region:

$$\int_{-1}^{3} [(2x+3)-x^2]\,dx = [x^2+3x-\frac{x^3}{3}]_{-1}^{3}$$

Evaluated, this becomes $\frac{32}{3}$. (Ans. B)

44. $\int_{2}^{4} \int_{0}^{3} (x^2y+x)\,dx\,dy = \int_{2}^{4} [\frac{x^3y}{3} + \frac{x^2}{2}]_{x=0}^{3} \, dy$

$= \int_{2}^{4} (9y+\frac{9}{2})\,dy = [\frac{9}{2}y^2+\frac{9}{2}y]_{2}^{4} = 63.$ (Ans. D)

45. The derivative of $y = \frac{1}{x}$ is $-\frac{1}{x^2}$, which is also the equation of the slope. At $(2,\frac{1}{2})$, the slope is $-\frac{1}{4}$. The equation of the tangent line is $y-\frac{1}{2} = -\frac{1}{4}(x-2)$, which simplifies to $x+4y=4$. (Ans. B)

46. $\sqrt{(1-\cos x)/(1+\cos x)} = \tan \frac{1}{2}x$. Since $\tan \frac{\pi}{2}$ does not exist

(as a finite quantity), when $x=\pi$, $\tan \frac{1}{2}x$ is not differentiable. (Ans. C)

47. $y=x^2-x$, so $y^2=x^4-2x^3+x^2$. Let $z=y^2$ and $u=x^2$.

Then, $z=u^2-2u^{\frac{3}{2}}+u$. $dz/du = 2u-3u^{\frac{1}{2}}+1$. Now, we get $d(y^2)/d(x^2) = 2x^2-3x+1$. (Ans. B)

48. Euler was involved in the discovery of transcendental numbers, such as e and π. One of his formulas is $e^{i\theta} = \cos\theta +i\sin\theta$. (Ans. C)

49. Probability of 4 right = $_5C_4(.5)^4(.5)^1$ = .15625

    Probability of 5 right = $_5C_5(.5)^5(.5)^0$ = .03125

    The sum of these probabilities = .1875 = $\dfrac{3}{16}$. (Ans. C)

50. Let P = probability. P(black ball) = P(black ball from A)·P(choosing A) + P(black ball from B)·P(choosing B) =

    $\dfrac{4}{9} \cdot \dfrac{1}{2} + \dfrac{6}{10} \cdot \dfrac{1}{2} = \dfrac{47}{90}$. (Ans. C)

    ———

EXAMINATION SECTION

1. The arithmetic mean of the measures 4.18, 4.23, 4.15, 1.___
   4.17, 4.09 is CLOSEST to which one of the following?
   A. 4.15   B. 4.16   C. 4.17   D. 4.18

2. Of the following pairs, the one containing two equivalent 2.___
   values is
   A. .0375, 3 3/4%   B. 2.75, .02 3/4%
   C. .8 1/3%, 1/12   D. .0125%, .01 1/4

3. If the original selling price of a certain article, 3.___
   including a profit of 40% of the cost, were $18.20, and
   if the profit were to be reduced to 30% of the cost, the
   selling price would become
   A. $13.39   B. $13.65   C. $16.38   D. $16.90

4. Assume that a gasoline tank was ½ full and the gasoline 4.___
   was used until the tank is only 1/8 full. If the tank is
   then filled to capacity by putting in 21 gallons, the
   capacity of the tank in gallons is
   A. 24   B. 42
   C. 56   D. none of these

5. If a 4% stock, whose par value is $60.00, is purchased at 5.___
   a price that will make the investment yield a return of
   5%, the purchase price is
   A. $30   B. $48   C. $75   D. $82

6. Assume that an investment depreciates 20% of the original 6.___
   value during the first year, and then during the second
   year depreciates 80% of the value it had at the beginning
   of the second year. The uniform yearly rate of decrease
   that would have yielded the same resulting value at the
   end of two years is
   A. 40%   B. 47%   C. 50%   D. 60%

7. The smallest subdivision on a certain accurately 7.___
   calibrated instrument is .01 inch. Assuming no human
   errors in use, the possible error of measurement in using
   the above instrument is
   A. .001"   B. .005"   C. .010"   D. .050"

8. The number 1011 to the base 2, if expressed to the base 10, 8.___
   would be
   A. 11   B. 14   C. 22   D. 38

9. If the integers 6 and 3 are interchanged in the number   9.____
   2635 now expressed to the base seven, the quantity
   expressed to the base 10 by which the number is reduced is
      A. 21   B. 30   C. 147   D. none of these

10. A number of the form an^4+bn^2+cn+d, where a=4, b=2, c=2,   10.____
    d=1, and n=10, is divisible by
       A. 2   B. 5   C. 7   D. 9

11. Of the following, the set in which all are units which   11.____
    may be used for measuring a one dimensional object is:
       A. Meter, liter, decimeter, kilometer
       B. Meter, kilometer, decimeter, millimeter
       C. Liter, decimeter, kilometer, millimeter
       D. Meter, liter, millimeter, decimeter

12. U represents the operation of the union of two sets. If   12.____
    A is the set of all numbers of the form 2n and B, the set
    of all numbers of the form 2n+1. n being any integer, than
    A U B is the set of all
       A. odd integers   B. even integers
       C. rational numbers   D. integers

13. Using a Venn diagram in which the   13.____
    circle A represents the set of
    rational numbers and B the set of
    non-terminating decimals, the
    section C represents the set of
    all
       A. transcendental numbers
       B. irrational numbers
       C. real numbers
       D. repeating decimals

14. If P implies Q, an equivalent statement is: 14.____
       A. Q implies P
       B. Q is a necessary condition for P
       C. P is a necessary condition for Q
       D. Not P implies not Q

15. The probability of obtaining 3 heads and 1 tail in a   15.____
    throw of 4 coins is
       A. 3/4   B. 1/2   C. 3/8   D. 1/4

16. The following "proof" was offered to show that 2=1.   16.____
    Suppose a and b are two names for the same number, then
    $a=b$, $a^2=ab$
    $a^2-b^2 = ab-b^2$
    $(a+b)(a-b) = b(a-b)$
    $a+b=b$
    $2b=b$
    $2=1$
    This "proof" is invalid because
       A. the commutative law does not hold for subtraction
       B. zero has no multiplicative inverse
       C. the commutative law does not hold for division
       D. the associative law does not hold for subtraction

17. Assume that for the first 90 miles of a 156 mile trip a man averages 36 miles per hour. To achieve an average rate of 39 miles per hour for the entire trip, his average rate for the remainder of the trip in miles per hour must be

    A. 40   B. 42   C. 44   D. 48

17.___

18. A varies directly as the square of b and inversely as the cube of c. If b is tripled and c is doubled, the value of A is

    A. multiplied by 3/2   B. multiplied by 6
    C. multiplied by 9/8   D. multiplied by 2

18.___

19. $\dfrac{10}{\sqrt{3}}$ x $\dfrac{3\sqrt{2}}{\sqrt{5}}$ equals which one of the following?

    A. $2\sqrt{2}$ B. $10\sqrt{6}$ C. $6\sqrt{10}$ D. $2\sqrt{30}$

19.___

20. The root (roots) of the equation $2\sqrt{x} = x-3$ is(are)

    A. 9,1   B. 9   C. -3,1   D. 3,-1

20.___

21. Of the following, an equivalent sentence to 5(x+3)-7 = 3x-4(1+x) is:

    A. 5x+15 = 3x+7-4-4x   B. 7x-5x = 8+4
    C. 5x+3x-4x = 7-15-4   D. 15-7-4 = 7x-5x

21.___

22. Of the following, the equation that expresses the relationship between the variables in the given table

x	-1	2	3	-2
y	-2	1	6	1

  is

    A. y=2x   B. $y-x^2=-3$
    C. y=x+3   D. y=x-1

22.___

23. If a certain wheel makes 100 revolutions in going a certain distance, and a wheel ½ foot less in diameter makes 25 more revolutions in going the same distance, then the diameter of the larger wheel is

    A. 2 ft.   B. 2.5 ft.   C. 4 ft.   D. 5 ft.

23.___

24. If 4 quarts of a certain mixture of alcohol and water is at 50% strength, the number of quarts of water that must be added to make the alcohol strength of the new mixture 40% is

    A. 1   B. 2   C. 3   D. 10

24.___

25. When the price of a certain article increases from 20 cents to 25 cents, the number of such articles that can be purchased for d dollars decreases by

    A. $\dfrac{d}{100}$ B. $\dfrac{d}{20}$ C. 5d   D. d

25.___

26. $\log (x^2-y^2)$ is equal to which one of the following?

    A. 2 log x - 2 log y
    B. log (x+y) + log(x-y)
    C. 2 log (x-y)
    D. none of these

26.___

27. If log x $\geq$ log 2+$\frac{1}{2}$log x, then   27. ___
    A. x $\geq$ 2   B. x $\leq$ 2   C. x $\leq$ 4   D. x $\geq$ 4

28. 2 cos^{3}A sin A + 2 sin^{3}A cos A equals which one of the   28. ___
    following?
    A. sin 2A   B. cos 2A   C. 2 sinA   D. 2 cosA

29. If in $\triangle$ABC, A=30^0 and B=120^0, BC:AC equals   29. ___
    A. $\frac{1}{4}$ B. $\frac{1}{\sqrt{3}}$ C. 1   D. $\frac{\sqrt{3}}{1}$

30. The point on the graph of y=x^2-x, at which the slope   30. ___
    exceeds the abscissa by 1, is
    A. (2,2)   B. (2,3)   C. (3,3)   D. (3,2)

31. The graph of y>x has points in quadrant(s)   31. ___
    A. I only   B. I and II only
    C. I, II, and III only   D. I and III only

32. The area bounded by y=x^2, y=0, x=2, and x=5 is   32. ___
    A. 27   B. 39   C. 43   D. 56

33. If 3x+5>x and n is a negative integer, an equivalent   33. ___
    sentence is:
    A. n(3x+5)>n x   B. 3x+5+n<n+x
    C. n-(3x+5)>n-x   D. $\frac{3x+5}{n} < \frac{x}{n}$

34. $\lim\limits_{x \to 1} \frac{x-1}{x^2-1}$ equals   34. ___

    A. 0   B. $\frac{1}{2}$ C. 1   D. infinity

35. If a point is equidistant from the sides of a triangle,   35. ___
    it must be the intersection of the three
    A. altitudes
    B. perpendicular bisectors of the sides
    C. medians
    D. angle bisectors

36. If triangle BAC with AB=15", AC=15", and BC=24" is   36. ___
    inscribed in a circle, the radius of the circle is
    A. 7"   B. 12$\frac{1}{2}$"   C. 25"   D. 25$\frac{1}{2}$"

37. If a chord 12 inches long is drawn in a circle and the   37. ___
    midpoint of the minor arc of the chord is 2 inches from
    the chord, then the radius of the circle, expressed in
    inches, is
    A. 8   B. 10   C. 18   D. 20

38. A pile of cement of conical shape has a height of 21 feet   38. ___
    and a base diameter of 36 feet. Using 22/7 as the value
    of π, the volume in cubic yards would be
    A. 264   B. 792   C. 1056   D. 1188

39. The system of numeration using the base 10 was first developed   39. ____
    by which one of the following?   The
       A. Babylonians   B. Egyptians   C. Hindus   D. Greeks

40. The sum of the angles of any triangle is always less than 180° 40. ____
    is a theorem in _____ geometry.
       A. Euclidean   B. Lobatchevskian
       C. Riemannian   D. spherical

_____

KEY (CORRECT ANSWERS)

1. B	11. B	21. A	31. C
2. A	12. D	22. B	32. B
3. D	13. D	23. B	33. D
4. A	14. B	24. C	34. B
5. B	15. D	25. D	35. D
6. D	16. B	26. B	36. B
7. B	17. C	27. A	37. B
8. A	18. C	28. A	38. A
9. D	19. D	29. B	39. C
10. D	20. B	30. A	40. B

_____

SOLUTIONS TO PROBLEMS

1. The arithmetic mean of the 5 numbers = $\frac{20.82}{5}$ = 4.164, which rounds off to 4.16. (Ans. B)

2. .0375 is equivalent to 3.75%, which equals $3\frac{3}{4}$%. (Ans. A)

3. Let C = cost. $18.20 = (1.40)(C), so C=$13.00. Now, the new profit = (13)(1.30) = $16.90. (Ans. D)

4. 21 gallons represents $\frac{7}{8}$ of the tank's capacity. Thus, the tank's capacity is (21)($\frac{8}{7}$) = 24 gallons. (Ans. A)

5. Let x = purchase price. Then, (60)(.04) = (x)(.05). Solving, x=$48. (Ans. B)

6. Let x = uniform yearly rate of decrease, expressed as a percent. Then, $(1 - \frac{x}{100})(1 - \frac{x}{100})$ = (.80)(.20) = .16. Solving, we get x=60. (Ans. D)

7. The error of measurement = $(\frac{1}{2})$(.01) = .005 inches. (Ans. B)

8. $1011_{\text{base 2}}$ = 8+2+1 = $11_{\text{base 10}}$

9. $2635_{\text{base 7}}$ = (2)(343)+(6)(49)+(3)(7)+5 = $1006_{\text{base 10}}$ and

   $2365_{\text{base 7}}$ = (2)(343)+(3)(49)+(6)(7)+5 = $880_{\text{base 10}}$

   The amount reduction is 126. (Ans. D)

10. The number's value is $4\times10^4+2\times10^2+2\times10+1$ = 40,221. Since the sum of the digits of this number is divisible by 9, then so must the number be divisible by 9. (Ans. D)

11. All four of the units, meter, kilometer, decimeter, and millimeter are linear measurements. Thus, they can be used to measure one-dimensional objects. (Ans. B)

12. All integers can be represented by either 2n or 2n+1, depending on whether the integer is even or odd. (Ans. D)

13. A repeating decimal is both non-terminating and rational. For example, $.\overline{6} = \frac{2}{3}$, which is rational. (Ans. D)

14. Q is a necessary condition for P, since if P occurs, Q must follow. Note that P is NOT a necessary condition for Q, since other events may also imply Q. (Ans. B)

15. Probability of any 3 heads and 1 tail out of 4 coins =

$$_4C_3 \ (\tfrac{1}{2})^3(\tfrac{1}{2}) = (4)(\tfrac{1}{16}) = \tfrac{1}{4}. \quad \text{(Ans. D)}$$

16. The fallacy of the argument occurs when one proceeds from line 3 to line 4. Dividing by a-b means dividing by zero, but zero has no multiplicative inverse. (Ans. B)

17. Let x = average rate for the remaining 66 miles. Since total distance ÷ total time = average rate for entire trip,

$$156 \div (\frac{90}{36} + \frac{66}{x}) = 39.$$ This equation could be simplified to

$36x/(90x+2376) = 39/156$. Solving, x=44. (Ans. C)

18. $A = Kb^2/c^3$, where K = constant. Let b be replaced by 3b and c be replaced by 2c. Then, $A = K(3b)^2/(2c)^3$ or $A = \frac{9}{8}Kb^2/c^3$.

Thus, the new value of A has been obtained by multiplying the original A value by $\frac{9}{8}$. (Ans. C)

19. $\frac{10}{\sqrt{3}} \cdot \frac{3\sqrt{2}}{\sqrt{5}} = \frac{30\sqrt{2}}{\sqrt{15}} = \frac{30\sqrt{2}}{\sqrt{15}} \cdot \frac{\sqrt{15}}{\sqrt{15}} = \frac{30\sqrt{30}}{15} = 2\sqrt{30}.$ (Ans. D)

20. $2\sqrt{x} = x-3$. Squaring both sides, $4x=x^2-6x+9$. This becomes $x^2-10x+9=0$, which factors as $(x-9)(x-1)=0$. Only 9 is a root (1 does not check the original equation). (Ans. B)

21. $5(x+3)-7 = 3x-4(1+x)$ is equivalent to $5x+15-7 = 3x-4-4x$, which is equivalent to $5x+15 = 3x+7-4-4x$. (Ans. A)

22. Since 4 ordered pairs are given, let $y = Ax^3+Bx^2+Cx+D$. By substituting ordered pairs, we get the following:
$-2 = -A+B-C+D$, $1 = 8A+4B+2C+D$.
$6 = 27A+9B+3C+D$, and $1 = -8A+4B-2C+D$.
Solving, A=0, B=1, C=0, and D=-3. Thus, $y=x^2-3$ or $y-x^2=-3$. (Ans. B)

23. Let D = diameter of larger wheel, D-.5 = diameter of smaller wheel. The respective circumferences are πD and πD-.5π. Then, $100\pi D = 125(\pi D-.5\pi)$. Solving, D = 2.5 ft. (Ans. B)

24. The original mixture has 2 quarts each of alcohol and water. Let x = amount of water added. Then $\frac{2}{2+x} = .40$. Solving, x=3. (Ans. C)

25. For d dollars, $\frac{100d}{20}$ = 5d articles can be bought, but when the price per article increases to 25 cents, the purchasing power of d dollars is $\frac{100d}{25}$ = 4d articles. The actual decrease is d articles. (Ans. D)

26. Log (x^2-y^2) = Log[$(x+y)(x-y)$] = Log$(x+y)$ + Log$(x-y)$. (Ans. B)

27. Log 2 + $\frac{1}{2}$Log x = Log $2x^{\frac{1}{2}}$. Now, since Log x ≥ Log $2x^{\frac{1}{2}}$,

x ≥ $2x^{\frac{1}{2}}$. This becomes x^2 ≥ 2x, which is solved as x ≥ 2. (Ans. A)

28. $2\cos^3 A \sin A + 2\sin^3 A \cos A = 2\sin A \cos A (\cos^2 A + \sin^2 A)$ = $2\sin A \cos A = \sin 2A$. (Ans. A)

29.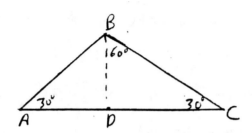

Draw $\overline{BD}$ perpendicular to $\overline{AC}$. Then, BC:DC = 2:$\sqrt{3}$. Since AC=2·DC, BC:AC=2:2$\sqrt{3}$ = 1:$\sqrt{3}$. (Ans. B)

30. Let the required point be (p, p^2-p). The slope at this point is 2p-1. Since 2p-1-p=1, p=2. Thus, the required point is (2,2). (Ans. A)

31.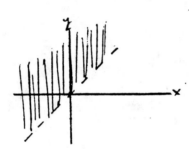

The dotted line represents y=x. The shaded area represents y>x and it occupies parts of quadrants I, III, and all of quadrant II. (Ans. C)

32.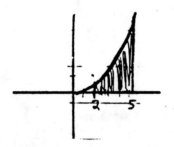

The area bounded by $y=x^2$, y=0, x=2, and x=5 is $\int_2^5 x^2 dx = [\frac{x^3}{3}]_2^5 = \frac{125}{3} - \frac{8}{3} = 39$.

(Ans. B)

33. If 3x+5>x and n<0, then $\frac{3x+5}{n} < \frac{x}{n}$, since dividing by a negative number reverses the inequality. (Ans. D)

34. $\lim\limits_{x \to 1} \frac{x-1}{x^2-1} = \lim\limits_{x \to 1} \frac{x-1}{(x-1)(x+1)} = \lim \frac{1}{x+1} = \frac{1}{2}$. (Ans. B)

35.

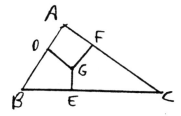

If G is located such that DG=FG=EG and ∠D=∠E=∠F=90°, then G lies at the intersection of the angle bisectors of △ABC. (Ans. D)

36.

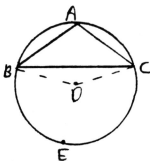

AB=AC=15, BC=24. Using △ABC, $24^2=15^2+15^2-(2)(15)(15)(\cos\angle A)$. Solving, ∠A=106° (approx.). This means B̂ÊC=212° and thus B̂ÂC=148°. Now, ∠BDC=148°. Using △DBC, letting BD=DC=x, $24^2=x^2+x^2-2x^2\cos 148°$. Solving, x=12.48 (approx.). Thus, the radius = 12½. (Ans. B)

37.

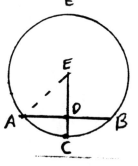

AB=12, DC=2, ÂC=ĈB. Now, AD=DB=6. Let AE=x, so that ED=x-2. Since ∠D=90°, $6^2+(x-2)^2=x^2$. Solving, x=10 = radius. (Ans. B)

38.

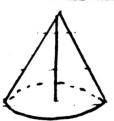

The radius is 18'. Volume = $\frac{1}{3}\pi R^2 H$

= $(\frac{1}{3})(\frac{22}{7})(18)^2(21)$ = 7128 cu.ft.,

which becomes 264 cu.yds. (Ans. A)

39. The Hindus invented the use of the so-called position system for digits 0 through 9.

40. By empirical knowledge.

———

BASIC FUNDAMENTALS OF MATHEMATICS

PRINCIPLES AND APPLICATIONS

CONCISE TEXT

WITH PROBLEMS AND ANSWERS

* ARITHMETIC

* ALGEBRA

* LOGARITHMS

* GEOMETRY

* TRIGONMETRY

———

BASIC FUNDAMENTALS OF MATHEMATICS

BASIC FUNDAMENTALS OF MATHEMATICS

CHAPTER 1

INTRODUCTION

1. PURPOSE AND SCOPE

a. Purpose. This section provides the basic mathematics required by students and candidates in all fields, including beginning and advanced students.

b. Scope. This section covers those principles and applications of arithmetic, algebra, logarithms, geometry, and trigonometry that are required for practical understanding.

2. MATHEMATICS AND TESTING

Skill in the use of mathematics, particularly arithmetic, algebra, and trigonometry, is essential in all fields of testing, including mental and general ability, school, college entrance, aptitude, achievement, civil service, professional, and advanced or graduate examinations.

CHAPTER 2
PERCENTAGE

3. General

a. *Definition.* Percentage is the process of computation in which the basis of comparison is a *hundred*. The term *percent*—from *per, by,* and *centum, hundred*—means *by* or *on the hundred*. Thus, 2 percent of a quantity means two parts of every hundred parts of the quantity.

b. *Symbol.* The symbol of percentage is %. Percent may also be indicated by a fraction or a decimal. Thus, $5\% = \frac{5}{100} = .05$. Figure 1 shows the relationship between fractions, decimals, and percentage.

c. *Base, Rate, and Percentage.*
(1) The *base* is the number on which the percentage is computed.
(2) The *rate* is the amount (in hundredths) of the base to be estimated.
(3) The *percentage* is a part or proportion of a whole expressed as so many per hundred. Percentage is the portion of the base determined by the rate.

4. Conversion of Decimal to Percent

To change a decimal to percent, move the decimal point two places to the right and add the percent symbol.

Example: Change .375 to percent.
Move decimal point two places to right: 37.5
Add percent symbol: 37.5%

5. Conversion of Fraction to Percent

To convert a fraction to percent, divide the numerator by the denominator and convert to a decimal. Then, convert the decimal to percent (par. 4).

Example: Change fraction $\frac{5}{8}$ to percent.
Divide numerator by denominator: $5 \div 8 = .625$
Convert decimal to percent: 6.25 $= 62.5\%$
Thus, $\frac{5}{8} = 62.5\%$.

6. Conversion of Percent to Decimal

To change a percent to a decimal, omit the percent symbol and move the decimal point two places to the left.

Example 1: Change 15% to a decimal.
Omit percent symbol: 15% becomes 15
Move decimal point two places to the left: 15 becomes .15
Thus, 15% = .15.

Example 2: Change 110% to a decimal.
Omit percent symbol: 110% becomes 110
Move the decimal point two places to the left: 110 becomes 1.10.
Thus, 110% = 1.10.

7. Conversion of Percent to Fraction

To change a percent to a fraction, first change the percent to a decimal (par. 6) and then to a fraction. Reduce the fraction to its lowest terms.

Example 1: Change 25% to a fraction.
Change to a decimal: 25% = .25
Change to a fraction: $.25 = \frac{25}{100}$
Reduce fraction to lowest terms: $\frac{25}{100} = \frac{1}{4}$
Thus, $25\% = \frac{1}{4}$.

Example 2: Change 37.5% to a fraction.
Change to a decimal: 37.5% = .375
Change to a fraction: $.375 = \frac{375}{1000}$
Reduce fraction to lowest terms: $\frac{375}{1000} = \frac{3}{8}$
Thus, $37.5\% = \frac{3}{8}$.

8. Finding Percentage

a. *General.* To find the percent of a number, write the percent as a decimal and multiply the number by this decimal. In this case, the *base* and *rate* are given. The problem is to find the percentage.

Example 1: Find 5% of 140 (140 is the base, 5% is the rate, and the product is the percentage).
5% of $140 = .05 \times 140 = 7$

Example 2: Find 5.2% of 140.
5.2% of $140 = .052 \times 140 = 7.28$

Example 3: Find 150% of 36.
150% of $36 = 1.50 \times 36 = 54$

Example 4: Find $\frac{1}{2}\%$ of 840.
$\frac{1}{2}\% = .5\%$
$.5\%$ of $840 = .005 \times 840 = 4.20$
Thus, $\frac{1}{2}\%$ of $840 = 4.20$.

b. *Application of Percentage.* In communications-electronics, typical applications of percentage computation are used in determining tolerance values of resistors or in determining the efficiencies of motors and generators.

9. Finding Rate

To find the percent one number is of another, write the problem as a fraction, change the fraction to a decimal, and write the decimal as a percent. In this case, the *percentage* and *base* are given. The problem is to find the *rate*.

Example 1: 3 is what percent of 8? (3 is the percentage, 8 is the base, and the quotient is the rate.)
$\frac{3}{8} = .375$

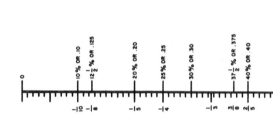

Figure 1. Relationship between fractions, decimals, and percentage.

.375 = 37.5% = $37\frac{1}{2}$%

Therefore, 3 is $37\frac{1}{2}$% of 8.

Example 2: What percent of 542 is 234?

$\frac{234}{542}$ = .4317 + (round off)

.432 = 43.2%

Therefore, 234 is 43.2% of 542.

Example 3: 125 is what percent of 50?

$\frac{125}{50}$ = 2.50

2.50 = 250%

Therefore, 125 is 250% of 50.

10. Finding Base Numbers

To find a number when a percent of the number is known, first find 1% of the number, and then find 100% of the number. In this case, the *percentage* of the number and the *rate* are given. The problem is to find the *base*.

Example 1: 42 is 12% of what number?

12% (base number) = 42

1% (base number) =

$\frac{42}{12}$ = 3.50

100% (base number) =

100 × 3.50 = 350

Therefore, the base number is 350.

Example 2: 45 is 150% of what number?

150% (base number) = 45

1% (base number) = $\frac{45}{150}$ = .3

100% (base number) =

100 × .3 = 30

Therefore, the base number is 30.

11. Expressing Accuracy of Measurements in Percent

a. *Relative error* is the accuracy of a measurement expressed in percent of the total measurement. In determining the relative error, it is first necessary to establish the *limit of error*.

b. The *limit of error* is the difference between the *true value* and the *measured value*. Assume that the reading on a scale, to the nearest tenth of an inch, is 2.2 inches. If the true value is 2.15 inches, the limit of error is the difference between 2.15 and 2.20, or .05 inch.

c. Relative error is computed by solving the ratio $\frac{\text{LIMIT OF ERROR}}{\text{MEASURED VALUE}}$, and expressing the result as a percent. In the scale reading above, the relative error = $\frac{.05}{2.2}$ = 2.27%, or 2.3%.

12. Review Problems—Percentage

a. Show each of the following in three forms —as a fraction or mixed number, as a decimal, and as a percent:

(1) $\frac{3}{5}$

(2) 50%

(3) .375

(4) $\frac{1}{4}$

(5) $62\frac{1}{2}$%

(6) .6

(7) $\frac{3}{10}$

(8) 70%

(9) 2.25

(10) $1\frac{7}{8}$

(11) .08

(12) $\frac{3}{50}$

(13) .18

(14) $1\frac{1}{4}$%

(15) .025

(16) .05

(17) $8\frac{1}{3}$%

(18) $37\frac{1}{2}$%

(19) 105%

(20) 4%

b. Evaluate the following:

(1) 250% of 60

(2) 125% of 40

(3) 200% of 2

(4) 225% of 400

c. What percent of a number is—

(1) 1.5 times the number?

(2) $2\frac{3}{4}$ times the number?

(3) $\frac{3}{2}$ times the number?

(4) $5\frac{1}{2}$ times the number?

d. Find the following:

(1) $\frac{2}{5}$% of 410

(2) $\frac{3}{5}$% of 416,000

(3) $\frac{2}{5}$ of 85

(4) 5.2% of 85

e. Solve the following problems:

(1) Find the relative error for a limit of error of .05 inch in measuring 24.2 inches.

(2) Find the relative error for a limit of error of 2 inches in measuring 200 yards.

f. Find the number when—

(1) 12% of the number is 52

(2) 15% of the number is 375

(3) 32% of the number is 166.4

(4) 8% of the number is 16

(5) 84% of the number is 168

CHAPTER 3
RATIO AND PROPORTION

Section I. RATIO

13. Understanding Ratio

It is often desirable, for the purpose of comparison, to express one quantity in terms of another quantity of the same kind. One way to express this relationship is by means of a *ratio*. For example, if one resistor has a resistance of 800 ohms and another has a resistance of 100 ohms, the first resistor has 8 times as much resistance as the second. In other words, the ratio between the resistors is 8 to 1.

14. Expressing Ratio

Ratio can be expressed in four different ways. For example, the ratio of 12 to 3 can be expressed as follows: 12 to 3, 12:3, 12 ÷ 3, or $\frac{12}{3}$. The numbers 12 and 3, which are the terms of the ratio, are called the *antecedent* and the *consequent*, respectively. The antecedent is the dividend or the numerator; the consequent is the divisor or denominator.

15. Obtaining Value of Ratio

Both terms of any ratio may be multiplied and divided by the same number without changing the value of the expression. In the ratio $\frac{12}{3}$, for example, the 12 is divided by 3, giving the value of 4. This means that the ratio 12:3 is equal to the ratio 4:1.

Example 1: What is the ratio of 6:2?

$$\frac{6}{2} = 3, \text{ or } 3{:}1$$

Example 2: What is the ratio of 7:3?

$$\frac{7}{3} = 2\frac{1}{3} \text{ or } 2\frac{1}{3}{:}1$$

Example 3: Find the ratio of the areas (par. 26) of two squares the sides of which are 6 and 8 inches, respectively. The areas of similar figures are in the same ratios as the squares of their like dimensions.

$$8^2{:}6^2 = 64{:}36$$
$$\frac{64}{36} = 1\frac{28}{36} = 1\frac{7}{9} \text{ or } 1\frac{7}{9}{:}1$$

Thus, the second square (8 inches on a side) is $1\frac{7}{9}$ times as large as the first square (6 inches on a side).

Section II. PROPORTIONS

16. Understanding Proportion

A proportion is a statement of equality between two ratios. If the value of one ratio is equal to the value of another ratio, they are said to be in proportion. For example, the ratio 3:6 is equal to the ratio 4:8. Therefore, this can be written 3:6 :: 4:8 or 3:6 = 4:8. In any proportion, the first and last terms are called the *extremes*; the second and third terms are called the *means* (fig. 2).

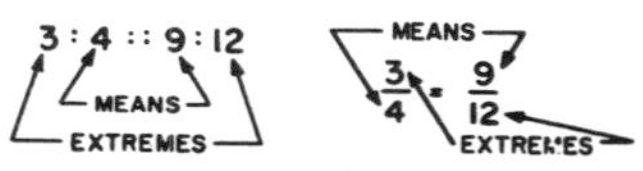

Figure 2. Terms of proportion.

17. Rules of Proportion

There are three rules of proportion that are used in determining an unknown quantity. They also can be used to prove that the proportion is true.

a. In any proportion, *the product of the means equals the product of the extremes.*

Example 1: 3:4 :: 9:12.

3 × 12 = 36 (product of extremes)

4 × 9 = 36 (product of means)

Example 2: $\frac{3}{4} = \frac{9}{12}$.

Note. When the proportion is expressed in fractional form, the numerator of one fraction is multiplied by the denominator of the other fraction. This process is called *cross-multiplication.*

3 × 12 = 36 (product of extremes)

4 × 9 = 36 (product of means)

b. In any proportion, *the product of the means divided by either extreme gives the other extreme.*

Example: 6:8 :: 18:24.

8 × 18 = 144 (product of means)

144 ÷ 6 = 24 (one extreme)

144 ÷ 24 = 6 (other extreme)

c. In any proportion, *the product of the extremes divided by either mean gives the other mean.*

Example: 5:7 :: 15:21

5 × 21 = 105 (product of extremes)

105 ÷ 7 = 15 (one mean)

105 ÷ 15 = 7 (other mean)

18. Solving for Unknown Term

As demonstrated in paragraph 49, the unknown term of a proportion can be determined if the other three terms are known.

Example 1: In the proportion $\frac{5}{10} = \frac{10}{y}$, solve for y (the unknown quantity).

Find the product of the means:

$$10 \times 10 = 100$$

Find the product of the extremes: $5 \times y = 5y$

The products of the means and extremes are equal: $5y = 100$

Divide both sides by 5:

$$\frac{\cancel{5}y}{\cancel{5}} = \frac{\overset{20}{\cancel{100}}}{\cancel{5}}$$
$$y = 20$$

Therefore, $\frac{5}{10} = \frac{10}{20}$.

Example 2: In the proportion 6:12 :: 24:y, solve for y.

Write the proportion in fractional form:

$$\frac{6}{12} = \frac{24}{y}$$

Cross-multiply.

$$6y = 288$$

Divide both sides by 6:

$$\frac{\cancel{6}y}{\cancel{6}} = \frac{\overset{48}{\cancel{288}}}{\cancel{6}}$$
$$y = 48$$

Therefore, 6:12 :: 24:48.

Example 3: In the proportion $\frac{z}{20} = \frac{5}{10}$, solve for z.

Cross-multiply.

$$10z = 100$$

Divide both sides by 10:

$$\frac{1\cancel{0}z}{1\cancel{0}} = \frac{1\overset{10}{\cancel{00}}}{1\cancel{0}}$$
$$z = 10$$

Therefore, $\frac{10}{20} = \frac{5}{10}$.

19. Stating Ratios for Problems in Proportion

When setting up a proportion problem, be sure to state the ratios correctly. Analyze each problem carefully to determine whether the unknown quantity will be greater or lesser than the known term of the ratio in which it occurs. Arrange the terms of the ratio as shown below, and solve for the unknown quantity as explained in paragraph 18.

$$\frac{LESSER}{GREATER} = \frac{LESSER}{GREATER}, \text{ or } LESSER : GREATER :: LESSER : GREATER$$

Example: The weight of 15 feet of iron pipe is 8 pounds.

What is the weight of 255 feet of the same pipe? Let the unknown quantity be represented by the letter y. Since ratios must express a relation between quantities of the same kind, one ratio must be between feet and feet and the other between pounds and pounds.

Study the problems; 255 feet of pipe will weigh more than 15 feet of pipe. Arrange the first ratio in the order LESSER to GREATER—15 feet: 255 feet, or $\frac{15}{255}$.

Arrange the second ratio in the same order—LESSER to GREATER—8 pounds: y pounds, or $\frac{8}{y}$.

Write the proportion and solve.

$15{:}255 = 8{:}y$, or
$\frac{15}{255} = \frac{8}{y}$
$15y = 255 \times 8$
$15y = 2040$
$y = \frac{2040}{15}$
$y = 136$ pounds

20. Inverse Proportion

a. The ratio 2:3 is the inverse of the ratio 3:2. In proportion, when a second ratio is equal to the inverse of the first ratio, the elements are said to be *inversely proportional.*

b. Two numbers are inversely proportional when one increases as the other decreases. In this case, their product is always the same. In problems dealing with pulleys, the speeds of different size pulleys connected by belts are inversely proportional to their diameters. A smaller pulley rotates faster than a larger pulley.

Example 1: A pulley 30 inches in diameter is turning at a speed of 300 revolutions per minute. If this pulley is belted to a pulley 15 inches in diameter (fig. 3), determine the speed at which the smaller pulley is turning.

Let the speed of the smaller pulley be represented by y. Study the problem; the first ratio will be between inches and the second will be between revolutions per minute (rpm). Also note that the second pulley is smaller than the first and must make more revolutions than the first. Therefore, the answer will be a number larger than 300.

Arrange the ratios in the order LESSER to GREATER.

First ratio:
$15{:}30$, or $\frac{15}{30}$

Second ratio:
$300{:}y$, or $\frac{300}{y}$

The proportion:
$15{:}30 = 300{:}y$, or $\frac{15}{30} = \frac{300}{y}$

Solve the proportion:
$\frac{15}{30} = \frac{300}{y}$
$15y = 300 \times 30$
$15y = 9000$
$y = \frac{9000}{15}$
$y = 600$ rpm

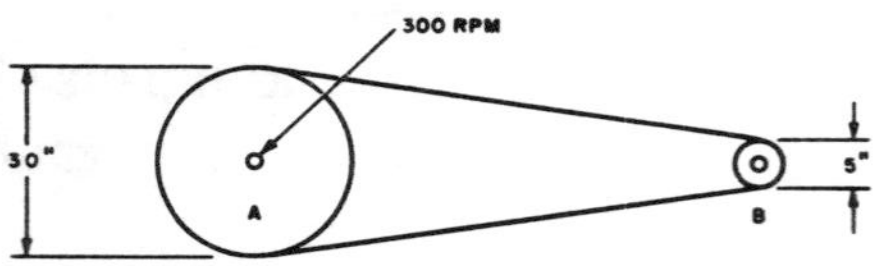

Example 2: A 24-inch pulley is fixed to a drive shaft that is turning at the rate of 400 rpm. This pulley is belted to a 6-inch pulley. Determine the speed of the smaller pulley in revolutions per minute.

Driving pulley (400 rpm, 24 inches in diameter).

Driven pulley (y rpm, 6 inches in diameter).

$\frac{6}{24} = \frac{400}{y}$
$6y = 400 \times 24 = 9,600$
$y = 1,600$ rpm

21. Problems Using Proportion

a. A steel plate ½ inch thick, 12 inches wide, and 9 feet long weighs 183.6 pounds. What is the weight of a piece of steel plate of the same thickness and width if it is 16 feet 6 inches long?

b. If three men complete a certain job in 8 days, how many days would it take seven men to complete the same job, considering that they will work at the same speed?

c. If 3 resistors cost 25 cents, find the cost of 60 resistors at the same rate?

d. If the upkeep on 62 trucks for a year is $3,100, what would be the upkeep on 28 such trucks for 1 year at the same rate?

e. At a given temperature, the resistance of a wire increases with its length. If the resistance of a wire per 1,000 feet at 68° F is .248 ohm, what is the resistance of 1,500 feet; of 1,200 feet; of 1,850 feet; of 3,600 feet?

f. If 21-gage wire weighs 2.452 pounds per 1,000 feet, what is the weight of 1,150 feet; 1,540 feet; 1,680 feet; 349 yards?

g. The speeds of gears running together are inversely proportional to the number of teeth in the gears. A driving gear with 48 teeth meshes with a driven gear with 16 teeth. If the driving gear turns at the rate of 100 rpm, how many rpm are made by the driven gear?

h. A 36-tooth gear running at a speed of 280 rpm drives another gear with 64 teeth. What is the speed of the other gear?

Figure 3. Pulleys and inverse ratio.

CHAPTER 4
POWERS AND ROOTS

22. Powers

There are many times in mathematics when a number must be multiplied by itself a number of times, such as $4 \times 4 \times 4 \times 4$. This is written as 4^5 and is described as 4 raised to the fifth power. A number multiplied by itself once is said to be raised to the second power (squared). Thus, 5×5 is written 5^2. The number 2, written to the right and above the number 5, is the *exponent*; the number 5 is the *base*. The base number is a *factor* of a number written in exponential form because the product is evenly divisible by the base.

23. Roots

The root of a number is that number which, when multiplied by itself a given number of times, will equal the given number. The square root of 25 is 5, since 5×5 or 5^2 equals 25. The third root (cube root) of 216 is 6, since $6 \times 6 \times 6$ or 6^3 equals 216. The fourth root of 81 is 3, since $3 \times 3 \times 3 \times 3$ or 3^4 equals 81. Extraction of a root is generally indicated by placing, in front of the number, a *radical sign* ($\sqrt{}$). A small figure is placed in the angle at the front of the sign to indicate the root to be taken. If the small figure is omitted, it is understood that the operation required is square root.

Thus,

$$\sqrt{25} = 5$$
$$\sqrt[3]{216} = 6$$
$$\sqrt[4]{81} = 3$$

24. Finding Square Root of a Number

a. Finding Square Root by Mental Calculation. In some instances, the square root can be determined mentally from a knowledge of common multiplication. For example, $\sqrt{25}$ is 5, since 5×5 or $5^2 = 25$. Similarly, $\sqrt{144}$ is 12, since 12×12 or $12^2 = 144$.

b. Finding Square Root by Arithmetical Process. In most cases, the square root of a number must be determined by a mathematical process. If the number is a perfect square, the square root will be an integral number; if the number is not a perfect square, the square root will be a continued decimal.

Example 1: Evaluate $\sqrt{3398.89}$.

Step 1. Starting at the decimal point, mark off the digits in pairs in both directions.

```
√33 98.89
```

Step 2. Place the decimal point for the answer directly above the decimal point that appears under the radical sign.

```
√33 98.89
```

Step 3. Determine by inspection the largest number that can be squared without exceeding the first pair of digits—33. The answer is 5, since the square of any number larger than 5 will be greater than 33. Place the 5 above the first pair of digits.

```
   5
 √33 98.89
```

Step 4. Square 5 to obtain 25, and place it under 33. Substract 25 from 33 and obtain 8. Bring down the next pair of digits—98.

```
   5
 √33 98.89
   25
   898
```

Step 5. Double the answer, 5, to obtain a trial divisor of 10. Divide the trial divisor into all but the last digit of the modified remainer. It will go into 89 eight times. Place the 8 above the second pair of digits, and also place the 8 to the right of the trail divisor. Thus, the true divisor is 108. Multiply 108 by 8 and obtain 864. Subtract 864 from 898 to obtain 34. Bring down the next pair of digits—89.

```
        5  8.
      √33 98.89
        25
        898
        864
        3489
2 × 5 = 10 8 =
   8 × 108 =
```

Note. With each new successive digit in the answer:

1. Place the digit in the answer above the pair of digits involved.
2. Place the same digit to the right of the trial divisor to obtain the true divisor.
3. Multiply the digit by the true divisor. (Do not use the square boxes in actual problems.)

Step 6. Double the answer, 58, to obtain a trial divisor of 116. Divide the trial divisor into all but the last digit of the remainder. It will go into 348 three times. Place the 3 above the third pair of digits, and also place the 3 to the right of the trial divisor. Thus, the true divisor is 1163. Multiply 1163 by 3 to obtain 3489. Subtract 3489 from 3489. There is no remainder. Therefore 3398.89 is a perfect square and its square root is 58.3.

Step 7. Check the answer by squaring 58.3—$58.3^2 = 3398.89$. The complete calculation is shown below:

```
          5  8. 3
        √33 98.89
          25
          898
          864
          3489
          3489
2 × 58 = 116 3
   3 × 1163 =
```

Example 2: Evaluate $\sqrt{786.308}$.

Step 1. Starting at the decimal point, mark off the digits in pairs in both directions.

```
√07 86.80 80
```

Note. The extreme left-hand group may have only one digit. However, there must be an even number of digits to the right of the decimal point. If necessary, add a zero.

Step 2. Place the decimal point for the answer directly above the decimal point that appears under the radical sign.

Step 3. Determine the largest number that can be squared without exceeding the first digit—7. The answer is 2, since the square of any whole number larger than 2 will be greater than 7. Place the 2 above the 7.

```
  2
√07 86.80 80
```

Step 4. Square 2 to obtain 4 and place it under 7. Subtract 4 from 7 to obtain 3. Bring down the next pair of digits—86.

```
  2
√07 86.80 80
  4
  386
```

Step 5. Double the answer, 2, to obtain a trial divisor of 4. Divide the trial divisor into all but the last digit of the modified remainder. It will go into 38 nine times. Place the 9 above the second pair of digits, and also place the 9 to the right of the trial divisor. The true divisor is 49. Multiply 49 by 9 to obtain 441. However,

```
          5  8. 8
        √33 98.89
          25
  5 × 5 = |   898
2 × 5 = 10 8 | 864
   8 × 108 = | 3489
2 × 58 = 116 3 | 3489
   3 × 1163 =
```

441 cannot be subtracted from 386, so the next lower digit must be tried. Substitute 8 for 9 in both the answer and the divisor and multiply 48 by 8 to obtain 384. Subtract 384 from 386 to obtain a remainder of 2. Bring down the next pair of digits—80.

```
        2  8.  9.
  √07 86.80 80
    4
    386
    441
```

$2 \times 2 = 4\ \boxed{9}$
$\boxed{9} \times 49 =$

```
        2  8.
  √07 86.80 80
    4
    386
    384
    280
```

$4\ \boxed{8}$
$\boxed{8} \times 48 =$

Step 6. Double the answer, 28, to obtain a trial divisor of 56. Divide the trial divisor into all but the last digit of the remainder. Since it is not possible to divide 56 into 28, place a zero above the third pair of digits and bring down the next pair of digits—80.

```
        2  8.  0
  √07 86.80 80
    4
    386
    384
    280
```

$2 \times 28 = 56$

Step 7. Multiply 280 by 2 to obtain a trial divisor of 560. Divide the trial divisor into all but the last digit of the remainder. It will go 5 times. Place the 5 above the fourth pair of digits, and also place the 5 to the right of the trial divisor. Thus, the true divisor is 5605. Multiply 5605 by 5 to obtain 28025. Subtract 28025 from 28080. There is a remainder of 55. Thus, the square root of 786.808 is 28.05, with a remainder of 55. A more exact answer can be obtained by adding pairs of zeros and continuing the square root process.

```
        2  8.  0  5
  √07 86.80 80
    4
    386
    384
    28080
    28025
       55
```

$2 \times 280 = 560\ \boxed{5}$
$\boxed{5} \times 5605 =$

Check the answer by squaring 28.05 and adding the remainder ($28.05^2 + .0055$). Place the extreme right digit of the remainder under the extreme right digit of the squared number. The complete calculation is shown below:

```
        2  8.  0  5
  √07 86.80 80
    4
    386
    384
    28080
    26025
       55
```

$2 \times 2 = 4\ \boxed{8}$
$\boxed{8} \times 48 =$
$2 \times 28 = 56$
$2 \times 280 = 560\ \boxed{5}$
$\boxed{5} \times 5605 =$

25. Review Problems—Square Root

a. Solve the following:

(1) $\sqrt{441}$
(2) $\sqrt{1089}$
(3) $\sqrt{2500}$
(4) $\sqrt{8.40}$
(5) $\sqrt{2510.01}$
(6) $\sqrt{4901.4001}$
(7) $\sqrt{7482.25}$
(8) $\sqrt{5759.2921}$

b. Solve the following to nearest thousandth.

(1) $\sqrt{5}$
(2) $\sqrt{7}$
(3) $\sqrt{11}$
(4) $\sqrt{13}$
(5) $\sqrt{15}$
(6) $\sqrt{17}$

c. The current (in amperes) flowing through a resistor can be determined by taking the square root of the quotient obtained by dividing the value of power supplied to the resistor (in watts) by value of the resistance (in ohms). Thus, if a resistance of 300 ohms is absorbing 60 watts of power, it is drawing a current of $\sqrt{\dfrac{60}{300}}$ amperes. This equals about .447 ampere. In the same manner, find the value of current for each of the following values of power and resistance:

	Power (watts)	Resistance (ohms)	Current (amperes)
(1)	25	1,000	?
(2)	50	7,000	?
(3)	40	500	?
(4)	75	60	?

8

CHAPTER 5

ALGEBRA

Section I. INTRODUCTION

26. General

a. Algebra is an extension of arithmetic. All of the four basic operations of arithmetic—addition, subtraction, multiplication and division—apply also to algebra. Arithmetic deals only with particular numbers; algebra may also employ letters or symbols to represent numbers.

b. Algebra is often referred to as the shorthand language of mathematicians. The simplest example of the algebraic language is the formula, in which letters are used to represent words or numbers. For example, the area (A) of a rectangle can be determined by multiplying the length (l) by the width (w). Algebraically, this is stated as $A = lw$.

27. Algebraic Expressions and Terms

a. An *algebraic expression* is the representation of any quantity in algebraic signs and symbols; for example, $2x - 7$. A *numerical algebraic expression* consists entirely of numerals and signs, such as $8 - (6 \times 2)$. A *literal algebraic expression* contains only letters and symbols, such as $ax - ay$.

b. Each algebraic expression contains two or more terms, separated by one of the signs of operation $(+, -, \div, \times)$. The expression $3x - 4xy - 2y$, for example, contains three terms: $3x$, $4xy$, and $2y$. If the terms have the same letters and exponents, such as $3a^2x$, $9a^2x$, and $12a^2x$, they are called *similar terms*. Terms that do not contain the same letters and exponents, such as $3ab^2$, $3a^2b$, and $3x^2y$, are *dissimilar terms*.

c. If an algebraic expression contains one term, such as $3abc$ or $5a^2x^2$, it is called a *monomial*; if it contains two terms, such as $x - y$,

it is called a *binomial*; and if it contains three terms, such as $5x^2 - 3xy - 2y^2$, it is called a *trinomial*. A more general rule of algebraic expressions states that any expression containing more than one term is called a *polynomial*.

28. Signs of Operation

In algebra, the conventional signs of operation $(+, -, \times$ and $\div)$ retain the same meaning as in arithmetic. In algebra, however, certain other signs may be used.

a. *Multiplication* may be indicated as follows:

Arithmetic	Algebra
$a \times b$	ab
$a \times b$	$a \cdot b$
$a \times b$	$(a)(b)$

b. *Division* may be indicated as follows:

Arithmetic	Algebra
$x \div y$	$\dfrac{x}{y}$
$(a + b) \div (a - b)$	$\dfrac{a+b}{a-b}$

c. The arithmetical signs for both *addition* and *subtraction* are retained in algebra.

Arithmetic	Algebra
$4 + 5$	$4 + 5$
$a - b$	$a - b$

29. Coefficients

Any factor of a product is known as a coefficient of the remaining factors. In the term $2\pi f$, 2 is the numerical coefficient of πf, f is the coefficient of 2π, and π is the coefficient of $2f$. However, it is common practice to speak of the numerical part of the term as the coefficient. If a term contains no numerical coefficient, the number 1 is understood. Thus, abc is $1\ abc$, and xyz is $1\ xyz$.

30. Subscripts

In expression such as $R_1 = R_1 + R_2 + R_3$, the small numbers or letters written to the right and below the literal terms are called subscripts. Subscripts are used to designate different values of a variable quantity. They are read: R sub 1, R sub 2, etc.

31. The Radical Sign

The radical sign ($\sqrt{}$) has the same meaning in algebra as in arithmetic (ch. 5). Thus, the expression $z = 2\sqrt{R^2 + x^2}$ states that z is equal to 2 times the square root of $R^2 + x^2$.

Section II. POSITIVE AND NEGATIVE NUMBERS

32. Signed Numbers

Only positive numbers are used in arithmetical operations, but both *positive* and *negative* numbers may appear in algebraic expressions. The plus sign ($+$) is used to indicate a positive number and the minus sign ($-$) to indicate a negative number. If the sign is omitted, the number is understood to be positive. Positive and negative numbers are called *signed numbers*.

33. Need for Negative Numbers

The need for negative numbers may be seen from the succession of subtraction below:

$$
\begin{array}{cccccccc}
6 & 6 & 6 & 6 & 6 & 6 & 6 & 6 \\
-0 & -1 & -2 & -3 & -4 & -5 & -6 & -7 & -8 & -9 \\
\hline
6 & 5 & 4 & 3 & 2 & 1 & 0 & -1 & -2 & -3
\end{array}
$$

When the subtrahend is greater than the minuend, the difference becomes less than zero and the negative sign is placed before the difference. Thus, a negative number may be defined as a number less than zero.

34. Application of Positive and Negative Numbers

In technical work, many scales are calibrated above and below (or to the right and left of)

a center point designated 0 (zero). For example, the degrees of temperature indicated on a thermometer scale are measurements of distance taken on a scale in opposite directions from some point chosen to represent a reference or zero point. Temperature is always so many degrees above or below zero. In mathematics, it is convenient to indicate that a temperature is so many degrees above or below zero by prefixing the reading with a positive or negative sign. Thus, 45° above zero is $+45°$ and 15° below zero is $-15°$. Similarly, in electronic and electrical measuring instruments, scales are often calibrated to read positive numbers on one side of a zero and negative numbers on the other.

35. Graphical Representation of Positive and Negative Numbers

a. *Principle.* Positive and negative numbers may be represented graphically as shown in figure 4. The zero is the reference point. This graph can be used to illustrate both addition and subtraction.

b. *Addition.* To add numbers graphically, start at the zero reference point and mark off the first number, going to the right if the number is positive, or to the left if the number is

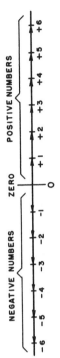

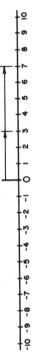

Figure 4. Graphical representation of positive and negative numbers.

Figure 5. Graphical representation of addition of positive numbers.

Figure 6. Graphical representation of addition of negative numbers (—1 and —5).

Figure 7. Graphical representation of addition of negative numbers (—3 and —2).

negative. From this new point, mark off the second number, again going to the right if the number is positive, or to the left if it is negative. The number of units between zero and the final point is the sum of the two numbers. This procedure can be continued for more than two numbers. Figure 5 shows graphical addition of positive numbers; figures 6 and 7 show graphical addition of negative numbers; and figure 8 shows the addition of a combination of a positive and a negative number. Figures 6 and 7 show that the order in which the negative numbers are taken does not affect the answer.

c. Subtraction. To subtract numbers graphically, change the sign of the subtrahend (number to be subtracted) and proceed as for addition. Figure 9 shows the subtraction of +3 from +5 to obtain the difference of +2.

36. Absolute Value of a Number

The numerical value of a number, without regard to its sign, is called the *absolute value* of the number. Thus, the absolute value of —3 or +3 is 3. This is written |3|.

37. Addition of Positive and Negative Numbers

a. Positive Numbers. To add two or more positive numbers, find the sum of their absolute values and prefix the sum with a plus sign. When there is no possibility of misunderstanding, the plus sign is usually omitted.

Example: Add +4, +5, and +6
$$+4 + (+5) + (+6) = +15 \text{ or } 15$$

b. Negative Numbers. To add two or more negative numbers, find the sum of their absolute values and prefix the sum with a minus sign.

Example: Add —4, —5, and —6
$$-4 + (-5) + (-6) = -15$$

c. Positive and Negative Numbers. To add a positive and a negative number, find the difference between their absolute values and prefix the sum with the sign of the number that has the greater absolute value. This is called *algebraic addition.* When three or more positive and negative numbers are to be added, first find the sum of all positive numbers, and then the sum of all negative numbers. Add these sums algebraically as above.

Example 1: Add +6 and —9.
$$+6 + (-9) = -3$$

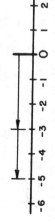

Figure 8. Graphical representation of addition of positive and negative numbers.

Example 2: Add +5, —8, +12, and —6.
$$+5 + (+12) = +17$$
$$-8 + (-6) = -14$$
$$(+17) + (-14) = +3$$

38. Subtraction of Positive and Negative Numbers

To subtract positive and negative numbers, change the sign of the subtrahend and proceed as in addition (par. 37).

a. Positive Numbers.

Example 1: Subtract +2 from +5.
$$+5 - (+2) = +5 - 2 = +3$$
or 3

Example 2: Subtract +5a² from +6a².
$$+6a^2 - (+5a^2) = +6a^2 - 5a^2$$
$$= +1a^2 = a^2$$

b. Negative Numbers.

Example 1: Subtract —3 from —5.
$$-5 - (-3) = -5 + 3 = -2$$

Example 2: Subtract —4a from —2a.
$$-2a - (-4a) = -2a + 4a =$$
+2a or 2a

c. Positive and Negative Numbers.

Example 1: Subtract —2 from +5.
$$+5 - (-2) = +5 + 2 = +7$$
or 7.

Example 2: Subtract —3x² from +5x².
$$+5x^2 - (-3x^2) = +5x^2 + 3x^2$$
$$= +8x^2 \text{ or } 8x^2$$

39. Multiplication of Positive and Negative Numbers

a. Numbers Having Like Signs. If the two numbers to be multiplied have the same signs, the product is positive.

Example 1: Multiply +5 by +3.
$$(+5)(+3) = +15 \text{ or } 15$$

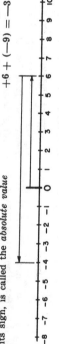
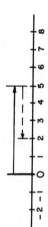

Figure 9. Graphical representation of subtraction of positive numbers.

Example 2: Multiply —5 by —3.
$$(-5)(3-3) = +15 \text{ or } 15$$

b. Numbers Having Unlike Signs. If the two numbers to be multiplied have unlike signs, the product is negative.

Example 1: Multiply —5 by +3.
$$(-5)(+3) = -15$$

Example 2: Multiply +5 by —3.
$$(+5)(-3) = -15$$

c. Several Positive and Negative Numbers. To multiply several positive and negative numbers, multiply the numbers in groups of two in the order in which they appear.

Example 1:
Multiply (—5)(+3)(+7)(—2)(—4).
$$
\begin{array}{llll}
(-5)(+3) & (+7)(-2) & (-4) \\
= (-15) & (-14) & (-4) \\
= & (+210) & (-4) \\
= & & -840
\end{array}
$$

Example 2:
Multiply (+7)(+2)(—5)(—3)(—1)(—4).
$$
\begin{array}{llll}
= (+7)(+2) & (-5)(-3) & (-1)(-4) \\
= (+14) & (+15) & (+4) \\
= & (+210) & (+4) \\
= & & 840
\end{array}
$$

40. Division of Positive and Negative Numbers

a. Numbers Having Like Signs. The quotient of two numbers that have the same signs is positive.

Example 1: Divide —15 by —5.
$$-15 \div -5 = +3 \text{ or } 3$$

Example 2: Divide +24 by +6.
$$+24 \div +6 = +4 \text{ or } 4$$

b. Numbers Having Unlike Signs. The quotient of two numbers that have opposite signs is negative.

Example 1: Divide 35 by —7.
$$+35 \div -7 = -5$$

Example 2: Divide —8,988 by 28.
$$-8988 \div 28 = -321$$

10

41. Order of Signs

When only addition and subtraction signs appear in a series of terms, addition and subtraction procedures may be performed in any order. However, when multiplication and division signs appear in the same series with addition and subtraction signs, the multiplication and division must be performed first, and then the addition and subtraction.

Example 1: Evaluate $15 + 5 - 3 + 4 - 8$.

Step 1. Add the + terms:
$15 + 5 + 4 = 24$

Step 2. Add the — terms:
$(-3) + (-8) = -11$

Step 3. Add the + terms and — terms algebraically:
$24 - 11 = 13$

Example 2: Evaluate $9 \times 4 + 6 - 3 + 5 \times 2$.

Step 1. Perform the multiplication first:
$(9 \times 4) + 6 - 3 + (5 \times 2) =$
$(36) + 6 - 3 + (10)$

Step 2. Add the + terms:
$36 + 6 + 10 = 52$

Step 3. Add the + terms and the — terms algebraically:
$52 - 3 = 49$

Example 3: Evaluate $81 \div 9 - 3 + 6 - 15 + 4 \times 5$.

Step 1. Perform the division:
$(81 \div 9) - 3 + 6 - 15 + (4 \times 5) = (9) - 3 + 6 - 15 + (4 \times 5)$

Step 2. Perform the multiplication:
$9 - 3 + 6 - 15 + (4 \times 5) = 9 - 3 + 6 - 15 + (20)$

Step 3. Add the + terms:
$9 + 6 + 20 = 35$

Step 4. Add the — terms:
$(-3) + (-15) = -18$

Step 5. Add the ÷ terms and the — terms algebraically:
$35 - 18 = 17$.

42. Review Problems—Positive and Negative Numbers

a. Add the following:
(1) 23 and —6
(2) 21 and 37
(3) —54 and 33
(4) —43° and —96°
(5) 682 volts and —934 volts

b. Subtract the following:
(1) —104 amperes from 147 amperes
(2) —37 volts from —45 volts
(3) .64cy from .0025cy
(4) $21.36az^2$ from $-10.63az^2$
(5) $-.986x^2y$ from $.824x^2y$

c. Find the product of the following:
(1) —6.4 and 2.8
(2) 3, —6, and 4
(3) $\frac{2}{3}$, $\frac{6}{7}$, and $\frac{2}{5}$
(4) 3.01, —.02, and —1.26
(5) —.0025, 150, —.10, and .075
(6) —2, 5, 3, —1, and 4

d. Divide:
(1) 36 by 4
(2) $-\frac{5}{7}$ by $\frac{3}{4}$
(3) —5.6 by —.008
(4) —750 by —3
(5) $\frac{1}{3}$ ampere by $\frac{1}{2}$ ampere
(6) —.3750 by 150

e. Evaluate the following:
(1) $2 + 3 - 9$
(2) $3 + 4 + 2 \times 5 - 3$
(3) $2 - 3 \times 9$
(4) $3 \times 4 + 2 \times 5 - 3$
(5) $5 + 3 \times 7 - 2 \times 11 + 7$
(6) $28 \div 14 - 8 + 16 + 3 \times 2$
(7) $46 - 18 + 3 \times 4 - 8 + 12$
(8) $5 - 3 + 6 \times 4 + 40$
(9) $8 - 16 + 4 \times 3 - 10 \times 5$
(10) $15 \div 5 - 3 + 2 \times 10 - 2$

Section III. FUNDAMENTAL OPERATIONS

43. Addition and Subtraction of Algebraic Expressions

a. *General.* Only similar algebraic terms—those that are exactly alike in all respects other than numerical coefficients—may be added or subtracted. For example, the sum of $3x^2y$ and $5x^2y$ is $8x^2y$. Dissimilar terms cannot be added or subtracted directly, but the processes of addition or subtraction can be indicated by the use of plus or minus signs. For example, the sum of $4x^2y$ and $2xy^2$ is $4x^2y + 2xy^2$.

b. *Procedure.* To add or subtract algebraic expressions, arrange the terms so that like terms are in the same vertical column, and preferably in descending order of powers. Add or subtract the terms according to the rules of signed numbers (pars. 37 and 38).

Example 1: Add $x^3 - 3x^2 + 1$, $x^3 + x - 3$, and $x^2 + x + 1$.

$$
\begin{aligned}
x^3 &- 3x^2 && + 1 \\
x^3 & && + x - 3 \\
& + x^2 && + x + 1 \\ \hline
2x^3 &- 2x^2 && + 2x - 1
\end{aligned}
$$

Example 2: Subtract $x^3 + 3x^2 - x + 1$ from $x^4 + x^3 - x + 2$.

$$
\begin{aligned}
x^4 + x^3 && - x + 2 \\
-(x^3 - 3x^2 && - x + 1)
\end{aligned}
$$

Remove parentheses and change signs.

$$
\begin{aligned}
x^4 + x^3 && - x + 2 \\
- x^3 - 3x^2 && - x + 1 \\ \hline
x^4 \quad\;\; - 3x^2 && - 2x + 3
\end{aligned}
$$

44. Multiplication and Division of Monomials

a. *Multiplication.* In multiplying monomials, multiply the numerical coefficients and write this result as the coefficient of the product. After the coefficient, write each literal factor with an exponent equal to the sum of all the exponents of that letter in the original factors. For example, $3a^n \cdot 2a^m = 6a^{n+m}$.

Example 1: Multiply x^2 by x^3.
$x^2 \cdot x^3 = x^{2+3} = x^5$

Example 2: Multiply x, x^3, and x^{10}.
$x^1 \cdot x^3 \cdot x^{10} = x^{1+3+10} = x^{14}$

Example 3: Multiply x^3y^6 by $3xy^2$.

Step 1. Multiply the coefficients:
$1 \cdot 3 = 3$

Step 2. Multiply the two factors having the base x:
$x^3 \cdot x = x^{3+1} = x^4$

Step 3. Multiply the two factors having the base y:
$y^6 \cdot y^2 = y^{6+2} = y^8$

Step 4. The product is:
$3x^3y^6 \cdot 3xy^2 = 3x^4y^8$

Example 4: Multiply x^2y^2z and wx^3y^5.

$x^2y^2z \cdot wx^3y^5 = wx^{2+3}y^{2+1+1}z^{1+5}$
$x^{2+3} = x^5$
$y^{4+1} = y^5$
$z^{1+5} = z^6$
Therefore, $x^2y^2z \cdot wx^3y^5 = wx^5y^5z^6$.

b. *Division.* In dividing a monomial by a monomial, divide the numerical coefficient of the dividend by the coefficient of the divisor and write the result as the coefficient of the quotient. After the coefficient, write each literal factor with an exponent equal to its exponent in the dividend minus its exponent in the divisor. Thus, to divide $6a^n$ by $3a^m$ (n greater than m), $\frac{6a^n}{3a^m} = 2a^{n-m}$.

Example 1: Divide x^3 by x^2.
$\frac{x^3}{x^2} = x^{3-2} = x^1 = x$

Example 2: Divide $5x^6yz^3$ by $6x^3z^2$.
$\frac{5x^6yz^3}{6x^3z^2} = \frac{5}{6}x^{6-3}yz^{3-2}$
$= \frac{5}{6}x^3yz$ or $\frac{5x^3yz}{6}$

c. *Removal of Parentheses and Brackets.*

(1) In multiplying a quantity in parentheses by a given factor, multiply each term inside the parentheses by that factor and drop the parentheses. If the factor is a negative quantity, the sign of every term inside the parentheses is changed. For example, $-5(a - b + c) = -5a + 5b - 5c$.

(2) When an algebraic expression, such as $5x - 4[x - 2(x - 3)]$, has more than one grouping symbol (parentheses and brackets), remove the inside grouping symbol first and then successively remove the outer grouping symbols.

Example 1: Simplify $5x — 4[x — 2(x — 3)]$.
$$5x — 4[x — 2(x — 3)] = 5x — 4[x — 2x + 6]$$
$$= 5x — 4x + 8x — 24$$
$$= 9x — 24$$
$$= 3(3x — 8)$$

Example 2: Simplify $4a — \{6a — 2b + 2[2a — b + 42] — (c + 2b)\}$.
$$4a — \{6a — 2b + 2[2a — b + 42] — (c + 2b)\}$$
$$= 4a — \{6a — 2b + 4a — 2b + 84 — c — 2b\}$$
$$= 4a — 6a + 2b — 4a + 2b — 84 + c + 2b$$
$$= —6a + 6b + c — 84$$

Example 3: Simplify $—\{—1[—(x — y — z) + 29] — 39 + 2y — z\}$.
$$= —\{—1[—(x — y — z) + 29] — 39 + 2y — z\}$$
$$= —\{—1[—x + y + z + 29] — 39 + 2y — z\}$$
$$= —\{+ x — y — z — 29 — 39 + 2y — z\}$$
$$= — x + y + z + 29 + 39 — 2y + z$$
$$= — x — y + 2z + 68$$

45. Raising Algebraic Functions to Powers

To raise an algebraic function to a power, multiply the exponents. Thus, $(a^n)^m = a^{nm}$.

Example 1: Simplify $(5^3)^4$.
$$(5^3)^4 = 5^{3.4} = 5^{12}$$

Example 2: Simplify $(2ab)^3$.
$$(2ab)^3 = 2ab \cdot 2ab \cdot 2ab = 8a^3 b^3$$
$$\text{or } 2^{1.3}a^{1.3}b^{1.3} = 8a^3b^3$$

Example 3: Simplify $(ax^2)^3$.
$$(ax^2)^3 = a^{1.3}x^{2.3} = a^3x^6$$

Example 4: Simplify $[(x^3)^4]^5$.
$$[(x^3)^4]^5 = [x^{3.4}]^5 = [x^{12}]^5 = x^{12.5} = x^{60}$$

Example 5: Simplify $\left(\dfrac{2}{x^2}\right)^5$
$$\left(\frac{2}{x^2}\right)^5 = \frac{2^{1.5}}{x^{2.5}} = \frac{2^5}{x^{10}} = \frac{32}{x^{10}}$$

46. Negative Exponents

The rule for dividing monomials (par. 44b) also holds when the exponents of the denominator is greater than the exponent of the numerator. For example, $a^3 \div a^5 = a^{3-5} = a^{-2}$; however, a quantity such as a^{-2} may be written as $\frac{1}{a^2}$.

Example: Multiply x^2, x^{-1}, and $\frac{1}{x^3}$.

Step 1. Write down the factors of the multiplication:
$$x^2 \cdot x^{-1} \cdot \frac{1}{x^3}$$

Step 2. Place all factors in the numerator:
$$x^2 \cdot x^{-1} \cdot x^3$$

Step 3. Multiply the factors (add their exponents):
$$x^{2-1+3} = x^4$$

47. Zero Exponents

The zero power of any quantity is equal to 1. For example $x^2 \cdot x^{-2} = x^0$ when the exponents are added. However, x^{-2} can also be written $\frac{1}{x^2}$; in this case, $x^2 \cdot x^{-2} = \frac{x^2}{x^2} = 1$.

Therefore, $x^0 = 1$. Any number (except zero) raised to the zero power is equal to 1.

Example: Solve $\dfrac{x^2y^3}{z} \cdot \dfrac{z^4}{xy} \div \dfrac{x^2y^2}{z^3}$.
$$\frac{x^2y^3}{z} \cdot \frac{z^4}{xy} \div \frac{x^2y^2}{z^3} = \frac{x^2y^3z^4}{xyz} \div \frac{x^2y^2}{z^3}$$
$$= \frac{x^2y^3z^4}{xyz} \div \frac{x^2y^2}{z^3} = x^{2-3}y^{3-3}z^{7-1}$$
$$= x^{-1}y^0z^6 = x^{-1} \cdot 1 \cdot z^6 = \frac{z^6}{x}$$

48. Multiplication of Polynomials

a. By a Monomial. To multiply a polynomial by a monomial, multiply each term in the polynomial separately by the monomial and add the products. Observe the rules for the multiplication of signed numbers (par. 39) and exponents (par. 44a).

Example 1: Multiply $3a + 2ab + 5c$ by $2b$.
$$3a + 2ab + 5c$$
$$2b$$
$$\overline{6ab + 4ab^2 + 10bc}$$

Example 2: Multiply $ad — ae + af$ by $3a^2$.
$$ad — ae + af$$
$$3a^2$$
$$\overline{3a^3d — 3a^3e + 3a^3f}$$

Example 3: Multiply $3x^2y^2 — 2xy^3 + 5x^4y$ by $4x^3y$.
$$3x^2y^2 — 2xy^3 + 5x^4y$$
$$4x^3y$$
$$\overline{12x^5y^3 — 8x^4y^4 + 20x^7y^2}$$

b. By a Polynomial. To multiply a polynomial by another polynomial, multiply each term of the one polynomial by each term of the other and add the products.

Example 1: Multiply $(a + b)$ by $(a + b)$.
$$a + b$$
$$a + b$$
$$\overline{a^2 + ab}$$
$$ab + b^2$$
$$\overline{a^2 + 2ab + b^2}$$

Example 2: Multiply $2x + 3y$ by $2x + 3z$.
$$2x + 3y$$
$$2x + 3z$$
$$\overline{4x^2 + 6xy}$$
$$+ 6xz + 9yz$$
$$\overline{4x^2 + 6xy + 6xz + 9yz}$$

Example 3: Multiply $5x^2 — 6xy + 3y^2$ by $x + y$.
$$5x^2 — 6xy + 3y^2$$
$$x + y$$
$$\overline{5x^3 — 6x^2y + 3xy^2}$$
$$+ 5x^2y — 6xy^2 + 3y^3$$
$$\overline{5x^3 — x^2y — 3xy^2 + 3y^3}$$

49. Division of Polynomials

a. By a Monomial. To divide a polynomial by a monomial, divide each term of the polynomial by the monomial.

Example 1: Divide $3a^2 + 4ab + 5ac$ by a.
$$\frac{3a^2 + 4ab + 5ac}{a} = 3a + 4b + 5c$$

Example 2: Divide $7x^2 + 14xy — 21ax^2$ by $7x$.
$$\frac{7x^2 + 14xy — 21ax^2}{7x} = x + 2y — 3ax$$

Example 3: Divide $4r(s + t) — r^3(s + t)^2 + qr^2(s + t)^3$ by $r^2(s + t)$.
$$\frac{4r(s + t) — r^3(s + t)^2 + qr^2(s + t)^3}{r^2(s + t)}$$
$$= \frac{4r(s + t)}{r^2(s + t)} — \frac{r^3(s + t)^2}{r^2(s + t)} + \frac{qr^2(s + t)^3}{r^2(s + t)}$$
$$= \frac{4}{r} — r(s + t) + q(s + t)^2$$

b. By a Polynomial. To divide a polynomial by a polynomial, just arrange the dividend and the divisor according to descending powers of one variable, starting with the highest powers at the left. Then proceed as shown in the examples below. If there is a remainder, write it as the numerator of a fraction the denominator of which is the divisor.

Example 1: Divide $ab + ac + db + dc$ by $a + d$.

Step 1. Divide the first term of the divisor, a, into the first term of the dividend, ab. The quantity a is contained in the first term, ab, b times. Write b as the first term of the quotient.

$$\begin{array}{r} b\phantom{+d\overline{)ab+ac+db+dc}} \\ a+d\,\overline{)\,ab+ac+db+dc} \end{array}$$

Step 2. Multiply both terms of the divisor by b:

$$\begin{array}{r} b\phantom{+d\overline{)ab+ac+db+dc}} \\ a+d\,\overline{)\,ab+ac+db+dc} \\ ab +db \end{array}$$

Step 3. Subtract the result from the original dividend:

$$\begin{array}{r} b\phantom{+d\overline{)ab+ac+db+dc}} \\ a+d\,\overline{)\,ab+ac+db+dc} \\ ab +db \\ \hline ac +dc \end{array}$$

Step 4. Divide the first term of the divisor into the first term of the

remainder. It is contained in the first term, ac, c times. Write c as the second term of the quotient.

$$\begin{array}{r} b+c\phantom{\overline{)ab+ac+db+dc}} \\ a+d\,\overline{)\,ab+ac+db+dc} \\ ab +db \\ \hline ac +dc \end{array}$$

Step 5. Multiply both terms of the divisor by c and subtract. There is no remainder:

$$\begin{array}{r} b+c\phantom{\overline{)ab+ac+db+dc}} \\ a+d\,\overline{)\,ab+ac+db+dc} \\ ab +db \\ \hline ac +dc \\ ac +dc \end{array}$$

Step 6. Therefore,
$$\frac{ab+ac+db+dc}{a+d} = b+c.$$

Example 2: Divide $x^2 + 2xy + y^2$ by $x + y$.

$$\begin{array}{r} x+y\phantom{\overline{)x^2+2xy+y^2}} \\ x+y\,\overline{)\,x^2+2xy+y^2} \\ x^2+xy \\ \hline xy+y^2 \\ xy+y^2 \end{array}$$

Therefore,
$$\frac{x^2+2xy+y^2}{x+y} = x+y.$$

Step 4. Divide the first term of the divisor into the first term of the

Example 3: Divide $6a^2 - ab - 27ac - 15b^2 + 7bc + 30c^2$ by $3a - 5b - 6c$.

$$\begin{array}{r} 2a+3b-5c\phantom{\overline{)6a^2-ab-27ac-15b^2+7bc+30c^2}} \\ 3a-5b-6c\,\overline{)\,6a^2-ab-27ac-15b^2+7bc+30c^2} \\ 6a^2-10ab-12ac \\ \hline 9ab-15ac-15b^2+7bc+30c^2 \\ 9ab -15b^2-18bc \\ \hline -15ac +25bc+30c^2 \\ -15ac +25bc+30c^2 \end{array}$$

50. Review Problems—Fundamental Operations

a. Add the following algebraic expressions:

(1) $2a^4 + 3a^2b^3 + 5b^4$, $a^v - 5a^2b^2 - 2b^4$, and $3a^4 - 2a^2b^2 + b^4$.

(2) $3E - 2RI - 15ZI$, $6RI + 24ZI$, and $-2E - RI + 11ZI$.

(3) $10w - 4x + 3y + 6z$, $2x - 5w + y$, $3z - 2x - y$, and $6y - 4w - z + 5x$.

b. Subtract the following algebraic expressions:

(1) $-7ax - 2by + cz$ from $12ax + 15by - 8cz$.

(2) $10w - 3y - 4z + 6x$ from $3x + 5y - 2z - 15w$.

(3) $8a^2 + 10ab - 4b^2$ from $12a^2 - 24ab + 2b^2$.

c. Simplify:

(1) $7a^0$

(2) $(5x + 9)^0$

(3) $(3x^2 + 7x + 1)^0$

d. Perform the indicated operations:

(1) $f^6 \cdot f^4$

(2) $y^a \cdot y^b$

(3) $y^{a+1} \cdot y^{a-1}$

(4) $\dfrac{r^{10}}{r^6}$

(5) $(R^3)^m$

(6) $\dfrac{r^{m+5}}{r^4}$

e. Express with positive exponents:

(1) $4z^{-4}$

(2) $r^{-3}x^{-4}$

(3) $(6a)^{-2b}$

(4) $I^{-2}R^{-1}$

(5) $2^{-3}a^2b^{-3}$

(6) $\dfrac{3EI^{-2}R^{-1}}{4}$

f. Perform the indicated operations:

(1) $(5ab)(2a^2 - 3ab + 7b^4)$

(2) $4a(a^2 + 3a + 1)$

(3) $(i^2 + 3i + 9)(i - 3)$

(4) $(2x^2 + 3xy - y^2)(x^2 + xy + y^4)$

(5) $(3x^2 - 2xy - 5y^2)(3x^2 + 2xy - 5y^4)$

(6) $[(x-1)a - (x-1)c] \div [(x-1)\,ac]$

(7) $(3rL - rR^2) \div rR$

(8) $(5a^4b - 10a^3b^2 + 15a^2b^4) \div 5a^2b$

(9) $(1 + 2x^4 + 4z^2 - z^3 + 7z) \div (3 + z^2 - z)$

(10) $(100b^3 - 13b^2 - 3b) \div (3 + 25b)$

Section IV. FACTORING

51. Understanding Factoring

Factoring is the breaking up of an expression into the *factors* or *individual parts* of which it is composed. In other words, to factor an algebraic expression means to find two or more expressions which, when multiplied together, will result in the original expression. For example, since $3 \cdot 5 = 15$, 3 and 5 are the factors of 15; since $4 \cdot b = 4ab$, 4, a, and b, are the factors of $4ab$; since $a(x + y) = ax + ay$, a and $(x + y)$ are the factors of $ax + ay$.

52. Factors of Positive Integers

It is often difficult to determine at a glance the factors of which a number is composed. For example, consider the numerical expression 36. There are many different combinations of numbers that would result in an answer of 36; for example, the desired factors for 36 in a certain problem might $36 \cdot 1$, $18 \cdot 2$, $12 \cdot 3$, $9 \cdot 4$, $6 \cdot 6$, $2 \cdot 2 \cdot 9$, $4 \cdot 3 \cdot 3$, $2 \cdot 3 \cdot 6$, and so on.

53. Factors of a Monomial

Because the factors of a monomial are evident, usually a monomial is not separated into its prime factors. The factors of a^4b^2c are $a \cdot a \cdot a \cdot b \cdot b \cdot c$, and the factors of $15a^2b^3$ are $3 \cdot 5 \cdot a \cdot a \cdot b \cdot b \cdot b$.

54. Square Root of a Monomial

The square root of an algebraic expression is one of its two equal factors. Thus, the square root of 49 is 7, the square root of 81 is 9, the square root of a^2 is a, and the square root of x^2y^2 is xy. As discussed in paragraph 31, the radical sign is used to indicate the square root of a number. Actually, every number has two square roots, one positive and one negative. If no sign precedes the radical, the positive or *principal root* is understood. For example, $\sqrt{9} = +3$. If a negative sign *precedes the radical*, however, the negative root is intended. Thus, $-\sqrt{9} = -3$. When dealing with literal terms, the values of the various factors often are unknown. Therefore, *when extracting the square root of a monomial, extract the square root of the numerical coefficient, divide the exponents of the literal terms by 2, and prefix the square root with the plus or minus (±) sign,* which denotes that either the positive or negative root may be the correct one.

Example 1: $\sqrt{x^{16}y^4} = \pm x^8y^2.$
Example 2: $\sqrt{49a^4b^2} = \pm 7a^2b.$

55. Cube Root of a Monomial

The cube root of a monomial is one of its three equal factors. The index 3 in the angle of the radical sign ($\sqrt[3]{\ }$) indicates cube root (par. 31). *To extract the cube root of a monomial, extract the cube root of the numerical coefficient, divide the exponents of the literal terms by 3, and prefix the cube with the same sign as that of the monomial.*

Example 1: $\sqrt[3]{a^6y^3} = a^2y.$
Example 2: $\sqrt[3]{27x^{12}y^6z^3} = 3x^4y^2z^3.$
Example 3: $\sqrt[3]{-64x^{21}z^8} = -4x^7z^8.$

56. Factors of a Polynomial

a. Common Monomial Factor. In an algebraic expression, the type of factor which can be recognized most easily is the monomial factor (single letter or number) which is common to each term in the expression. For instance, in the expression $xa + xb + xc$, the x is a factor common to each of the terms. Thus, the expression $xa + xb + xc$ can be written $x(a + b + c)$. This relationship is shown pictorially in figure 10. Since the area of a rectangle is equal to its base multiplied by its altitude (par. 136b), the area of the uppermost rectangle in figure 10 is x times a, or xa. The areas of the center and lower rectangles are xb and xc, respectively. The area of the large rectangle formed by the three small rectangles is equal to its base x times its altitude $(a + b + c)$, or $x(a + b + c)$. Since the area of the large

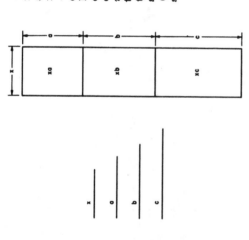

Figure 10. Common monomial factors.

$x(a + b + c) = xa + xb + xc$

rectangle is equal to the sum of the areas of the three smaller rectangles, then $x(a + b + c)$ is equal to $xa + xb + xc$. This shows that the factor x can be removed from $xa + xb + xc$ and the expression written $x(a + b + c)$. Accuracy of factoring can be checked by multiplying the two factors together—the product should be the original expression. Thus, $x(a + b + c) = xa + xb + xc$. *To factor a polynomial the terms of which have a common monomial factor, determine the largest factor common to all of the terms, divide the polynomial by this factor, and write the quotient in parentheses preceded by the monomial factor.* The first factor contains all that is common to all of the terms; it may consist of more than one literal number and may be to a power higher than the first.

Example 1: Factor $x^3 - 7x^2 + 4x$.
$$x^3 - 7x^2 + 4x = x(x^2 - 7x + 4)$$

Example 2: Factor $abx + aby - abz$.
$$abx + aby - abz = ab(x + y - z)$$

Example 3: Factor $2az^2 - 4bz^2 + 6cz^2$.
$$2az^2 - 4bz^2 + 6cz^2 = 2z^2(a - 2b + 3c)$$

b. Binomial Factors. Sometimes binomial factors are not immediately apparent, and an algebraic term may appear to have no common factors. For example, the expression $am + bm + an + bn$ may seem to have no factors in common. However, the first pair, $am + bm$, has a common factor, m, and the second pair, $an + bn$, has a common factor, n. Factoring out the common factors, the expression becomes $m(a + b) + n(a + b)$. Since there are two terms containing a common factor $(a + b)$, this factor can be removed to make the expression $(a + b) (m + n)$. Thus, the factors are $(a + b)$ and $(m + n)$. This relationship is shown pictorially in figure 11. Starting with

the upper left-hand rectangle and going clockwise, the areas of the four rectangles are am, bm, and bn. The area of the large rectangle formed by the four smaller rectangles is its base $(m + n)$ times its altitude $(a + b)$, or $(m + n) (a + b)$. Since the area of the large rectangle is equal to the sum of the areas of the four smaller rectangles, then $(m + n) (a + b)$ is equal to $am + am + bm + bn$. This shows that the expression $am + bm + an + bn$ can be factored into $(m + n)$ and $(a + b)$. To check the factoring, multiply $(a + b)$ by $(m + n)$. Since the product is $am + an + bm + bn$, the addition of terms can be expressed in any order, the factoring is correct.

Example 1: Factor $py - pz - qy + qz$.
$$py - pz - qy + qz = p(y - z) - q(y - z)$$
$$= (p - q)\,(y - z)$$

Example 2: Factor $4za - 8zb - 6ya - 4zb + 8za + 6yb$.
$$4za - 8zb - 6ya - 4zb + 8za + 6yb$$
$$= 2a(2x - 3y + 4z) - 2b(2x - 3y + 4z)$$
$$= (2a - 2b)\,(2x - 3y + 4z)$$
$$= 2(a - b)\,(2x - 3y + 4z)$$

Example 3: Factor $da + db - dc - ea - eb + ec + fa + fb - fc$.
$$da + db - dc - ea - eb + ec + fa + fb - fc$$
$$= d(a + b - c) - e(a + b - c) + f(a + b - c)$$
$$= (d - e + f)\,(a + b - c)$$

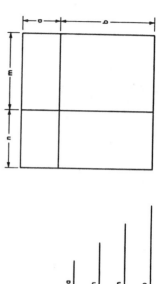

$(m+n)(a+b) = am + bm + an + bn$

Figure 11. Binomial factors.

14

57. Factors of the Square of a Binomial.

a. Square of Sum of Two Numbers. The square of the sum of two numbers is a special product that should be readily recognized. *To aid in factoring algebraic expressions, the square of the sum of two numbers equals the square of the first, plus twice the product of the first and second, plus the square of the second.* To illustrate, $(a + b)^2 = a^2 + 2ab + b^2$. Conversely, the factors of $a^2 + 2ab + b^2$ are $(a + b) (a + b)$ or $(a + b)^2$. This relationship is shown in figure 12. The areas of the four rectangles, as shown on the figure, are a^2, ab, ab, and b^2. The area of the large rectangle formed by the four smaller rectangles is equal to its base $(a + b)$ times its altitude $(a + b)$, or $(a + b)^2$. Since the area of the large rectangle is equal to the sum of the areas of the four smaller rectangles, then $(a + b)^2$ is equal to $a^2 + ab + ab + b^2$, or $a^2 + 2ab + b^2$. This shows that the expression $a^2 + 2ab + b^2$ can be factored into $(a + b) (a + b)$, or $(a + b)^2$. Figure 13 shows a similar relationship in which nine small rectangles form one large rectangle.

In this case, the area of the large rectangle is $(a + 2b)^2$ and the sum of the areas of the nine smaller rectangles is $a^2 + 4ab + 4b^2$; consequently, $(a + 2b)$ and $(a + 2b)$ are factors of $a^2 + 4ab + 4b^2$. Thus, the factors of the square of one number, plus twice the product of the first and second number, plus the square of the second number are the square of the sum of the two numbers.

Example: Factor $4b^2 + 16db + 16d^2$.
$$4b^2 + 16db + 16d^2 = (2b + 4d) (2b + 4d)$$
$$= (2b + 4d)^2$$
$$= [2(b + 2d)]^2$$
$$= 2^2 (b + 2d)^2$$

To prove the factoring:
$$(2b + 4d)^2 = (2b)^2 + 2(2b) (4d) + (4d)^2$$
$$= 4b^2 + 16db + 16d^2$$

Note that 4 (that is, 2^2) may be removed before factoring the rest of the expression—this often simplifies computation.

$$4(b^2 + 4bd + 4d^2) = 4(b + 2d)^2$$

b. Square of Difference of Two Numbers. The square of the difference of two numbers equals the square of the first, minus twice the product of the first and second, plus the square of the second. For example, $(a - b)^2 = a^2 - 2ab + b^2$. The factors of $a^2 - 2ab + b^2$ are $(a - b) (a - b)$ or $(a - b)^2$. This relationship is shown pictorially in figure 14. The area of the large rectangle formed by the four small rectangles is a^2. The areas of the four smaller rectangles are shown on the illustration. The area of the upper left-hand rectangle is $(a - b)^2$. It is also equal to the area of the large rectangle minus the areas of the other three rectangles, or $a^2 - b (a - b) - b (a - b) - b^2$. This can be further simplified as follows:

$$a^2 - b(a - b) - b(a - b) - b^2$$
$$a^2 - 2b(a - b) - b^2$$
$$a^2 - 2ab + 2b^2 - b^2$$
$$a^2 - 2ab + b^2$$

Therefore, $(a - b)^2 = a^2 - 2ab + b^2$, and $(a - b)$ and $(a - b)$ are factors of $a^2 - 2ab + b^2$. Thus, the factors of the square of one number, minus twice the product of the first and the second, plus the square of the second are the square of the difference of the two numbers.

Example:

Factor $9b^2 - 12bd + 4d^2$.
$$9b^2 - 12bd + 4d^2 = (3b - 2d) (3b - 2d)$$
$$= (3b - 2d)^2$$

To prove the factoring:
$$(3b - 2d)^2 = (3b)^2 - 2 (3b) (2d) + (2d)^2$$
$$= 9b^2 - 12bd + 4d^2$$

58. Factors of Difference of Two Squares

The product of the sum and difference of two numbers is equal to the difference of their squares. Thus, $(a + b) (a - b) = a^2 - b^2$. To factor the difference of two squares, extract the square root for the difference of two squares, then write the sum of the roots as one factor and the difference of the roots as the other factor. Thus, the factors of $a^2 - b^2$ are $(a + b) (a - b)$.

Example:

Factor $4x^2 - 9y^2$.
$$4x^2 - 9y^2 = (2x + 3y) (2x - 3y)$$

To prove the factoring:
$$(2x + 3y) (2x - 3y)$$
$$= (2x)^2 + (2x)(3y) - (2x)(3y) - (3y)^2$$
$$= 4x^2 - 9y^2$$

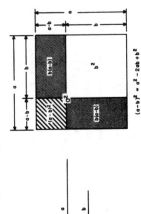

$$(a-b)^2 = a^2 - 2ab + b^2$$

Figure 14. Square of difference of two numbers.

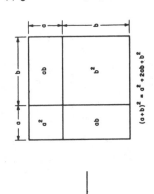

$$(a+b)^2 = a^2 + 2ab + b^2$$

Figure 12. Square of sum of two numbers.

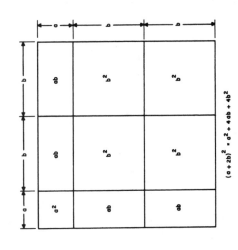

$$(a+2b)^2 = a^2 + 4ab + 4b^2$$

Figure 13. Factors of square of positive binomial.

15

59. Factors of Trinomials

a. *Trinomials Such as* $x^2 + x(a + b) + ab$. The factors of a trinomial consisting of the square of the common term, the product of the common term and the algebraic sum of the unlike terms, and the product of the unlike terms are two binomials that have one term in common and the other term unlike. Thus, the factors of $x^2 + x(a + b) + ab$ are $(x + a)(x + b)$ where x is the common term, and a and b are the unlike terms. As proof, the product of $(x + a)(x + b)$ is $x^2 + xa + xb + xb + ab$. By factoring the two terms which have a common factor, x, the original trinomial $x^2 + x(a + b) + ab$ is obtained.

Example: Factor $9r^2 + 6r(s + t) + 4st$.

$9r^2 + 6r(s + t) + 4st = (3r + 2s)(3r + 2t)$

To prove the factoring:

$$(3r + 2s)(3r + 2t) = (3r)^2 + (3r)(2s) + (3r)(2t) + (2s)(2t)$$
$$= 9r^2 + 6rs + 6rt + 4st$$
$$= 9r^2 + 6r(s + t) + 4st$$

b. *Trinomials Such as* $x^2 + 6x + 8$. To factor a trinomial of the form $x^2 + 6x + 8$, or $x^2 - 6x - 8$, much of the work is done by trial and error. The problem is to find two factors of the final term which, when added together, will give the coefficient of the middle term. Taking the first of the trinomials above, the factors of 8 are $8 \cdot 1$ and $4 \cdot 2$. Since $4 + 2 = 6$ and $8 + 1 = 9$, the factors that will be used are 4 and 2. With regards to signs, *if the sign of the final term is positive, the signs of the two factors are alike and will be the same as the sign of the middle term.* Thus, the factors $x^2 + 6x + 8$ are $(x + 4)$ and $(x + 2)$, and the factors of $x^2 - 6x - 8$ are $(x - 4)$ and $(x - 2)$. *If the sign of the final term is negative, however, the signs containing the two terms of each binomial factor are unlike; the larger factor will take the sign of the middle term.* For example, the factors of $x^2 + 2x - 8$ are $(x + 4)$ and $(x - 2)$, and the factors of $x^2 - 2x - 8$ are $(x - 4)$ and $(x + 2)$.

Example 1: Factor $y^2 + 12y + 32$.

$y^2 + 12y + 32 = (y + 8)(y + 4)$

Example 2: Factor $z^2 - 11z + 30$.

$z^2 - 11z + 30 = (z - 6)(z - 5)$

Example 3: Factor $r^2 + 4r - 12$.

$r^2 + 4r - 12 = (r + 6)(r - 2)$

Example 4: Factor $s^2 - s - 20$.

$s^2 - s - 20 = (s - 5)(s + 4)$

c. *Trinomials Such as* $6a^2 - 11a - 10$. The procedure used to factor trinomials of this type is an extension of the procedure described in b above and as shown in the example below.

Example: Factor $6a^2 - 11a - 10$.

Step 1. Find two numbers that, when multiplied together, form the left-hand term, $6a^2$.

$$(6a)(a) = 6a^2$$
$$(2a)(3a) = 6a^2$$

Step 2. Find two numbers that, when multiplied together, form the right-hand term, -10.

$$(10)(-1) = -10$$
$$(5)(-2) = -10$$
$$(-10)(1) = -10$$
$$(-5)(2) = -10$$

Step 3. By trial and error, set up two binomial expressions containing factors from step 1 in the left-hand term and factors from step 2 in the right-hand term. The proper selection of factors should give the middle term of the trinomial when the binomials are multiplied.

$$(2a + 5)(3a - 2) \text{ (first trial)}$$
$$6a^2 + 15a - 4a - 10 = 6a^2$$
$$+ 11a - 10 \text{ (multiplying out)}$$

The middle term obtained does not match the middle term of the given trinomial. The numerical value is correct, but the sign is wrong. Make a second trial with the signs in the binomials changed.

$$(2a - 5)(3a + 2)$$
$$6a^2 - 15a + 4a - 10 = 6a^2$$
$$- 11a - 10$$

Step 4. Since the second trial results in the correct trinomial, the factors of $6a^2 - 11a - 10$ are $(2a - 5)$ and $(3a + 2)$.

Note. The method of trial and error used above may not work in every case. Other arrangements of factors and signs must be tried until the correct results are obtained.

60. Factors of Two Cubes

a. *Sum of Two Cubes.* The factors of the sum of two cubes, such as $x^3 + y^3$, are $(x + y)$ and $(x^2 - xy + y^2)$. In this case, the binomial is an expression of the sum of the primes times the product of the primes minus the product of the primes. This is seen readily by dividing $x^3 + y^3$ by $x + y$.

Thus,

```
              x² − xy  + y²
        ┌─────────────────────
x + y   │ x³            + y³
          x³ + x²y
          ─────────
             − x²y
             − x²y − xy²
             ──────────────
                    xy² + y³
                    xy² + y³
```

Example 1: Factor $z^3 + 8$.

$z^3 + 8 = (z + 2)(z^2 - 2z + 4)$

To prove the factoring:

```
              z² − 2z  + 4
        ┌─────────────────────
z + 2   │ z³           + 8
          z³ + 2z²
          ─────────
             − 2z²
             − 2z² − 4z
             ──────────────
                    4z + 8
                    4z + 8
```

Example 2: Factor $r^3 + 125x^3$.

$r^3 + 125x^3 = (r + 5x)(r^2 - 5rx + 25x^2)$

To prove the factoring:

```
              r² − 5rx  + 25x²
        ┌──────────────────────────
r + 5x  │ r³            + 125x³
          r³ + 5r²x
          ─────────
             − 5r²x
             − 5r²x − 25rx²
             ──────────────────
                    25rx² + 125x³
                    25rx² + 125x³
```

b. *Difference of Two Cubes.* The factors of the difference of two cubes, such as $x^3 - y^3$, are an expression of the difference of the primes times the sum of the squares plus the product of the primes. As in the sum of two cubes, the factoring can be proved by dividing the product by the binomial factor.

Example 1: Factor $a^3 - b^3$.

$a^3 - b^3 = (a - b)(a^2 + ab + b^2)$

To prove the factoring:

```
              a² + ab  + b²
        ┌─────────────────────
a − b   │ a³           − b³
          a³ − a²b
          ─────────
             + a²b
             a²b − ab²
             ──────────────
                    ab² − b³
                    ab² − b³
```

Example 2: Factor $z^3 - 27$.

$z^3 - 27 = (z - 3)(z^2 + 3z + 9)$

To prove the factoring:

```
              z² + 3z  + 9
        ┌─────────────────────
z − 3   │ z³           − 27
          z³ − 3z²
          ─────────
             + 3z²
             3z² − 9z
             ──────────────
                    9z − 27
                    9z − 27
```

Example 3: Factor $64s^3 - 216t^3$.

$64s^3 - 216t^3 = (4s - 6t)(16s^2 + 24st + 36t^2)$

To prove the factoring:

```
              16s²    + 24 st   + 36t²
4s — 6t /64s³                   + 36t²
         64s³                   — 216t³
         — 96s²t
         96s²t      — 144st²
         96s²t      — 216t³
                    — 144st²  — 216t³
                    — 144st²
```

61. Review Problems—Factoring

a. Factor:

(1) $25 + 5 - 30$
(2) $8 + 4 - 32$
(3) $9 - 18 + 21$
(4) $7r - 21r + 35r$
(5) $10x + 8y + 6z$

b. Find the values of the indicated powers:

(1) $(7xy^9)^2$
(2) $(-2w^5)^2$
(3) $(8a^2b^4)^2$
(4) $(9a^3x)^3$
(5) $(-3bz^4)^3$

c. Find the value of each of the following:

(1) $\sqrt{5^2}$
(2) $\sqrt{4^8}$
(3) $\sqrt{a^2b^6}$
(4) $\sqrt{36y^2z^4}$
(5) $\sqrt{100a^2b^{10}}$
(6) $\sqrt{16a^2 \cdot 5^2}$
(7) $\sqrt[3]{27}$
(8) $\sqrt[3]{-x^9}$
(9) $\sqrt[3]{(-8)^2}$
(10) $\sqrt[3]{125x^{12}y^{18}z^6}$

d. Factor:

(1) $3x + 6$
(2) $5a^2 + 15a$
(3) $10x^3 - 14x^2 - 2x$
(4) $6axy + 9bzx - 12cz$
(5) $m^3 + m^2 - 5mx$
(6) $3a^5 - 6a^4b - 3a^3b^2$
(7) $7ry^3 - 14ry^3 + 21ry^3$
(8) $12x^2am + 14xa^2m + 16xam^2$
(9) $\pi r_1^2 + \pi r_2^2$
(10) $\frac{1}{4}c^9d - \frac{1}{8}c^3d^2 + \frac{1}{16}cd^3$

Section V. ALGEBRAIC FRACTIONS

62. General

Algebraic fractions play an important part in equations for electrical and electronic circuits. These fractions can be added, subtracted, multiplied, and divided in the same manner as arithmetical fractions.

63. Changing Signs of Fractions

a. The sign preceding a fraction is the sign of the fraction. It refers to the fraction as a whole and not to either the numerator or the denominator. In addition, the numerator and denominator each has a sign. For example, in the fraction $-\frac{3a}{5b}$, the sign of the fraction is minus, the sign of the numerator is plus, and the sign of the denominator is plus. Any two of the three signs can be changed without changing the value of the fraction.

Thus, $-\dfrac{3a}{5b} = \dfrac{-3a}{5b} = \dfrac{3a}{-5b}$.

Therefore, the sign of the fraction is not changed if the signs of both the numerator and the denominator are changed. Also, the sign of the fraction must be changed if the sign of either the numerator or denominator, but not both, is changed.

b. If the numerator or denominator is a polynomial, the sign of each term should be changed, not just the first sign. For example,

$$-\frac{a-b}{c-d} = + \frac{-(a-b)}{c-d} = \frac{-a+b}{c-d} = \frac{b-a}{c-d}$$

c. If the numerator or denominator is in factored form, change only the sign of one of the factors, not both. Thus,

$$-\frac{(x-y)(x-2y)}{x+y} = \frac{(x+y)(x-2y)}{x+y} = \frac{(y-x)(x-2y)}{x+y}.$$

64. Changing Form of Algebraic Fractions

In algebra, as in arithmetic, any fraction can be changed to an equivalent fraction by multiplying or dividing both the numerator and denominator by the same term or number except zero. This will not change the value of the fraction. For example, to change the fraction $\frac{3}{5}$ to a fraction with 10 as its denominator, multiply both the numerator and the denominator by 2. Thus,

$$\frac{3}{5} = \frac{3 \cdot 2}{5 \cdot 2} = \frac{6}{10}.$$

Similarly, to change the fraction $\frac{x}{y}$ to a fraction with yz as its denominator, the denominator is changed to yz by multiplying by z; the numerator also is multiplied by z to become xz. Thus,

$$\frac{x}{y} = \frac{x \cdot z}{y \cdot z} = \frac{xz}{yz}.$$

Example 1: Change $\dfrac{4}{a-3}$ to a fraction with $a^2 - 9$ as its denominator.

$$\frac{4}{a-3} = \frac{4 \cdot (a+3)}{(a-3)(a+3)}$$
$$= \frac{4(a+3)}{a^2-9}$$

Example 2: Change $\dfrac{4r-3}{6r}$ to a fraction with $18r^2s$ as its denominator.

$$\frac{4r-3}{6r} = \frac{(4r-3) \cdot 3rs}{6r \cdot 3rs} = \frac{3rs(4r-3)}{18r^2s}$$

65. Reducing Fractions to Lowest Terms

As in arithmetic, when the numerator and denominator of a fraction have no common factor other than 1, the fraction is said to be in its lowest terms. The fraction $\frac{3}{8}$, $\frac{a}{b}$, and $\frac{p+q}{p-q}$, therefore, are in their lowest terms since the numerator and denominator of each fraction have no other factor except 1. The fractions $\frac{6}{12}$ and $\frac{3a}{9a^2}$ are not in their lowest terms. The fraction $\frac{6}{12}$ can be reduced to its lowest term by dividing both the numerator and denominator by 6. Similarly, the fraction $\frac{5y}{15y^2}$ can be reduced to $\frac{1}{3y}$ by dividing the numerator and denominator by $5y$. Thus, to reduce a fraction to its lowest terms, factor the numerator and denominator into prime factors and cancel the factors common to both (since they are equal to $\frac{1}{1}$).

Example 1: Reduce $\dfrac{6y}{8y^2}$ to lowest terms.

$$\frac{6y}{8y^2} = \frac{2y(3)}{2y(4y)} = \frac{3}{4y}$$

Example 2: Reduce $\dfrac{xab^2}{xcb}$ to lowest terms.

$$\frac{xab^2}{xcb} = \frac{xb(ab)}{xb(c)} = \frac{ab}{c}$$

Example 3: Reduce $\dfrac{a^2-b^2}{4a+4b}$ to lowest terms.

$$\frac{a^2-b^2}{4a+4b} = \frac{(a+b)(a-b)}{4(a+b)} = \frac{a-b}{4}$$

Example 4: Reduce $\dfrac{2a^2+4ab+2b^2}{2a+2b}$ to lowest terms.

$$\frac{2a^2+4ab+2b^2}{2a+2b} = \frac{2(a+b)(a+b)}{2(a+b)} = \frac{a+b}{1} = a+b$$

66. Finding Lowest Common Denominator

The lowest common denominator (LCD) of two or more fractions is the smallest term or number that is divisible by each of the denominators. Inspect to find this term or number, divide the LCD by the denominator of each fraction, and multiply both the numerator and denominator by the quotient. For example, when changing the fractions $\frac{2}{3}$ and $\frac{4}{5}$ to fractions which have an LCD, inspection shows that 15 is the smallest number which is divisible by both 3 and 5. Thus, the fractions $\frac{2}{3}$ and $\frac{3}{5}$ become $\frac{10}{15}$ and $\frac{9}{15}$. Similarly, the LCD of $\frac{4xy}{3a^2}$ and $\frac{6z}{4ab}$ is $12a^2b$ because this is the smallest term that is divisible by both $3a^2$ and $4ab$. Thus, the fraction $\frac{4xy}{3a^2}$ and $\frac{6z}{4ab}$ become $\frac{16xyb}{12a^2b}$ and $\frac{18za}{12a^2b}$ respectively. When fractions have factors with exponents in the denominators, the highest power of each distinct factor is used to form the LCD. For example, consider the problem of finding the LCD of fractions having the following denominators: x^3y^2z, $x^2y^3z^2$, y^4z^3, x^2y^4. The LCD is $x^3y^4z^3$ because x^3, y^4, and z^3 are the highest powers of x, y, and z in any one denominator.

Example: Change $\dfrac{3a}{a^2-b^2}$ and $\dfrac{4b}{a^2-ab-2b^2}$ to equivalent fractions having an LCD.

Step 1. Factor each denominator into its prime factors:

$$\frac{3a}{a^2-b^2} = \frac{3a}{(a+b)(a-b)}$$
$$\frac{4b}{a^2-ab-2b^2} = \frac{4b}{(a+b)(a-2b)}$$

Step 2. The lowest common multiple of the denominators is the LCD:

$$(a+b)(a-b)(a-2b)$$

Step 3. Divide the LCD by the denominators:

$$(a+b)(a-b)(a-2b) \div (a+b)(a-b) = a-2b$$
$$(a+b)(a-b)(a-2b) \div (a+b)(a-2b) = a-b$$

Step 4. Change $\dfrac{3a}{(a+b)(a-b)}$ into a fraction having $(a+b)(a-b)(a-2b)$ as its denominator:

$$\frac{3a}{(a+b)(a-b)} = \frac{3a(a-2b)}{(a+b)(a-b)(a-2b)}$$

Step 5. Change $\dfrac{4b}{(a+b)(a-2b)}$ into a fraction having $(a-b)(a-2b)$ as its denominator.

$$\frac{4b}{(a+b)(a-2b)} = \frac{4b(a-b)}{(a+b)(a-b)(a-2b)}$$

Step 6. Therefore, $\dfrac{3a}{a^2-b^2} = \dfrac{3a(a-2b)}{(a+b)(a-b)(a-2b)}$

and $\dfrac{4b}{a^2-ab-2b^2} = \dfrac{4b(a-b)}{(a+b)(a-b)(a-2b)}$

67. Addition and Subtraction of Algebraic Fractions

a. Addition. The addition of algebraic fractions is similar to the corresponding operation in arithmetic. To add two or more fractions having a common denominator, add the numerators and place the result over the common denominator. If the fractions have different denominators, convert them to fractions with an LCD. The sum of the fractions is equal to the algebraic sum of the numerators divided by the LCD. Simplify the numerator and reduce the result to its lowest terms. If possible, factor or combine for further simplification.

Example: Find the sum of $\dfrac{2x}{x+y}$ and $\dfrac{2y}{x-y}$.

The LCD is $(x+y)(x-y)$. Therefore,

$$\frac{2x}{x+y} + \frac{2y}{x-y} = \frac{2x(x-y)}{(x+y)(x-y)} + \frac{2y(x+y)}{(x+y)(x-y)}$$
$$= \frac{2x(x-y)+2y(x+y)}{(x+y)(x-y)}$$
$$= \frac{2x^2-2xy+2xy+2y^2}{(x+y)(x-y)}$$
$$= \frac{2x^2+2y^2}{(x+y)(x-y)}$$
$$= \frac{2(x^2+y^2)}{x^2-y^2}$$

b. Subtraction. To subtract two fractions having a common denominator, subtract the numerator of the subtrahend from the numerator of the minuend and place the result over the common denominator. If the denominators are different, find the LCD and subtract, as shown below.

Example: Subtract $\dfrac{8}{x^2+6x-16}$ from $\dfrac{9}{x^2+7x-18}$. Therefore,

The LCD is $(x-2)(x+8)(x+9)$.

$$\frac{9}{x^2+7x-18} - \frac{8}{x^2+6x-16}$$
$$= \frac{9(x+8)}{(x-2)(x+8)(x+9)} - \frac{8(x+9)}{(x-2)(x+8)(x+9)}$$
$$= \frac{9(x+8)-8(x+9)}{(x-2)(x+8)(x+9)}$$
$$= \frac{9x+72-8x-72}{(x-2)(x+8)(x+9)}$$
$$= \frac{x}{(x-2)(x+8)(x+9)}$$

68. Multiplication and Division of Algebraic Fractions

a. *Multiplication.* The process of multiplication of algebraic fractions is the same as in arithmetic. The product of two or more fractions is the product of the numerators divided by the product of the denominators. The operation may be simplified by dividing common factors in the numerator and denominator by the same factor.

Example 1: Multiply $\frac{6a^2b}{7x}$ by $\frac{21x^2y}{24a^2b}$.

The first numerator and the second denominator are divisible by $6a^2b$; the first denominator and the second numerator are divisible by $7x$. Therefore:

$$\frac{\cancel{6a^2b}}{\cancel{7x}}\cdot\frac{\cancel{21x^2y}}{\cancel{24a^2b}}=\frac{3xy}{4}$$

Example 2: Multiply $\frac{a^2+2ab+b^2}{a-b}$ by $\frac{a^2-2ab+b^2}{a+b}$.

$$\frac{a^2+2ab+b^2}{a-b}\cdot\frac{a^2-2ab+b^2}{a+b}=\frac{(a+b)(a+b)}{a-b}\cdot\frac{(a-b)(a-b)}{a+b}$$

$$=\frac{\cancel{(a+b)}(a+b)\,\cancel{(a-b)}(a-b)}{\cancel{(a-b)}\,\cancel{(a+b)}}$$

$$=(a+b)(a-b)$$
$$=a^2-b^2$$

b. *Division.* To divide algebraic fractions, multiply the dividend by the reciprocal of the divisor. Thus, to divide by x, multiply by the reciprocal of x, that is $\frac{1}{x}$. In other words, invert the divisor and proceed as in multiplication.

Example 1: Divide $\frac{2a+2b}{a-3}$ by $\frac{a^2-b^2}{2a-6}$.

$$\frac{2a+2b}{a-3}\div\frac{a^2-b^2}{2a-6}=\frac{2a+2b}{a-3}\cdot\frac{2a-6}{a^2-b^2}$$

$$=\frac{2(a+b)}{a-3}\cdot\frac{2(a-3)}{(a+b)(a-b)}$$

$$=\frac{2\cdot2}{a-b}$$
$$=\frac{4}{a-b}$$

Example 2: Divide $\frac{z^2-z-6}{z^2-25}$ by $\frac{z^2+z-12}{z^2-z-20}$.

$$\frac{z^2-z-6}{z^2-25}\div\frac{z^2+z-12}{z^2-z-20}=\frac{z^2-z-6}{z^2-25}\cdot\frac{z^2-z-20}{z^2+z-12}$$

$$=\frac{(z-3)(z+2)}{(z+5)(z-5)}\cdot\frac{(z-5)(z+4)}{(z-3)(z+4)}$$

$$=\frac{z+2}{z+5}$$

69. Review Problems—Algebraic Fractions

a. *Changing Signs of Fractions.* Solve for the unknown.

(1) $\frac{4x+3}{6}-\frac{x-9}{4}=5$

(2) $\frac{x-2}{4}=\frac{1}{2}$

(3) $\frac{r+4}{3}-\frac{r-2}{5}=2$

(4) $\frac{4x-3}{6x}-\frac{4x+5}{3x}=2$

(5) $\frac{7t+2}{3}=3$

(6) $\frac{x-4}{3}+\frac{2x-5}{6}=3$

(7) $\frac{2r+3}{2}-\frac{3r+2}{4}=2$

(8) $\frac{7x-4}{3}+\frac{x-5}{5}=\frac{1}{5}$

b. *Equivalent Fractions.* Supply missing terms.

(1) $\frac{4}{8}=\frac{?}{16}$

(2) $\frac{1}{c}=\frac{?}{cx}$

(3) $\frac{3}{r-s}=\frac{?}{r^2-s^2}$

(4) $\frac{a-8}{1}=\frac{?}{3}$

(5) $\frac{I-6}{I-3}=\frac{?}{(I-3)(I-9)}$

(6) Change $\frac{4E^2}{R}$ into an equivalent fraction of which the denominator is $2I^2R$.

(7) Change $\frac{1}{3\pi fc}$ into an equivalent fraction of which the denominator is $6\pi f^2c$.

c. *Lowest Common Denominator.* Reduce to equivalent fractions having an LCD.

(1) $\frac{1}{R},\frac{1}{R^2},\frac{1}{r}$

(2) $\frac{1}{a+1},\frac{x}{a-1}$

(3) $\frac{b}{2x},\frac{c}{3x}$

(4) $\frac{y}{2},\frac{y}{2y+6}$

(5) $\frac{2}{c},\frac{3}{c+1}$

(6) $\frac{i}{e-5},\frac{i}{2e-10}$

(7) $\frac{y}{c^2-d^2},\frac{z}{c-d}$

d. *Addition and Subtraction of Fractions.* Perform the indicated operations.

(1) $\frac{1}{a}+\frac{4}{a}+\frac{7}{a}$

(2) $\frac{8}{t}+\frac{8+4}{2t}+\frac{8+3}{4t}$

(3) $\frac{3a}{4x^2y}+\frac{5b}{6xy^3}$

(4) $\frac{2}{z^2-1}+\frac{4}{z^2-4}$

(5) $\frac{3c-2d}{4cd^2}+\frac{2c-3d}{3c^2d}$

(6) $\frac{(r+1)(r-3)}{r^2+2r-15}+\frac{(r-2)(r+5)}{r^2+2r-15}$

(7) $3y-\frac{1}{4}$

(8) $\frac{a+b}{a-b}-\frac{a-b}{a+b}$

(9) $\frac{32}{25q^2}-\frac{16}{5q}$

(10) $\frac{3t-2t}{4tv^2}-\frac{2t-3t}{3t^2v}$

e. *Multiplication and Division of Fractions.* Perform the indicated operations.

(1) $\frac{9y^2}{16}\cdot\frac{2}{3}$

(2) $\frac{a^3}{b^4}\cdot\frac{a^6}{b^2}$

(3) $\frac{3x^2}{49y^2z}\cdot\frac{7yz^2}{9xm}$

(4) $\left(\frac{1}{r}-\frac{1}{s}\right)\left(r-\frac{r^2}{s}\right)$

(5) $\frac{2x^2-5xy-3y^2}{x^2-9y^2}\cdot\frac{3x+9xy}{10x^2+5xy}$

(6) $\frac{a-b}{a^2+2ab+b^2}\cdot\frac{a+b}{a^2-2ab+b^2}\cdot\frac{a^2-b^2}{a^3}$

(7) $3z\div\frac{1}{5}$

(8) $\frac{5ba^3}{6cd}\div5b$

(9) $\frac{12s^2t}{20uv}\div\frac{3st}{4u^2v}$

(10) $\left(e+2-\frac{3}{e}\right)\div\left(e+1-\frac{2}{e}\right)$

Section VI. EXPONENTS AND RADICALS

70. General

Chapter 4 presents exponents and roots consisting only of whole numbers. However, to use exponents and radicals to solve many equations and formulas, a knowledge of additional operations is required.

71. Fractional Exponents

a. *General.* A fractional exponent is merely another way of expressing the root of a number. For example, the cube root of x usually is written $\sqrt[3]{x}$; however, it also can be written $x^{\frac{1}{3}}$. Similarly, $\sqrt{x}$ also can be written $x^{\frac{1}{2}}$.

b. *Application.* Fractional exponents have a practical value in simplifying algebraic problems. They follow the same rules as exponents that consist of integers, and can be added, subtracted, multiplied, or divided in the same way; thus

$$a^{\frac{1}{2}} \cdot a^{\frac{1}{2}} = a^{\frac{1}{2}+\frac{1}{2}} = a^1 = a, \text{ and } a^{\frac{1}{3}} \cdot a^{\frac{1}{3}} \cdot a^{\frac{1}{3}} = a^{\frac{1}{3}+\frac{1}{3}+\frac{1}{3}} = a^1 = a.$$

In other words, $a^{\frac{1}{2}}$ is one of two equal factors of a or the square root of a, and $a^{\frac{2}{3}}$ is two of three equal factors of a or the square cube root of a; therefore, $a^{\frac{1}{2}} = \sqrt{a}$ and $a^{\frac{2}{3}} = \sqrt[3]{a^2}$.

c. *Changing from Radical Form to Exponential Form.* To change a radical expression to exponential form, remove the radical sign and annex a fractional exponent to the radicand (number under the radical sign). The numerator of the fractional exponent is the power of the radicand, and the denominator is the index of the root.

Example 1: Change $\sqrt[4]{a^2}$ to exponential form and simplify.

$$\sqrt[4]{a^2} = (a^2)^{\frac{1}{4}}$$
$$(a^2)^{\frac{1}{4}} = a^{2\cdot\frac{1}{4}} = a^{\frac{2}{4}} = a^{\frac{1}{2}} = \sqrt{a}$$

Therefore, $\sqrt[4]{a^2} = \sqrt{a}$.

Example 2: Change $\sqrt[3]{8a^2b^3}$ to exponential form and simplifying:

$$\sqrt[3]{8a^2b^3} = \sqrt[3]{2^3a^2b^3} = (2^3a^2b^3)^{\frac{1}{3}} = 2^{3\cdot\frac{1}{3}} \, a^{2\cdot\frac{1}{3}} \, b^{3\cdot\frac{1}{3}}$$
$$= 2^{\frac{3}{3}}a^{\frac{2}{3}}b^{\frac{3}{3}} = 2b\sqrt[3]{a^2}$$

d. *Changing from Exponential Form to Radical Form.* To change an expression with a fractional exponent to a radical form, make the base of the fractional exponent the radicand, the numerator of the fractional exponent the power of the radicand, and the denominator of the exponent the index of the root.

Example 1: Change $4^{\frac{1}{2}}$ to radical form.

$$4^{\frac{1}{2}} = \sqrt{4}$$

Example 2: Change $3^{\frac{1}{3}}$ to radical form.

$$3^{\frac{1}{3}} = \sqrt[3]{3^1} = \sqrt[3]{3}$$

Example 3: Change $(5a^2b)^{\frac{1}{2}}$ to radical form.

$$(5a^2b)^{\frac{2}{4}} = \sqrt[4]{(5a^2b)^2}$$
$$= \sqrt[4]{25a^4b^2}$$

72. Simplification of Radicals

a. *Removing a Factor from the Radicand.* The form in which a radical expression is written may be changed without altering its numerical value. Sometimes there is a question as to what actually is the simplest form for an expression. For instance, consider the simplification of an expression such as $\sqrt{1250}$: $\sqrt{1250} = \sqrt{2 \cdot 5^4} = 5^2\sqrt{2} = 25\sqrt{2}$. The expression $25\sqrt{2}$ usually is accepted as being simpler than $\sqrt{1250}$. As a general rule, the fewer the factors under the radical sign, the simpler the expression. Thus, a radicand may be separated into two factors, one of which is the greater power whose root can be taken. The root of this factor may then be written as the coefficient of a radical of which the other factor is the radicand.

Example 1: Simplify $\sqrt{50}$.

$$\sqrt{50} = \sqrt{25 \cdot 2}$$
$$= \sqrt{25} \cdot \sqrt{2}$$
$$= 5\sqrt{2}$$

Example 2: Simplify $\sqrt[4]{32a^7b^3}$.

$$\sqrt[4]{32a^7b^3} = (2^5a^7b^3)^{\frac{1}{4}}$$
$$= 2^{\frac{5}{4}}a^{\frac{7}{4}}b^{\frac{3}{4}}$$
$$= 2^{\frac{4}{4}} \cdot 2^{\frac{1}{4}} \, a^{\frac{4}{4}} \cdot a^{\frac{3}{4}} \, b^{\frac{3}{4}}$$
$$= 2a\sqrt[4]{2a^3b^3}$$

b. *Rationalizing Denominator.* Rationalizing a denominator containing a radical means to eliminate the radical in the denominator. For example, to rationalize the expression $\frac{1}{\sqrt[3]{2}}$, first change the denominator into an expression having a fractional exponent; thus, $\frac{1}{\sqrt[3]{2}} = \frac{1}{2^{\frac{1}{3}}}$. Then multiply the denominator by a number that will make its exponent equal to 1. This operation eliminates the radical sign below the line. In this case, $2^{\frac{2}{3}}$ is such a factor; thus $2^{\frac{1}{3}} \cdot 2^{\frac{2}{3}} = 2^{\frac{1}{3}+\frac{2}{3}} = 2^1 = 2$. Such multiplication can be performed without changing the value of the fraction if the numerator also is multiplied by the same number; thus $\frac{1}{2^{\frac{1}{3}}} \cdot \frac{2^{\frac{2}{3}}}{2^{\frac{2}{3}}} = \frac{2^{\frac{2}{3}}}{2^{\frac{1}{3}+\frac{2}{3}}} = \frac{2^{\frac{2}{3}}}{2}$. Finally, changing the numerator into radical form, $\frac{2^{\frac{2}{3}}}{2} = \frac{\sqrt[3]{2^2}}{2} = \frac{\sqrt[3]{4}}{2}$. Therefore, to rationalize a denominator, multiply both the numerator and the denominator by a number that will make the exponent in the denominator equal to 1; then simplify the radicand in the numerator. The examples below illustrate the method of rationalizing a few different types of denominators.

Example 1: Rationalize $\frac{1}{3^{\frac{2}{7}}}$.

$$\frac{1}{3^{\frac{2}{7}}} = \frac{1}{3^{\frac{2}{7}}} \cdot \frac{3^{\frac{5}{7}}}{3^{\frac{5}{7}}} = \frac{3^{\frac{5}{7}}}{3^{\frac{7}{7}}} = \frac{3^{\frac{5}{7}}}{3} = \frac{\sqrt[7]{3^5}}{3}$$

Example 2: Rationalize $\frac{1}{\sqrt{8}}$.

First simplify $\sqrt{8}$.

$$\sqrt{8} = \sqrt{4 \cdot 2} = \sqrt{4} \cdot \sqrt{2} = 2 \cdot 2^{\frac{1}{2}}$$
$$\frac{1}{\sqrt{8}} = \frac{1}{2 \cdot 2^{\frac{1}{2}}} = \frac{2^{\frac{1}{2}}}{2 \cdot 2^{\frac{1}{2}} \cdot 2^{\frac{1}{2}}} = \frac{2^{\frac{1}{2}}}{2 \cdot 2} = \frac{\sqrt{2}}{4}$$

Example 3: Rationalize $\frac{1}{\sqrt{7}}$.

Here the square root in the denominator is being multiplied by itself, making the number a perfect square.

$$\frac{1}{\sqrt{7}} = \frac{1}{\sqrt{7}} \cdot \frac{\sqrt{7}}{\sqrt{7}} = \frac{\sqrt{7}}{\sqrt{7} \cdot \sqrt{7}} = \frac{\sqrt{7}}{7}$$

c. *Practical Application.* The processes of the simplification of radicals and rationalization of denominators are useful when computing decimals. It is necessary to know, however, that $\sqrt{2} = 1.414$, $\sqrt{3} = 1.732$, etc. For example, consider the problem of evaluating $\frac{1}{\sqrt{2}}$. One way of evaluating this problem is to divide 1 by 1.414. This evaluation is a long-division problem of some length, however. A much more simple way is to rationalize—thus $\frac{1}{\sqrt{2}} = \frac{\sqrt{2}}{2}$, and dividing 1.414 by 2 gives the result, 0.707.

73. Addition and Subtraction of Radicals

As discussed in paragraph 27b, terms that are alike in all respects, except for their coefficients, are called *similar terms*. Similarly, radicals that have the same index and the same radicand and differ only in their coefficients are called *similar radicals*. For example, $-5\sqrt{3}$, $2\sqrt{3}$, and $\sqrt{3}$ are similar radicals. Similar radicals may be added or subtracted in the same way that similar terms are added and subtracted. However, if the radicands are not alike and cannot be reduced to a common radicand, they are dissimilar and addition and subtraction can only be indicated; thus to add or subtract radicals, reduce them to their simplest form, then combine similar radicals, and indicate the addition or subtraction of dissimilar radicals.

Example 1: Perform the indicated operations.

$$4\sqrt{6} - 5\sqrt{6} - \sqrt{6} + 10\sqrt{6} = 8\sqrt{6}$$

Example 2: Add.

$$\sqrt{48a} + \sqrt{\frac{a}{3}} + \sqrt{3a} = 4\sqrt{3a} + \tfrac{1}{3}\sqrt{3a} + \sqrt{3a}$$
$$= \frac{16}{3}\sqrt{3a}$$

Example 3: Perform the indicated operations.

$$\sqrt[6]{16r^2} - r\sqrt[3]{4r} + \sqrt[9]{64r^3} = \sqrt[6]{(4r)^2} - r\sqrt[3]{4r} + \sqrt[9]{(4r)^3}$$
$$= (4r)^{\frac{2}{6}} - r(4r)^{\frac{1}{3}} + (4r)^{\frac{3}{9}}$$
$$= \sqrt[3]{4r} - r\sqrt[3]{4r} + \sqrt[3]{4r}$$
$$= \sqrt[3]{4r}\,(2-r)$$

Example 4: Perform the indicated operations.

$$2\sqrt{6} + 9\sqrt{\frac{2}{3}} - \sqrt[4]{36} = 2\sqrt{6} + 9\sqrt{\frac{2}{3}} - \sqrt[4]{6^2}$$
$$= 2\sqrt{6} + \frac{9}{3}\sqrt{6} - \sqrt[4]{6^2}$$
$$= 2\sqrt{6} + 3\sqrt{6} - \sqrt{6}$$
$$= 4\sqrt{6}$$

74. Multiplication of Radicals

a. *Radicals With Same Indexes.* Radicals can be multiplied and combined under the same radical sign even though they differ in value, provided the index of the radicals are the same. To multiply a radical expression when radicals are of the same order, first multiply the coefficients, then multiply the radicands, and then simplify, if possible. For example, $2\sqrt{3} \cdot 3\sqrt{5} = 6\sqrt{15}$. If the radicand is a perfect square, simplify the result by extracting the square root. Remember that there are two square roots, one positive and one negative; thus, $6\sqrt{3} \cdot 4\sqrt{3} = 24\sqrt{9} = 24(\pm3) = \pm72$. When polynomial expressions, either or both of which involve radicals, are to be multiplied, proceed in the same manner as with literal polynominal expressions (par. 48). For example, $(\sqrt{3} + 2\sqrt{5}) \times (\sqrt{3} - 2\sqrt{5}) =$

$$\begin{array}{r}
\sqrt{3} + 2\sqrt{5} \\
\sqrt{3} - 2\sqrt{5} \\ \hline
\sqrt{9} + 2\sqrt{15} \\
-2\sqrt{15} - 4\sqrt{25} \\ \hline
\sqrt{9} \qquad\quad\; - 4\sqrt{25}
\end{array}$$
$$= \pm3 - 4(\pm5)$$
$$= \pm3 \pm20$$
$$= 3 \pm20 \text{ or } -3 \pm20$$
$$= \pm17 \text{ or } \pm23$$

Example 1: Multiply $2\sqrt[3]{3a}$, $5\sqrt[3]{4a}$, and $3\sqrt[3]{18a}$.

$$2\sqrt[3]{3a} \cdot 5\sqrt[3]{4a} \cdot 3\sqrt[3]{18a} = 2\cdot3\cdot5 \cdot \sqrt[3]{3a}\cdot\sqrt[3]{4a}\cdot\sqrt[3]{18a}$$
$$= 30\sqrt[3]{216a^3}$$
$$= 30 \cdot 6a$$
$$= 180a$$

Example 2: Multiply $\sqrt[4]{8t^3}$ and $\sqrt[4]{4t^2s}$.

$$\sqrt[4]{8t^3} \cdot \sqrt[4]{4t^2s} = \sqrt[4]{32t^5s}$$
$$= \sqrt[4]{2^4 \cdot 2 \cdot t^4 \cdot t \cdot s}$$
$$= 2t\sqrt[4]{2ts}$$

b. *Radicals With Different Indexes.* To multiply radicals when the indexes are different, first express them as radicals with a common index (or common fractional exponent) and proceed as in *a* above. The common index is the lowest common multiple of the indexes of the original radicals.

Example 1: Multiply $\sqrt{2} \cdot \sqrt[3]{4}$.

$$\sqrt{2} \cdot \sqrt[3]{4} = \sqrt{2} \cdot \sqrt[3]{2^2}$$
$$= 2^{\frac{1}{2}} \cdot 2^{\frac{2}{3}}$$
$$= 2^{\frac{3}{6}} \cdot 2^{\frac{4}{6}}$$
$$= 2^{\frac{7}{6}}$$
$$= 2^{\frac{6}{6}} \cdot 2^{\frac{1}{6}}$$
$$= 2 \cdot 2^{\frac{1}{6}} \text{ or } 2\sqrt[6]{2}$$

Example 2: Multiply $\sqrt[3]{4x} \cdot \sqrt[4]{8x^3}$.

$$\sqrt[3]{4x} \cdot \sqrt[4]{8x^3} = \sqrt[12]{(4x)^4} \cdot \sqrt[12]{(8x^3)^3}$$
$$= \sqrt[12]{(2^2x)^4 \cdot (2^3x^3)^3}$$
$$= \sqrt[12]{2^8 \cdot 2^9 \cdot x^{13}}$$
$$= \sqrt[12]{2^{17} \cdot x^{13}}$$
$$= \sqrt[12]{2^{12} \cdot 2^5 \cdot x^{12} \cdot x}$$
$$= 2x\sqrt[12]{2^5 \cdot x}$$
$$= 2x\sqrt[12]{32x}$$

75. Division of Radicals

a. *Monomial Radical Expressions.* The division of radicals is essentially the opposite of multiplication. When radicals are of the same order, the division of two radicals may be expressed under one radical sign—for example, $\frac{\sqrt{4}}{\sqrt{2}} = \sqrt{\frac{4}{2}} = \sqrt{2}$. When radicals are of different orders, they must be expressed as radicals having the same index or be changed to fractional exponents.

Example 1: Divide $\sqrt{15}$ by $\sqrt{5}$.

$$\frac{\sqrt{15}}{\sqrt{5}} = \sqrt{\frac{15}{5}} = \sqrt{3}$$

Example 2: Divide $\sqrt[3]{x^4y}$ by $\sqrt[3]{y^7}$.

$$\frac{\sqrt[3]{x^4y}}{\sqrt[3]{y^7}} = \sqrt[3]{\frac{x^4y}{y^7}}$$
$$= \sqrt[3]{\frac{x^4}{y^6}}$$
$$= \frac{x}{y^2}\sqrt[3]{x}$$

Example 3: Divide $\sqrt{35}$ by $\sqrt{15}$.

$$\frac{\sqrt{35}}{\sqrt{15}} = \sqrt{\frac{35}{15}}$$
$$= \sqrt{\frac{7}{3}}$$
$$= \frac{1}{3}\sqrt{21}$$

Example 4: Divide $\sqrt{4ab}\,\sqrt[3]{2ab}$ by $\sqrt[6]{4a^5b^3}$.

$$\frac{\sqrt{4ab}\,\sqrt[3]{2ab}}{\sqrt[6]{4a^5b^3}} = \frac{\sqrt[6]{(4ab)^3}\cdot\sqrt[6]{(2ab)^2}}{\sqrt[6]{4a^5b^3}}$$
$$= \sqrt[6]{\frac{64a^3b^3 \cdot 4a^2b^2}{4a^5b^3}}$$
$$= \sqrt[6]{64b^2}$$
$$= \sqrt[6]{2^6b^2} \text{ or } (2^6b^2)^{\frac{1}{6}}$$
$$= 2\sqrt[3]{b}$$

b. *Binomial Expressions With Radical in Divisor.* When the divisor is a binomial in which one or more of the terms contains a square root, division is performed by first rationalizing the divisor. Multiply the numerator and denominator of the fraction by the denominator with the sign between the terms changed; then simplify the numerator and the denominator.

Example 1: Divide 3 by $4 + \sqrt{6}$.

$$\frac{3}{4+\sqrt{6}} = \frac{3}{4+\sqrt{6}} \cdot \frac{4-\sqrt{6}}{4-\sqrt{6}}$$
$$= \frac{3(4-\sqrt{6})}{16-6}$$
$$= \frac{3}{10}(4-\sqrt{6})$$

Example 2: Divide $\sqrt{1+x}-\sqrt{1-x}$ by $\sqrt{1+x}+\sqrt{1-x}$.

$$\frac{\sqrt{1+x}-\sqrt{1-x}}{\sqrt{1+x}+\sqrt{1-x}}\cdot\frac{\sqrt{1+x}-\sqrt{1-x}}{\sqrt{1+x}-\sqrt{1-x}}$$

$$=\frac{(1+x)-2\sqrt{1-x^{2}}+(1-x)}{(1+x)-(1-x)}$$

$$=\frac{2-2\sqrt{1-x^{2}}}{2x}$$

$$=\frac{1-\sqrt{1-x^{2}}}{x}$$

76. Review Problems—Exponents and Radicals

a. Simplify.
(1) $2^{\frac{1}{3}}(2^{3})$
(2) $(8^{3})^{2}$
(3) $\sqrt{50}$
(4) $\sqrt[3]{\frac{7}{16}}$
(5) $\sqrt{18x-9}$
(6) $\sqrt[a]{\frac{6z^{3n}}{y^{6}}}$
(7) $(x^{10}y^{6})^{\frac{1}{5}}$
(8) $(d^{9}e^{4})^{\frac{3}{4}}$
(9) $\left(\dfrac{64x^{6}}{g^{3}}\right)^{\frac{1}{3}}$
(10) $(a^{9}b^{4})^{6}$

b. Express with radical signs.
(1) $\dfrac{1}{4^{\frac{1}{3}}}$
(2) $\dfrac{3}{a^{2}b^{3}}$
(3) $\dfrac{2}{6^{3}}$
(4) $(8f)^{\frac{1}{2}}$
(5) $5x^{5}$
(6) $\dfrac{3}{a^{2}c^{1.5}}$
(7) $\dfrac{1}{6x^{3}}$
(8) $(8a^{2}b^{3})^{\frac{1}{3}}$
(9) $(2r_{1}+3r_{2})^{\frac{1}{2}}$
(10) $3\left(\tfrac{1}{4}x^{4}y^{2}\right)^{\frac{1}{2}}$

c. Express with fractional exponents.
(1) $\sqrt[4]{a^{3}}$
(2) $\sqrt[3]{5x}$
(3) $6x\sqrt[3]{a^{x}}$
(4) $\sqrt[5]{z^{2}}$
(5) $\sqrt[3]{3a^{3}b^{5}}$
(6) $y^{3}\sqrt[4]{a^{3}}$
(7) $8\sqrt[3]{3e}$
(8) $9\sqrt[5]{g^{7}}$
(9) $3b\sqrt[5]{cd^{2}}$
(10) $\sqrt[3]{(x-y)^{2}}$

d. Simplify by removing suitable factors from radicand.
(1) $\sqrt{12}$
(2) $\sqrt{63}$
(3) $\sqrt{63x^{4}}$
(4) $2\sqrt{72a^{2}b^{4}}$
(5) $\sqrt{50b^{2}d^{2}}$
(6) $\sqrt{8f^{2}R^{2}}$
(7) $3\sqrt{63p^{3}z^{2}}$
(8) $2d\sqrt{108d^{7}g^{3}}$
(9) $5a\sqrt{81a^{2}b}$
(10) $16w^{2}x\sqrt{98w^{4}x^{2}y^{2}z}$

e. Rationalize denominators.
(1) $\dfrac{1}{\sqrt{50}}$
(2) $\dfrac{1}{\sqrt{4x}}$
(3) $\dfrac{2a}{\sqrt{3a}}$
(4) $\dfrac{1}{\sqrt[3]{x}}$
(5) $\dfrac{1}{\sqrt[3]{8ax^{2}}}$
(6) $\dfrac{1}{\sqrt[3]{9}-2x}$
(7) $\dfrac{a+b}{\sqrt[3]{a^{2}}}$
(8) $\dfrac{a}{\sqrt[3]{a^{2}bc}}$
(9) $\dfrac{1}{\sqrt[3]{(s+1)^{2}}}$
(10) $\dfrac{i+3}{\sqrt[5]{(i+3)^{2}}}$

f. Simplify.
(1) $6\sqrt{4}-3\sqrt{4}+2\sqrt{4}$
(2) $6\sqrt{45}-2\sqrt{20}$
(3) $x-\sqrt{\dfrac{3x^{2}}{4}}$
(4) $\dfrac{a}{2}+\sqrt{\dfrac{9a^{2}}{2}}$
(5) $r\sqrt{r8t}+rt\sqrt{\dfrac{5}{rt}}$
(6) $\sqrt{\dfrac{x+y}{x-y}}-\sqrt{\dfrac{x-y}{x+y}}$
(7) $\sqrt{5}+3\sqrt{x}+5\sqrt{x}$
(8) $7\sqrt{a}-4\sqrt{5}-2\sqrt{5}$
(9) $4\sqrt{x-y}+3\sqrt{x+y}-8\sqrt{x-y}$
(10) $3\sqrt{125a^{3}b^{4}}+b\sqrt{20a^{5}}-\sqrt{500a^{3}b^{3}}$

g. Find product and simplify.
(1) $3\sqrt{5}\cdot 4\sqrt{2}$
(2) $2\sqrt[3]{9}\cdot 3\sqrt[3]{3}$
(3) $4\sqrt[3]{a^{2}b^{4}}\cdot 2\sqrt[3]{ab^{3}}$
(4) $\sqrt{4z^{4}}\cdot z\sqrt{3z^{3}}$
(5) $\sqrt[5]{4x^{2}y^{2}}\cdot\sqrt[5]{2x^{4}y^{2}}\cdot\sqrt[5]{4xy^{2}}$
(6) $2\sqrt[3]{2pq^{4}r}\cdot\sqrt[3]{4pq^{4}r^{2}}\cdot 3\sqrt[3]{8pq^{4}r^{3}}$
(7) $(\sqrt{a}+\sqrt{b}+\sqrt{c})^{2}$
(8) $a\sqrt{x}(a\sqrt{ax}+x\sqrt{ax}+\sqrt{ax})$
(9) $\sqrt{9}-\sqrt{17}\cdot\sqrt{9}+\sqrt{17}$
(10) $\sqrt[3]{x^{3}y^{6}}\,\sqrt{256a^{8}}$

h. Divide and simplify.
(1) $\dfrac{\sqrt{12}}{\sqrt{3}}$
(2) $\dfrac{\sqrt[3]{625y}}{\sqrt[3]{5y}}$
(3) $\dfrac{\sqrt[3]{16x^{4}}}{\sqrt[3]{2x}}$
(4) $\dfrac{3zy}{\dfrac{\sqrt{zu}}{2}}$
(5) $\dfrac{\sqrt{6}-2}{\sqrt[4]{5a}}$
(6) $\dfrac{\sqrt{30a}\;\sqrt[4]{24a^{2}}\;\sqrt[3]{72a}}{\sqrt[4]{5a}}$
(7) $\dfrac{\sqrt{2}+\sqrt{c}}{\sqrt{c}+2\sqrt{2}}$
(8) $\dfrac{4\sqrt{3}-3\sqrt{2}}{\sqrt{6}}\div\dfrac{\sqrt{10}}{4\sqrt{3}+3\sqrt{2}}$
(9) $\dfrac{\sqrt{e^{2}+f^{2}+f}}{\sqrt{e^{2}+f^{2}-f}}$
(10) $\dfrac{2b+\sqrt{1-4b^{2}}}{2b-\sqrt{1-4b^{2}}}$

Section VII. IMAGINARY AND COMPLEX NUMBERS

77. Imaginary Numbers

a. Indicated Square Root of Negative Numbers.

(1) In the study of roots to this point, only the roots of positive numbers have been considered. Sometimes a negative expression will appear under the radical. Such an expression was given the designation *imaginary number* to distinguish it from real numbers. In electricity and electronics, however, so-called imaginary numbers are used for real physical calculations—the reactance of a large capacitor or inductor must be calculated by using this type of number.

(2) In multiplication, when a real number is multiplied by itself the result is always positive. For example, $+5 \cdot +5 = 25$, and $-5 \cdot -5 = 25$. Therefore, any number raised to a power having an even exponent will be positive because like signs are being multiplied. However, this is not true for the interpretation of an expression such as $\sqrt{-9}$. Any negative number can be regarded as the product of a positive number of the same absolute value and -1, and the square root of a negative

number can be written as the square root of a positive number times $\sqrt{-1}$; thus, $\sqrt{-9} = \sqrt{9}\sqrt{-1} = 3\sqrt{-1}$, with $\sqrt{-1}$ being the imaginary number. Most mathematics texts represent the imaginary number $\sqrt{-1}$ by the letter i. However, the letter I or i means current in electrical formulas; therefore, the letter j, commonly called the *operator j*, is used in electronics.

Example 1: $\sqrt{-36} = \sqrt{(-1)36} = \sqrt{-1} \cdot \sqrt{36} = j6$

Example 2: $\sqrt{-Z^2} = \sqrt{(-1)Z^2} = \sqrt{-1} \cdot \sqrt{Z^2} = \sqrt{-1} \cdot Z = jZ$

Example 3: $-\sqrt{-9a^2} = -\sqrt{(-1)9a^2} = -\sqrt{-1} \cdot \sqrt{9a^2} = -\sqrt{-1} \cdot 3a = -j3a$

b. *Powers of Operator j.* Imaginary numbers follow the fundamental laws of addition, subtraction, multiplication, and division. They also can be raised to a power; thus, $j^3 = j^2 \cdot j = -1(j) = -j$, and $j^4 = j^2 \cdot j^2 = -1(-1) = 1$. The values of the powers of j are obtained as follows:

$j^2 = j \cdot j = \sqrt{-1} \cdot \sqrt{-1} = -1;$

$j^3 = j \cdot j \cdot j = \sqrt{-1} \cdot \sqrt{-1} \cdot \sqrt{-1} = -1\sqrt{-1} = -j;$ and

$j^4 = j \cdot j \cdot j \cdot j = \sqrt{-1} \cdot \sqrt{-1} \cdot \sqrt{-1} \cdot \sqrt{-1} = -1 \cdot -1 = 1;$ but

$j^5 = j \cdot j \cdot j \cdot j \cdot j = j^4 \cdot j = j^1 = \sqrt{-1}$, and the whole cycle starts over again. Therefore, j^4 can be eliminated as many times as it is contained in an expression, reducing the quantity to j, j^2, or j^3 and getting its value from the following:

$$j = j = \sqrt{-1}$$
$$j^2 = -1$$
$$j^3 = -j$$
$$j^4 = 1$$

Example 1: Simplify j^{13}.
$$j^{13} = j^{12} \cdot j = j = \sqrt{-1}$$

Example 2: Simplify j^{27}.
$$j^{27} = j^{24} \cdot j^3 = j^3 = -j = -\sqrt{-1}$$

d. *Multiplication of Simple Imaginary Numbers.* When multiplying two imaginary numbers, remember that $j^2 = -1$, $j^3 = -j$, and $j^4 = 1$ (b above); then, proceed as with any problem in multiplication (par. 45).

Example 1: Multiply $\sqrt{-16}$ and $\sqrt{-4}$.
$$\sqrt{-16} \cdot \sqrt{-4} = j4 \cdot j2 = j^2 8 = (-1)8 = -8$$

Example 2: Multiply $\sqrt{-81}$, $\sqrt{-25}$, and $\sqrt{-49}$.
$$\sqrt{-81} \cdot \sqrt{-25} \cdot \sqrt{-49} = j9 \cdot j5 \cdot j7 = j^3 315 = (-j)315 = -j315$$

e. *Division of Single Imaginary Numbers.* In the division of two simple imaginary numbers, when both the dividend and divisor contain operator j, divide both by j and proceed as with ordinary integers. If a j remains in the denominator, the denominator must be rationalized because the j represents a radical expression. To rationalize, multiply both the numerator and denominator by the imaginary number.

Example 1: Divide $\sqrt{-100}$ by $\sqrt{-16}$.
$$\frac{\sqrt{-100}}{\sqrt{-16}} = \frac{j \cdot 10}{j \cdot 4} = \frac{10}{4} = 2\tfrac{1}{2}$$

Example 2: Divide 12 by $\sqrt{-6}$.
$$\frac{12}{\sqrt{-6}} = \frac{12}{j\sqrt{6}} = \frac{12 \cdot j\sqrt{6}}{j\sqrt{6} \cdot j\sqrt{6}} = \frac{j12\sqrt{6}}{j^2 6} = \frac{j12\sqrt{6}}{-6} = -j2\sqrt{6}$$

Example 3: Divide $\sqrt{-3}$ by $\sqrt{-4}$.
$$\frac{\sqrt{-3}}{\sqrt{-4}} = \frac{j\sqrt{3}}{j2} = \frac{\sqrt{3}}{2} \text{ or } \frac{1}{2}\sqrt{3}$$

Example 4: Divide 6 by j.
$$\frac{6}{j} = \frac{6}{j} \cdot \frac{j}{j} = \frac{j6}{j^2} = \frac{j6}{-1} = -j6$$

c. *Addition and Subtraction of Imaginary Numbers.* These numbers may be added or subtracted in the same manner that any algebraic expression is added or subtracted (par. 44). First change the expression to the j form; then treat the j as any other letter in an algebraic expression.

Example 1: Add $\sqrt{-25}$, $\sqrt{-36}$, and $\sqrt{-9}$.
$$\sqrt{-25} + \sqrt{-36} + \sqrt{-9} = j5 + j6 + j3 = j14$$

Example 2: Add $6\sqrt{-2} + 5\sqrt{-8} + 8\sqrt{-18}$.
$$6\sqrt{-2} + 5\sqrt{-8} + 8\sqrt{-18} = j6\sqrt{2} + j5\sqrt{8} + j8\sqrt{18}$$
$$= j6\sqrt{2} + j5(5 \cdot 2)\sqrt{2} + j8(8 \cdot 3)\sqrt{2}$$
$$= (j6 + j10 + j24)\sqrt{2}$$
$$= j40\sqrt{2}$$

Example 3: Subtract $\sqrt{-64}$ from $\sqrt{-36}$.
$$\sqrt{-36} - \sqrt{-64} = j6 - j8 = -j2$$

Example 4: Subtract $4\sqrt{-8}$ from $6\sqrt{-18}$.
$$6\sqrt{-18} - 4\sqrt{-8} = j(6 \cdot 3)\sqrt{2} - j(4 \cdot 2)\sqrt{2}$$
$$= (j18 - j8)\sqrt{2}$$
$$= j10\sqrt{2}$$

78. Complex Numbers

a. *Operations With Complex Numbers.* A *complex number* is a real number united to an imaginary number by a plus or minus sign; thus, $10 - j5$, $x + jy$, and $R + jx$ are complex numbers. Complex numbers are of great importance in alternating-current electricity in which many problems would be difficult to solve without their use. A complex number expressed in the form $x + jy$ may be considered a bi-nominal; thus, the addition, subtraction, multiplication, and division of complex numbers are reduced to the corresponding operations with binomials in which one term is real and the other imaginary.

b. *Addition and Subtraction of Complex Numbers.* To add or subtract complex numbers, first combine the real parts, then combine the imaginary parts, and write the results as a binomial with the appropriate sign separating the real and imaginary terms.

Example 1: Add $3 + j5$ and $5 - j$.
$$(3 + j5) + (5 - j) = 3 + j5 + 5 - j$$
$$= 8 + j4$$

Example 2: Add $6 + \sqrt{-25}$ and $8\sqrt{-16}$.

$$(6 + \sqrt{-25}) + (8\sqrt{-16}) = 6 + j5 + (8 \cdot j4)$$
$$= 6 + j5 + j32$$
$$= 6 + j37$$

Example 3: Add $8 + \sqrt{-12}$ and $9 + \sqrt{-75}$.

$$(8 + \sqrt{-12}) + (9 + \sqrt{-75}) = 8 + j2\sqrt{3} + 9 + j5\sqrt{3}$$
$$= 17 + j7\sqrt{3}$$

Example 4: Subtract $7 - j6$ from $3 - j2$.

$$(3 - j2) - (7 - j6) = 3 - j2 - 7 + j6$$
$$= -4 + j4$$

Example 5: Subtract $2 - 3\sqrt{-4}$ from $10 + \sqrt{-4}$.

$$(10 + \sqrt{-4}) - (2 - 3\sqrt{-4}) = (10 + j2) - (2 - j6)$$
$$= 10 + j2 - 2 + j6$$
$$= 8 + j8 \text{ or } 8(1 + j)$$

Example 6: Subtract $3 + 7\sqrt{-24}$ from $5 + 3\sqrt{-6}$.

$$(5 + 3\sqrt{-6}) - (3 + 7\sqrt{-24}) = 5 + j3\sqrt{6} - [3 + j(7 \cdot 2)\sqrt{6}]$$
$$= 5 + j3\sqrt{6} - 3 - j14\sqrt{6}$$
$$= 2 - j11\sqrt{6}$$

c. Multiplication of Complex Numbers. As in addition and subtraction, when complex numbers are multiplied they are treated as ordinary binomials. Remember, however, that $j^2 = -1$.

Example 1: Multiply $3 - j6$ by $4 + j2$.

$$\begin{array}{r} 3 - j6 \\ 4 + j2 \\ \hline 12 - j24 \\ +j6 - j^2 12 \\ \hline 12 - j18 - j^2 12 \end{array} = j12 - j18 - (-1)(12)$$
$$= 12 - j18 + 12$$
$$= \underline{24 - j18}$$

Example 2: Multiply $8 \cdot -\sqrt{-5}$ by $-2 + \sqrt{-6}$.

$$\begin{array}{r} 8 - j\sqrt{5} \\ -2 + j\sqrt{6} \\ \hline -16 + j2\sqrt{5} + j8\sqrt{6} - j^2\sqrt{30} \end{array} = -16 + j2\sqrt{5} + j8\sqrt{6} - (-1)\sqrt{30}$$
$$= -16 + j2\sqrt{5} + j8\sqrt{6} + \sqrt{30}$$
$$= -16 + \sqrt{30} + j(2\sqrt{5} + 8\sqrt{6})$$

d. Division of Complex Numbers. When dividing complex numbers, the denominator of the expression in its fractional form must first be rationalized (par. 74). To obtain a real number as a divisor, multiply both the numerator and denominator by the complex number of the denominator with its sign changed (called the *conjugate* of the complex number). In carrying out the multiplication, the radical expression is eliminated. Since $j^2 = -1$, the sign of the coefficient of j^2 is changed; the complex number thus becomes a real number to combine with the other real number in the denominator.

Example 1: Divide $3 + j4$ by $1 + j$.

$$\frac{3 + j4}{1 + j} = \frac{3 + j4}{1 + j} \cdot \frac{1 - j}{1 - j}$$
$$= \frac{3 + j - j^2 4}{1 - j^2}$$
$$= \frac{3 + j - (-1)4}{1 - (-1)}$$
$$= \frac{3 + j + 4}{2}$$
$$= \frac{7}{2} + j\frac{1}{2}$$

Example 2: Divide 6 by $3 + \sqrt{-2}$.

$$\frac{6}{3 + \sqrt{-2}} = \frac{6}{3 + j\sqrt{2}} \cdot \frac{3 - j\sqrt{2}}{3 - j\sqrt{2}}$$
$$= \frac{6(3 - j\sqrt{2})}{(3 + j\sqrt{2})(3 - j\sqrt{2})}$$
$$= \frac{18 - j6\sqrt{2}}{9 - j^2 2}$$
$$= \frac{18 - j6\sqrt{2}}{11}$$

79. Review Problems—Imaginary and Complex Numbers

a. Simplify the radical, using operator j.

(1) $\sqrt{-75}$

(2) $\sqrt{-23}$

(3) $-\sqrt{-64ax^5}$

(4) $-\sqrt{-100x^4y^4}$

(5) $\sqrt{\dfrac{1}{9}}$

(6) $\sqrt[3]{-128x^7y^8}$

b. Add.

(1) $-47 + j17$ and $63 + j92$

(2) $27 - j11$ and $14 - j11$

(3) $123 - j114$ and $-62 - j137$

(4) $44 + j17$ and $-j7$

(5) $6 + j10$ and $j1$

(6) $14 + j15$ and $-16 - j62$

c. Subtract.

(1) $-69 + j432$ from $710 + j61$

(2) $14 - j121$ from $73 - j7$

(3) $84 - j62$ from $62 - j47$

(4) $-74 - j20$ from $81 - j81$

(5) $-87 - j7$ from $82 + j16$

(6) $-9 + j$ from $-j7$

d. Multiply.

(1) $4 + \sqrt{-81}$ by $2 + \sqrt{-49}$

(2) $2 + 2\sqrt{-2}$ by $3 + 3\sqrt{-3}$

(3) $2 - j3$ by $2 + j3$

(4) $(2 - j3)^2$

(5) $(j^4 + j^2 2 + j^3 3 + j4)^2$

(6) $4 - j7$ by $8 + j2$

(7) $f + jg$ by $f + jg$

(8) $I + jE$ by $I - jE$

(9) $8 - j13$ by $11 - j12$

(10) $5 + \sqrt{-16}$ by $7 - \sqrt{-81}$

e. Divide.

(1) 1 by $3 + j2$

(2) $6 + j$ by j

(3) $2 + j3$ by $3 - j4$

(4) $4 + \sqrt{-9}$ by $2 - \sqrt{-1}$

(5) $x + jy$ by $x - jy$

(6) 10 by $1 + j2$

(7) 3 by $1 - j$

(8) $3 + \sqrt{-25}$ by $4 - \sqrt{-4}$

(9) $6 - j2$ by $4 - j7$

(10) $I + jE$ by $I - jE$

Section VIII. EQUATIONS

80. General

An *equation* is a statement of equality between two expressions. For example, $x + y = 12$, $3x + 5 = 20$, and $3 \cdot 9 = 27$ are equations; therefore, all expressions separated by the equality sign are equations, whether the expressions are algebraic or arithmetical. The expression to the left of the equality sign is called the *left-hand member* of the equation; the expression to the right of the equality sign is known as the *right-hand member*. Finding the values of the unknown quantities of an algebraic equation is known as solving the equation, and the answer is called the *solution*. If only one unknown is involved, the solution is also called the *root*.

81. Solving Simple Equations

a. Adding Same Quantity to Both Members of Equation. Equal quantities may be added to both sides of an equation without changing the equality.

Example 1: Solve the equation $x - 4 = 7$ for x.

$$x - 4 = 7$$
$$x - 4 + 4 = 7 + 4$$
$$x = 11$$

Example 2: Solve the equation $x - 7 = 14$ for x.

$$x - 7 = 14$$
$$x - 7 + 7 = 14 + 7$$
$$x = 21$$

b. Subtracting Same Quantity From Both Members of Equation. Equal quantities may be subtracted from both sides of an equation.

Example 1: Solve the equation $x + 2 = 5$ for x.

$$x + 2 = 5$$
$$x + 2 - 2 = 5 - 2$$
$$x = 3$$

Example 2: Solve the equation $x + 5 = 12$ for x.

$$x + 5 = 12$$
$$x + 5 - 5 = 12 - 5$$
$$x = 7$$

c. Multiplying Both Members of Equation by Same Quantity. Both sides of an equation can be multiplied by the same quantity.

Example 1: Solve the equation $\frac{x}{3} = 5$ for x.

$$\frac{x}{3} = 5$$
$$\frac{x}{3} \cdot \frac{3}{1} = 5 \cdot 3$$
$$x = 15$$

Example 2: Solve the equation $\frac{z}{3} + \frac{z}{9} = 4$ for z.

Multiply both sides of the equation by 9.

$$\left(\frac{z}{3} \cdot \frac{9}{1}\right) + \left(\frac{z}{9} \cdot \frac{9}{1}\right) = 4 \cdot 9$$
$$3z + z = 36$$
$$4z = 36$$
$$z = 9$$

d. Dividing Both Members of Equation by Same Quantity. Both sides of an equation may be divided by the same quantity.

Example 1: Solve the equation $3x = 12$ for x.

$$3x = 12$$
$$\frac{3x}{3} = \frac{12}{3}$$
$$x = 4$$

Example 2: Solve the equation $PV = RT$ for T.

$$PV = RT$$
$$\frac{PV}{R} = \frac{RT}{R}$$
$$T = \frac{PV}{R}$$

82. Solving More Difficult Equations

a. Transposition. The process of adding to or subtracting from both members of an equation (par. 81a and b) can be shortened by shifting a term or terms from one side of the equation to the other and changing the signs. This operation is called transposition.

Example 1: Solve the equation $6x + 4 = x - 16$ for x.

$$6x + 4 = x - 16$$
$$6x - x = -16 - 4$$
$$5x = -20$$
$$x = -4$$

Example 2: Solve the equation $5a - 7 = 2a + 2$ for a.

$$5a - 7 = 2a + 2$$
$$5a - 2a = 2 + 7$$
$$3a = 9$$
$$a = 3$$

b. Equations With Fractions. In solving a fractional equation, first find the LCD and multiply both members of the equation, term by term; then perform the operations in paragraph 81 or a above.

Example 1: Solve the equation $\frac{x}{2} + \frac{x}{3} = 10$ for x.

$$\frac{x}{2} + \frac{x}{3} = 10$$
$$\frac{3x + 2x}{6} = 10$$
$$\frac{5x}{6} = \frac{10}{1}$$
$$5x = 60$$
$$x = 12$$

Example 2: Solve the equation $\frac{x-1}{2} = 3 + x$ for x.

$$\frac{x-1}{2} = 3 + x$$
$$\frac{x-1}{2} = \frac{3+x}{1}$$
$$1(x-1) = 2(3+x)$$
$$x - 1 = 6 + 2x$$
$$x - 2x = 6 + 1$$
$$-x = 7$$
$$x = -7$$

Example 3: Solve the equation $\frac{2}{x-2} + \frac{2}{x+4} = \frac{4}{x-3}$ for x.

$$\frac{2}{x-2} + \frac{2}{x+4} = \frac{4}{x-3}$$
$$\frac{2(x+4) + 2(x-2)}{(x-2)(x+4)} = \frac{4}{x-3}$$
$$\frac{2x+8+2x-4}{(x-2)(x+4)} = \frac{4}{x-3}$$
$$\frac{4x+4}{(x-2)(x+4)} = \frac{4}{x-3}$$
$$(4x+4)(x-3) = 4(x-2)(x+4)$$
$$4x^2 - 8x - 12 = 4(x^2 + 2x - 8)$$
$$4x^2 - 8x - 12 = 4x^2 + 8x - 32$$
$$4x^2 - 4x^2 - 8x - 8x = -32 + 12$$
$$-16x = -20$$
$$x = \frac{20}{16} = \frac{5}{4} = 1\frac{1}{4}$$

83. Written Equations

Many practical problems are stated in words and must be translated into symbols before the rules of algebra can be applied. There are no specific rules for the translation of a written problem into an equation of numbers, signs, and symbols. The following general suggestions may be helpful in developing equations:

a. From the worded statement of the problem, select the unknown quantity (or one of the unknown quantities) and represent it by a letter, such as x. Write the expression, stating exactly what x represents and the units in which it is measured.

b. If there is more than one unknown quantity in the problem, try to represent each unknown in terms of the first unknown.

Example 1: In simple problems, an equation may be written by an almost direct translation into algebraic symbols; thus,

Seven times a certain voltage diminished by 3
$$7 \times E - 3$$

gives the same result as the voltage increased by 75.
$$= E + 75$$

Solving the equation:

$$7E - 3 = E + 75$$
$$7E - E = 75 + 3$$
$$6E = 78$$
$$E = 13$$

expressed in an equation by using letters, symbols, and constant terms. For example, a formula in electricity states that the voltage across any part of a circuit is equal to the product of the current and resistance of that part of the circuit. In formula form, this is expressed as $E = IR$, where E is the *voltage or difference in potential* expressed in *volts*, I is the *current* expressed in *amperes*, and R is the *resistance* expressed in *ohms*.

b. *Solving the Formula.* To solve a formula, perform the same operations on both members of an equation until the desired unknown can be isolated in one member of the equation. If the numerical values for some variables are given, substitute in the formula and solve for the unknown as in any other equation.

Example 1: Solve the formula $T = \frac{12(D-d)}{l}$ for D.

$$T = \frac{12(D-d)}{l}$$

Multiply both sides by l:
$$Tl = 12D - 12d$$

Transpose and change signs:
$$12D = Tl + 12d$$

Divide both sides by 12:
$$\frac{12D}{12} = \frac{Tl}{12} + \frac{12d}{12}$$

$$D = \frac{Tl}{12} + d$$

Example 2: Given the formula for electrical power, $P = I^2R$, find the value of P in watts when $I = 15.4$ amperes and $R = 25.7$ ohms.

$$P = I^2R$$

Substituting the given numerical values for I and R:
$$P = (15.4)^2 \times 25.7$$
$$= 237.16 \times 25.7$$
$$= 6,095 \text{ watts}$$

Example 3: Given the formula for the total resistance of two resistors in parallel,
$R_T = \frac{R_1 R_2}{R_1 + R_2}$, solve for R_T in ohms when

84. Simultaneous Equations

a. *Definition.* Simultaneous equations are two or more equations satisfied by the same sets of values of the unknown quantities. They are used to solve a problem with two or more unknown quantities.

b. *Example.* Assume that the sum of two numbers is 17, and that three times the first number less two times the second number is equal to 6. What are the numbers? In setting up equations for this problem, let x equal the first number and y equal the second number. The first equation is $x + y = 17$, and the second equation is $3x - 2y = 6$. This problem can be solved in three ways: by substitution, by addition, or by subtraction. All three methods are explained below.

(1) *Substitution.*

$x + y = 17$ or $x = 17 - y$

Substitute $x = 17 - y$ in the second equation:
$$3x - 2y = 6$$
$$3(17 - y) - 2y = 6$$
Remove the parentheses:
$$51 - 3y - 2y = 6$$
Transpose:
$$-5y = 6 - 51$$
$$-5y = -45$$
$$5y = 45$$
$$y = 9$$

Substitute $y = 9$ in the first equation and solve for x:
$$x + y = 17 \text{ or } x + 9 = 17$$
Transpose:
$$x = 17 - 9$$
$$x = 8$$

(2) *Addition.*

$$x + y = 17$$
$$3x - 2y = 6$$

Before adding, change the y in the first equation to $2y$ so that the y terms drop out when added; thus, the first equation must be multiplied by 2.
$$2x + 2y = 34$$
$$3x - 2y = 6$$
$$5x = 40$$
$$x = 8$$

Substitute $x = 8$ in the first equation and solve for y:
$$x + y = 17 \text{ or } 8 + y = 17$$
$$y = 17 - 8$$
$$y = 9$$

(3) *Subtraction.*

Before subtracting, multiply the first equation by 3 so that the x terms drop out when subtracted.
$$3x + 3y = 51$$
$$3x - 2y = 6$$
Subtract the second equation from the first equation:

$$3x + 3y = 51$$
$$-3x + 2y = -6$$
$$5y = 45$$
$$y = 9$$

Substitute $y = 9$ in the first equation and solve for x: Refer to (1) and (2) above.

c. *Additional Examples.* If the coefficients of the unknowns differ (for example, $3x$ and x and $2y$ and $4y$), multiply one or both equations to establish equal coefficients for one of the unknowns (x or y).

Example 1: Solve for x and y if $3x + 2y = 7$ and $x + 4y = 9$.

Multiply the first equation by 2 so that $2y$ will become $4y$:
$$6x + 4y = 14$$
$$x + 4y = 9$$

Subtract the second equation from the first equation:
$$6x + 4y = 14$$
$$-x - 4y = -9$$
$$5x = 5$$
$$x = 1$$

Solve for y by substituting $x = 1$ in either equation.

Example 2: Solve for x and y if $2x + 3y = 24$ and $3x - 4y = 2$.
$$2x + 3y = 24$$
$$3x - 4y = 2$$

Multiply the first equation by 4 to change $3y$ to $12y$; multiply the second equation by 3 to change $4y$ to $12y$; then add the two equations:
$$8x + 12y = 96$$
$$9x - 12y = 6$$
$$17x = 102$$
$$x = 6$$

Solve for y by substituting $x = 6$ in either equation.

85. Solving Formulas

a. *The Formula.* A formula is a rule or law that states a scientific relationship. It can be

Check: $7(13) - 3 = 13 + 75$
$$91 - 3 = 13 + 75$$
$$88 = 88$$

Example 2: A triangle has a perimeter of 30 inches. The longest side is 7 inches longer than the shortest side, and the third side is 5 inches longer than the shortest side. Find the length of the three sides.

Let x = length of shortest side.
$x + 7$ = length of longest side.
$x + 5$ = length of third side.
$$x + (x+5) + (x+7) = 30$$
Solving the equation:
$$x + x + 5 + x + 7 = 30$$
$$3x + 12 = 30$$
$$3x = 30 - 12$$
$$3x = 18$$
$$x = 6 = \text{shortest side.}$$
$$6 + 5 = 11 = \text{third side.}$$
$$6 + 7 = 13 = \text{longest side.}$$

$R_1 = 40$ ohms and $R_2 = 60$ ohms.

$$R_T = \frac{R_1 R_2}{R_1 + R_2}$$

Substitute the given numerical values for R_1 and R_2:

$$R_T = \frac{40 \times 60}{40 + 60}$$
$$= \frac{2,400}{100}$$
$$= 24 \text{ ohms}$$

86. Review Problems—Equations

a. Solve for the unknown quantity in each of the following:

(1) $y + 12 = 15$

(2) $\dfrac{n}{8} = \dfrac{1}{4}$

(3) $0.638s = 53.55$

(4) $47x - 17 = 235 - 37x$

(5) $(10m + 6) - (11 - 15m) = 14m + 6m$

(6) $x + y = 3$
$3x + 2y = 1$

(7) $a - 3b = 0$
$5a - 4b = 11$

(8) $7x - 5y = 1$
$5x + y = 19$

(9) $4m - 2n = 2$
$3m + n = 14$

(10) $3r - 9s = 15$
$6r - 7s = 41$

b. Solve the following formulas for the quantity indicated:

(1) $Fd = Wh$ for d

(2) $v^2 = v_0^2 + 2gh$ for g

(3) $F = \dfrac{w}{g} a$ for a

(4) $H = \dfrac{D^2 N}{2.534}$ for N

(5) $F = \dfrac{22.5\, BIl}{10^8}$ for l

c. Solve the following linear equations for the unknown quantity:

(1) $7(2x - 6) - 8 = 10x + 10$

(2) $10(x - 2) - 10(2 - x) = 4x - 40$

(3) $9.8a - 9.4 = 6.8a + .6$

(4) $2x + 3 + \dfrac{11x - 11}{3} = 22$

(5) $3R + 2(R - 4) = 6R - 10(R - 2)$

(6) $\dfrac{5Z}{4} + 2Z = \dfrac{3 + Z}{3} - 7Z$

(7) $-(5x + 15) = 5x + 21 - \dfrac{5(2 - x)}{2}$

(8) $\dfrac{11y - 13}{25} + \dfrac{17y + 4}{21} + \dfrac{19y + 3}{7} =$
$28\frac{1}{7} + \dfrac{5y - 25\frac{1}{4}}{4}$

(9) $\dfrac{4X_L}{5} - 6X_L + 2 = \dfrac{X_L}{4}$

(10) $(x - 1)(x + 1) + x(1 - x) = 4x(2x + 1) - 8x(x - 2)$

d. Solve the following sets of simultaneous linear equations:

(1) $5x - 2y = 10$
$3x - y = 7$

(2) $6a + 15b = 69$
$6a - 6b = 14$

(3) $x - 3y = -17$
$2x + 6y = 50$

(4) $6x - 8y = 20$
$3x + 2y = -14$

(5) $-4x + y = 13$
$8x - 5y = -29$

(6) $2I + \dfrac{2Z - 22}{3} = 30$
$\dfrac{3I - 15}{4} + 6Z = 108$

(7) $\dfrac{2}{x} + y = 1$
$\dfrac{1}{x} + 2y = 1\frac{1}{4}$

(8) $\dfrac{a}{3} + \dfrac{b}{4} = 1$
$\dfrac{a}{5} + \dfrac{b}{2} = -\frac{4}{5}$

(9) $\dfrac{5}{x} + \dfrac{2}{y} = -1$
$\dfrac{3}{x} + \dfrac{1}{y} = 1\frac{1}{8}$

(10) Solve for r and s:
$(a - b)r + (a + b)s = a^2 - b^2$
$(a + b)r - (a - b)s = 2ab$

e. Solve the following problems:

(1) Three times a voltage (E) diminished by 2 is equal to that voltage. What is the voltage?

(2) The sum of two resistances in series is 20 ohms. One resistance is 20 ohms. Give the algebraic expression for the other.

(3) If a certain voltage (E) is tripled and the result is diminished by 220 volts, the remainder is equal to the original voltage. What is the voltage?

(4) When two resistors are connected in series, the total resistance (R) is the sum of the two resistances. If one resistor is 25 ohms and the total resistance is 100 ohms, what is the value of the other resistor?

(5) The current (I) from a battery is divided among three circuits. The first circuit draws 20 milliamperes more than the second circuit, and the second circuit draws 20 milliamperes more than the third circuit. If the total current drawn is 240 milliamperes, what is the current in each circuit?

(6) Solving by the formula $I = \dfrac{E}{R}$, how much current (I) does an electric circuit having a resistance (R) of 20 ohms take if the voltage (E) is 110 volts?

Section IX. QUADRATIC EQUATIONS

87. General

A quadratic equation is one which can be reduced to the form $ax^2 + bx + c = 0$ where a, b, and c are known and x is the unknown quantity. In other words, a quadratic equation contains the square of the unknown quantity, such as x^2, but no higher power. For example, $3x^2 + 5x - 2 = 0$ and $x^2 - 4x + 3 = 0$ are quadratic equations. The form $ax^2 + bx + c = 0$ is called the *general quadratic equation.*

88. Pure Quadratic Equations

A pure quadratic equation is obtained from the general quadratic equation when b is equal to zero and the middle term (bx) does not appear. The equation then becomes $ax^2 + c = 0$. The pure quadratic equation has two roots that are equal in absolute value but have opposite signs. As discussed in paragraph 49, all numbers have two square roots. The equation $x^2 - 36 = 0$ is a pure quadratic equation since there are two numbers which, when substituted for x, will satisfy the equation. Thus $(+6)^2 - 36 = 0$ since $36 - 36 = 0$; also, $(-6)^2 - 36 = 0$ since $36 - 36 = 0$. Therefore, $x = \pm 6$.

Example: Solve the equation $x^2 - 5 = 20$ for x.

$$x^2 - 5 = 20$$
$$x^2 = 25$$
$$x = \pm 5$$

Check:

$$(\pm 5)^2 - 5 = 20$$
$$25 - 5 = 20$$
$$20 = 20$$

89. Solution by Factoring

a. Quadratic equations are found in many applications of even the simplest nature. For example, suppose that a sheet of metal is to be cut so that it has an area of 30 square inches, and that the length of the piece will be 1 inch longer than the width. With x representing the unknown width and $x + 1$ the unknown length, $x(x + 1)$ equals the area; therefore, the equation that must be satisfied is $x(x + 1) = 30$. By performing the indicated multiplication and subtracting 30 from each side, the equation now can be written in the form of a quadratic equation, as $x^2 + x - 30 = 0$.

b. To solve this equation, factor the left-hand side into the equivalent equation: $(x - 5)(x + 6) = 0$. The product of two factors is zero if either of the factors is zero (par. 53). Thus, each factor is set equal to zero and solved for the unknown. The equation is satisfied if $x - 5 = 0$ or $x = 5$. Note that the equation also is satisfied if $x + 6 = 0$. This illustrates an important fact concerning quadratic equations: *Every quadratic equation has two solutions.* Only one solution, however, may be appropriate when quadratic equations are used to solve actual problems. The quadratic equation only gives two *possible* solutions—the *actual* solution must be determined by referring to the facts in the original problem.

Example 1: Solve the equation $x^2 - 2x = 0$ for x.

$$x^2 - 2x = 0$$

Factoring:
$$x(x - 2) = 0$$
$$x = 0$$
or $\quad x - 2 = 0$
$$x = 2$$

Thus, 0 or 2 are the roots of the equation $x^2 - 2x = 0$.

Example 2: Solve the equation $2x^2 - 3x - 5 = 0$ for x.

$$2x^2 - 3x - 5 = 0$$

Factoring:
$$(2x - 5)(x + 1) = 0$$
so $\quad x + 1 = 0$
and $\quad x = -1$
or $\quad 2x - 5 = 0$
$$2x = 5$$
and $\quad x = \frac{r}{2}$ or $2\frac{1}{2}$

Thus, -1 and $2\frac{1}{2}$ are the roots of the equation $2x^2 - 3x - 5 = 0$.

90. Solution by Completing the Square

In solving quadratic equations, the method of factoring described in paragraph 89 usually is best if the factors are immediately apparent by inspection. When the values of the unknown are not whole numbers or rational fractions, a quadratic equation can be solved more easily by the method of *completing the square*. This method also is used to derive the quadratic formula (par. 91). For example, to solve the equation $2x^2 - x - 2 = 0$ by completing the square, proceed as follows:

a. Transpose all terms involving x to the left-hand side of the equation and all other terms to the right-hand side. The equation is now in the form $2x^2 - x = 2$, or $x^2 - \frac{1}{2}x = 1$. When using this method, the coefficient of the squared term must be unity (one).

b. Add a number to both sides of the equation so that the left-hand side will be a perfect trinomial square. To determine this number, divide the coefficient of the middle term ($-\frac{1}{2}$) by 2 and square the resulting number.

$$x^2 - \frac{1}{2}x = 1$$

$$x^2 - \frac{1}{2}x + \frac{1}{16} = 1 + \frac{1}{16}$$

c. Replace the trinomial square on the left-hand side of the equation with the square of a binomial.

$$\left(x - \frac{1}{4}\right)^2 = \frac{17}{16}$$

d. Extract the square root of both sides of the equation.

$$x - \frac{1}{4} = \frac{\pm\sqrt{17}}{4}$$

Thus, $\qquad x = \frac{1 \pm \sqrt{17}}{4}$

91. The General Quadratic Equation

a. *General.* Another method of solving quadratic equations consists of substitution in a formula derived from the general quadratic equation (b below). The general quadratic equation is in the form $ax^2 + bx + c = 0$, and any quadratic equation can be written in this form (par. 87). Thus, in the equation $2x^2 + 5x - 3 = 0$, $a = 2$, $b = 5$, and $c = -3$. Similarly, in the equation $9x^2 - 25 = 0$, $a = 9$, $b = 0$, and $c = -25$.

b. *Deriving Formula for Solving any Quadratic Equation.* Since the general quadratic equation, $ax^2 + bx + c = 0$, represents any quadratic equation, the roots of this equation will represent the roots of any quadratic equation; then, if the general quadratic equation is solved for the unknown values, the roots obtained will serve as a formula for finding the roots of any quadratic equation. The formula is derived from the general form by the method of completing the square; thus, given the general equation $ax^2 + bx + c = 0$, proceed as follows:

(1) Divide through by the coefficient a.

$$x^2 + \frac{bx}{a} + \frac{c}{a} = 0$$

(2) Subtract the term $\frac{c}{a}$ from both sides of the equation.

$$x^2 + \frac{bx}{a} = -\frac{c}{a}$$

This operation prepares the equation for the addition of a quantity to both sides of the equation that will make the left-hand side a perfect square. This quantity is obtained by dividing the coefficient of the x term by 2, and squaring the quotient. Since the coefficient of the x term is $\frac{b}{a}$, the quantity to be added to both sides of the equation is $\left(\frac{b}{2a}\right)^2$, or $\frac{b^2}{4a^2}$.

(3) Add $\frac{b^2}{4a^2}$ to both sides of the equation.

$$x^2 + \frac{bx}{a} + \frac{b^2}{4a^2} = \frac{b^2}{4a^2} - \frac{c}{a}$$

(4) Factor the left-hand side of the equation, and add the fraction on the right-hand side.

$$\left(x + \frac{b}{2a}\right)^2 = \frac{b^2 - 4ac}{4a^2}$$

(5) Take the square root of both sides of the equation.

$$x + \frac{b}{2a} = \pm\frac{\sqrt{b^2 - 4ac}}{2a}$$

(6) Subtract $\frac{b}{2a}$ from both sides of the equation.

$$x = -\frac{b}{2a} \pm \frac{\sqrt{b^2 - 4ac}}{2a}$$

(7) Collect the terms on the right-hand side of the equation.

$$x = \frac{-b \pm \sqrt{b^2 - 4ac}}{2a}$$

This equation is known as the *quadratic formula*. The two roots of any quadratic equation can be obtained by substituting in the formula the particular values of a, b, and c.

92. Solution by the Quadratic Formula

In practical problems, pure quadratic equations (par. 88) are seldom found, and solution by factoring (par. 89) can be used only occasionally. However, any quadratic equation can be solved by the method of completing the square (par. 90)—the method used to derive the quadratic formula (par. 91). This method is unnecessary, however, when the values for a, b, and c for any quadratic equation can be substituted in the formula $x = \frac{-b \pm \sqrt{b^2 - 4ac}}{2a}$

Example 1: Solve the equation $2x^2 - 6x + 3 = 0$ by using the quadratic formula.

$$2x^2 - 6x + 3 = 0$$
$$a = 2; \ b = -6; \ c = 3$$

Substituting in the formula:

$$x = \frac{-b \pm \sqrt{b^2 - 4ac}}{2a}$$

$$x = \frac{-(-6) \pm \sqrt{36 - (4)(2)(3)}}{4}$$

$$= \frac{6 \pm \sqrt{12}}{4}$$

$$= \frac{3 \pm \sqrt{3}}{2}$$

Thus, $x = \frac{3 + \sqrt{3}}{2}$ or $x = \frac{3 - \sqrt{3}}{2}$.

Check: $x = \frac{3 + \sqrt{3}}{2}$

$$x = \frac{3 + 1.732}{2} = 2.366$$

Substituting in the equation:
$$2(2.366)^2 - 6(2.366) + 3 = 0$$
$$11.20 - 14.20 + 3 = 0$$
$$14.20 - 14.20 = 0$$

$$x = \frac{3 - \sqrt{3}}{2}$$

$$x = \frac{3 - 1.732}{2} = .634$$

Substituting in the equation:
$$2(.634)^2 - 6(.634) + 3 = 0$$
$$2(.40) - 3.80 + 3 = 0$$
$$3.80 - 3.80 = 0$$

Example 2: **Solve the equation $3x^2 + 5x - 2 = 0$ by using the quadratic formula.**

$$3x^2 + 5x - 2 = 0$$
$$a = 3;\ b = 5;\ c = -2$$

Substituting in the formula:
$$x = \frac{-b \pm \sqrt{b^2 - 4ac}}{2a}$$
$$x = \frac{-5 \pm \sqrt{25 - (4)(3)(-2)}}{(2)(3)}$$
$$= \frac{-5 \pm 7}{6}$$

Thus, $x = \frac{1}{3}$ or $x = -2$.

Check: $x = \frac{1}{3}$

Substituting in the equation:
$$3\left(\frac{1}{3}\right)^2 + 5\left(\frac{1}{3}\right) - 2 = 0$$
$$\frac{3}{9} + \frac{5}{3} - 2 = 0$$
$$\frac{1}{3} + \frac{5}{3} - \frac{6}{3} = 0$$
$$\frac{6}{3} - \frac{6}{3} = 0$$
$$12 - 12 = 0$$

$x = -2$

Substituting in the equation:
$$3(-2)^2 + 5(-2) - 2 = 0$$
$$12 - 10 - 2 = 0$$
$$12 - 12 = 0$$

93. Character of the Roots

a. The values for unknowns that are not whole numbers or rational fractions are called *irrational roots*. A *rational* number is a number which can be expressed as the ratio of two integers. For example, 9, $\frac{7}{3}$, $\frac{1}{8}$, and $\sqrt{16}$ are rational numbers. Any whole number is rational since it is the quotient of itself and unity; thus, $9 = \frac{9}{1}$. Numbers such as $\frac{7}{3}$ and $\frac{1}{8}$ are often referred to as rational fractions. A radical is rational if it can be expressed as the quotient of two whole numbers. Thus $\sqrt{16}$ is rational since

$\sqrt{16} = 4 = \frac{4}{1}$. A number such as $\sqrt{3}$ which cannot be written as the ratio of two whole numbers is called irrational. Rational and irrational numbers, taken together, make up the system of real numbers. Any number, such as $3 + \sqrt{3}$, which contains a radical sign that cannot be removed also is considered irrational. Roots of quadratic equations are real if a minus sign does not occur under a radical. For example, $x = 5$ is a real root—roots such as $x = \frac{3 + \sqrt{3}}{2}$ or $x = \frac{3 - \sqrt{3}}{2}$ are real, but irrational.

b. One important fact to be remembered when using the quadratic formula is that the expression under the radical sign, $b^2 - 4ac$, must be regarded as a whole before the square root can be taken. The quantity $b^2 - 4ac$ is called the *discriminant* of the quadratic equation. Many things can be learned about a quadratic equation merely by inspecting the discriminant. If the value of the discriminant is positive, real roots will be obtained when the equation is solved. These roots are either rational or irrational—rational when the discriminant is a perfect square, irrational when it is not. The roots are equal only when the value of $b^2 - 4ac$ is zero. When $b^2 - 4ac$ is negative, the square root will be that of a negative number and the roots will be imaginary.

c. In summary, *a quadratic equation always has two solutions*. The solutions will be:

Real and equal_____ if $b^2 - 4ac$ equals 0.
Unequal but real____ if $b^2 - 4ac$ is positive.
Real and rational___ if $b^2 - 4ac$ is a perfect square.
Imaginary_____ if $b^2 - 4ac$ is negative.

94. Review Problems—Quadratic Equations

a. Solve by factoring.

(1) $2x^2 + 3x = 0$
(2) $(x - 4)x = 0$
(3) $(x + 3)\frac{x}{3} = 0$
(4) $\frac{1}{4}x^2 + \frac{1}{4}x = 0$
(5) $2x^2 - 128 = 0$
(6) $\frac{1}{3}x^2 - 2 = 1$
(7) $3x^2 - 25 = 2$
(8) $3x(x - 2) + 2x(3 - x) = 16$
(9) $x^2 - x - 42 = 0$
(10) $x^2 - 13x + 12 = 0$

b. Solve by completing the square.

(1) $x^2 + 3x - 1 = 0$
(2) $y^2 + 6y - 10 = 0$
(3) $x^2 + 4x - 1 = 0$
(4) $2E^2 + 8E - 3 = 0$
(5) $8H^2 - 8H = 5$
(6) $5L^2 - 5 = 2L^2 - 10L$
(7) $14r^2 - 28r - 42 = 0$
(8) $\frac{1}{v^2} - \frac{4}{v} = 2$
(9) $y^2 - 5 = 2y$
(10) $8x^2 - 8x = 8$

c. Solve by using the quadratic formula.

(1) $a^2 + 2a + 1 = 0$
(2) $12y^2 - 6 + y = 0$
(3) $0 = 1 + 5E + 3E^2$
(4) $6I^2 + I - 12 = 0$
(5) $2z^2 + 4c - 6 = 0$
(6) $15R^2 = 22R + 5$
(7) $\frac{Z - 2}{Z} = 1 - Z$
(8) $\frac{3}{r - 2} = 1 + \frac{2}{r + 3}$
(9) $\frac{3x + 2}{2x + 4} = \frac{x + 2}{2x}$
(10) $0 = 6 - \frac{b - 2}{b + 2} - \frac{b - 1}{b + 1}$

CHAPTER 6
GRAPHS

Section I. BASIC CHARACTERISTICS OF GRAPHS

95. General

A graph is a pictorial representation of the relation between two or more quantities. In many instances, problems are more clearly understood when solved graphically than when solved by other methods. Numerical data taken from an experiment or calculations derived from a formula require interpretation, and a curve on a graph depicting such data will provide a picture that shows at a glance how one factor or function depends on another.

96. The Number Line

a. In figure 15, on a straight line of indeterminate length, a point 0 has been chosen from which to measure distances. The point 0 is called the origin. A unit of measurement also has been chosen, and positive and negative integers have been marked off and labeled. The usual choice for a positive direction is shown by the arrow. On the number line, Z_1 corresponds to -4, Z_2 corresponds to $3\frac{1}{2}$, and Z_3 corresponds to 5.2.

b. Consider a number x as corresponding to a point a distance of x units from 0. If x is positive, the point will be in the direction of the arrow from 0; if x is negative, the point will be in the opposite direction from 0. The relative size of two numbers is indicated graphically by the relative positions on the number line of points corresponding to the two numbers. For example, if x is greater than w, the point corresponding to x will be to the right of the point corresponding to w; if x is less than w, the point corresponding to x will be to the left of the point corresponding to w. The number of units from the origin to the point representing a certain number, regardless of direction, is the absolute value (par. 35) of the number.

97. Rectangular Coordinates

a. In the preceding paragraph, a relationship was given between numbers and points on a straight line. A similar relationship can be established between a pair of numbers and a point on a plane. In figure 16, two number lines are drawn perpendicular to each other at their origins for form a set of axes. The horizontal axis is commonly called the x axis;

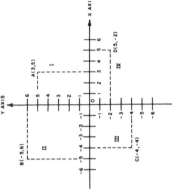

Figure 16. Rectangular coordinates.

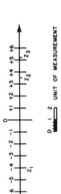

Figure 15. The number line.

the vertical axis is commonly called the *y axis*. Any point on the plane can be located with reference to the two axes: It must lie a certain number of units to the left (negative) or to the right (positive) of the *y* axis; and it must lie a certain number of units above (positive) or below (negative) the *x*-axis. To locate a point with reference to the set of axes, it is necessary only to know the *x* value and the *y* value of the point. These two values are known as the *coordinates* of the point. The *x* value, called the *abscissa*, is written first; the *y* value, called the *ordinate*, follows. The two numbers are separated by a comma and are usually inclosed in parentheses. Thus, in figure 16, the correct notation for the coordinates at point A is (3,5), because the *x* value is 3 and the *y* value 5.

b. The axes divide the graph into sections, or *quadrants*, identified by the Roman numerals I, II, III, and IV in figure 16. The signs of the abscissa and the ordinate in each of the quadrants are given in the chart below.

Quadrant	Abscissa	Ordinate
I	+	+
II	−	+
III	−	−
IV	+	−

98. Plotting Points

The procedure for locating points by their coordinates is called *plotting* the points. To plot the point D (5, —2) in figure 16, for example, erect a perpendicular on the *x* axis five units to the right of the *y* axis; then erect a perpendicular to the *y* axis two units below the *x* axis; the point of intersection of these two perpendiculars is the point D (5,—2).

99. Review Problems—Plotting Points

a. Plot each of the following points and state the quadrant, if any, in which each lies:

(1) (4,2)
(2) (4,—2)
(3) (—1,3)
(4) (6,—1)
(5) (3,0)
(6) (0,—3)
(7) (—15,—27)
(8) (3¼,4¼)
(9) (5.6,—6.5)

b. Plot the points in the following chart and connect them by straight segments in the order of increasing values of *x*:

x	—3	—2	—1	0	1	2	3	4
y	18	8	2	0	2	8	18	32

c. Plot the points in the following chart and sketch a smooth curve passing through them in the order of increasing values of *x*:

x	—3	—2	—1	0	1	2	3
y	—37	8	5	8	7	7	17

d. If $y = 2x - 3$, plot the points for which x = 4, 2, 1, 0, —1, —2, and —4 after finding the corresponding values of *y*.

e. Draw the triangle of which the vertices are (—2,6), (3,2), and (0,—3).

f. Draw the quadrilateral of which the vertices, connected in the order given, are (1,3), (—3,4), (—2,—5), and (3,—2).

Section II. GRAPHING EQUATIONS

100. Graphing Linear Equations

a. General. An equation in the first degree in two unknowns is called a *linear equation* since its graph is a straight line. For example, $x + y = 5$, $2x + y = 12$, and $x - 6y = 6$ are linear equations. An equation is said to be of the first degree in two unknowns if only the first power of either unknown is involved and if neither of the unknowns appears in a denominator.

b. Plotting Graphs of Linear Equations.

(1) The first step in plotting the graph of a linear equation (or of any other equation or formula) is to set up a table of values for both unknowns that will satisfy the equation. In the equation $x + y = 5$, for example, it is apparent that there are a number of values for *x* and *y* that will satisfy the equation. For any number assigned to *x*, there is a corresponding number for *y* which will satisfy the equation. Consider that 4 and —4 will be the maximum plus and minus values for *x*. Using the values 4, 3, 2, 1, 0, —1, —2, —3, and —4 for *x*, the equation is solved for *y* at each value of *x*. These are arranged in tabular form as shown on figure 17.

(2) Each of these pairs of values gives a point on a graph. Consider each of the corresponding points as coordinates—the value of *x* the abscissa and the value of *y* the ordinate. The line joining these points (fig. 17) is the graph of the equation $x + y = 5$. Note that the coordinates for any two points are sufficient to determine its graph. Therefore, plotting the coordinates for any two points is sufficient to determine the graph of a first degree equation. Plotting a third point, however, will serve as a check, for if the three points are not on the same straight line, one of them is in error.

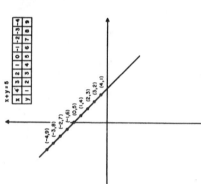

x	4	3	2	1	0	-1	-2	-3	-4
y	1	2	3	4	5	6	7	8	9

Figure 17. Graph of linear equation.

101. Graphical Solution of Simultaneous Linear Equations

a. When two *independent* linear equations contain the same two related unknowns, there will be an unlimited number of solutions for each equation. However, *there can be only one set of values that will satisfy both equations.* Determining the one set of values is known as the simultaneous solution of the two independent equations.

b. Graphically, the two equations can be solved simultaneously by plotting them on the same graph and locating their point of intersection (if there is one). For example, consider the graphical solution of the equations $3x - 2y = 0$ and $3x + 2y = 6$. Selecting 6 and —6 as the maximum plus and minus values for *x* and using x = 4 as a checkpoint, the coordinates for both equations are determined. For the equation $3x - 2y = 0$, the coordinates are (6,9), (4,6), and (—6,—9); for the equation $3x + 2y = 6$, (6,—6), (4,—3), and (—6,12). These coordinates are plotted on an axis and a line is drawn joining the plotted points of each equation (fig. 18). The graphs of the two independent linear equation lines cross at point P, where x = 1 and y = 1.5. To check the graphical solution of the equations, substitute these values for *x* and *y* in the original equations. Since they satisfy both equation, the graphical solution is correct.

c. If two *dependent* equations are plotted on a graph, their lines will coincide. For example, the equations $x + y = 4$ and $2x + 2y = 8$

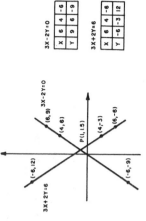

3X − 2Y = 0

x	6	4	-6
Y	9	6	-9

3X + 2Y = 6

x	6	4	-6
Y	-6	-3	12

Figure 18. Graphical solution of simultaneous linear equations.

are dependent, since they can be reduced to identical forms. Selecting the same plus and minus values for x and the same checkpoint as in b above, the coordinates for both equations are found to be $(6,-2)$, $(4,0)$, and $(-6,10)$. Plotted on a graph, both equations form a single line (fig. 19).

d. Simultaneous equations that have no common solution are called *inconsistent*. No solution is possible for the equations $x + y = 3$ and $x + y = 5$, because there are no values for x and y which, when added together to make 3, will also equal 5. Using 6 and -6 as maximum plus and minus values for x, and using $x = 4$ as a checkpoint, the coordinates for equation $x + y = 3$ are found to be $(6,-3)$, $(4,-1)$, and $(-6,9)$; the coordinates for $x + y = 5$ are $(6,-1)$, $(4,1)$, and $(-6,11)$. Plotted on a graph, these equations form parallel lines (fig. 20).

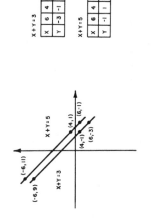

Figure 20. Graph of inconsistent simultaneous linear equations.

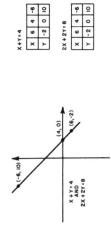

Figure 19. Graph of dependent simultaneous linear equations.

102. Graphing Quadratic Equations

a. The Dependent Variable. In graphing a quadratic equation, only two values, or points, for plotting the equation can be obtained by finding the roots of the equation (par. 88). These values do not give a complete picture of the equation. To get a continuous graph, a *dependent variable* is introduced. This variable, usually identified by the letter y, gets its name from the fact that it depends on another quantity for its value. For example, in the equation $y = x^2 - 6x + 5$, the value of y depends on the value of x; therefore, y is a dependent variable. The quantity on which y depends is called the *independent variable*. A more accurate designation for the dependent variable is $f(x)$, meaning *function of x*. Using

this designation, the equation given above would be written $f(x) = x^2 - 6x + 5$. If the independent variable in the equation were z, the equation would be written $f(z) = z^2 - 6z + 5$.

b. Graphical Solution of Quadratic Equations. In the original equation $f(x) = x^2 - 6x + 5$, different values are substituted for the unknown to find the corresponding values of the function; thus if x equals -1, the equation becomes $f(-1) = (-1)^2 - 6(-1) + 5 = 12$; if x equals zero, the equation becomes $f(0) = 0 - 0 + 5 = 5$; if x equals 1, the equations becomes $f(1) = (1)^2 - 6(1) + 5 = 0$, etc. Compile a table of enough values to make it possible to plot the equation, as shown in figure 21. The graph of the function crosses the x-axis at two points, 1 and 5, which give a graphical solution of the equation $x^2 - 6x + 5 = 0$. The equation also may be solved by factoring, as follows:

$$(x-1)(x-5) = 0$$
$$x - 1 = 0 \text{ and } x - 5 = 0$$
$$x = 1 \text{ and } x = 5$$

Thus, the solutions or the roots of the equation are obtained when $f(x) = 0$. These roots represent the points where the graph of $f(x) = x^2 - 6x + 5$ crosses the x-axis.

c. Properties of Functions. In addition to the original equation, $f(x) = x^2 - 6x + 5$, consider three equations that differ in one respect —their constant terms are not the same. For example:

$$f(x) = x^2 - 6x + 8$$
$$f(x) = x^2 - 6x + 9$$
$$f(x) = x^2 - 6x + 12$$

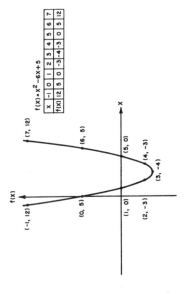

x	-1	0	1	2	3	4	5	6	7
$f(x)$	12	5	0	-3	-4	-3	0	5	12

$f(x) = x^2 - 6x + 5$

Figure 21. Graph of function of quadratic equation.

The graphs of the four corresponding functions have interesting properties and can be studied more advantageously when plotted on the same graph, as shown in figure 22.

(1) The function of $x^2 - 6x + 5$ crosses the horizontal or x-axis at two points, 1 and 5. These points indicate that the roots of the equation are $x = 1$ and $x = 5$. To compare this information with the discussion on quadratic equations in chapter 5, the discriminant of the equation must be investigated. The discriminant of $x^2 - 6x + 5$ is $(b^2 - 4ac) = (36 - 4 \cdot 1 \cdot 5) = 36 - 20 = 16$. Referring to the summary of the character of roots in paragraph 93, the roots are real and rational. To prove this, substitute the value of the discriminant in the quadratic formula.

$$x = \frac{-b \pm \sqrt{b^2 - 4ac}}{2a}$$

$$x = \frac{-(-6) \pm \sqrt{16}}{2}$$

$$x = \frac{6 + 4}{2} = 5 \text{ or } \frac{6 - 4}{2} = 1$$

Thus, the discriminant is a perfect square and the roots are real and rational.

(2) The function of $x^2 - 6x + 8$ crosses the horizontal axis at 2 and 4, indicating that the roots are $x = 2$ and $x = 4$. Calculating the discriminant,

$(b^2 - 4ac) = (36 - 4 \cdot 2 \cdot 2) = 36 - 32 = 4$. Thus, the discriminant is a perfect square and will give real and rational roots.

(3) The function of $x^2 - 6x + 9$ touches the x-axis at only one point, 3. Thus, both roots of the equation are $x = 3$. Calculating the discriminant, $(b^2 - 4ac) = (36 - 4 \cdot 9) = 0$, which indicates that the roots are real and equal. Check the graph of this equation (fig. 22); it will be seen that the curve just touches the x-axis at one point. Thus, the root $x = 3$ must be counted twice and may be called a double root.

(4) The equation $f(x) - x^2 - 6x + 12$ has a discriminant equal to $(36 - 4 \cdot 12)$ or -12. Solving for the roots of this equation,

$$x = \frac{6 \pm \sqrt{-12}}{2} = 3 \pm \sqrt{-3}.$$

This is imaginary, but the meaning becomes apparent when the graph of the function of the equation is inspected. The plot does not cross the x-axis and, therefore, both roots must be imaginary.

d. Minimum Value of a Quadratic.

(1) The minimum value of a quadratic function will occur at $x = \frac{-b}{2a}$ when

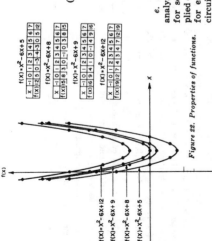

f(x)→x²-6x+12

f(x)→x²-6x+9

f(x)→x²-6x+8

f(x)→x²-6x+5

f(x)=x²-6x+5									
x	-1	0	1	2	3	4	5	6	7
f(x)	12	5	0	-3	-4	-3	0	5	12

f(x)→x²-6x+8									
x	-1	0	1	2	3	4	5	6	7
f(x)	15	8	3	0	-1	0	3	8	15

f(x)→x²-6x+9									
x	-1	0	1	2	3	4	5	6	7
f(x)	16	9	4	1	0	1	4	9	16

f(x)→x²-6x+12									
x	-1	0	1	2	3	4	5	6	7
f(x)	19	12	7	4	3	4	7	12	19

Figure 22. Properties of functions.

the general quadratic equation $ax^2 + bx + c = y$ (par. 91) defines the coefficients a and b. This relation can be checked by calculating the value of x at which the minimum value of the function $x^2 - 6x + 5$ occurs and comparing this calculated value with the plot of the equation (fig. 21 or 22). Thus,

$$x = \frac{-b}{2a} = -\frac{(-6)}{2(1)} = \frac{6}{2} = 3,$$

and the minimum value of the function $x^2 - 6x + 5$ occurs at $x = 3$. Checking the graph verifies this statement. The minimum value of the functions $x^2 - 6x + 8$, $x^2 - 6x + 9$, and $x^2 - 6x + 12$ also occurs at $x = 3$.

(2) To find the value of the function at the minimum point, substitute for x. The minimum occurs at $x = \frac{-b}{2a}$; therefore, substitute $\frac{-b}{2a}$ for x in the function of the general quadratic equation.

$$f(x) = ax^2 + bx + c$$
$$= a\left(\frac{-b}{2a}\right)^2 + b\left(\frac{-b}{2a}\right) + c$$
$$= \frac{b^2}{4a} - \frac{b^2}{2a} + c = \frac{b^2}{4a} - \frac{2b^2}{4a} + c$$
$$= \frac{-b^2}{4a} + c$$

Thus, to find the value of the function $f(x) = x^2 - 6x + 5$ at the minimum point:

$$f(x) = \frac{-b^2}{4a} + c = \frac{-36}{4} + 5 =$$
$$-9 + 5 = -4$$

This method can be used to find the minimum value of the function if the value of x at which the minimum occurs is *not* known. However if it is known that the minimum value occurs at $x = 3$, merely substitute this value for x in the original equation.

$$f(x) = x^2 - 6x + 5$$
$$= 9 - 6 \cdot 3 + 5$$
$$= 14 - 18$$
$$f(x)\text{min} = -4$$

(3) Note that in all cases where the word *minimum* is used, the word *maximum* is applicable if the equation $y = f(x)$ is such that its graph has a maximum instead of a minimum. If the equation were $f(x) = 3 + 6x - x^2$, the minus sign preceding the term x^2 would indicate that the curve has a maximum.

e. *Practical Application.* The methods of analysis presented in c and d above can be used for some very important relationships in applied electricity and electronics. It may be used, for example, to find the load resistance of a circuit in terms of the circuit components necessary to obtain maximum power transfer.

103. Review Problems—Graphs

a. Plot the graphs of the following linear equations:

(1) $2x - 5 = y$
(2) $5 - 2x = y$
(3) $y = 5x$
(4) $3x + 2y = 18$
(5) $5x - 5y = 20$
(6) $3x + y + 14 = 0$

b. Plot the graphs of the following sets of simultaneous equations:

(1) $2x + 3y = 12$
    $3x - y = 7$
(2) $x + y = 9$
    $5x + y = 17$
(3) $x + 5y = 22$
    $3x - 2y = -2$
(4) $3x - 2y = 0$
    $x - 5y = 13$
(5) $6x + 2y = 12$
    $4y + 2y = 10$
(6) $x - 2y = 0$
    $y = 1 + x$

c. Find the roots of the following quadratic equations to the nearest tenth by plotting their graphs:

(1) $y^2 - 2y - 2 = 0$
(2) $x^2 - 1 + x = 0$
(3) $9 - t^2$
(4) $x^2 - 2x + 2 = 0$
(5) $x^2 - 5x + 3 = 0$
(6) $10 - 3x - x^2 = 0$

CHAPTER 7
POWERS OF 10

104. General

The technique of using powers of 10 can greatly simplify mathematical calculations. A number containing many zeros to the right or to the left of the decimal point can be dealt with much more readily when put in the form of powers of 10. For example, .0000037 × .000021 can be handled more easily when put in the form $3.7 \times 10^{-6} \times 2.1 \times 10^{-5}$.

105. Table of Powers of 10

The table below gives some of the values of the powers of 10. In a whole number, the exponent is positive and equals the number of zeros following the 1; in decimals, the exponent is negative and equals one more than the number of zeros immediately following the decimal point.

Number	Power of 10	Number	Power of 10
.000001	10^{-6}	1	10^{0}
.00001	10^{-5}	10	10^{1}
.0001	10^{-4}	100	10^{2}
.001	10^{-3}	1,000	10^{3}
.01	10^{-2}	10,000	10^{4}
.1	10^{-1}	100,000	10^{5}
		1,000,000	10^{6}

106. Expressing Numbers in Scientific Notation

Any number written as the product of an integral power of 10 and a number between 1 and 10 is said to be expressed in *scientific notation*.

Example 1: $81,000,000 = 8.1 \times 10,000,000 = 8.1 \times 10^{7}$

Example 2: $600,000,000 = 6 \times 100,000,000 = 6 \times 10^{8}$

Example 3: $.000,000,000,9 = 9 \times .000,000,000,1 = 9 \times 10^{-10}$

107. Addition and Subtraction of Numbers in Scientific Notation

Numbers expressed in scientific notation can only be added or subtracted if the powers of 10 are the same. For example, 3×10^{5} can be added to 2×10^{5} to get 5×10^{5}; however, 3×10^{6} cannot be added to 2×10^{5} because the powers of 10 are not the same. The number 3×10^{6} can be changed to 30×10^{5}, however, and it can then be added to 2×10^{5} to obtain 32×10^{5}. The answers to problems solved by using scientific notation can be left in the exponential form. In the examples below, however, the answers are converted to the decimal form to aid in understanding this technique.

Example 1: Add 450,000 and 763,000.
$$450,000 + 763,000 = 45 \times 10^{4} + 76.3 \times 10^{4}$$
$$= 121.3 \times 10^{4}$$
$$= 1,213,000$$

Example 2: Add .000,068,25 and .000,007,54.
$$.000,068,25 + .000,007,54 = 6825 \times 10^{-8} + 754 \times 10^{-8}$$
$$= 7579 \times 10^{-8}$$
$$= .000,075,79$$

Example 3: Subtract .000,004,33 from .000,05.
$$.000,05 - .000,004,33 = 5000 \times 10^{-8} - 433 \times 10^{-8}$$
$$= 4567 \times 10^{-8}$$
$$= .000,045,67$$

108. Multiplication of Numbers in Scientific Notation

The general rules covering the multiplication of radicals (par. 74) also apply in the multiplication of numbers that are expressed in scientific notation.

Example 1: Multiply 100,000 by 1,000.
$$100,000 \times 1,000 = 10^5 \times 10^3 = 10^{5+3} = 10^8 = 100,000,000$$

Example 2: Multiply 25,000 by 5,000.
$$25,000 \times 5,000 = 2.5 \times 10^4 \times 5 \times 10^3 = 2.5 \times 5 \times 10^{4+3}$$
$$= 12.5 \times 10^7$$
$$= 125,000,000$$

Example 3: Multiply 1,800, .000015, 300, and .0048.
$$1,800 \times .000015 \times 300 \times .0048$$
$$= 1.8 \times 10^3 \times 1.5 \times 10^{-5} \times 3 \times 10^2 \times 4.8 \times 10^{-3}$$
$$= 1.8 \times 1.5 \times 3 \times 4.8 \times 10^{3-5+2-3}$$
$$= 38.88 \times 10^{-3}$$
$$= .03888$$

109. Division of Numbers in Scientific Notation

The general rules covering the division of radicals (par. 75) also apply in the division of numbers that are expressed in scientific notation.

Example 1: Divide 75,000 by .0005.
$$\frac{75,000}{.0005} = \frac{75 \times 10^3}{5 \times 10^{-4}} = \frac{75}{5} \times 10^{3+4} = 15 \times 10^7 = 150,000,000$$

Example 2: Divide 14,400,000 by 1,200,000.
$$\frac{14,400,000}{1,200,000} = \frac{144 \times 10^5}{12 \times 10^5} = \frac{144}{12} = 12$$

Example 3: Divide 98,100 by .0025, 180, and 1,090,000.
$$\frac{98,100}{.0025 \times 180 \times 1,090,000}$$
$$= \frac{9.81 \times 10^4}{2.5 \times 10^{-3} \times 1.8 \times 10^2 \times 1.09 \times 10^6}$$
$$= \frac{9.81 \times 10^4}{2.5 \times 1.8 \times 1.09 \times 10^{-3+2+6}}$$
$$= \frac{9.81 \times 10^4}{4.905 \times 10^5}$$
$$= 2 \times 10^{-1}$$
$$= .2$$

110. Finding the Power or Root of a Number in Scientific Notation

The general rules covering powers and roots (pars. 71 and 72) also apply to numbers expressed in scientific notation.

Example 1: Find the square root of 144,000,000.
$$\sqrt{144,000,000} = \sqrt{144 \times 10^6} = 12 \times 10^3 = 12,000$$

Example 2: Find the cube root of .000,008.
$$\sqrt[3]{.000,008} = \sqrt[3]{8 \times 10^{-6}} = 2 \times 10^{-2} = .02$$

Example 3: Square 15,000.
$$(15,000)^2 = (15 \times 10^3)^2 = 225 \times 10^6 = 225,000,000$$

Example 4: Find the square root of (160,000)³.
$$\sqrt{160,000^3} = (160,000)^{3/2} = (16 \times 10^4)^{3/2} = 64 \times 10^6 = 64,000,000$$

Example 5: Find the square root of $\dfrac{86,900}{3,560,000}$.
$$\sqrt{\frac{86,900}{3,560,000}} = \sqrt{\frac{8.69 \times 10^4}{3.56 \times 10^6}} = \sqrt{2.44 \times 10^{-2}}$$
$$= 1.56 \times 10^{-1}$$
$$= .156$$

111. Review Problems—Powers of 10

In the following problems, leave the answer in powers of ten:

a. Convert the following numbers to powers of 10 and add:

  (1) 1,245,000 + 368,000
  (2) 79,000 + 421,000
  (3) .000,067,66 + .000,054

b. Convert the following numbers to powers of 10 and subtract:

  (1) 333,400 — 22,500
  (2) .000,068 — .000,049
  (3) .000,004,89 — .000,000,398

c. Convert the following numbers to powers of 10 and multiply:

  (1) 446,000 × 200
  (2) 7,700 × .008,2
  (3) .000,096 × .000,33
  (4) .003,66 × 4,000,000

d. Convert the following numbers to powers of 10 and divide:

  (1) 668,000 ÷ 4,000
  (2) 88,445,000 ÷ .000,55
  (3) .000,963 ÷ .000,009
  (4) .006,93 ÷ 21

e. Convert the following numbers to powers of 10 and perform the indicated operations:

  (1) $\sqrt[3]{64,000,000}$
  (2) $\sqrt[3]{.000,169}$
  (3) $.003^3$
  (4) $27,000^{4/3}$

CHAPTER 8
LOGARITHMS

112. General

Many lengthy mathematical operations may be accomplished more easily through the use of logarithms. With logarithms (also called logs), multiplication of numbers is reduced to a simple process of addition, division becomes a process of subtraction, raising a number to a power becomes simple multiplication, and extraction of roots is done by simple division.

113. Definition

The logarithm of a given number is the power to which another number (called the base) must be raised to equal the given number. The word "logarithm" has the same meaning as the word "exponent."

Example: Find the logarithm of 1,000 to the base 10.

From the definition, the logarithm of a number (1,000) is the power (x) to which another number called the base (10) must be raised to equal the given number (1,000).

Thus, $10^x = 1,000$. Since $10^3 = 1,000$, then:

$10^x = 10^3$ and by inspection:

$$x = 3$$

Therefore, the logarithm of 1,000 to the base 10 equals 3 or $\log_{10} 1,000 = 3$.

114. Types of Logarithms

a. *Common Logarithms.* Common logarithms use the number 10 as a base. They are so universally used that the 10 usually is omitted; the answer in paragraph 113 could be log 1,000 = 3. Some values of common logarithms are included in the table below. The common logarithm of any number between these values consists of the logarithm of the smaller number plus a decimal. For example, the log of a number between 100 and 1,000, such as 157, consists of the log of the smaller number (10) plus a decimal. The log of 157 is 2.1959.

log 1	= 0	log .1	= —1
log 10	= 1	log .01	= —2
log 100	= 2	log .001	= —3
log 1,000	= 3	log .0001	= —4
log 10,000	= 4		

b. *Natural Logarithms.* Natural logarithms are based upon the irrational number e, and are written both as $\log_e$ and $\ln$. Natural logarithms are used in special applications and as such are not explained further in this text.

115. Parts of Logarithms

a. Logarithms are divided into two parts, the integral and the decimal. The integral part is known as the *characteristic,* and the decimal part is called the *mantissa.*

(1) *The characteristic of any number is one less than the number of digits to the left of the decimal point.* Thus, the characteristic for the number 3 is 1 — 1 or zero, since there is one number to the left of the decimal point. The characteristic for 30, with two numbers to the left of the decimal point, is 2 — 1 or 1. Similarly, the characteristic for 300 is 2, and the characteristic for 3,000 is 3. The characteristic of the log of a decimal is negative and is based upon the position of the first rational number to the right of the decimal point. *If there are no numbers to the left of the decimal point, the characteristic is negative.* In the number 327, for example, the first rational number is in the first decimal place and the characteristic is —1; in the number .03, the first rational number is in the second decimal place and the characteristic is —2. Similarly, the characteristic for .003 is —3, and the characteristic for .0003 is —4.

(2) The mantissa is always the same for a given sequence of integers, regardless of where the decimal point appears among them. Thus, the *mantissa* is the same for 1570, 157, 15.7, 1.57, .157, and .0157, and the logs of these numbers differ only in respect to their characteristics. Their logarithms, respectively, are 3.1959, 2.1959, 1.1959, 0.1959, —1.1959 and —2.1959.

b. The mantissa is always positive—even when the characteristic is negative. This fact poses a problem of notation, and also complicates the addition and subtraction of logarithms.

(1) In the notation of logarithms, to say that log .157 is —1.1959 is not strictly true, for what we mean to say is —1 plus .1959. To overcome this problem, the minus sign is generally written above the characteristic, and is made long enough to cover the entire negative portion of the logarithm. More properly, therefore, log .157 is written $\bar{1}$.1959.

(2) In the addition and subtraction of logarithms, the complication can be removed by expressing the negative characteristic in a positive manner; more precisely, by adding a large enough number to the characteristic and by subtracting the same number from the entire logarithm. Thus, the log of .157 is written 9.1959-10, and the log of .0157 is written 8.1959—10.

116. Finding a Logarithm

The characteristic must be obtained, in each instance, by following the rules given in paragraph 115a(1).

Example 1: Find the logarithm of 333.

Determine the characteristic of 333. The characteristic is 3 —1, or 2.

Determine the mantissa of 333. In the table of common logarithms, look down the N column for the number 33. The mantissa for 333 is in this horizontal row in the column headed by the number 3. The mantissa is .5224.

Log 333 = 2.5224.

Example 2: Find the logarithm of .127.

Determine the characteristic of .127. The characteristic is —1 or 9. ------- —10.

Determine the mantissa of .127. In the table of common logarithms, look down the N column for 12. The mantissa for 127 is in this horizontal row in the column headed by the number 7. The mantissa is .1038.

Log .127 = 9.1038—10.

117. Logarithmic Interpolation

The table of common logarithms given in appendix is adequate if the given number has three or less integers. If it has four or more integers, however, it is necessary to interpolate—that is, to find the proportional part of the difference between the logarithms shown in the table.

Example 1: Find the logarithm of 2.369.

Step 1.

The characteristic of 2.369 is 0. Since the mantissa for this number cannot be found in the table, it is necessary to interpolate. Look for the mantissa of the numbers next lower and higher than 2369. The mantissa of the number 2360 is .3729 and the mantissa of the number 2370 is .3747. Since 2369 lies between 2360 and 2370, the mantissa of

Step 2. 2369 must lie between .3729 and .3747. This may be written:

log 2360 = .3729
log 2369 = .3729 + x
log 2370 = .3747

Step 2. Set up the proportions. The difference between 2369 and 2360 is 9. The difference between 2370 and 2360 is 10. Therefore, the desired mantissa is $\frac{9}{10}$ of the difference between these two. Let the difference between the mantissa of 2369 and 2360 equal x. The difference between .3747 and .3729 is .0018. The proportion is $\frac{x}{.0018}$.

Step 3. Solve the problem.

$$\frac{9}{10} = \frac{x}{.0018}$$
$$10x = .0162$$
$$x = .0016$$

Step 4. Since the value of x is .0016, the mantissa of 2369 is .3729 + .0016 or .3745. Therefore, log 2.369 = 0.3745.

Example 2: Find the logarithm of .017234.

Step 1. The characteristic of .017234 is −2 or 8. ------ −10. The numbers in the table lower and higher than 17234 are 17200 and 17300. The mantissa of 17200 is .2355; the mantissa of 17300 is .2380. The difference between 17234 and 17200 is 34; the difference between 17300 and 17200 is 100; the difference between .2380 and .2355 is .0025. This may be written:

log 17200 = .2355
log 17234 = .2355 + x
log 17300 = .2380

Step 2. Let the difference between the mantissas of 17234 and 17200 equal x. The equation is as follows:

$$\frac{34}{100} = \frac{x}{.0025}$$
$$100x = .0850$$
$$x = .00085 = .0009$$

Step 3. Since the value of x is .0009, the mantissa of 17234 is .2355 + .0009 or .2364. Therefore, log .017234 is .2364 —10.
.017234 = 8.2364—10.

118. Reading Antilogarithms

The process of finding the antilogarithm (also called antilog), consists of determining the number from which the logarithm was derived. This process is essentially the reverse of finding the logarithm (par. 116). Consequently, the location of the decimal point is determined from the characteristic, and the numerical value of the number is determined from the mantissa.

Example 1: Find the antilog of 1.8954.

Step 1. Since the characteristic of the logarithm is 1, there will be two digits to the left of the decimal point in the number.

Step 2. Look in the table for the mantissa, .8954. The number given for .8954 is 786.

Step 3. Count off two digits from the left and insert the decimal point. The antilog of 1.8954 is 78.6.

Example 2: Find the antilog of 7.0828—10.

Step 1. Since the characteristic of the logarithm is —3, the first significant figure will be in the third decimal place.

Step 2. Look for the mantissa .0828 in the table. The number given for .0828 is 121.

Step 3. Add two zeros to the right of the decimal point and before the first significant figure. Thus, the antilog of 7.0828—10 is .0021.

119. Antilogarithmic Interpolation

If the mantissa of a logarithm does not appear in the table, it is necessary to interpolate.

Example 1: Find the antilog of 2.7654.

Step 1. Since the characteristic of the logarithm is 2, there will be three digits to the left of the decimal point in the number.

Step 2. The mantissa in the table lower than .7654 is .7649. The number with .7649 as a mantissa is 582.

The mantissa higher than .7654 is .7657. The number with .7657 as a mantissa is 583.

Step 4. Set up the proportions. The difference between .7654 and .7649 is .0005; the difference between .7657 and .7649 is .0008. The proportional difference is $\frac{.0005}{.0008}$ or $\frac{5}{8}$. The difference between 583 and 582 is 1. This can be written:

antilog .7649 = 582
antilog .7654 = 582 + x
antilog .7657 = 583

Step 5. Let x equal the difference between the number represented by the mantissa .7654 and the number 582. The equation is as follows:

$$\frac{5}{8} = \frac{x}{1}$$
$$8x = 5$$
$$x = .625$$

Step 6. The number is 582 + .625. Since there are three digits to the left of the decimal point, the antilog of 2.7654 is 582.625.

Example 2: Find the antilog of 6.7166—10.

Step 1. Since the characteristic of the logarithm is —4, the first rational number will be in the fourth decimal place.

Step 2. The mantissa in the table lower than .8166 is .8162; the number with .8162 as a mantissa is 655.

Step 3. The mantissa in the table higher than .8166 is .8169; the number with .8169 as a mantissa is 656.

Step 4. The difference between .8162 and .8166 is .0004; the difference between .8169 and .8162 is .0007. The proportional difference is $\frac{.0004}{.0007}$ or $\frac{4}{7}$. The difference between 656 and 655 is 1. This may be written:

antilog .8162 = 655
antilog .8166 = 655 + x
antilog .8169 = 656

Step 5. Let x equal the difference between the number represented by the mantissa .8166 and the number 655. The equation is as follows:

$$\frac{4}{7} = \frac{x}{1}$$
$$7x = 4$$
$$x = .57$$

Step 6. The number is 655 + .57. Since the first rational figure is in the fourth decimal place, the antilog of 6.7166—10 is .00065557.

120. Addition and Subtraction of Logarithms

Logarithms are added and subtracted arithmetically. Since every mantissa is positive (par. 115b), however, every negative characteristic should be expressed as a positive (par. 115b).

Example 1: Add the logarithms 3.7493 and 2.4036.

3.7493
+2.4036
6.1529

Example 2: Add the logarithms 3.4287 and 6.3982.

3.4287
+4.3982—10
7.8269—10

Example 3: Add the logarithms 8.9324—10, 7.2812—10, 5.4138—10, and 9.9918—10.

8.9324—10
7.2812—10
5.4138—10
+9.9918—10
31.6192—40
—(30   —30)
1.6192—10

Example 4: Subtract the logarithm 9.1245 from the logarithm 6.3058.

To subtract a larger logarithm from a smaller logarithm, add 10 or a multiple of 10 to the smaller logarithm, and subtract the same number from the logarithm by writing that number with a minus sign to the right of the logarithm. The number chosen for this purpose should be the least that will cause the smaller logarithm to exceed the larger.

$$\begin{array}{r} 16.3058{-}10 \\ {-\ }9.1245 \\ \hline 7.1813{-}10 \end{array}$$

Example 5: Subtract the logarithm 3.7980—10 from 2.8686. When subtracting a negative logarithm from a positive logarithm, where that part of the characteristic of the negative logarithm to the left of the mantissa is larger than the characteristic of the positive logarithm, add 10 or a multiple of 10 to the characteristic of the positive logarithm, and subtract that same amount from the right of the positive logarithm.

$$\begin{array}{r} 12.8686{-}10 \\ 3.7980{-}10 \\ \hline 9.0706 \end{array}$$

121. Multiplication by Use of Logarithms

The logarithm of the product of two numbers is equal to the sum of the logarithms of the numbers. Thus, log (2 × 6) = log 2 + log 6; and log (12 × 8) = log 12 + log 8.

Example 1: Multiply 68.2 by 40.8 by using logarithms.

log (68.2 × 40.8) = log 68.2 + log 40.8.

$$\begin{array}{r} \log 68.2 = 1.8338 \\ \log 40.8 = 1.6107 \\ \hline \log (68.2 \times 40.8) = 3.4445 \end{array}$$

antilog .4440 = 278
antilog .4445 = 278 + x
antilog .4455 = 279

$$\frac{5}{15} = \frac{x}{1}$$
$$15x = 5$$
$$x = .33$$

antilog .4445 = 2783
68.2 × 40.8 = 2,783

Example 2: Find the product of 2.11 and 41.3 by using logarithms.

log (2.11 × 41.3) = log 2.11 + log 41.3.

$$\begin{array}{r} \log 2.11 = 0.3243 \\ \log 41.3 = 1.6160 \\ \hline \log (2.11 \times 41.3) = 1.9403 \end{array}$$

antilog .9400 = 871
antilog .9403 = 871 + x
antilog .9405 = 872

$$\frac{3}{5} = \frac{x}{1}$$
$$5x = 3$$
$$x = .6$$

antilog 1.9403 = 87.16
2.11 × 41.3 = 87.16

122. Division by Use of Logarithms

The logarithm of the quotient of two numbers is equal to the difference between the logarithms of the numbers. Thus, log (75 ÷ 83) = log 75 — log 83, and log (8 ÷ 2) = log 8 — log 2.

Example 1: Divide 785 by 329 by using logarithms.

log (785 ÷ 329) = log 785 — log 329.

$$\begin{array}{r} \log 785 = 2.8949 \\ \log 329 = 2.5172 \\ \hline \log (785 \div 329) = 0.3777 \end{array}$$

antilog .3766 = 238
antilog .3777 = 238 + x
antilog .3784 = 239

$$\frac{11}{18} = \frac{x}{1}$$
$$18x = 11$$
$$x = .611$$

antilog 0.3777 = 2.386
785 ÷ 329 = 2.386

Example 2: Find the value of $\frac{3}{7}$ by using logarithms.

$$\log \frac{3}{7} = \log 3 - \log 7.$$

log 3 = 0.4771
log 7 = 0.8451

Since the logarithm of 7 is greater than the logarithm of 3, it is necessary to add 10. ——— —10 to the logarithm of 3 before subtracting the logarithm of 7.

$$\begin{array}{r} \log 3 = 10.4771{-}10 \\ \log 7 = 0.8451 \\ \hline \log (3 \div 7) = 9.6320{-}10 \end{array}$$

antilog .6314 = 428
antilog .6320 = 428 + x
antilog .6325 = 429

$$\frac{6}{11} = \frac{x}{1}$$
$$11x = 6$$
$$x = .55$$

antilog 9.6320—10 = .42855
3 ÷ 7 = .42855

123. Finding the Power of a Number by Logarithms

The logarithm of a number raised to a power is equal to the logarithm of the number multiplied by the power.

Example 1: Evaluate (18.7)³.

$$\begin{aligned} \log (18.7)^3 &= 3 \log 18.7 \\ &= 3 \times 1.2718 \\ &= 3.8154 \end{aligned}$$

antilog .8149 = 653
antilog .8154 = 653 + x
antilog .8156 = 654

$$\frac{5}{7} = \frac{x}{1}$$
$$7x = 5$$
$$x = .7$$

antilog 3.8154 = 6537
(18.7)³ = 6,537

Example 2: Evaluate (.03625)⁴.

$$\log (.03625)^4 = 4 \log .03625$$

$$\begin{array}{ll} \log 3620 = .5587 \\ \log 3625 = .5587 + x \\ \log 3630 = .5599 \end{array}$$

$$\frac{5}{10} = \frac{x}{1}$$

$$\begin{array}{r} .0012 \\ .0006 \end{array}$$

$$\begin{array}{r} = 4\ (8.5593{-}10) \\ 34.2372{-}40 \\ \text{(Subtract)}\quad 30.0000{-}30 \\ \hline 4.2372{-}10 \end{array}$$

antilog .2355 = 172
antilog .2372 = 172 + x
antilog .2380 = 173

$$\frac{17}{25} = \frac{x}{1}$$
$$25x = 17$$
$$x = .68 = .7$$

antilog 4.2372—10 = .000001727
(.03625)⁴ = .000001727

Example 3: Evaluate (2.13)⁴.

$$\begin{aligned} \log (2.13)^4 &= \tfrac{2}{3} \log 2.13 \\ &= \tfrac{2}{3} \times 0.3284 \\ &= 0.2189 \end{aligned}$$

antilog .2175 = 165
antilog .2189 = 165 + x
antilog .2201 = 166

$$\frac{14}{26} = \frac{x}{1}$$
$$26x = 14$$
$$x = .5$$

antilog 0.2189 = 1.655
(2.13)³ = 1.655

124. Finding the Root of a Number by Logarithms

The logarithm of the root of a number is equal to the logarithm of the number divided by the root.

Example 1: Evaluate √34987.

$$\log \sqrt{34987} = \frac{\log 34987}{4}$$

$$\begin{array}{l} \log 34900 = .5428 \\ \log 34987 = .5428 + x \\ \log 35000 = .5441 \end{array}$$

$$\frac{87}{100} = \frac{x}{}$$
$$100x = .0013$$

$$\begin{array}{r} .1131 \\ .0011 \end{array}$$

$$\begin{array}{r} = 4.5439 \\ = 4 \\ \hline = 1.135975 = 1.1360 \end{array}$$

antilog .1335 = 136
antilog .1360 = 136 + x
antilog .1367 = 137

$$\frac{25}{32} = \frac{x}{1}$$
$$32x = 25$$
$$x = .78$$

antilog 1.1360 = 13.678
√34987 = 13.678

Example 2: Evaluate ∛76.24.

$$\log \sqrt[3]{76.24} = \frac{\log 76.24}{3}$$

$$\begin{array}{l} \log 7620 = .8820 \\ \log 7624 = .8820 + x \\ \log 7630 = .8825 \end{array}$$

$$\frac{4}{10} = \frac{x}{}$$
$$.0005$$

$$10x = .0020$$
$$x = .0002$$
$$= \frac{1.8822}{3}$$
$$= 0.6274$$

antilog $0.6274 = 4.24$

$\sqrt[3]{76.24} = 4.24$

$$\frac{27.8667—30}{3} = 9.2889—10$$

antilog $.2878 = 194$
antilog $.2889 = 194 + x$
antilog $.2900 = 195$

$$\frac{11}{22} = \frac{x}{1}$$
$$22x = 11$$
$$x = .5$$

antilog $9.2889—10 = .1945$

$\sqrt[3]{.0073573} = .1945$

Example 3: Evaluate $\sqrt[3]{.0073573}$.

$$\log \sqrt[3]{.0073573} = \frac{\log .0073573}{3}$$

$\log 73500 = .8663$
$\log 73573 = .8663 + x$
$\log 73600 = .8669$

$$\frac{73}{100} = \frac{x}{.0006}$$
$$100x = .0438$$
$$x = .0004$$
$$= \frac{7.8667—10}{3}$$

The quotient of $7.8667—10$ divided by 3 is $2.6222—3\tfrac{1}{3}$. By adding $20.0000—20$ to $7.8667—10$, the sum, $27.8667—30$, can be divided by 3 and the quotient will be a workable logarithm.

$\log .0073573 = 7.8667—10$
add $ 20.0000—20$
$ 27.8667—30$

125. Cologarithms

The *cologarithms* of a number is the logarithm of the reciprocal of the number. For example, colog $N = \log \frac{1}{N}$. However,

$$\log \frac{1}{N} = \log 1 — \log N$$
$$\log \frac{1}{N} = 0 — \log N$$
$$\log \frac{1}{N} = — \log N$$

Therefore, colog $N = \log \frac{1}{N} = — \log N$. Thus the cologarithm of a number is the logarithm of the number subtracted from the logarithm of 1 (0.0000 or, to avoid a negative mantissa, $10.0000—10$).

Example 1: Evaluate the cologarithm of 373.

$$\text{colog } 373 = \log \frac{1}{373}$$
$$\log 1 = 10.0000—10$$
$$\log 373 = 2.5717$$
$$\text{colog } 373 = 7.4283—10$$

Example 2: Evaluate $\frac{2.37}{3.61}$.

$$\log \frac{2.37}{3.61} = \log 2.37 — \log 3.61$$
$$= \log 2.37 + \text{colog } 3.61$$
$$\log 1 = 10.0000—10$$
$$\log 3.61 = 0.5575$$
$$\text{colog } 3.61 = 9.4425—10$$
$$\log 2.37 = 0.3747$$
$$9.8172—10$$

antilog $9.8172—10 = .65643$

126. Computation by logarithms

In performing logarithmic computations, follow the principles given in paragraphs 117 through 125. When negative quantities are involved (in multiplication and division), disregard the minus sign when making logarithmic calculations. After calculating the antilog, the sign is determined in accordance with the algebraic law of signs for multiplication and division.

Example 1: Evaluate $\sqrt[3]{\dfrac{(94.7)^2 \, (.00789)}{(3.71)^3 \, (.345)}}$.

$$\log (94.7)^2 = 2 \log 94.7$$
$$= 2 \times 1.9763$$
$$= 3.9526$$

$$\log (.00789) = 7.8971—10$$
$$\log (94.7)^2 + \log (.00789) = 11.8497—10 = 1.8497$$

$$\log (3.71)^3 = 3 \log 3.71$$
$$= 3 \times 0.5694$$
$$= 1.7082$$

$$\log (3.71)^3 + \log (.345) = 9.5378—10$$
$$\log (94.7)^2 \, (.00789) = 11.2460—10 = 1.2460$$

$$\log (94.7)^2 \, (.00789) = 1.8497$$
$$\log (3.71)^3 \, (.345) = 1.2460$$
$$0.6037$$

$$\log \sqrt[3]{\frac{(94.7)^2 \, (.00789)}{(3.71)^3 \, (.345)}} = \frac{0.6037}{3}$$
$$= .2012$$

antilog $.2012 = 1.5892$

Example 2: Evaluate $\sqrt[4]{\dfrac{(6.484)^2 \cdot \sqrt[3]{7.667}}{(12.35)^2 \cdot \sqrt[3]{3007}}}$.

$$\log (6.484)^2 = 2 \log 6.484$$
$$= 2 \times 0.8118$$
$$= 1.6236$$

$$\log \sqrt[3]{7.667} = \frac{\log 7.667}{3}$$
$$= \frac{0.8846}{3}$$
$$= 0.2949$$

$$\log (6.484)^2 + \log \sqrt[3]{7.667} = 1.6236 + .2949$$
$$= 1.9185$$

$$\log (12.35)^2 = 2 \log 12.35$$
$$= 2 \times 1.0917$$
$$= 2.1834$$

$$\log \sqrt[3]{3007} = \frac{\log 3007}{3}$$
$$= \frac{3.4782}{3}$$
$$= 1.1594$$

$$\log (12.35)^2 + \log \sqrt[3]{3007} = 2.1834 + 1.1594$$
$$= 3.3428$$

$$\log (6.484)^2 \, \sqrt[3]{7.667} = 11.9185—10$$
$$\log (12.35)^2 \, \sqrt[3]{3007} = 3.3428$$
$$8.5757—10$$

$$\log \sqrt[4]{\frac{(6.484)^2 \cdot \sqrt[3]{7.667}}{(12.35)^2 \cdot \sqrt[3]{300?}}} = \frac{38.5757-40}{4} = 9.6439-10$$

antilog 9.6439—10 = .4405

127. Review Problems—Logarithms

a. Find the logarithms of the following numbers to the base 10:

(1) 785
(2) 3.57
(3) .0345
(4) .000476
(5) 49.6
(6) 273.5
(7) 760.1
(8) 7.234
(9) .009875
(10) .00005254

b. Find the antilogs of the following logarithms:

(1) 4.8457
(2) 2.4330
(3) 9.5453—10
(4) 6.8299—10
(5) 0.6010
(6) 2.5690
(7) 5.4343—10
(8) 5.6994
(9) 0.2018
(10) 4.5372—10

c. Using logarithms, find the products of the following to four significant figures:

(1) 6.93 × 23.7
(2) 186 × 215
(3) 64.3 × 21.4
(4) .089 × .076
(5) 135 × 42.3

d. Using logarithms, find the quotients of the following to four significant figures:

(1) 148 ÷ 297
(2) $\dfrac{251}{648}$

(3) 14.9 ÷ 37.4
(4) 47.38 ÷ 63.29
(5) $\dfrac{1.06}{4.35}$

e. Using logarithms, evaluate the following:

(1) $(.0293)^4$
(2) $(1.756)^7$
(3) $(7.953)^8$
(4) $(69.37)^{.7}$
(5) $(27.98)^2$
(6) $\sqrt[3]{.01325}$
(7) $\sqrt[4]{815}$
(8) $\sqrt{7698}$
(9) $\sqrt[5]{8.942}$
(10) $\sqrt[4]{.000079911}$

f. Using logarithms, compute the following:

(1) $\dfrac{3.8 \times 2.6}{4.3}$

(2) $\sqrt[3]{\dfrac{.541 \times 47.3}{.0157}}$

(3) $\dfrac{44.1 \times 1.82}{10.27 \times .32}$

(4) $\dfrac{85.21 \times \sqrt[3]{4651}}{\sqrt{46.82} \times 6.230}$

(5) $\left(\dfrac{31.21}{40.70}\right)^3$

(6) $\sqrt[3]{\dfrac{(57.20)^2}{(31.42)^3}}$

(7) $\sqrt{\dfrac{.08152 \times 1.953}{95.27}}$

(8) $\sqrt[3]{\dfrac{.8531}{9.327}} \times \sqrt[3]{\dfrac{518.2}{61.52}}$

(9) $\dfrac{48.19 \times \sqrt{56.02}}{431.6 \times \sqrt[3]{46.25} \times \sqrt{16.34}}$

(10) $\sqrt{\dfrac{.008150 \times .08532}{.01234 \times \sqrt[3]{.09156}}}$

CHAPTER 9

PLANE GEOMETRY

128. Introduction

Plane geometry is that part of geometry which deals with plane figures. In electronics, as in many other fields, it is necessary to know how to deal with areas of common plane figures. This chapter presents the formulas for finding the areas of triangles, quadrilaterals (plane figures having four sides and four angles), and circles. No effort has been made to cover the entire field of geometry. Only those principles and proofs are presented that are of value in practical work.

129. Definitions

a. *Lines.* A line has length, but no width or thickness. What is drawn on paper and called a line has thickness and breadth because of the material used to draw it—however, this mark only *represents* the actual line.

b. *Angles.* An angle, such as *ABC* in *A*, figure 23, is formed by the intersection of two lines. An angle, therefore, is the measure of the difference in direction of two straight lines that meet. The lines which form the angle, *AB* or *BC*, are called the *sides* of the angle, and the point of meeting, *B*, the vertex. The symbol ∠ is used to indicate angles. Angles usually are measured in *degrees*. A complete circle or rotation consists of 360 degrees. The symbol ° is used to indicate degrees; it is written to the right and slightly above the number. For example, 30 degrees is written 30°. Each degree consists of 60 *minutes*, and each minute is further broken down into 60 *seconds*. The symbol ' is used to indicate minutes; the symbol " indicates seconds. For example, 20 minutes is written 20'; 15 seconds is written 15".

(1) When one straight line is *perpendicular* to another straight line, the angle formed is a right angle (90°) (B, fig. 23).

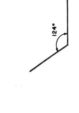

(2) Two right angles, added together, form a *straight angle*. A straight angle, therefore, is an angle of 180°.

(3) Any angle less than a right angle is an *acute angle* (C, fig. 23).

(4) Any angle greater than a right angle and less than 180° is an *obtuse angle* (D, fig. 23).

(5) Two angles whose sum is one right angle are called *complementary angles* (E, fig. 23).

(6) Two angles whose sum is a straight angle are called *supplementary angles* (F, fig. 23).

Figure 23. Angles.

130. Basic Principles of Geometric Construction

a. *Reproducing Angles.* To draw an angle equal to a given angle *BAC* (fig. 24)—

(1) Draw a line, *A'C'*.

(2) With *A* as the center, use a compass to strike an arc that cuts the sides of the given angle at *X* and *Y*. Using the same radius, strike a similar arc, *X'Y'*, on the line, *A'C'*.

(3) Measure the opening of the given angle by setting one point of the compass at *Y* and the other at *X*. With the compass at this distance and with *Y'* as the center, strike an arc as shown in figure 24. This will cut the first arc at point *X'*.

(4) Draw a line, *A'B'*, through *X'*. The new angle, *B'A'C'*, is the same size as angle *BAC*.

Figure 24. Reproducing an angle.

b. *Finding the Midpoint of a Straight Line Segment.* To find the midpoint of any straight line segment, such as *AB* in figure 25—

(1) Use a radius greater than half the length of *AB*. Using point *A* as the center, draw arcs *CD* and *C'D'*. With point *B* as the center, and using the same radius, draw arcs *EF* and *E'F'*.

(2) Draw a straight line to connect the points where the arcs intersect. Point *X*, where this line intersects *AB*, is the midpoint of straight line segment *AB*.

c. *Constructing a Perpendicular.* To construct a perpendicular to a straight line at a given point—

(1) On the straight line, such as *AB* in figure 26, mark point *P* at which the perpendicular is to be constructed.

(2) Set a compass for a radius less than the shorter of the two segments, *AP*

or *PB*. With *P* as a center, draw arcs, cutting line *AB* at points *X* and *Y*.

(3) Set the compass for a radius greater than *PX*. With *X* as a center, draw an arc above point *P* (fig. 26). Keep the compass at the same setting and, with *Y* as a center, draw another arc intersecting the one drawn with *X* as a center. (The two arcs may be drawn to intersect below point *P* instead of above.)

(4) Draw a straight line from the point where the two arcs intersect to point *P*. The line is perpendicular to *AB*.

(5) To construct the perpendicular bisector of a straight line segment, first find the midpoint of the line segment (*b* above), and construct the perpendicular at that point.

Figure 26. Constructing a perpendicular to a straight line at a point on the line.

d. *Constructing a Perpendicular to a Straight Line from a Point Not on the Line.* To draw a perpendicular to a straight line from a point outside the line, such as point *P* in figure 27—

(1) With point *P* as the center, draw an arc cutting line *AB* at points *X* and *Y*.

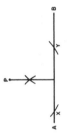

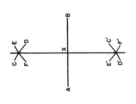

Figure 25. Bisecting a straight line segment.

(2) Using a radius greater than one-half the distance between *X* and *Y* and, with points *X* and *Y* as centers, draw arcs that intersect.

(3) Draw a straight line from point *P*, through the point where the two arcs intersect, to line *AB*. The line is perpendicular to *AB*.

e. *Finding the Center of a Circle.*

(1) Draw any two chords, such as *AB* and *AC* in figure 28.

(2) Construct the perpendicular bisector of each chord (*c* above). Point *X*, where the two perpendicular bisectors meet, is the center of the circle.

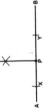

Figure 28. Finding the center of a circle.

f. *Bisecting an Angle.* Any angle, such as angle *CAB* in figure 29, can be divided into two equal angles. An angle, thus divided, is said to be bisected. To bisect an angle—

(1) Using *A* as a center, draw an arc cutting the sides of angle *CAB* at *X* and *Y*.

(2) With *X* and *Y* as centers, draw intersecting arcs.

(3) Draw a straight line from *A* through the point where the arcs intersect. The line divides angles *CAB* into two

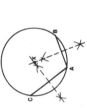

Figure 27. Constructing a perpendicular to a straight line from a point not on the line.

equal angles and is called the bisector of angle *CAB*.

Figure 29. Bisecting an angle.

131. Triangles

a. *General.* A triangle is a plane figure bounded by three straight lines. There are several different kinds of triangles.

(1) An *equilateral triangle* (A, fig. 30) has three equal sides and three equal angles; each angle equals 60°.

(2) An *isosceles triangle* has two equal

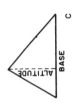

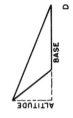

Figure 30. Triangles.

sides and two equal angles. The equal angles are opposite the equal sides.

(3) A *right triangle* (B, fig. 30) has one right angle.

(4) An *oblique triangle* (C and D, fig. 30) is one that does not contain a right angle. Thus, all except right triangles are oblique triangles.

b. *Base.* The base of a triangle is the side on which the triangle is supposed to stand. However, any side of a triangle may be used as the base.

c. *Altitude.* The altitude is the perpendicular line distance from the vertex of the triangle to the base or the base extended. In B, figure 30, the altitude of a right triangle is shown, in C, figure 30, the altitude of an acute triangle, and in D, figure 30, the altitude of an obtuse triangle. Note that in an obtuse triangle, it is necessary to extend the base of the triangle to find the altitude.

d. *Area.* The area of a triangle is the entire surface within the perimeter.

e. *Hypotenuse.* The side opposite the right angle of any right triangle is the hypotenuse (B, fig. 30).

132. Law of Angles of Any Triangle

The sum of the angles of any triangle is equal to 180°. When given any two of the three angles of a triangle, the third angle can be found by subtracting the sum of the given angles from 180°

Example 1:

If two angles of a triangle are 90° and 45°, what is the size of the third angle?

90° + 45° = 135°

180° — 135° = 45°

Therefore, the third angle is 45°.

Example 2:

Angle A of triangle ABC is 100°; angle B is 30°. What is the size of angle C?

$\angle A + \angle B + \angle C = 180°$
$\angle A = 100°$
$\angle B = 30°$
$\angle A + \angle B = 130°$
$\angle C = 180° - 130°$
$\angle C = 50°$

133. Law of Right Triangles

a. *The Pythagorean Theorem.* This theorem, which applies to any right triangle, states that *the square of the hypotenuse is equal to the sum of the squares of the other two sides.* The Pythagorean theorem is of prime importance in trigonometry (ch. 10) since the value of one side of a right triangle can be found if the other two sides are known. Thus, in figure 31:

$c^2 = a^2 + b^2$ or $25 = 16 + 9$
$a^2 = c^2 - b^2$ or $16 = 25 - 9$
$b^2 = c^2 - a^2$ or $9 = 25 - 16$

Example 1: Find the hypotenuse of a right triangle if the sides are 3 and 4 inches long, respectively.

$c^2 = a^2 + b^2$
$c^2 = 9 + 16$
$c^2 = 25$
$c = \sqrt{25}$
$c = 5$ inches

Example 2: The hypotenuse of a right triangle is 13 inches long and one side is 5 inches long. Find the length of the other side.

$c^2 = a^2 + b^2$
$13^2 = 5^2 + b^2$
$b^2 = 169 - 25$
$b^2 = 144$
$b = \sqrt{144}$
$b = 12$ inches

Example 3: Given the right triangle ABC (fig. 31), find c if a = 7 and b = 6.

$c^2 = a^2 + b^2$
$c^2 = 49 + 36$
$c^2 = 85$
$c = \sqrt{85}$
$c = 9.22—$

$$\begin{array}{r} 9.\ 2\ 2 \\ \sqrt{85.00\ 00} \\ 81 \\ \end{array}$$
182 | 400
364
1842 | 3600
3684

Example 4: Given the right triangle ABC (fig. 31), find b if a = 9 and

$c = 12.$
$b^2 = c^2 - a^2$
$b^2 = 144 - 81$
$b^2 = 63$
$b = \sqrt{63}$
$b = 7.93+$

$$\begin{array}{r} 7.\ 9\ 3 \\ \sqrt{63.00\ 00} \\ 49 \\ \end{array}$$
149 | 1400
1341
1583 | 5900
4749

Example 5: Given the right triangle ABC (fig. 31), find a if b = 6 and

$c = 13.$
$a^2 = c^2 - b^2$
$a^2 = 169 - 36$
$a^2 = 133$
$a = \sqrt{133}$
$a = 11.53+$

$$\begin{array}{r} 1\ 1.5\ 3 \\ \sqrt{01\ 33.00\ 00} \\ 1 \\ \end{array}$$
21 | 33
21
225 | 1200
1125
2303 | 7500
6909

b. *Special Right Triangles.* The two right triangles in examples 1 and 2 of a above are special right triangles with sides that have whole numbers. These triangles are called the 3-4-5 right triangle and the 5-12-13 right triangle, although their sides may also be multiples of these numbers. For example, a triangle having sides of 6, 8, and 10 inches is also a 3-4-5 right triangle, because its sides are multiples of 3, 4, and 5. When determining the unknown side of a right triangle, the process is greatly simplified if the triangle is a 3-4-5 or 5-12-13 right triangle. In these cases, the unknown side can often be determined by inspection.

Example 1: The hypotenuse of a right triangle is 15 inches long, and one side is 12 inches long. Find the other side.

Since 15 and 12 can be divided by 3 to give 5 and 4, the triangle is a 3-4-5 right triangle. The third side, therefore, is equal to 3 times 3, or

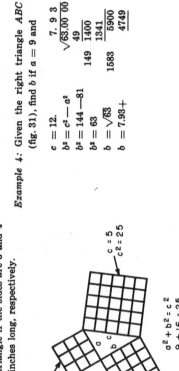
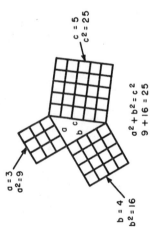

a = 3
a² = 9

b = 4
b² = 16

c = 5
c² = 25

a² + b² = c²
9 + 16 = 25

Figure 31. The Pythagorean theorem.

9 inches. The answer can be checked by the Pythagorean theorem.

Example 2: The two sides of a triangle are 10 and 24 feet long. Find the length of the hypotenuse.

Dividing 10 and 24 by 2 gives 5 and 12, the two sides of a 5–12–13 right triangle. Therefore, the hypotenuse is 2 times 13, or 26 inches.

134. Area of Any Triangle

The area of any triangle is equal to one-half the product of its base and altitude. The formula for finding the area is $A = \frac{bh}{2}$ where b is the base of the triangle and h is the altitude.

Example 1:
What is the area of a triangle with a base of 15 inches and an altitude of 10 inches?

$$A = \frac{bh}{2}$$
$$= \frac{15 \times 10}{2}$$
$$= \frac{150}{2}$$
$$= 75 \text{ square inches}$$

Example 2:
Find the area of a right triangle if the base measures 7 feet and the hypotenuse 25 feet.

$$c^2 - b^2 = a^2$$
$$a^2 = 25^2 - 7^2 = 625 - 49$$
$$a^2 = 576$$
$$a = \sqrt{576} = 24 \text{ feet altitude}$$
$$A = \frac{bh}{2}$$
$$= \frac{7 \times 24}{2} = \frac{168}{2}$$
$$= 84 \text{ square feet}$$

135. Quadrilaterals

A quadrilateral is a plane figure bounded by four straight lines.

a. A *parallelogram* (A, fig. 32) is a quadrilateral having both pairs of opposite sides parallel.

b. A *rectangle* (B, fig. 32) is a parallelogram that has four right angles.

c. A *square* (C, fig. 32) is a rectangle, all four sides of which are equal.

d. A *trapezoid* (D, fig. 32) is a quadrilateral with two sides (called bases) parallel and unequal.

136. Area of Any Parallelogram

The area of any parallelogram is equal to the product of the base by the altitude. The formula for finding the area is $A = bh$ where b is the base and h is the height or altitude.

Example 1: Find the area of a square, each side of which is 15 inches.

$$A = bh$$
$$= 15 \times 15$$
$$= 225 \text{ square inches}$$

Example 2: What is the area of a rectangle with a base of 12 inches and an altitude of 7 inches?

$$A = bh$$
$$= 12 \times 7$$
$$= 84 \text{ square inches}$$

137. Area of Trapezoid

The area of a trapezoid is determined by multiplying one-half the sum of the bases by the altitude of the trapezoid.

Thus, $A = \left(\frac{B+b}{2}\right)h$.

Figure 32. Quadrilaterals.

Example: Find the area of a trapezoid the bases of which are 16 and 10 inches long and the altitude is 8 inches.

$$A = \left(\frac{B+b}{2}\right)h$$
$$= \left(\frac{16+10}{2}\right)8$$
$$= \frac{26}{2} \times 8$$
$$= 104 \text{ square inches}$$

138. Circles

a. *General.* A circle is a plane figure bounded by a closed curve, every point of which is equidistant from the center.

b. *Circumference.* The circumference is the curved line that bounds a circle (A, fig. 33).

c. *Chord.* A chord is a straight line drawn through a circle and terminated at its intersections with the circumference (B, fig. 33).

d. *Diameter.* The diameter of a circle is a chord that passes through the center of the circle (A, fig. 33).

e. *Radius.* The radius of a circle is a straight line from the center to a point on the circumference (A, fig. 33). All radii of the same circle are of equal length, one-half of the diameter.

f. *Arc.* An arc is any part of the circumference of a circle.

g. *Segment.* A segment is that area of a circle bounded by a chord and the arc subtended by that chord (C, fig. 33).

h. *Sector.* A sector is the area between an arc and two radii drawn to the ends of the arc (C, fig. 33).

i. *Tangent.* A tangent is a straight line that touches the circumference of a circle at only one point and is perpendicular to the radius drawn to the point of contact (B, fig. 33). This

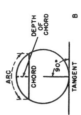

Figure 33. Circles.

point is called the *point of tangency* or the *point of contact*.

j. Concentric Circles. Concentric circles are circles having a common center (D, fig. 33).

k. Pi(π). The Greek letter π is used to represent the relationship of the circumference of any circle to its diameter. Roughly, it equals $\frac{22}{7}$. More approximately, it equals 3.1416. In many applications, it is rounded off to 3.14.

139. Circumference of Any Circle

The circumference of any circle is π times the diameter; therefore, $C = \pi D$.

Example 1: Find the circumference of a circle if the diameter is 6½ inches.

$C = \pi D$
$= 3.14 \times 6.5$
$= 20.42$ inches

Example 2: Find the diameter of a circular tank having a circumference of 31½ inches.

When the circumference of a circle is given, the diameter is calculated by dividing the circumference by π — $D = \frac{C}{\pi}$.

$D = \frac{C}{\pi}$
$= \frac{31.5}{3.1416}$
$= 10.03$ inches

140. Area of Any Circle

a. The area of any circle is equal to π multiplied by the radius squared; therefore, $a = \pi r^2$.

Example 1: Find the area of a circle having a diameter of 5 feet 6 inches.

$A = \pi r^2$
$= \pi \left(\frac{5.5}{2}\right)^2$
$= \pi (2.75)^2$
$= 3.14 \times 7.56$
$= 23.76$ square feet

Example 2: What is the diameter of a circle the area of which is 78.54 square rods?

$A = \pi r^2$ and $r = \frac{D}{2}$

$A = \pi \left(\frac{D}{2}\right)^2$

$A = \frac{\pi D^2}{4}$

Transposing:

$D^2 = \frac{4A}{\pi}$

$D = \sqrt{\frac{4A}{\pi}}$

$D = 2\sqrt{\frac{A}{\pi}}$

Substituting and solving for D:

$D = 2\sqrt{\frac{78.54}{3.1416}}$

$D = 2\sqrt{25}$

$D = 2 \times 5$

$D = 10$ rods

b. The area of any circle also is equal to one-half the product of the circumference and the radius.

Example: If the diameter of a circle is 10 inches, and the circumference of the circle is 31.416 inches, what is the area of the circle?

$A = \frac{1}{2}Cr$

$r = \frac{1}{2}D$ or $r = 5$

$A = \frac{1}{2}(31.416 \times 5)$
$= \frac{157.08}{2}$
$= 78.54$ square inches

141. Area of Ring

A ring is the area between the circumferences of two concentric circles. The area of a ring may be found by subtracting the area of the small circle from the area of the large circle. If R is the radius of the large circle and r is the radius of the small circle, a simplified formula for the area of the ring can be developed as follows:

Area of ring = area of large circle — area of small circle
$= \pi R^2 — \pi r^2$
$= \pi (R^2 — r^2)$

By factoring $(R^2 — r^2)$ into $(R + r)(R — r)$, the formula also can be written:

$A = \pi (R + r)(R — r)$

Example: Find the area of a ring having an inside diameter of 8 inches and an outside diameter of 12 inches.

$A = \pi (R + r)(R — r)$
$= 3.14(6 + 4)(6 — 4)$
$= 3.14 \times 10 \times 2$
$= 62.8$ square inches

142. Review Problems—Plane Geometry

a. Find the area of a rectangle having a base of 12 inches and an altitude of 8 inches.

b. What is the area of a square, each side of which is 6 inches?

c. Find the area of a triangle of which the altitude is 5 inches and the base is 10 inches.

d. Find the area of a triangle having an altitude of 15 inches and a base of 2 inches.

e. What is the hypotenuse of a right triangle the sides of which are 12 and 8 inches?

f. Find the third side of a right triangle if one side is 7 inches and the hypotenuse is 9 inches.

g. Identify the following figures, give the formulas, and solve for the required quantity.

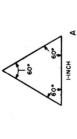

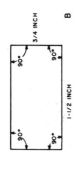

A

B

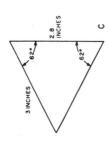

C

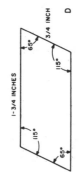

D

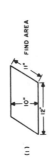

(1) FIND AREA

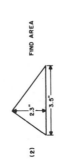

(2) FIND AREA

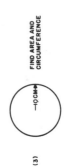

(3) FIND AREA AND CIRCUMFERENCE

(4) FIND AREA

i. Find the area of the largest circle that can be cut from a square piece of sheet metal with sides of 10 inches.

j. If the height of an antenna is 80 feet, how far from its top is an object on the ground 60 feet from the base of the pole?

k. How many square feet of lumber are needed to build 10 boxes 18 inches by 16 inches by 9 inches?

l. A metal plate is in the shape of an equilateral triangle. If the altitude is 14 inches, what is the perimeter?

h. What are the perimeters of the following figures?

CHAPTER 10

TRIGONOMETRY

Section I. BASIC TRIGONOMETRIC THEORY

143. Introduction

a. *Definition.* Trigonometry deals with the relationships between the sides and angles of triangles. It uses the theories of basic mathematics—the numbers of arithmetic, the equations of algebra, and the theorems of geometry—to aid in the measurement of the sides and angles of triangles.

b. *Application.* The ability to use angles and their trigonometric relationships in electrical calculations is especially important in the study of alternating current (ac). Most effects of ac circuit components can be studied or described only in terms of the part of a cycle by which a current lags behind a corresponding voltage, or vice versa. A large percentage of the problems relating to the analysis of ac circuits and communication networks involves the solution of the right triangle in some form. Certain facts about right triangles are familiar (ch 9)—namely, that the square of the hypotenuse is equal to the sum of the squares of the other two sides ($c^2 = a^2 + b^2$), that the sum of the acute angles of a right triangle is 90°, and that the sum of the interior angles of any triangle is 180°. However, it would be impossible to solve certain problems with only this information. After learning other relationships between the sides and angles of triangles, it will be found that trigonometry is an easy and accurate method of solving many problems in ac electricity.

144. Trigonometric Functions

a. *General.* Trigonometry is based on the six trigonometric functions involved in the study of the right angle. If the value of one quantity depends on the value of a second quantity, the first quantity is said to be a function of the second. The six trigonometric functions —sine (sin), cosine (cos), tangent (tan), co-

tangent (cot), secant (sec), and cosecant (csc) —are derived from the ratios of the sides of a right triangle to each other.

b. *The Right Triangle.* Figure 34 shows a right triangle, with the angles labeled A, B, and C; C is the right angle. The sides of the triangle are labeled a, b, and c, with the side opposite each angle given the same letter as the angle. The following are the trigonometric ratios of the sides of a triangle:

$$\sin = \frac{\text{opposite side}}{\text{hypotenuse}}$$

$$\cos = \frac{\text{adjacent side}}{\text{hypotenuse}}$$

$$\tan = \frac{\text{opposite side}}{\text{adjacent side}}$$

$$\cot = \frac{\text{adjacent side}}{\text{opposite side}}$$

$$\sec = \frac{\text{hypotenuse}}{\text{adjacent side}}$$

$$\csc = \frac{\text{hypotenuse}}{\text{opposite side}}$$

c. *Angle A.* Refer again to figure 34. Using the acute angle A, a is the opposite side, b is the adjacent side, and c, which is the side opposite the right angle, is the hypotenuse. Therefore,

$$\sin A = \frac{a}{c}$$

$$\cos A = \frac{b}{c}$$

$$\tan A = \frac{a}{b}$$

$$\cot A = \frac{b}{a}$$

$$\sec A = \frac{c}{b}$$

$$\csc A = \frac{c}{a}$$

d. *Angle B.* Using the acute angle B in figure 34, b is the opposite side, a is the adjacent side, and c is the hypotenuse. Therefore,

$$\sin B = \frac{b}{c}$$

$$\cos B = \frac{a}{c}$$

$$\tan B = \frac{b}{a}$$

$$\cot B = \frac{a}{b}$$

$$\sec B = \frac{c}{a}$$

$$\csc B = \frac{c}{b}$$

e. *Angle C.* Right angle C is the angle which establishes the relationship between the other sides and other angles and thus may be called a constant. Although it is possible to obtain functions for angle C, they are not covered here because they are not needed in solving problems of this type.

Example:

Determine the values of the trigonometric functions of a right triangle with sides as follows: $a = 3$, $b = 4$, $c = 5$ (fig. 35).

Functions of angle A:

$$\sin A = \frac{a}{c} = \frac{3}{5}$$

$$\cos A = \frac{b}{c} = \frac{4}{5}$$

$$\tan A = \frac{a}{b} = \frac{3}{4}$$

$$\cot A = \frac{b}{a} = \frac{4}{3}$$

$$\sec A = \frac{c}{b} = \frac{5}{4}$$

$$\csc A = \frac{c}{a} = \frac{5}{3}$$

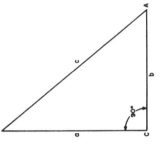

Figure 34. Trigonometric functions of the right triangle.

Functions of angle B:

$$\sin B = \frac{b}{c} = \frac{4}{5}$$

$$\cos B = \frac{a}{c} = \frac{3}{5}$$

$$\tan B = \frac{b}{a} = \frac{4}{3}$$

$$\cot B = \frac{a}{b} = \frac{3}{4}$$

$$\sec B = \frac{c}{a} = \frac{5}{3}$$

$$\csc B = \frac{c}{b} = \frac{5}{4}$$

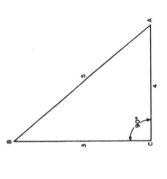

Figure 35. Right triangle with sides known.

145. Reciprocal Relations of Trigonometric Functions

From the definitions of the six trigononometric functions (par. 144), the reciprocal relations (listed below) can be determined. The cosecant, secant, and cotangent should always be thought of as the reciprocals of the sine, cosine, and tangent, respectively.

$$\sin A = \frac{a}{c} = \frac{1}{\frac{c}{a}} = \frac{1}{\csc A}$$

$$\cos A = \frac{b}{c} = \frac{1}{\frac{c}{b}} = \frac{1}{\sec A}$$

$$\tan A = \frac{a}{b} = \frac{1}{\frac{b}{a}} = \frac{1}{\cot A}$$

$$\csc A = \frac{c}{a} = \frac{1}{\frac{a}{c}} = \frac{1}{\sin A}$$

$$\sec A = \frac{c}{b} = \frac{1}{\frac{b}{c}} = \frac{1}{\cos A}$$

$$\cot A = \frac{b}{a} = \frac{1}{\frac{a}{b}} = \frac{1}{\tan A}$$

147. Solving for Unknown Functions

If one trigonometric function of a right triangle is known, the other trigonometric functions can be determined. This is done by using the Pythagorean theorem (par. 133).

Example 1: Given the right triangle ABC (fig. 23): side a is 4; side C is 9. Since $\sin A = \frac{4}{9}$; also, $\sin A = \frac{4}{9}$, find the other trigonometric functions of angle A.

$\sin A = \frac{a}{c}$; also, $\sin A = \frac{4}{9}$.

Therefore, $a = 4$, $c = 9$

$$b^2 = c^2 - a^2$$
$$b^2 = 81 - 16$$
$$b^2 = 65$$
$$b = \sqrt{65}$$
$$b = 8.06$$

```
        8. 0 6
  √65.00 00
    64
1606  10000
       9636
```

146. Functions of Complementary Angles

a. The function of an acute angle is equal to the cofunction of its complementary angle. Apply the definitions of the trigonometric functions (par. 144) to angles A and B to obtain the following relations:

$$\sin B = \frac{b}{c} = \cos A$$

$$\tan B = \frac{b}{a} = \cot A$$

$$\sec B = \frac{c}{a} = \csc A$$

$$\cos B = \frac{a}{c} = \sin A$$

$$\cot B = \frac{a}{b} = \tan A$$

$$\csc B = \frac{c}{b} = \sec A$$

b. With angle B equal to 90° — A, these relations may be written:

$$\sin (90° - A) = \cos A$$
$$\tan (90° - A) = \cot A$$
$$\sec (90° - A) = \csc A$$
$$\cos (90° - A) = \sin A$$
$$\cot (90° - A) = \tan A$$
$$\csc (90° - A) = \sec A$$

$$\sin A = \frac{4}{9}$$
$$\cos A = \frac{8.06}{9}$$
$$\tan A = \frac{4}{8.06}$$
$$\cot A = \frac{8.06}{4}$$
$$\sec A = \frac{9}{8.06}$$
$$\csc A = \frac{9}{4}$$

Example 2: Given the right triangle ABC (fig. 23): side A is $\sqrt{3}$; side b is 7. Since $\tan A = \frac{\sqrt{3}}{7}$ or $\frac{1}{7}\sqrt{3}$, find the other trigonometric functions of angle A.

$\tan A = \frac{a}{b}$; also, $\tan A = \frac{1}{7}\sqrt{3} = \frac{\sqrt{3}}{7}$.

Therefore,
$$a = \sqrt{3}, \ b = 7$$
$$c^2 = a^2 + b^2$$
$$c^2 = 3 + 49$$
$$c^2 = 52$$
$$c = \sqrt{52}$$
$$c = \sqrt{4} \cdot \sqrt{13}$$
$$c = 2\sqrt{13}$$

$$\sin A = \frac{\sqrt{3}}{2\sqrt{13}}$$
$$\cos A = \frac{7}{2\sqrt{13}}$$
$$\tan A = \frac{\sqrt{3}}{7}$$
$$\cot A = \frac{7}{\sqrt{3}}$$
$$\sec A = \frac{2\sqrt{13}}{7}$$
$$\csc A = \frac{2\sqrt{13}}{\sqrt{3}}$$

148. Solving for Sides and Trigonometric Functions When One Side and One Function Are Given

When one side and one function of an angle of a right triangle are given, the two other sides and the remaining trigonometric functions of the given angle can be found. These are determined by use of the Pythagorean theorem.

Example 1: Given the right triangle ABC (fig. 34): if the hypotenuse is 30 inches and sec $A = 5$, solve for sides a and b and the trigonometric functions of angle A.

$\sec A = \frac{c}{b}$; also, $\sec A = \frac{30}{b}$; but $\sec A = 5$ or $\frac{5}{1}$.

Therefore, $\frac{30}{b} = \frac{5}{1}$

$$5b = 30$$
$$b = 6 \text{ inches}$$

$$a^2 = c^2 - b^2$$
$$a^2 = 900 - 36$$
$$a^2 = 864$$
$$a = \sqrt{864}$$
$$a = \sqrt{144}\ \sqrt{6}$$
$$a = 12\ \sqrt{6} \text{ inches}, \ b = 6 \text{ inches}, \ c = 30 \text{ inches}$$

$\sin A = \dfrac{12\sqrt{6}}{30} = \dfrac{12}{30}\sqrt{6} = \dfrac{2}{5}\sqrt{6}$

$\cos A = \dfrac{6}{30} = \dfrac{1}{5}$

$\tan A = \dfrac{12\sqrt{6}}{6} = 2\sqrt{6}$

$\cot A = \dfrac{6}{12\sqrt{6}} = \dfrac{1}{2\sqrt{6}} = \dfrac{\sqrt{6}}{(2)(6)} = \dfrac{\sqrt{6}}{12} = \dfrac{1}{12}\sqrt{6}$

$\sec A = \dfrac{30}{6} = 5$

$\csc A = \dfrac{30}{12\sqrt{6}} = \dfrac{5}{2\sqrt{6}} = \dfrac{5}{2\sqrt{6}}\cdot\dfrac{\sqrt{6}}{\sqrt{6}} = \dfrac{5\sqrt{6}}{(2)(6)} = \dfrac{5\sqrt{6}}{12} = \dfrac{5}{12}\sqrt{6}$

Example 2: Given the right triangle ABC (fig. 34): solve for sides b and c and the trigonometric functions of angle A when side a is 21.2 inches and sin A = 4/7.

$\sin A = \dfrac{a}{c}$; also, $\sin a = \dfrac{21.2}{c}$, but $\sin A = \dfrac{4}{7}$.

Therefore, $\dfrac{21.2}{c} = \dfrac{4}{7}$

$4c = 148.4$

$c = 37.1$ inches

$b^2 = c^2 - a^2$

$b^2 = 1376.41 - 449.44$

$b^2 = 926.97$

$b = \sqrt{926.97}$

$b = 30.4$ inches, $a = 21.2$ inches, $c = 37.1$ inches

$\sin A = \dfrac{21.2}{37.1} = \dfrac{4}{7}$

$\cos A = \dfrac{30.4}{37.1}$

$\tan A = \dfrac{21.2}{30.4} = \dfrac{5.3}{7.6}$

$\cot A = \dfrac{30.4}{21.2} = \dfrac{7.6}{5.3}$

$\sec A = \dfrac{37.1}{30.4}$

$\csc A = \dfrac{37.1}{21.2} = \dfrac{7}{4}$

149. Constructing an Acute Angle of Right Triangle When One Trigonometric Function Is Known

When the trigonometric function of an acute angle is given, the angle may be constructed geometrically. Use the definition given for the given function.

Example: Construct the acute angle A of right triangle ABC if tan A = ¼.

Step 1. Let a = 1 unit and b = 4 units.

Step 2. Erect perpendicular lines AC and BC. Use cross-sectional paper if available.

Step 3. Measure off 1 unit along BC and 4 units along AC (A, fig. 36).

Step 4. Join A and B, thus forming the right triangle ABC (B, fig. 36).

Step 5. Tan A = ¼; therefore, A is the required angle. Measuring angle A with a protractor shows it to be an angle of approximately 14°.

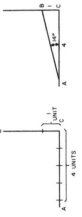

Figure 36. Constructing an angle when one function is known.

150. Common Trigonometric Functions

a. General. There are two special-case right triangles that are commonly used in solving mathematical problems. These are the right isosceles triangle (par. 131a) (fig. 37) with equal acute angles of 45° (fig. 37) and the right triangle with acute angles of 30° and 60°. The functions of these angles are tabulated in appendix III.

Figure 37. Right isosceles triangle—trigonometric functions of 45°.

b. Trigonometric Functions of 45°. Draw the right triangle ABC (fig. 37) with angle A equal to 45°. Because the acute angles of a right triangle are complementary, angle A plus angle B equals 90°. Thus, angle B is also 45°. Since sides opposite equal angles are equal, side a is equal to side b.

Let a = 1 and b = 1.

$c^2 = a^2 + b^2$

$c^2 = 1 + 1$

$c^2 = 2$

$c = \sqrt{2}$

$\sin 45° = \dfrac{1}{\sqrt{2}} \cdot \dfrac{\sqrt{2}}{\sqrt{2}} = \dfrac{\sqrt{2}}{2} = \dfrac{1}{2}\sqrt{2}$

$\cos 45° = \dfrac{1}{\sqrt{2}} \cdot \dfrac{\sqrt{2}}{\sqrt{2}} = \dfrac{\sqrt{2}}{2} = \dfrac{1}{2}\sqrt{2}$

$\tan 45° = \dfrac{1}{1} = 1$

$\cot 45° = \dfrac{1}{1} = 1$

$\sec 45° = \dfrac{\sqrt{2}}{1} = \sqrt{2}$

$\csc 45° = \dfrac{\sqrt{2}}{1} = \sqrt{2}$

c. Trigonometric Functions of 30° and 60°. Draw the equilateral triangle ABX (fig. 38). The angles of any equilateral triangle are 60° and the sides are equal (par. 131a). Drop a perpendicular BC to the center of the base AX. Right angles ACB and BCX are formed by the perpendicular and the base. The angles ABC and XBC are 30° angles. Since the sides of the equilateral triangle are equal, the perpendicular bisecting the base makes the base AC of the right triangle ABC one-half the length of the base AX of the equilateral triangle. Thus, the side opposite the right angle in a right triangle is twice the length of the side opposite the 30° angle.

Let b = 1 and c = 2.

$a^2 = c^2 - b^2$

$a^2 = 4 - 1$

$a^2 = 3$

$a = \sqrt{3}$

$\sin 60° = \dfrac{\sqrt{3}}{2} = \dfrac{1}{2}\sqrt{3}$

$\cos 60° = \dfrac{1}{2}$

$\tan 60° = \dfrac{\sqrt{3}}{1} = \sqrt{3}$

$\cot 60° = \dfrac{1}{\sqrt{3}} \cdot \dfrac{\sqrt{3}}{\sqrt{3}} = \dfrac{\sqrt{3}}{3} = \dfrac{1}{3}\sqrt{3}$

$\sec 60° = \dfrac{2}{1} = 2$

$\csc 60° = \dfrac{2}{\sqrt{3}} \cdot \dfrac{\sqrt{3}}{\sqrt{3}} = \dfrac{2\sqrt{3}}{3} = \dfrac{2}{3}\sqrt{3}$

$\sin 30° = \dfrac{1}{2}$

$\cos 30° = \dfrac{\sqrt{3}}{2} = \dfrac{1}{2}\sqrt{3}$

$\tan 30° = \dfrac{1}{\sqrt{3}} \cdot \dfrac{\sqrt{3}}{\sqrt{3}} = \dfrac{\sqrt{3}}{3} = \dfrac{1}{3}\sqrt{3}$

$\cot 30° = \dfrac{\sqrt{3}}{1} = \sqrt{3}$

$\sec 30° = \dfrac{2}{\sqrt{3}} \cdot \dfrac{\sqrt{3}}{\sqrt{3}} = \dfrac{2\sqrt{3}}{3} = \dfrac{2}{3}\sqrt{3}$

$\csc 30° = \dfrac{2}{1} = 2$

151. Solving for Sides of 45°–45°–90° or 30°–60°–90° Triangles When One Side Is Given

In special cases, right triangles can be solved when only one side is given. These are the 45°–45°–90° isosceles triangle and the 30°–60°–90° triangle.

Example 1: Solve for the unknown sides of right triangle *ABC* if angle $A = 60°$ and $b = 4$ inches.

$\text{Tan } 60° = \dfrac{a}{b} = \dfrac{a}{4}$; however, $\tan 60° = \sqrt{3}$.

Therefore,

$$\frac{a}{4} = \frac{\sqrt{3}}{1}$$

$$a = 4\sqrt{3} \text{ inches}$$

$\text{Cos } 60° = \dfrac{b}{c} = \dfrac{4}{c}$; however, $\cos 60° = \dfrac{1}{2}$.

Therefore,

$$\frac{4}{c} = \frac{1}{2}$$

$$c = 8 \text{ inches}$$

Thus, $a = 4\sqrt{3}$ inches, $b = 4$ inches, $c = 8$ inches.

Example 2: Solve for the unknown sides of right triangle *ABC* if angle $A = 45°$ and $c = 6$ inches.

$\text{Sin } 45° = \dfrac{a}{c} = \dfrac{a}{6}$; however, $\sin 45° = \dfrac{\sqrt{2}}{2}$.

Therefore,

$$\frac{a}{6} = \frac{\sqrt{2}}{2}$$

$$2a = 6\sqrt{2}$$

$$a = 3\sqrt{2}$$

$\text{Cos } 45° = \dfrac{b}{c} = \dfrac{b}{6}$; however, $\cos 45° = \dfrac{\sqrt{2}}{2}$.

Therefore,

$$\frac{b}{6} = \frac{\sqrt{2}}{2}$$

$$2b = 6\sqrt{2}$$

$$b = 3\sqrt{2} \text{ inches}$$

Thus, $a = 3\sqrt{2}$ inches, $b = 3\sqrt{2}$ inches, $c = 6$ inches.

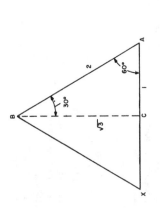

Figure 38. Equilateral right triangle—trigonometric functions of a right triangle with angles of 30° and 60°.

152. Calculations Involving Angles

a. Addition. To add angles, arrange the degrees, minutes, and seconds in separate columns and add each column separately. If the sum of the seconds column is 60 or more, subtract 60 or a multiple of 60 from that column, and add 1 minute or the same multiple of 1 minute to the minutes column. If the sum of the minutes column is 60 or more, subtract 60 from that column and add 1° to the degree column.

Example 1: Add 20° 40′ 25″, 8° 35′ 5″, and 30° 58′ 51″.

```
20°  40′  25″
 8°  35′   5″
30°  58′  51″
58° 133′  81″
```

Subtract 60″ from 81″ and add 1′ to 133′.

```
58° 133′   81″
    + 1′  −60″
58° 134′   21″
```

Subtract 120′ from 134′ and add 2° to 58°.

```
 58°  134′  21″
+ 2°  −120′
 60°   14′  21″
```

Example 2: Add 15° 44′ 36″ and 12° 38′ 35″.

```
15°  44′  36″
12°  38′  35″
27°  82′  71″ = 27° 83′ 11″ = 28° 23′ 11″.
```

b. Subtraction. To subtract angles, arrange the degrees, minutes, and seconds in separate columns with the larger angle on top. Then, subtract the individual columns. If the upper number in a column is too small to allow subtraction, one unit must be taken away from the preceding column and 60 units added to the insufficient number to make subtraction possible.

Example 1: Subtract 14° 51′ 30″ from 86° 45′ 10″.

```
86°  45′  10″
−14°  51′  30″
```

Subtraction cannot be performed in either the seconds or minutes columns. Subtract 1′ from 45′ leaving 44′, and add 60″ to 10″ for a total of 70″.

```
86°  44′  70″
−14°  51′  30″
```

Subtraction still cannot be performed in the minutes column. Subtract 1° from 86°, leaving 85°, and add 60′ to 44′ for a total of 104′.

```
85° 104′  70″
−14°  51′  30″
 71°  53′  40″
```

Example 2: Subtract 10° 35′ 42″ from 19° 20′ 20″.

```
19°  20′  20″
−10°  35′  42″
```

Subtraction cannot be performed in either the minutes or seconds columns. Therefore, change 19° 20' 20" to 18° 79' 80" and subtract.

$$18°\ 79'\ 80''$$
$$\underline{-10°\ 35'\ 42''}$$
$$8°\ 44'\ 38''$$

c. *Multiplication.* To multiply an angle by a given number, multiply each column by the number. If the answer in the seconds or minutes column is greater than 60, reduce as in the addition of angles (a above).

Example 1: Multiply 15° 21' 40" by 3:

$$15°\ 21'\ 40''$$
$$\underline{\qquad\qquad 3}$$
$$45°\ 63'\ 120'' = 45°\ 65'\ 0'' = 46°\ 5'$$

Example 2: Multiply 12° 14' 36" by 5.

$$12°\ 14'\ 36''$$
$$\underline{\qquad\qquad 5}$$
$$60°\ 70'\ 180'' = 60°\ 73' = 61°\ 13'$$

d. *Division.* To divide an angle by a given number, divide each column by the number (beginning with the degrees column). Change the remainder in degrees, if any, into minutes and add it to the numbers in the minutes column. Change the remainder in minutes, if any, to seconds and add it to the seconds column; then, perform division on the numbers in the seconds column.

Example 1: Divide 71° 22' 21" by 3.

```
      23°  47'   27"
  3)71°   22'   21"
    69
    2° = 120'
         142'
         141'
          1' = 60"
               81"
               81"
```

Example 2: Divide 166° 17' 36" by 6.

```
      27°  42'   56"
  6)166°  17'   36"
    162°
    4° = 240'
         257'
         252'
          5' = 300"
               336"
               336"
```

Section II. NATURAL TRIGONOMETRIC FUNCTIONS

154. Tables and Their Uses

For convenience in computing, trigonometric functions are arranged in tables similar to the tables of logarithms. The ratios themselves are called *natural* sines, cosines, tangents, cotangents, etc. The tables give the sines and cosines, the tangents and cotangents, and the secants and cosecants of the angles from 0° to 90°. Angles less than 45° are read down the page; the degrees are at the top of the page and the minutes are on the left. Angles greater than 45° are read up the page; the degrees are at the bottom of the page and the minutes are on the right. As with logarithms, it is necessary to interpolate to find the function of an angle which does not reduce to an integral number of minutes. When working with the sine and tangent, which are increasing in size from 0° to 90°, it is necessary to add in interpolation. When working with the cosine and cotangent, which are decreasing in size from 0° to 90°, it is necessary to subtract.

155. Finding the Function of an Angle From the Table

To find the function of an angle from the table, proceed much the same as with the table of logarithms.

a. *When an Angle Is Given in the Table.*

Example 1: Find the cosine of 44° 27'

Step 1. Turn to the table of sines and cosines.
Step 2. Locate the 44° column at the top of the page.
Step 3. Locate the 27' column at the left of the page.
Step 4. Read .71386 in the column headed Cosin.
Step 5. Cos 44° 27' = .71386.

Example 2: Fine the tangent of 86° 18'.

Step 1. Turn to the table of tangents and cotangents.
Step 2. Locate the 86° column at the bottom of the page.
Step 3. Locate the 18' at the right of the page.
Step 4. Read 15.4638 in the column headed Tang.
Step 5. Tan 86° 18' = 15.4638.

b. *When an Angle Is Not Given in the Table.*

Example 1: Find the sine of 32° 46' 36".

$$\sin 32°\ 46' = .54122$$
$$\sin 32°\ 46'\ 36'' = .54122 + x$$
$$\sin 32°\ 47' = .54146$$

153. Review Problems—Basic Trigonometry

Note. In the following problems, angle C is the right angle and equals 90°.

a. Find the third side of each of the following right triangles ABC, if two sides are:

(1) $a = 5,\ b = 7$
(2) $b = 18,\ c = 19$
(3) $a = 17,\ c = 43$
(4) $a = 3b$
(5) $a = 2m,\ c = m^2 + 1$

b. Given the right triangle ABC, solve for the trigonometric functions of angle A in each of the following cases:

(1) $\sin A = \dfrac{4}{7}$
(2) $\tan A = \dfrac{2}{3}$
(3) $\cos A = \dfrac{\sqrt{3}}{2}$
(4) $\csc A = 2.4$
(5) $\cot A = \dfrac{1}{y}$
(6) $\sec A = 2\dfrac{2}{3}$

c. Solve each of the right triangles (ABC) for the two unknown sides:

(1) $\sin A = \dfrac{1}{2},\ a = 17$
(2) $\tan A = \dfrac{3}{4},\ b = 12$
(3) $\cos A = \dfrac{4}{5},\ c = 20$
(4) $\csc A = \dfrac{15}{7},\ c = 37.5$
(5) $\cot A = \dfrac{3}{5},\ a = 10$
(6) $\sec A = \dfrac{9}{4},\ b = 18.4$

d. Solve each of the following right triangles (ABC) for the unknown sides:

(1) $A = 30°,\ a = 10$
(2) $B = 45°,\ b = 7$
(3) $A = 60°,\ c = 8$
(4) $B = 30°,\ a = 9$
(5) $B = 60°,\ c = 25$

sin 32° 46' 36"
−32° 46'
36"

32' 46'   32' 47'
            1' = 60"

.54146
−.54122 = .00024

ratio $= \dfrac{36}{60} = \dfrac{6}{10} = \dfrac{3}{5}$

ratio $= \dfrac{x}{.00024}$

$\dfrac{3}{5} = \dfrac{x}{.00024}$

5x = .00072

x = .000144

sin 32° 46' 36" = .54122 + .000144 = .54136

Example 2: Find the tangent of 56° 43' 27".

tan 56° 43'   = 1.52332
tan 56° 43' 27" = 1.52332 + x
tan 56° 44'   = 1.52429

$\dfrac{27}{60}$ or $\dfrac{9}{20} = \dfrac{x}{.00097}$

20x = .00873

x = .000436 or .00044

tan 56° 43' 27" = 1.52332 + .00044 = 1.52376

156. Finding an Angle When the Trigonometric Function Is Given

The procedure for using the table to find an angle corresponding to a function is similar to that of logarithms. This is illustrated in the examples in a and b below.

a. When the Function Is Given in the Table.

Example: Find the value of angle A if sine A = .27284.

Step 1. Find .27284 in the Sine column of the Sines and Cosines table.

Step 2. Reading 15° at the top of the column and 50' in the minutes column on the left, angle A = 15° 50'.

b. When the Function Is Not Given in the Table.

Example 1: Find the value of angle A when sine A = .78112.

.78098 = sin 51° 21'
.78112 = sin 51° 21' + x
.78116 = sin 51° 22'

51° 22' — 51° 21' 1' = 60"

.78112
−.78098
.00014

.78116
−.78098
.00018

ratio $= \dfrac{.00014}{.00018} = \dfrac{14}{18} = \dfrac{7}{9}$

ratio $= \dfrac{x}{60}$

$\dfrac{7}{9} = \dfrac{x}{60}$

9x = 420

x = 47

angle A = 51° 21' 47"

Example 2: Find the value of angle A when cot A = .33820.

.33848 = cot 71° 18'
.33820 = cot 71° 18' + x
.33816 = cot 71° 19'

$\dfrac{28}{32}$ or $\dfrac{7}{8} = \dfrac{x}{60}$

8x = 420

x = 53

angle A = 71° 18' 53"

157. Solving a Right Triangle When an Acute Angle and the Hypotenuse Are Given

To solve for the unknowns in a right triangle when an acute angle and the hypotenuse are given, proceed as in a and b below. In both examples, angle C is the right angle; therefore, angle C = 90°.

Example 1: Find the unknown sides a and b, and the value of angle B in right triangle ABC (fig. 39) if angle A is 33° 15' and the hypotenuse, c is 9 inches.

∠A + ∠B + ∠C = 180°
∠B = 180° − ∠A − ∠C
∠B = 180° − 33° 15' − 90°
∠B = 56° 45'

$\sin A = \dfrac{a}{c}$

$\sin 33° \, 15' = \dfrac{a}{9}$

a = 9 sin 33° 15'
a = 9 × .54829 = 4.93461
a = 4.93461

$\cos A = \dfrac{b}{c}$

$\cos 33° \, 15' = \dfrac{b}{9}$

b = 9 cos 33° 15'
b = 9 × .83629
b = 7.52661

Therefore, ∠A = 33° 15'
∠B = 56° 45'
∠C = 90°
a, = 4.93461 inches
b = 7.52661 inches
c = 9 inches

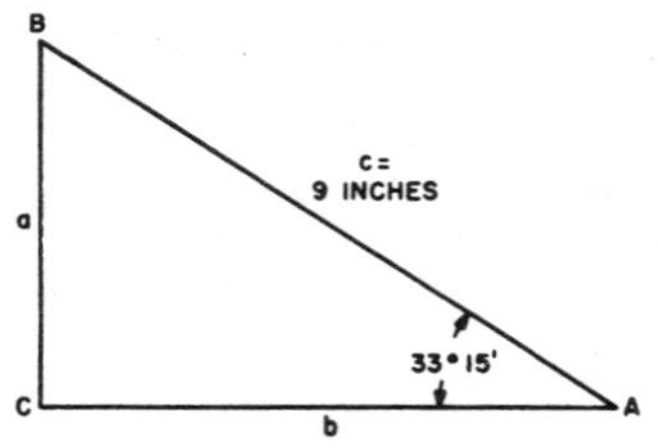

Figure 39. Solving a right triangle when an acute angle (33° 15') and the hypotenuse are given.

158. Solving a Right Triangle When an Acute Angle and the Adjacent Side Are Given

To solve a right triangle when an acute angle and the adjacent side are given, proceed as shown in the example below. Angle C is the right angle.

Example: Find the unknown sides a and c and the value of angle B in the right triangle ABC (fig. 41) if angle A is 37° 42' 42" and the side adjacent to angle A is 8 inches.

$$\angle B = 180° - 90° - 37°\ 42'\ 42"$$
$$\angle B = 52°\ 17'\ 18"$$

$$\cos A = \frac{b}{c}$$

$$\cos 37°\ 42'\ 42" = \frac{8}{c}$$

$$c\ (\cos 37°\ 42'\ 42") = 8$$

$$\cos 37°\ 42' \qquad\quad = .79122$$
$$\cos 37°\ 42'\ 42" = .79122 - x$$
$$\cos 37°\ 43' \qquad\quad = .79105$$

$$\frac{42}{60}\ \text{or}\ \frac{7}{10} = \frac{x}{.00017}$$
$$10x = .00119$$
$$x = .00012$$

$$\cos 37°\ 42'\ 42" = .79122 - .00012 = .79110$$

$$.79110c = 8$$
$$c = \frac{8}{.79110}$$
$$c = 10.11$$

$$\tan A = \frac{a}{b}$$

$$\tan 37°\ 42'\ 42" = \frac{a}{8}$$

$$a = 8 \tan 37°\ 42'\ 42"$$

$$\tan 37°\ 42' \qquad\quad = .77289$$
$$\tan 37°\ 42'\ 42" = .77289 + x$$
$$\tan 37°\ 43' \qquad\quad = .77335$$

$$\frac{42}{60}\ \text{or}\ \frac{7}{10} = \frac{x}{.00046}$$
$$10x = .00322$$
$$x = .00032$$

$$\tan 37°\ 42'\ 42" = .77289 + .00032 = .77321$$

$$a = 8 \times .77321$$
$$a = 6.18568$$

Therefore, $\angle A = 37°\ 42'\ 42"$ $a = 6.18568$ inches
$\angle B = 52°\ 17'\ 18"$ $b = 8$ inches
$\angle C = 90°$ $c = 10.11$ inches

Example 2: Solve for the unknown sides a and b, and the value of angle B in right triangle ABC (fig. 40) if angle A is 24° 35' 36" and the hypotenuse, c, is 12 inches.

$$\angle B = 180° - \angle A - \angle C$$
$$\angle B = 180° - 24°\ 35'\ 36" - 90°$$
$$\angle B = 65°\ 24'\ 24"$$

$$\sin A = \frac{a}{c}$$

$$\sin 24°\ 35'\ 36" = \frac{a}{12}$$

$$a = 12 \sin 24°\ 35'\ 36"$$

$$\sin 24°\ 35' \qquad\quad = .41602$$
$$\sin 24°\ 35'\ 36" = .41602 + x$$
$$\sin 24°\ 36' \qquad\quad = .41628$$

$$\frac{36}{60}\ \text{or}\ \frac{3}{5} = \frac{x}{.00026}$$
$$5x = .00078$$
$$x = .00016$$

$$\sin 24°\ 35'\ 36" = .41602 + .00016 = .41618$$

$$a = 12 \times .41618$$
$$a = 4.99416$$

$$\cos A = \frac{b}{c}$$

$$\cos 24°\ 35'\ 36" = \frac{b}{12}$$

$$b = 12 \cos 24°\ 35'\ 36"$$

$$\cos 24°\ 35' \qquad\quad = .90936$$
$$\cos 24°\ 35'\ 36" = .90936 - x$$
$$\cos 24°\ 36' \qquad\quad = .90924$$

$$\frac{36}{60}\ \text{or}\ \frac{3}{5} = \frac{x}{.00012}$$
$$5x = .00036$$
$$x = .00007$$

$$\cos 24°\ 35'\ 36" = .90936 - .00007 = .90929$$

$$b = 12 \times .90929$$
$$b = 10.91148$$

Therefore, $\angle A = 24°\ 35'\ 36"$ $a = 4.99416$ inches
$\angle B = 65°\ 24'\ 24"$ $b = 10.91148$ inches
$\angle C = 90°$ $c = 12$ inches

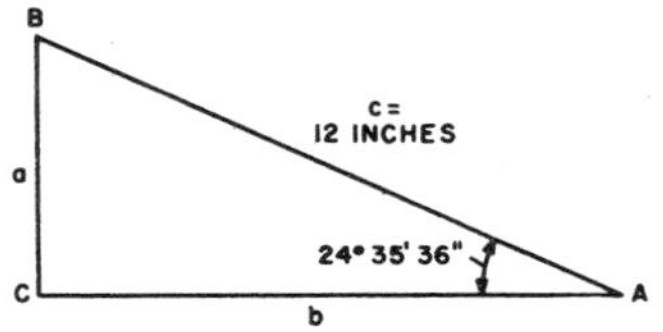

Figure 40. Solving a right triangle when an acute angle (24°35'36") and the hypotenuse are given.

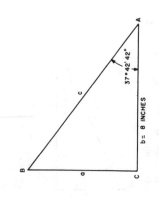

Figure 41. Solving a right triangle when an acute angle and the adjacent side are given.

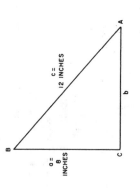

Figure 42. Solving a right triangle, when the hypotenuse and one side are given.

159. Solving a Right Triangle When Hypotenuse and One Side Are Given

Given the hypotenuse and one other side of a right triangle, solve for the unknown angles and the opposite side as illustrated in the example below.

Example: Find the unknown angles A and B, and side c of right triangle ABC (fig. 42) if the hypotenuse is 12 inches and the side opposite angle A is 8 inches.

$$b^2 = c^2 - a^2$$
$$b^2 = 12^2 - 8^2$$
$$b^2 = 144 - 64$$
$$b^2 = 80$$
$$b = \sqrt{80}$$
$$b = 8.94$$

$$\sin A = \frac{a}{c}$$
$$\sin A = \frac{8}{12} = \frac{2}{3}$$
$$\sin A = .66667$$

$$.66653 = \sin 41° \ 48'$$
$$.66667 = \sin 41° \ 48' + x$$
$$.66675 = \sin 41° \ 49'$$

$$\frac{14}{22} = \frac{x}{60}$$
$$22x = 840$$
$$x = \frac{840}{22} = 38$$

$$.66667 = \sin 41° \ 48' \ 38''$$

$$\text{angle } A = 41° \ 48' \ 38''$$
$$\angle B = 180° - \angle C - \angle A$$
$$\angle B = 180° - 90° - 41° \ 48' \ 38''$$
$$\angle B = 48° \ 11' \ 22''$$

Therefore, $\angle A = 41° \ 48' \ 38''$ $a = 8$ inches
$\angle B = 48° \ 11' \ 22''$ $b = 8.94$ inches
$\angle C = 90°$ $c = 12$ inches

Figure 42. Solving a right triangle, when the hypotenuse and one side are given.

160. Solving a Right Triangle When Two Sides Are Given

When two sides of a right triangle are given, solve for the unknown angles and the hypotenuse as shown in the example below.

Example: Find the unknown angles A and B and side c in right triangle ABC (fig. 43) if side a is 8 inches and side b is 10 inches.

$$c^2 = a^2 + b^2$$
$$c^2 = 64 + 100$$
$$c^2 = 164$$
$$c = \sqrt{164}$$
$$c = 12.8$$

$$\tan A = \frac{a}{b}$$
$$\tan A = \frac{8}{10}$$
$$\tan A = .80000$$

$$.79972 = \tan 38° \ 39'$$
$$.80000 = \tan 38° \ 39' + x$$
$$.80020 = \tan 38° \ 40'$$

$$\frac{28}{48} \text{ or } \frac{7}{12} = \frac{x}{60}$$
$$12x = 420$$
$$x = 35$$

$$.80000 = \tan 38° \ 39' \ 35''$$

$$\text{angle } A = 38° \ 39' \ 35''$$
$$\angle B = 180° - \angle C - \angle A$$
$$\angle B = 180° - 90° - 38° \ 39' \ 35''$$
$$\angle B = 51° \ 20' \ 25''$$

Therefore, $\angle A = 38° \ 39' \ 35''$ $a = 8$ inches
$\angle B = 51° \ 20' \ 25''$ $b = 10$ inches
$\angle C = 90°$ $c = 12.8$ inches

161. Solving a 30°–60°–90° Triangle When One Side Is Given

In a 30°–60°–90° triangle, the side opposite the 30° angle is equal to one-half the hypotenuse. Refer to paragraph 150c for the derivation of the trigonometric functions. Solve for the unknown sides as shown in the example below.

Example: Find the unknown sides b and c of 30°–60°–90° triangle ABC (fig. 44) if the side opposite the 60° angle is 6 inches.

$$\sin 60° = \frac{\sqrt{3}}{2}; \text{ also, } \sin 60° = \frac{a}{c} = \frac{6}{c}$$

$$\frac{\sqrt{3}}{2} = \frac{6}{c}$$

$$\sqrt{3}c = 12$$

$$c = \frac{12}{\sqrt{3}}$$

Eliminate $\sqrt{3}$ in the denominator by multiplying $\frac{12}{\sqrt{3}}$ by $\frac{\sqrt{3}}{\sqrt{3}}$:

$$c = \frac{12}{\sqrt{3}} \cdot \frac{\sqrt{3}}{\sqrt{3}} = \frac{12\sqrt{3}}{\sqrt{9}} = \frac{12\sqrt{3}}{3} = 4\sqrt{3}$$

$$c = 4\sqrt{3} = 4 \times 1.7321 = 6.9284$$

$$\tan 60° = \frac{\sqrt{3}}{1}; \text{ also, } \tan 60° = \frac{a}{b} = \frac{6}{b}$$

$$\frac{\sqrt{3}}{1} = \frac{6}{b}$$

$$\sqrt{3}b = 6$$

$$b = \frac{6}{\sqrt{3}} \cdot \frac{\sqrt{3}}{\sqrt{3}} = \frac{6\sqrt{3}}{\sqrt{9}} = \frac{6\sqrt{3}}{3} = 2\sqrt{3}$$

$$b = 2\sqrt{3} = 2 \times 1.7321 = 3.4642$$

Therefore, $a = 6$ inches

$b = 3.4642$ inches

$c = 6.9284$ inches

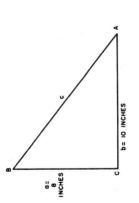

Figure 43. Solving a right triangle when two sides are given.

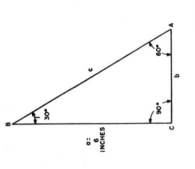

Figure 44. Solving a 30°–60°–90° triangle when one side is given.

162. Solving a 45°–45°–90° Triangle When One Side Is Given

In a 45°–45°–90° triangle, the sides opposite the equal angles are equal. Refer to paragraph 150b for the derivation of the trigonometric functions. Solve for the unknown sides as shown in the example below.

Example: Find the unknown sides a, b, and c of 45°–45°–90° triangle ABC (fig. 45) if the side opposite acute angle A is 5 inches.

$$\sin 45° = \frac{1}{\sqrt{2}}; \text{ also, } \sin A = \frac{a}{c} = \frac{5}{c}$$

$$\frac{1}{\sqrt{2}} = \frac{5}{c}$$

$$c = 5\sqrt{2}$$

$$c = 5 \times 1.4142 = 7.0710$$

$$\tan 45° = \frac{1}{1}; \text{ also, } \tan A = \frac{a}{b} = \frac{5}{b}$$

$$\frac{1}{1} = \frac{5}{b}$$

$$[b = 5]$$

Therefore, $a = 5$ inches

$b = 5$ inches

$c = 7.071$ inches

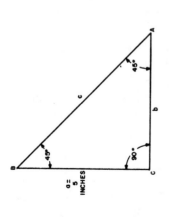

Figure 45. Solving a 45°–45°–90° triangle when one side is given.

163. Angles of Elevation and Depression

When an object is higher than the observer's eye, the angle between the horizontal and the line of sight to the object is called the *angle of elevation* (A, fig. 46). When an object is lower than the observer's eye, the angle between the line of sight to the object and the horizontal is called the *angle of depression* (B, fig. 46).

Example:

A television antenna mast is 450 feet high (fig. 47). Find to the nearest second the angle of elevation to its top at a point 200 feet from the base of the mast.

$$\tan A = \frac{a}{b}$$
$$\tan A = \frac{450}{200}$$
$$\tan A = 2.2500$$

$$2.2496 = \tan 66° \ 2'$$
$$2.2500 = \tan 66° \ 2' + x$$
$$2.2513 = \tan 66° \ 3'$$

$$\frac{4}{17} = \frac{x}{60}$$
$$17x = 240$$
$$x = 14$$

$$2.2500 = \tan 66° \ 2' \ 14''$$
$$A = 66° \ 2' \ 14''$$

Figure 46. Angles of elevation and depression.

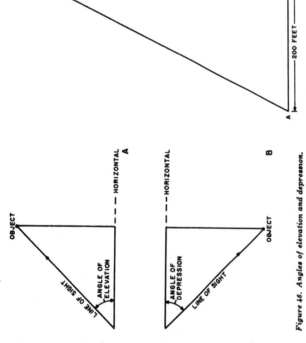

Figure 47. Finding the angle of elevation to top of an antenna mast.

164. Review Problems—Natural Trigonometric Functions

a. Find the sine, cosine, tangent, and cotangent of the following angles:

(1) 1° 30'
(2) 15° 25'
(3) 32° 10'
(4) 36° 39'
(5) 44° 59'
(6) 44° 59' 45"
(7) 35° 12' 15"
(8) 54° 27' 32"
(9) 48° 25' 37"
(10) 67° 33' 42"

b. Solve for the values of the following angles in degrees, minutes and seconds:

(1) sin A = .25737
(2) cot A = .43279
(3) cos A = .94000
(4) tan A = .47237
(5) cot A = 1.17529
(6) cos A = .36243
(7) sin A = .37778
(8) tan A = .67676
(9) tan A = 1.29000
(10) cot A = .79553

c. Solve for the following (angle C = 90°):

(1) Angle A in right triangle ABC when a = 19 and c = 27.
(2) Side a in right triangle ABC when A = 37° 15' and c = 17.
(3) Side c in right triangle ABC when A = 42° 37' 15" and a = 22.
(4) Side B in right triangle ABC when A = 37° 45' 42" and c = 25.
(5) Side c in right triangle ABC when A = 14° 35' and b = 12.
(6) Angle A in right triangle ABC when b = 7 and c = 12.
(7) Side a in right triangle ABC when A = 47° 22' 52" and b = 31.
(8) Side b in right triangle ABC when A = 56° 31' 25" and a = 25.
(9) Angle A in right triangle ABC when a = 17 and b = 23.
(10) Side b in right triangle ABC when A = 7° 32' 54" and a = 17.
(11) Side c in right triangle ABC when a = 15 and b = 27.
(12) Angle A in right triangle ABC when a = 15 and b = 27.

d. Solve the following problems:

(1) Over a distance of 300 feet, the angle of elevation of a road is 8° 24' 30". What is the rise in feet?

(2) The angle of elevation to the top of an antenna mast is 34° 17' 50". If the distance from the transit to the center of the mast is 110 feet, how high is the mast? The transit is 5 feet high.

(3) If a ladder 15 feet long just touches the top of a wall and subtends an angle of 35° 24' 16" with the ground, how far is the lower end of the ladder from the wall and how high is the wall?

(4) A captive balloon is anchored by 950 feet of cable. A man observes that the angle of elevation from his point of observation to the bottom of the balloon is 16° 47' 12". How far is he from the balloon anchor?

(5) An excavation is 33 feet wide. The angle of depression from the top of one side to the bottom of the other side is 19° 34' 24". How deep is the excavation?

(6) The angle of elevation from a given

point to the top of a tower is 17° 37' 15". Moving back 40 feet in a direct line, the angle of elevation from this point to the top of the tower is 15° 35' 20". Find the height of the tower.

(7) To determine the height of a tower, two sights are taken on a straight line perpendicular to the tower. If the distance between the points of observation is 60 feet and the angles of elevation are 32° 30' 15" and 28° 15' 30", respectively, what is the height of the tower?

(8) From a point in an open field a man sights on two mileposts along the side of a highway. The angles formed by an imaginary line perpendicular to the highway and the sights on the mileposts are 33° 20' and 39° 17' 30". How far is the man from the closest point on the highway?

(9) An airplane is flying between two towns at an altitude of 5,000 feet. The angle of depression to the outskirts of one town is 50° 26' 14", while the angle to the outskirts of the other town is 64° 44' 12". How far apart, in a direct line, are the two towns?

(10) A radio antenna on top of a building is 10 feet high. The angle of elevation to the base of the pole is 37° 17' 20"; the angle of elevation to the top of the antenna is 40° 30' 15". How high is the building?

(11) In a 45°–45°–90° right triangle the hypotenuse is 2 inches long. Find the length of the other two sides.

(12) In a 30°–60°–90° right triangle the hypotenuse is 6 inches long. Find the length of the other two sides.

Section III. TRIGONOMETRIC LAWS

165. Solving Oblique Triangles

An oblique triangle is one in which one of the angles is a right angle. The formulas in this section are used primarily to solve oblique triangles, but may also be used to solve right triangles. In the solution of triangles, the four following cases arise:

a. When any side and any two angles are given.

b. When any two sides and the angle opposite one of them are given.

c. When any two sides and the angle included between them are given.

d. When the three sides are given.

166. Law of Sines

In any triangle, the sides are proportional to the sines of the opposite angles.

Thus, $\dfrac{a}{\sin A} = \dfrac{b}{\sin B} = \dfrac{c}{\sin C}$.

b. *Two Angles and One Side Given.*

Example: Solve for the unknowns in oblique triangle ABC (fig. 48) when angle $A = 35° 47' 36''$, angle $B = 68° 42' 27''$, and the side opposite angle A is 15 inches.

$\angle C = 180° - \angle A - \angle B$
$\angle C = 180° - 35° 47' 36'' - 68° 42' 27''$
$\angle C = 75° 29' 57''$

$\dfrac{a}{\sin A} = \dfrac{b}{\sin B}$
$b \sin A = a \sin B$
$b = \dfrac{a \sin B}{\sin A}$
$b = \dfrac{15 \sin 68° 42' 27''}{\sin 35° 47' 36''}$

sin 68° 42' $= .93169$
sin 68° 42' 27" $= .93169 + x$
sin 68° 43' $= .93180$

$\dfrac{27}{60}$ or $\dfrac{9}{20} = \dfrac{x}{.00011}$

$20x = .00099$
$x = .000049 = .00005$

sin 68° 42' 27" $= .93169 + .00005 = .93174$
sin 35° 47' $= .58472$
sin 35° 47' 36" $= .58472 + x$
sin 35° 48' $= .58496$

$\dfrac{36}{60}$ or $\dfrac{3}{5} = \dfrac{x}{.00024}$

$5x = .00072$
$x = .00014$

sin 35° 47' 36" $= .58472 + .00014 = .58486$

$b = \dfrac{15 \times .93174}{.58486}$
$b = \dfrac{13.97610}{.58486}$
$b = 23.89$

$\dfrac{a}{\sin A} = \dfrac{c}{\sin C}$
$c \sin A = a \sin C$
$c = \dfrac{a \sin C}{\sin A}$
$c = \dfrac{15 \sin 75° 29' 57''}{\sin 35° 47' 36''}$

sin 75° 29' $= .96807$
sin 75° 29' 57" $= .96807 + x$
sin 75° 30' $= .96815$

$\dfrac{57}{60}$ or $\dfrac{19}{20} = \dfrac{x}{.00008}$

$20x = .00152$
$x = .000076 = .00008$

sin 75° 29' 57" $= .96807 + .00008 = .96815$

$c = \dfrac{15 \times .96815}{.58486}$
$c = \dfrac{14.52225}{.58486}$
$c = 24.83$

Therefore, $\angle A = 35° 47' 36''$
$\angle B = 68° 42' 27''$
$\angle C = 75° 29' 57''$
$a = 15$ inches
$b = 23.89$ inches
$c = 24.83$ inches

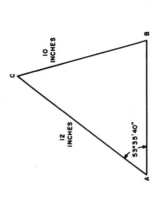

$\angle C = 180° - 53° \ 35' \ 40'' - 74° \ 58' \ 17''$
$\angle C = 51° \ 26' \ 3''$

$$\frac{a}{\sin A} = \frac{c}{\sin C}$$
$$c \sin A = a \sin C$$
$$c = \frac{a \sin C}{\sin A}$$
$$c = \frac{10 \sin 51° \ 26' \ 3''}{\sin 53° \ 35' \ 40''}$$

$\sin 51° \ 26' = .78188$
$\sin 51° \ 26' \ 3'' = .78188 + x$
$\sin 51° \ 27' = .78206$

$$\frac{3}{60} \text{ or } \frac{1}{20} = \frac{x}{.00018}$$
$$20x = .00018$$
$$x = .000009 = .00001$$
$$\sin 51° \ 26' \ 3'' = .78188 + .00001 = .78189$$

$$c = \frac{10 \times .78189}{.80483}$$
$$c = \frac{7.8189}{.80483}$$
$$c = 9.71$$

Therefore, $\angle A = 53° \ 35' \ 40''$ $a = 10$ inches
$\angle B = 74° \ 58' \ 17''$ $b = 12$ inches
$\angle C = 51° \ 26' \ 3''$ $c = 9.71$ inches

Figure 49. Solving an oblique triangle by the law of sines when two sides and an angle are given.

167. Law of Cosines

In any triangle, the square of any side equals the sum of the squares of the other two sides minus twice the product of these two sides times the cosine of the angle between them.

Thus, $a^2 = b^2 + c^2 - 2bc \cos A$
$b^2 = a^2 + c^2 - 2ac \cos B$
$c^2 = a^2 + b^2 - 2ab \cos C$

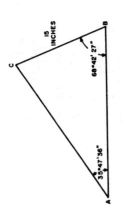

Figure 48. Solving an oblique triangle by the law of sines when two angles and a side are given.

b. Two Sides and One Angle Given.

Example: Find the unknowns in oblique triangle ABC (fig. 49) when angle $A = 53° \ 35' \ 40'$, the side opposite angle A is 10 inches, and the side opposite angle B is 12 inches.

$$\frac{a}{\sin A} = \frac{b}{\sin B}$$
$$a \sin B = b \sin A$$
$$\sin B = \frac{b \sin A}{a}$$
$$\sin B = \frac{12 \sin 53° \ 35' \ 40''}{10}$$

$\sin 53° \ 35' = .80472$
$\sin 53° \ 35' \ 40'' = .80472 + x$
$\sin 53° \ 36' = .80489$

$$\frac{40}{60} \text{ or } \frac{2}{3} = \frac{x}{.00017}$$
$$3x = .00034$$
$$x = .00011$$
$$\sin 53° \ 35' \ 40'' = .80472 + .00011 = .80483$$

$$\sin B = \frac{\overset{6}{\cancel{12}} \times .80483}{\underset{5}{\cancel{10}}}$$
$$\sin B = \frac{4.82898}{5}$$
$$\sin B = .965796 = .96580$$

$.96578 = \sin 74° \ 58'$
$.96580 = \sin 74° \ 58' + x$
$.96585 = \sin 74° \ 59'$

$$\frac{2}{7} = \frac{x}{60}$$
$$7x = 120$$
$$x = 17$$

$.96580 = \sin 74° \ 58' \ 17''$
$\angle B = 74° \ 58' \ 17''$
$\angle C = 180° - \angle A - \angle B$

54

Example: Find the unknowns in oblique triangle ABC (fig. 50) when angle $C = 56° \; 45' \; 24''$, the side opposite angle A is 6 inches, and the side opposite angle B is 8 inches.

$$
\begin{aligned}
c^2 &= a^2 + b^2 - 2ab \cos C \\
c^2 &= 6^2 + 8^2 - 2(6)(8) \cos 56° \; 45' \; 24'' \\
c^2 &= 36 + 64 - 96 \cos 56° \; 45' \; 24'' \\
c^2 &= 100 - 96 \cos 56° \; 45' \; 24''
\end{aligned}
$$

$$
\begin{aligned}
\cos 56° \; 45' &= .54829 \\
\cos 56° \; 45' \; 24'' &= .54829 - x \\
\cos 56° \; 46' &= .54805 \\
\frac{24}{60} \text{ or } \frac{2}{5} &= \frac{x}{.00024} \\
5x &= .00048 \\
x &= .000096 \text{ or } .00010 \\
\cos 56° \; 45' \; 24'' &= .54829 - .00010 = .54819
\end{aligned}
$$

$$
\begin{aligned}
c^2 &= 100 - 96(.54819) \\
c^2 &= 100 - 52.62624 \\
c^2 &= 47.37376 \\
c &= \sqrt{47.37376} \\
c &= 6.882
\end{aligned}
$$

$$
\begin{aligned}
\frac{a}{\sin A} &= \frac{c}{\sin C} \\
c \sin A &= a \sin C \\
\sin A &= \frac{a \sin C}{c} \\
\sin A &= \frac{6 \sin 56° \; 45' \; 24''}{6.882}
\end{aligned}
$$

$$
\begin{aligned}
\sin 56° \; 45' &= .83629 \\
\sin 56° \; 45' \; 24'' &= .83629 + x \\
\sin 56° \; 46' &= .83645 \\
\frac{24}{60} \text{ or } \frac{2}{5} &= \frac{x}{.00016} \\
5x &= .00032 \\
x &= .000064 = .00006 \\
\sin 56° \; 45' \; 24'' &= .83629 + .00006 = .83635
\end{aligned}
$$

$$
\begin{aligned}
\sin A &= \frac{6(.83635)}{6.882} \\
\sin A &= \frac{5.01810}{6.882} \\
\sin A &= .72916
\end{aligned}
$$

$$
\begin{aligned}
.72897 &= \sin 46° \; 48' \\
.72916 &= \sin 46° \; 48' + x \\
.72917 &= \sin 46° \; 49' \\
\frac{19}{20} &= \frac{x}{60} \\
20x &= 1140 \\
x &= 57 \\
.72917 &= \sin 46° \; 48' \; 57''
\end{aligned}
$$

$$
\begin{aligned}
\angle A &= 46° \; 48' \; 57'' \\
\angle B &= 180° - \angle C - \angle A \\
\angle B &= 180° - 56° \; 45' \; 24'' - 46° \; 48' \; 57'' \\
\angle B &= 76° \; 25' \; 39''
\end{aligned}
$$

Therefore, $\angle A = 46° \; 48' \; 57''$ $\qquad a = 6$ inches
$\angle B = 76° \; 25' \; 39''$ $\qquad b = 8$ inches
$\angle C = 56° \; 45' \; 24''$ $\qquad c = 6.882$ inches

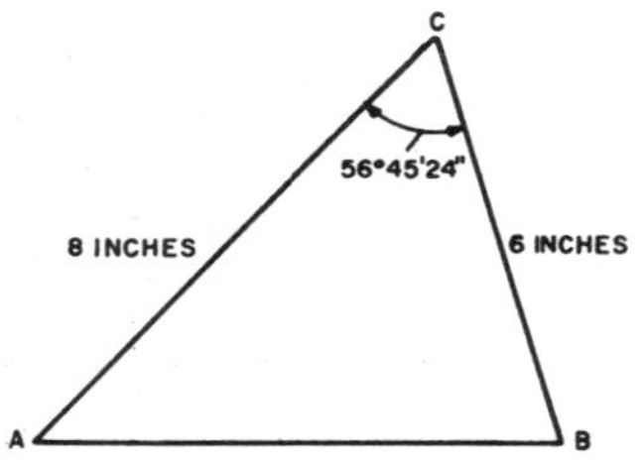

Figure 50. Solving an oblique triangle by the law of cosines when an angle and two sides are given.

168. Law of Tangents

The law of tangents is expressed by the formula $\frac{a - b}{a + b} = \frac{\tan \frac{1}{2}(A - B)}{\tan \frac{1}{2}(A + B)}$ where a and b are any two sides and A and B are the angles opposite these sides.

Example: Find the unknowns in oblique triangle ABC (fig. 51) when two sides of the triangle are 9 and 11 inches, respectively, and angle C, the angle included between these two sides, is $40° \; 40' \; 40''$.

$$
\begin{aligned}
\angle A + \angle B + \angle C &= 180° \\
\angle A + \angle B + 40° \; 40' \; 40'' &= 180° \\
\angle A + \angle B &= 180° - 40° \; 40' \; 40'' \\
\angle A + \angle B &= 139° \; 19' \; 20'' \\
\tfrac{1}{2}(A + B) &= \frac{139° \; 19' \; 20''}{2} \\
\tfrac{1}{2}(A + B) &= 69° \; 39' \; 40'' \\
\frac{a - b}{a + b} &= \frac{\tan \frac{1}{2}(A - B)}{\tan \frac{1}{2}(A + B)} \\
\frac{11 - 9}{11 + 9} \text{ or } \frac{2}{20} &= \frac{\tan \frac{1}{2}(A - B)}{\tan 69° \; 39' \; 40''} \\
20 \tan \tfrac{1}{2}(A - B) &= 2 \tan 69° \; 39' \; 40'' \\
10 \tan \tfrac{1}{2}(A - B) &= \tan 69° \; 39' \; 40'' \\
\tan \tfrac{1}{2}(A - B) &= \frac{\tan 69° \; 39' \; 40''}{10}
\end{aligned}
$$

$$
\begin{aligned}
\tan 69° \; 39' &= 2.69612 \\
\tan 69° \; 39' \; 40'' &= 2.69612 + x \\
\tan 69° \; 40' &= 2.69853 \\
\frac{40}{60} \text{ or } \frac{2}{3} &= \frac{x}{.00241} \\
3x &= .00482 \\
x &= .00161 \\
\tan 69° \; 39' \; 40'' &= 2.69612 + .00161 = 2.69773
\end{aligned}
$$

$$\tan \tfrac{1}{2}(A - B) = \frac{2.69773}{10}$$

$$\tan \tfrac{1}{2}(A - B) = .26977$$

$$.26951 = \tan 15° \ 5'$$
$$.26977 = \tan 15° \ 5' + x$$
$$.26982 = \tan 15° \ 6'$$

$$\frac{26}{31} = \frac{x}{60}$$
$$31x = 1560$$
$$x = 50$$

$$.26977 = \tan 15° \ 5' \ 50"$$

$$\tfrac{1}{2}(A - B) = 15° \ 5' \ 50"$$

$$\tfrac{1}{2}(A + B) = \tfrac{1}{2}A + \tfrac{1}{2}B = 69° \ 39' \ 40"$$
$$\tfrac{1}{2}(A - B) = \tfrac{1}{2}A - \tfrac{1}{2}B = 15° \ 5' \ 50"$$
$$\text{(add)}$$
$$A = 84° \ 44' \ 90"$$
$$\angle A = 84° \ 45' \ 30"$$

$$\tfrac{1}{2}(A + B) = \tfrac{1}{2}A + \tfrac{1}{2}B = 69° \ 38' \ 100"$$
$$\tfrac{1}{2}(A - B) = \tfrac{1}{2}A - \tfrac{1}{2}B = 15° \ 5' \ 50"$$
$$\text{(subtract)}$$
$$B = 54° \ 33' \ 50"$$
$$\angle B = 54° \ 33' \ 50"$$

$$\frac{a}{\sin A} = \frac{c}{\sin c}$$
$$c \sin A = a \sin C$$
$$c = \frac{a \sin C}{\sin A}$$
$$c = \frac{11 \sin 40° \ 40' \ 40"}{\sin 84° \ 45' \ 30"}$$

$$\sin 40° \ 40' = .65166$$
$$\sin 40° \ 40' \ 40" = .65166 + x$$
$$\sin 40° \ 41" = .65188$$

$$\frac{40}{60} \text{ or } \frac{2}{3} = \frac{x}{.00022}$$
$$3x = .00044$$
$$x = .000146 = .00015$$

$$\sin 40° \ 40' \ 40" = .65166 + .00015 = .65181$$

$$\sin 84° \ 45' = .99580$$
$$\sin 84° \ 45' \ 30" = .99580 + x$$
$$\sin 84° \ 46' = .99583$$

$$\frac{30}{60} \text{ or } \frac{1}{2} = \frac{x}{.00003}$$
$$2x = .00003$$
$$x = .000015 = .00002$$

$$\sin 84° \ 45' \ 30" = .99580 + .00002 = .99582$$

$$c = \frac{11 \sin 40° \ 40' \ 40"}{\sin 84° \ 45' \ 30"}$$
$$c = \frac{11 \times .65181}{.99582}$$
$$c = \frac{7.16991}{.99582}$$
$$c = 7.2$$

Therefore, $\angle A = 84° \ 45' \ 30"$ $a = 11$ inches
              $\angle B = 54° \ 33' \ 50"$ $b = 9$ inches
              $\angle C = 40° \ 40' \ 40"$ $c = 7.2$ inches

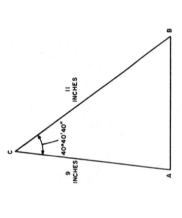

Figure 51. Solving an oblique triangle by the law of tangents when an angle and two sides are given.

169. Finding an Angle When Three Sides Are Given

The following formulas are used to find the angles of a triangle when three sides of the triangle are given:

$$\sin \tfrac{1}{2}A = \sqrt{\frac{(s - b)(s - c)}{bc}}$$

$$\sin \tfrac{1}{2}B = \sqrt{\frac{(s - a)(s - c)}{ac}}$$

$$\sin \tfrac{1}{2}C = \sqrt{\frac{(s - a)(s - b)}{ab}}$$

In these formulas, a, b, and c are three sides of the triangle, and $s = \tfrac{1}{2}(a + b + c)$.

Example: Find the angles of an oblique triangle if $a = 5$ inches, $b = 8$ inches, and $c = 11$ inches.

$$s = \tfrac{1}{2}(a + b + c)$$
$$s = \tfrac{1}{2}(5 + 8 + 11)$$
$$s = \tfrac{1}{2}(24)$$
$$s = 12$$

$$\sin \tfrac{1}{2}A = \sqrt{\frac{(s - b)(s - c)}{bc}}$$

$$\sin \tfrac{1}{2}A = \sqrt{\frac{(12 - 8)(12 - 11)}{(8)(11)}}$$

$$\sin \tfrac{1}{2}A = \sqrt{\frac{(4)(1)}{88}}$$

$$\sin \tfrac{1}{2}A = \sqrt{\frac{4}{88}} = \sqrt{\frac{1}{22}}$$

$$\sin \tfrac{1}{2}A = \sqrt{.0454545}$$

$$\sin \tfrac{1}{4}A = .21319$$
$$.21303 = \sin 12° \ 18'$$
$$.21319 = \sin 12° \ 18' + x$$
$$.21331 = \sin 12° \ 19'$$
$$\frac{16}{28} \text{ or } \frac{4}{7} = \frac{x}{60}$$
$$7x = 240$$
$$x = 34$$
$$.21319 = \sin 12° \ 18' \ 34''$$
$$\tfrac{1}{4}A = 12° \ 18' \ 34''$$
$$\angle A = 24° \ 36' \ 68'' \text{ or } 24° \ 37' \ 8''$$

$$\sin \tfrac{1}{4}B = \sqrt{\frac{(s-a)(s-c)}{ac}}$$
$$\sin \tfrac{1}{4}B = \sqrt{\frac{(12-5)(12-11)}{(5)(11)}}$$
$$\sin \tfrac{1}{4}B = \sqrt{\frac{(7)(1)}{55}}$$
$$\sin \tfrac{1}{4}B = \sqrt{\frac{7}{55}}$$
$$\sin \tfrac{1}{4}B = \sqrt{.1272727}$$
$$\sin \tfrac{1}{4}B = .35675$$
$$.35674 = \sin 20° \ 54'$$
$$.35675 = \sin 20° \ 54' + x$$
$$.35701 = \sin 20° \ 55'$$
$$\frac{1}{27} = \frac{x}{60}$$
$$27x = 60$$
$$x = 2$$
$$.35675 = \sin 20° \ 54' \ 2''$$
$$\tfrac{1}{4}B = 20° \ 54' \ 2''$$
$$\angle B = 40° \ 108' \ 4'' \text{ or } 41° \ 48' \ 4''$$
$$\angle C = 180° - \angle A - \angle B$$
$$\angle C = 180° - 24° \ 37' \ 8'' - 41° \ 48' \ 4''$$
$$\angle C = 180° - 66° \ 25' \ 12''$$
$$\angle C = 113° \ 34' \ 48''$$

Therefore, $\angle A = 24° \ 37' \ 8''$
$$\angle B = 41° \ 48' \ 4''$$
$$\angle C = 113° \ 34' \ 48''$$

170. Finding the Area of a Triangle When Two Sides and the Included Angle Are Given

The formula for finding the area of a triangle when two sides and the included angle are given is $S = \tfrac{1}{2} ab \sin C$ where S is the area of the triangle, a and b are the given sides, and C is the included angle.

Example: Find the area of oblique triangle ABC (fig. 52) when two sides are 7 and 8 inches, respectively, and the included angle is 50° 50' 50".

$$S = \tfrac{1}{2} ab \sin C$$
$$S = \tfrac{1}{2} \times 7 \times 8 \times \sin 50° \ 50' \ 50''$$
$$\sin 50° \ 50' = .77531$$
$$\sin 50° \ 50' \ 50'' = .77531 + x$$

$$\sin 50° \ 51' = .77550$$
$$= x$$
$$= .00019$$
$$\frac{50}{60} \text{ or } \frac{5}{6} = \frac{x}{.00019}$$
$$6x = .00095$$
$$x = .00016$$
$$\sin 50° \ 50' \ 50'' = .77531 + .00016 = .77547$$
$$S = \tfrac{1}{2} \times 7 \times 8 \times .77547 = 21.71316$$
$$S = 21.71316 \text{ square inches}$$

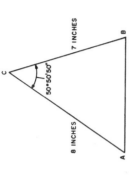

Figure 52. Solving for the area of an oblique triangle when two sides and the included angle are given.

171. Finding the Area of a Triangle When Two Angles and a Side Are Given

The formula for finding the area of a triangle when two angles and a side are given is $S = \dfrac{a^2 \sin B \sin C}{2 \sin A}$ where S is the area of the triangle, B and C are the given angles, and a is the given side.

Example: Find the area of oblique triangle ABC (fig. 53) when the two angles are 38° 42' 48" and 68° 52' 42" and the side is 10 inches.

$$\angle A = 180° - \angle B - \angle C$$
$$\angle A = 180° - 38° \ 42' \ 48'' - 68° \ 52' \ 42''$$
$$\angle A = 180° - 107° \ 35' \ 30''$$
$$\angle A = 72° \ 24' \ 30''$$

$$S = \frac{a^2 \sin B \sin C}{2 \sin A}$$
$$S = \frac{10^2 \sin 38° \ 42' \ 48'' \sin 68° \ 52' \ 42''}{2 \sin 72° \ 24' \ 30''}$$

$$\sin 38° \ 42' = .62524$$
$$\sin 38° \ 42' \ 48'' = .62524 + x$$
$$\sin 38° \ 43' = .62547$$
$$\frac{48}{60} \text{ or } \frac{4}{5} = \frac{x}{.00023}$$
$$5x = .00092$$
$$x = .00018$$
$$\sin 38° \ 42' \ 48'' = .62524 + .00018 = .62542$$

$$\sin 68° \ 52' = .93274$$
$$\sin 68° \ 52' \ 42'' = .93274 + x$$

sin 68° 53'   = .93285

$\dfrac{42}{60}$ or $\dfrac{7}{10} = \dfrac{x}{.00011}$

$10x = .00077$

$x = .000077$ or $.00008$

sin 68° 53' 42" = .93274 + .00008 = .93282

sin 72° 24'   = .95319

sin 72° 24' 30" = .95319 + x

sin 72° 25'   = .95328

$\dfrac{30}{60}$ or $\dfrac{1}{2} = \dfrac{x}{.00009}$

$2x = .00009$

$x = .000045$ or $.00005$

sin 72° 24' 30" = .95319 + .00005 = .95324

$$S = \dfrac{100 \times .62542 \times .93282}{2 \times .95324}$$

$$S = \dfrac{50 \times .62542 \times .93282}{.95324}$$

$S = \log 50 + \log .62542 + \log .93282 - \log .95324$

log 50   = 1.6990

log .62500 = 9.7959—10

log .62542 = 9.7959—10 + x

log .62600 = 9.7966—10

$\dfrac{42}{100} = \dfrac{x}{.0007}$

$100x = .0294$

$x = .000294$ or $.0003$

log .62542 = 9.7959—10 + .0003 = 9.7962—10

log .93200 = 9.9694—10

log .93282 = 9.9694—10 + x

log .93300 = 9.9699—10

$\dfrac{82}{100} = \dfrac{x}{.0005}$

$100x = .0410$

$x = .00041$ or $.0004$

log .93282 = 9.9694—10 + .0004 = 9.9698—10

log .95300 = 9.9791—10

log .95324 = 9.9791—10 + x

log .95400 = 9.9795—10

$\dfrac{24}{100} = \dfrac{x}{.0004}$

$100x = .0096$

$x = .000096$ or $.0001$

log .95324 = 9.9791—10 + .0001 = 9.9792—10

$S = 1.6990 + 9.7962—10 + 9.9698—10 - 9.9792—10$

1.6990

9.7962—10

+ 9.9698—10

21.4650—20

— 9.9792—10

11.4858—10 or 1.4858

antilog 1.4857 = 30.6

antilog 1.4858 = 30.6 + x

antilog 1.4871 = 30.7

$\dfrac{1}{14} = \dfrac{x}{.1}$

$14x = .1$

$x = .007$

S = antilog 1.4858 = 30.6 + .007 = 30.607

S = 30.607 square inches

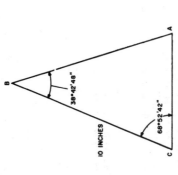

B

A

38°42'48"

10 INCHES

68°52'42"

C

Figure 55. Solving for the area of an oblique triangle when two angles and a side are given.

172. Finding the Area of Triangle When Three Sides Are Given

To find the area of triangle when three sides are given, use the formula

$$S = \sqrt{s(s - a)(s - b)(s - c)}$$

where a, b, and c are the sides of the triangle and $s = \tfrac{1}{2}(a + b + c)$.

Example: Find the area of an oblique triangle when the sides are 8, 11, and 15 inches, respectively.

$s = \tfrac{1}{2}(a + b + c)$

$s = \tfrac{1}{2}(8 + 11 + 15)$

$s = \tfrac{1}{2}(34)$

$s = 17$

$S = \sqrt{s(s - a)(s - b)(s - c)}$

$S = \sqrt{17(17 - 8)(17 - 11)(17 - 15)}$

$S = \sqrt{17(9)(6)(2)}$

$S = \sqrt{1836}$

$S = 42.84$ square inches

173. Review Problems—Trigonometric Laws

a. In an oblique triangle ABC, angle $A = 42° 15' 12''$, angle $B = 75° 28' 10''$, and side b measures 21 inches. Solve the triangle for angle C and side a.

b. In an oblique triangle ABC, angle $C = 52° 30'$, side $b = 45$ inches, and side $c = 38$ inches. Solve for angle B.

c. In an oblique triangle ABC, sides a, b, and c opposite angles A, B, and C have lengths of 9, 16, and 21 inches, respectively. Find the three angles of the triangle.

d. In an oblique triangle where a and b are any two sides and A and B are the angles opposite these sides, angle $C = 57° 20' 45''$, $a =$ 9.73 inches, and $b = 6.47$ inches. Find angles A and B.

e. The three sides of a triangle are 40, 37, and 13 inches, respectively. Find the area of the triangle.

f. Two sides of an oblique triangle measure 12 and 18 feet, respectively. The angle between the two sides is 115°. Find the area of the triangle.

g. In a triangle ABC, angle $A = 30°$ and angle $B = 60°$. The side opposite angle $C = 16$ inches. Find the area of the triangle.

h. In an oblique triangle ABC, angle $C = 62° 50'$. The side opposite angle A measures 9.65 inches, and the side opposite angle B measures 17.85 inches. Find the length of the side opposite angle C.

CHAPTER 11

RADIANS

174. Angular Measurement Using Radians

a. Definition. A radian is a unit of angular measurement equal to that angle which, when its vertex is upon the center of a circle, intercepts an arc that is equal in length to the radius of the circle. Thus, in figure 54, central angle AOB is equal to 1 radian because arc AB is equal to radius OA.

(1) The system that makes use of the radian is called the *natural system* of angular measurement because it has no arbitrary unit, such as the degree, but is founded upon the observation that the absolute size of any angle is the ratio of its arc to the radius of that arc. Where the arc and radius are equal, the ratio is 1, and this unit is the radian.

(2) The natural system of angular measurement—also called the circular system and the radian system—is used extensively in electrical formulas (part II).

b. Finding Any Angle. To find any angle, such as angle AOC in figure 54, when the length of arc AB is known, determine the number of times that radius r will go into arc length ABC, thus determining the number of radians in the angle.

Thus,

$$\text{Angle} = \frac{\text{arc}}{\text{radius}}$$

or, if angle AOC is denoted by the Greek letter θ (Theta) and arc ABC by s,

$$\theta = \frac{s}{r} \text{ radians}$$

Example: A circle has a radius of 6 inches. Find the angle subtended at the center of the circle by an arc 9 inches in length.

$$\theta = \frac{s}{r}$$
$$= \frac{9}{6}$$
$$= 1.5 \text{ radians}$$

c. Finding Length of Arc. To find the length of an arc intercepted by a central angle when the radius of the circle and the number of radians in the angle are known, use the formula in *b* above in the form—

$$s = r\theta$$

Example: A circle has a radius of 5 feet. How long is the arc intercepted by a central angle of 1.5 radians?

$$s = r\theta$$
$$= 5 \times 1.5$$
$$= 7.5 \text{ feet}$$

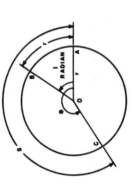

Figure 54. The radian or circular system of measurement.

175. The Relation Between Degrees and Radians

a. *General.* It is often necessary to convert an angle from degrees to radians or from radians to degrees. If the angle is one complete revolution, the arc is one complete circumference of a circle; thus, it is 2π times the radius. Therefore, the angle is equal to $2\pi r$ divided by r—that is, 2π radians ($\pi = 3.1416$).

Therefore,

$$1 \text{ revolution} = 2\pi \text{ radians}$$

also

$$1 \text{ revolution} = 360°$$

Thus,

$$2\pi \text{ radians} = 360°$$

$$1 \text{ radian} = \frac{360°}{2\pi} = \frac{180°}{\pi} = 57.29578°$$

and since

$$360° = 2\pi \text{ radians}$$

$$1° = \frac{2\pi}{360} = \frac{\pi}{180} = 0.017453 \text{ radians}$$

To change radians to degrees, accurate to seconds, use figures accurate to at least five decimal places.

b. *Changing Degrees to Radians and Radians to Degrees.*

Example 1: Change 2.74 radians to degrees, minutes, and seconds.

$$1 \text{ radian} = 57.29578°$$
$$2.74 \text{ radians} = 2.74(57.29578)$$
$$= 156.99044°$$

$$1° = 60'$$
$$.99044° = .99044(60)'$$
$$= 59.4264'$$

$$.4264' = .4264(60)''$$
$$= 25.5''$$

$$2.74 \text{ radians} = 156° \ 59' \ 25.5''$$

Example 2: Change 57° 15' 18" to radians.

Step 1.   Change the minutes and seconds to decimals of a degree:

$$1' = 60''$$
$$18'' = \frac{18}{60}$$
$$= .3'$$

$$15.3' = \frac{15.3}{60}$$
$$= .255°$$

$$57° \ 15' \ 18'' = 57.255°$$

Step 2.   Change to radians:

$$1° = .017453 \text{ radian}$$
$$57.255° = 57.255(.017453)$$
$$= .99927 \text{ radian}$$

c. *Expressing Angles in Radians as Multiples of π.* It is often convenient to express angles in radians as multiples of π. Since $360° = 2\pi$ radians, $90° = \frac{1}{2}\pi$ radians, $40° = \frac{1}{9}\pi$ radians, etc. It is necessary only to multiply the degrees by $\frac{\pi}{180}$ to change to radians.

Example: Express 135° in radians as a multiple of π.

$$135° = 135\left(\frac{\pi}{180}\right)$$
$$= \frac{3}{4}\pi \text{ radians}$$

176. Review Problems—Radians

a. Find the angle θ for the following arc lengths and radii:

(1) $r = 5$ inches, $s = 2$ inches.
(2) $r = 3$ feet, $s = 12$ feet.
(3) $r = .8$ miles, $s = 6.4$ miles.
(4) $r = 27$ meters, $s = 75$ meters

b. Find the arc lengths for the following angles and radii:

(1) $\theta = 5$ radians, $r = 7$ inches
(2) $\theta = 8$ radians, $r = 2.2$ feet
(3) $\theta = 2.1$ radians, $r = 9$ miles
(4) $\theta = .03$ radians, $r = .066$ inch

c. Express the following angles in radians:

(1) 30°
(2) 263° 12'
(3) 158° 33'
(4) 336° 24' 22"

d. Express the following angles in degrees:

(1) .8 radians
(2) 25 radians
(3) 3.45 radians
(4) 3π radians

e. Express the following angles as multiples of π:

(1) 30°
(2) 60°
(3) 225°
(4) 720°

CHAPTER 12

VECTORS

177. Plane Vectors

a. A line segment used to represent a quantity that has direction as well as magnitude is called a vector. The length of a vector is proportionate to the magnitude, and the arrow, or head, of the vector indicates the direction of the quantity represented.

b. The quantity represented by a vector is called a vector quantity. This is the directed magnitude itself. Electrical quantities, such as current and voltage, are vector quantities in ac circuits.

Example: An airplane is flying northeast at 120 miles per hour. Its speed is represented on figure 55 by line OA. The direction in which the airplane is traveling is represented by the direction of the line.

178. Vector Notation

Because a vector quantity has direction as well as magnitude, the methods of denoting a vector are different from the methods of denoting a scaler quantity. A vector may be denoted by two letters, the first indicating the origin, or initial point, and the other indicating the head or terminal point. For example, a vector may be represented by the letters *AB*, indicating that the quantity went from *A* to *B*. A small arrow sometimes is placed over the letters for emphasis; for example, $\overrightarrow{AB}$. Another method of notation is $A\underline{/\theta}$, where *A* represents the magnitude of the quantity, and $\underline{/\theta}$ represents the angle the vector makes with some reference line. For example, if line *OE* in figure 55 were used as the reference line, vector *OA* could be represented by the notation $120\underline{/45°}$, where 120 represents the magnitude of the quantity, and $\underline{/45°}$ represents the direction with respect to line *OE*. With respect to line *ON*, vector *OA*, would be represented by the notation $120 \underline{/-45°}$.

179. Addition of Vectors, Parallelogram Method

The addition of vectors by the parallelogram method is shown in figure 56. To add vector *OA* to *OC*, draw a vector *OC* with its initial point located at the initial point of vector *OA*, and complete the parallelogram with these vectors forming two sides. The diagonal vector *OB*, with its initial point at the same initial point of *OA* and *OC* and its terminal point at the opposite vertex of the parallelogram, is the sum of *OA* and *OC*. Thus, two vectors (*OA* and *OC*) acting simultaneously on a point or object may be replaced by a single vector called the *resultant* (*OB*). The resultant vector will produce the same effect on the object as the joint action of the two vectors.

180. Addition of More Than Two Vectors

a. In determining the resultant (par. 179) of vectors when more than two quantities are represented, proceed as follows:

(1) Find the resultant of two of the vector quantities,

(2) Determine the final resultant between the third quantity and the resultant obtained from (1), above.

b. Assume three forces U, V, and W are acting on point O as shown in A, figure 57. Force U exerts 150 pounds at an angle of 60°, V exerts 100 pounds at an angle of 135°, and W exerts 150 pounds at an angle of 260°. Find the resultant of forces on point O.

(1) The resultant of any two vectors, such as U and W, are determined graphically by the line R_1 (B, fig. 57). To solve this problem first draw the vectors to scale at the designated angles; then construct the parallelogram OUTW with adjacent sides WT and UT. The resultant R_1 of OW and OU will be the diagonal OT.

(2) Combine the resultant R_1 with force V, then construct another parallelogram to scale as in (1), above. The final resultant R_2 is similarly determined by the line SO (C, fig. 57).

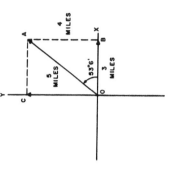

Figure 58. Horizontal and vertical components of vector.

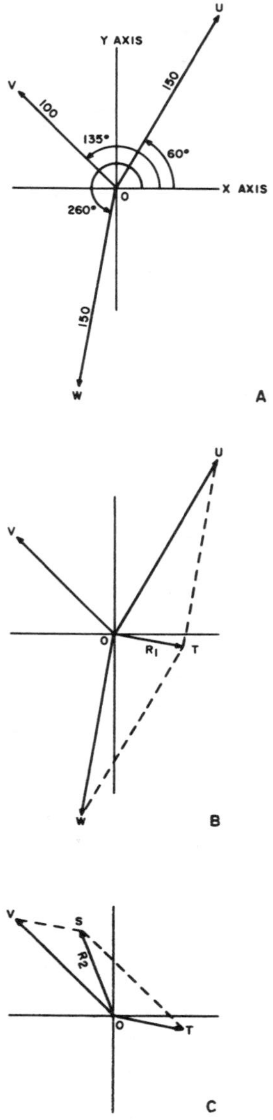

Figure 57. Resolution of three vectors.

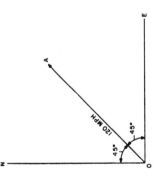

Figure 56. Adding vectors, parallelogram method.

Figure 55. The velocity of an airplane described by a vector.

61

This, then, is the resolution of all three forces U, V, and W acting on point O.

181. Components of a Vector

a. A vector may be resolved into components along any two specified directions. If the directions of the components are chosen so that they are at right angles to each other, the components are called *rectangular components*.

b. By placing the initial point of a vector at the origin of the X and Y axes, the rectangular components are readily obtained either graphically or by computation. In figure 58, a vector with a magnitude of 5 and a direction of 53° 6' is shown broken down into a horizontal compo- nent of 3 and a vertical component of 4. This is done by using the sine and cosine function as follows:

$$\sin 53° 6' = \frac{BA}{5}$$
$$.79968 = \frac{BA}{5}$$
$$BA = 5 \times .79968$$
$$= 4 \text{ (approx)}$$
$$\cos 53° 6' = \frac{OB}{5}$$
$$.60042 = \frac{OB}{5}$$
$$OB = 5 \times .60042$$
$$= 3 \text{ (approx)}$$

ANSWERS TO PROBLEMS

Paragraph 12.

a(1) $\frac{3}{5}$; .6; 60%. (2) $\frac{1}{2}$; .5; 50%. (3) $\frac{3}{8}$; .375; $37\frac{1}{2}$%. (4) $\frac{1}{4}$; .25; 25%. (5) $\frac{5}{8}$; .625; $62\frac{1}{2}$%. (6) $\frac{3}{5}$; .6; 60%. (7) $\frac{3}{10}$; .3; 30%. (8) $\frac{7}{10}$; .7; 70%. (9) $2\frac{1}{4}$; 2.25; 225%. (10) $1\frac{7}{8}$; 1.875; $187\frac{1}{2}$%. (11) $\frac{2}{25}$; .08; 8%. (12) $\frac{3}{50}$; .06; 6%. (13) $\frac{9}{50}$; .18; 18%. (14) $\frac{1}{400}$; .0025; .25%. (15) $\frac{1}{40}$; .025; $2\frac{1}{2}$%. (16) $\frac{1}{20}$; .05; 5%. (17) $\frac{1}{12}$; $.08\frac{1}{3}$ (See note be- low) $8\frac{1}{3}$%. (18) $\frac{3}{8}$; .375; $37\frac{1}{2}$% (19) $\frac{1}{20}$; 1.05; 105%. (20) $\frac{1}{25}$; .04; 4%.

Note. This mixed decimal and fractional form is often used when an unending decimal would result.

b(1) 150; (2) 50; (3) 4; (4) 900.
c(1) 150%; (2) 275%; (3) 150%; (4) 550%.
d(1) 1.64; (2) 2,496; (3) .34; (4) 4.42.
e(1) .207%; (2) .028%.
f(1) $433\frac{1}{3}$; (2) 2,500; (3) 520; (4) 200; (5) 200.

Paragraph 21.

a 336.6 pounds. b $3\frac{3}{7}$ aays. c $5.00. d $1400.00. e .372 ohm. .298 ohm; .459 ohm; .893 ohm. f 2.820 pounds; 3.776 pounds; 4.119 pounds; 2,567 pounds. g 300 rpm. h 157.5 rpm.

Paragraph 25.

a(1) 21; (2) 33; (3) 50; (4) 2.90; (5) 50.1; (6) 70.01; (7) 86.5; (8) 75.89.
b(1) 2.236; (2) 2.646; (3) 3.317; (4) 3.606; (5) 3.873; (6) 4.123.
c(1) .158 ampere; (2) .085 ampere; (3) .283 ampere; (4) 1.118 amperes.

Paragraph 42.

a(1) 17; (2) 58; (3) −21; (4) −139°; (5) −252 volts.
b(1) 251 amperes; (2) −8 volts; (3) −.6375cy; (4) −31.99ax^2; (5) 1.810x^2y.
c(1) −17.92; (2) −72; (3) $-\frac{8}{35}$; (4) .075852; (5) .0028125; (6) 120.
d(1) 9; (2) $-\frac{20}{21}$; (3) 700; (4) 250; (5) $+\frac{2}{3}$ ampere; (6) −.0025.
e(1) −4; (2) 14; (3) −25; (4) 19; (5) 11; (6) 16; (7) 44; (8) 66; (9) +2; (10) 18.

Paragraph 50.

a(1) $6a^4 - 4a^2b^2 + 4b^4$. (2) $E + 3RI + 20ZI$. (3) $w + x + 9y + 8z$.
b(1) $19ax + 17by - 9cz$. (2) $-25w - 3x + 8y + 2z$. (3) $4a^2 - 34ab + 6b^2$.
c(1) 7. (2) 1. (3) 1.
d(1) f^{10}. (2) y^{a+b}. (3) v^{2m}. (4) r^5. (5) R^{3m}. (6) r^{m+1}.
e(1) $\frac{4}{x^4}$. (2) $\frac{1}{r^3 x^4}$. (3) $\frac{1}{36^a a^{2b}}$. (4) $\frac{1}{FR}$. (5) $\frac{a^2}{8b^4}$. (6) $\frac{3E}{4FR}$.
f(1) $10a^3b - 15a^2b^2 + 35ab^3$. (2) $4a^3 + 12a^2 + 4a$. (3) $i^3 - 27$. (4) $2x^4 + 5x^2y + 4x^2y^2 + 2xy^3 - y^4$. (5) $9x^4 - 34x^2y^2$

$+ 25y^4$. (6) $\dfrac{a-c}{ca}$. (7) $\dfrac{3L - R^2}{R}$.

(8) $1 - 2a^2b + 3a^4b^3$. (9) $2z^2 + z - 1 + \dfrac{3z + 4}{z^2 - z + 3}$. (10) $4b^2 - b$.

Paragraph 61.

a(1) $5(5 + 1 - 6)$; (2) $4(2 + 1 - 8)$;
(3) $3(3 - 6 + 7)$; (4) $7r(1 - 3 + 5)$;
(5) $2(5x + 4y + 3z)$.

b(1) $49x^2y^6$; (2) $4w^{10}$; (3) $64a^4b^8$; (4) $729a^9x^3$; (5) $-27b^3z^{12}$.

c(1) 5; (2) $+8$; (3) $\pm ab^3$; (4) $\pm 6yz^2$;
(5) $\pm 10ab^5$; (6) $\pm 20a$; (7) -3; (8) $-x^3$; (9) 4; (10) $5x^4y^5z^2$.

d(1) $3(x + 2)$; (2) $5a(a + 3)$; (3) $2x(5x^2 - 7x - 1)$; (4) $3z(2ay + 3bx - 4c)$; (5) $m(m^2 + m - 5x)$; (6) $3a^3(a^2 - 2ab - b^2)$; (7) $7ry^3(1 - 2 + 3)$ or 14^3ry; (8) $2xzam(6x + 7a + 8m)$; (9) $\pi(r_1^2 + r_2^2)$; (10) $\tfrac{1}{16}cd(4c^2 - 2cd + d^2)$.

Paragraph 69.

a(1) $x = 5\tfrac{2}{5}$; (2) $x = 4$; (3) $r = 2$; (4) $x = \dfrac{-13}{16}$; (5) $t = 1$; (6) $x = 7\tfrac{3}{4}$; (7) $r = 4$; (8) $x = 1$.

b(1) 8; (2) x; (3) $3(r + s)$; (4) $3(a - s)$; (5) $(I - 6)(I - 9)$; (6) $\dfrac{8E^2I^2}{2I^2R}$; (7) $\dfrac{2f}{6rf^2c}$.

c(1) $\dfrac{rR}{rR^2}, \dfrac{r}{rR^2}, \dfrac{R^2}{rR^2}$; (2) $\dfrac{a-1}{a^2-1}, \dfrac{x(a+1)}{a^2-1}$; (3) $\dfrac{3b}{6x}, \dfrac{2c}{6x}$; (4) $\dfrac{y(y+3)}{2(y+3)}, \dfrac{y}{2(y+3)}$; (5) $\dfrac{2(c+1)}{c(c+1)}, \dfrac{3c}{c(c+1)}$; (6) $\dfrac{i}{2e-10}, \dfrac{i}{2e-10}$; (7) $\dfrac{y}{C^2-d^2}, \dfrac{z(c+d)}{C^2-d^2}$.

d(1) $\dfrac{12}{a}$; (2) $\dfrac{7s + 11}{4t}$;
(3) $\dfrac{9y^2a + 10xb}{12x^2y^3}$; (4) $\dfrac{6(z^2 - 2)}{z^4 - 5z^2 + 4}$;
(5) $\dfrac{9c^2 + 2cd - 12d^2}{12c^2d^2}$; (6) $\dfrac{2r^2 + r - 13}{r^2 + 2r - 15}$;
(7) $\dfrac{12y - 1}{4}$; (8) $\dfrac{4ab}{a^2 - b^2}$;
(9) $\dfrac{16(2 - 5q)}{25q^2}$; (10) $\dfrac{3t + 4w}{12tv^2}$;

e(1) $\dfrac{3y^2}{8}$; (2) $\dfrac{a^9}{b^6}$; (3) $\dfrac{xz}{21my}$;
(4) $\dfrac{(s - r)^2}{s^2}$; (5) $\dfrac{3}{5x}$; (6) $\dfrac{1}{a^3}$;
(7) $15z$; (8) $\dfrac{a^3}{6cd}$; (9) $\dfrac{48u}{5}$;
(10) $\dfrac{e + 3}{e + 2}$.

Paragraph 76.

a(1) 2; (2) 16; (3) $5\sqrt{2}$; (4) $\dfrac{\sqrt[5]{4}}{4}$;
(5) $3\sqrt{2x - 1}$; (6) $\dfrac{x^{2\cdot n}\sqrt{6}}{y}$; (7) x^2y;
(8) d^2e^3; (9) $\dfrac{4r^2}{s}$; (10) a^3b.

b(1) $\sqrt[3]{4}$; (2) $\sqrt[6]{a^9}\,{}^{5}4$; (3) $\sqrt[3]{6^2}$; (4) $2 \cdot \dfrac{\sqrt[3]{2f}}{\sqrt{a^2}}$;
(5) $\sqrt[5]{5\sqrt{x}}$; (6) $\sqrt[12]{a^3c^2}$; (7) $6\sqrt[3]{r}$; (8) $2b \cdot \sqrt[3]{\sqrt{a^2}}$;
(9) $\sqrt{2r_1 + 3r_2}$; (10) $3y\sqrt[8]{x}$.

c(1) $a^{\frac{1}{3}}$; (2) $(5x)^{\frac{1}{4}}$; (3) $6xd^{\frac{1}{4}}$; (4) $z^{\frac{1}{3}}$;
(5) $(3a^3b^5)^{\frac{1}{2}}$; (6) $y^3d^{\frac{1}{2}}$; (7) $8(3e)^{\frac{1}{4}}$;
(8) $9g^{\frac{1}{4}}$; (9) $3bc^{\frac{1}{4}}d^{\frac{1}{4}}$; (10) $(x - y)^{\frac{1}{4}}$.

d(1) $2\sqrt{3}$; (2) $3\sqrt{7}$; (3) $3x\sqrt{7}$;
(4) $12ab^2\sqrt{2}$; (5) $2bd\sqrt{15}$; (6) $2I\sqrt{2R}$;
(7) $9pz\sqrt{7p}$; (8) $12d^4s\sqrt{3ds}$; (9) $45a^2\sqrt{b}$; (10) $112w^4z^2y\sqrt{2xz}$.

e(1) $\dfrac{\sqrt{2}}{10}$; (2) $\dfrac{\sqrt{x}}{2x}$; (3) $\dfrac{2\sqrt{3a}}{3}$,
(5) $\dfrac{\sqrt[3]{27a^3x^2}}{3ax}$; (6) $\dfrac{\sqrt[3]{(3 - 2x)^2}}{3 - 2x}$,
(7) $\dfrac{\sqrt[3]{a(a + b)}}{a}$; (8) $\dfrac{\sqrt[3]{a^5b^2e^2}}{bc}$;
(9) $\dfrac{\sqrt[3]{s + 1}}{s + 1}$; (10) $\sqrt[5]{(i + 3)^3}$.

f(1) 10; (2) $14\sqrt{5}$; (3) $x - \dfrac{x\sqrt{3}}{2}$; (4) $\dfrac{3a\sqrt{2} + a}{2}$; (5) $(r + 1)\sqrt{rst}$; (6) $\dfrac{2y\sqrt{x^2 - y^2}}{x^2 - y^2}$; (7) $\sqrt[3]{5} + 8\sqrt{x}$; (8) $7\sqrt{a} - 6\sqrt{b}$; (9) $3\sqrt{x + y} - 4\sqrt{x - y}$; (10) $7ab\sqrt{5a}$.

g(1) $12\sqrt{10}$; (2) 18; (3) $8ab^2$; (4) $2z^3\sqrt{3z}$; (5) $2xy\sqrt{5xy}$; (6) $24pq^2\sqrt[3]{q^2b^2}$; (7) $a + b + c + 2(\sqrt{ab} + \sqrt{ac} + \sqrt{bc})$; (8) $ax\sqrt{a}\,(a + x + 1)$; (9) 8; (10) $2axy^2\sqrt[3]{2a}$.

h(1) 2; (2) 5; (3) $2\sqrt[3]{x}$; (4) $3\sqrt{zy}$; (5) $\sqrt{6} + 2$; (6) $12a^{12}\sqrt{2^3 \cdot 3^5 \cdot 5^4 \cdot a^2}$; (7) $\dfrac{c - \sqrt{7c} - 4}{c - 8}$; (8) $\sqrt{15}$; (9) $\dfrac{e^2 + f^2 + 2f\sqrt{e^2 + f^2}}{e^2}$; (10) $\dfrac{4b\sqrt{1 - 4b^2} + 1}{8b^2 - 1}$

Paragraph 79.

a(1) $j5\sqrt{3}$; (2) $j\sqrt{25}$; (3) $\dfrac{j}{3}$;
(4) $-j10x^2y^2\sqrt{x}$; (5) $\dfrac{j}{3}$;
(6) $-4xy\sqrt[3]{2x^2y^2}$.

b(1) $16 + j109$; (2) $41 - j22$; (3) $61 - j251$; (4) $44 + j10$; (5) $6 + j11$; (6) $-2 - j47$.

c(1) $779 - j371$; (2) $59 + j114$; (3) $-22 + j15$; (4) $155 - j61$; (5) $169 + j23$; (6) $9 - j8$.

d(1) $-55 + j46$; (2) $6 - 6\sqrt{6} + j(6\sqrt{2} + 6\sqrt{3})$; (3) 13; (4) $-5 - j12$; (5) $-j8$; (6) $46 - j48$; (7) $f^2 + j2fg - g^2$; (8) $I^2 + E^2$; (9) $-68 - j239$; (10) $71 - j17$.

e(1) $\dfrac{3}{13} - j\dfrac{2}{13}$; (2) $1 - j6$; (3) $-\dfrac{6}{25} + j\dfrac{17}{25}$; (4) $1 + j2$; (5) $\dfrac{x^2 + j2xy - y^2}{x^2 + y^2}$; (6) $2(1 - j2)$; (7) $\dfrac{3(1 + j)}{2}$; (8) $\dfrac{I^2 + j2IE - E^2}{I^2 + E^2}$; (9) $\dfrac{38 + j34}{65}$; (10) $\dfrac{I^2 + j2IE - E^2}{I^2 + E^2}$.

Paragraph 86.

a(1) 3; (2) 2; (3) 85; (4) 3; (5) 1;
(6) $x = -5, y = 8$; (7) $a = 3, b = 1$;
(8) $x = 3, y = 4$; (9) $m = 3, n = 5$;
(10) $r = 8, s = 1$.

b(1) $d = \dfrac{Wh}{F}$. (2) $g = \dfrac{v^2 - v_0^2}{2h}$.
(3) $a = \dfrac{Fg}{w}$. (4) $N = \dfrac{2.534H}{D^2}$. (5) $l = \dfrac{10^8F}{22.5BI}$.

c(1) 15; (2) 0; (3) $\dfrac{10}{3}$; (4) 4; (5) $\dfrac{28}{9}$;
(6) $\dfrac{12}{119}$; (7) $-2\dfrac{12}{25}$; (8) 8; (9) $\dfrac{40}{109}$;
(10) $-\dfrac{1}{19}$.

d(1) $x = 4, y = 5$; (2) $a = 4.95, b = 2.62$
(3) $x = 4, y = 7$; (4) $x = -2, y = -4$;
(5) $x = -3, y = 1$; (6) $I = 13, Z = 17$;
(7) $x = 4, y = \dfrac{1}{2}$; (8) $a = 6, b = -4$;
(9) $x = 5, y = -1$; (10) $r = \dfrac{(a + b)}{2}$;
$s = \dfrac{(a - b)}{2}$.

e(1) 1 volt; (2) R — 20 ohms; (3) 110 volts; (4) 75 ohms; (5) 100 milliamperes, 80 milliamperes, 60 milliamperes; (6) 5.5 amperes.

Paragraph 94.

a(1) $0, -\dfrac{3}{2}$; (2) 0, 4; (3) 0, -3; (4) 0, -2; (5) ± 8; (6) ± 3; (7) ± 3; (8) ± 4; (9) 7, -6; (10) 1, 12.

b(1) $\dfrac{-3 \pm \sqrt{13}}{2}$; (2) $-3 \pm \sqrt{19}$; (3) $2 \pm \sqrt{3}$; (4) $-2 \pm \dfrac{\sqrt{22}}{2}$; (5) $\dfrac{1}{2} \pm \dfrac{\sqrt{14}}{4}$; (6) $-\dfrac{5}{3} \pm \dfrac{2\sqrt{10}}{3}$; (7) $-1, 3$; (8) $-1 \pm \dfrac{\sqrt{6}}{2}$; (9) $1 \pm \sqrt{6}$; (10) $\dfrac{1}{2} \pm \dfrac{\sqrt{5}}{2}$

$c(1)$ —1; (2)—$\frac{3}{4}$, $\frac{2}{3}$; (3) $\dfrac{-5\pm\sqrt{13}}{6}$;
(4)$-\frac{3}{2}$, $\frac{4}{3}$; (5) —3, 1; (6)-1, $\frac{5}{3}$;
(7) $\pm\sqrt{2}$; (8) $\pm\sqrt{19}$; (9) —1, 2;
(10)$\dfrac{-5\pm\sqrt{7}}{3}$

Paragraph 111.
$a(1)$ 1,613 × 10³; (2) 500 × 10³, or 5 × 10⁵; (3) 6,166 × 10⁻⁸.
$b(1)$ 3,109 × 10²; (2) 19 × 10⁻⁶; (3) 4,492 × 10⁻⁹.
$c(1)$ 892 × 10⁶; (2) 2,464 × 10⁻², or 24.64; (3) 3,168 × 10⁻¹¹; (4) 14,640.
$d(1)$ 167; (2) 1,608 ×10⁸ (3) 107; (4) 33 × 10⁻⁵.
$e(1)$ 4 × 10², or 400; (2) 19 × 10⁻³; (3) 27 × 10⁻⁹; (4) 9 × 10², or 900.

Paragraph 127.
$a(1)$ 2.8949; (2) 0.5527; (3) 8.5378-10; (4) 6.6776-10; (5) 1.6955; (6) 2.4370; (7) 2.8809; (8) 0.8593; (9) 7.9946-10; (10) 5.7205-10.
$b(1)$70,097 (2) 271; (3) .351; (4) .000676; (5) 3.99; (6) 370.67; (7) .0002718; (8) 500,500; (9) 1.5915; (10) .00003445.
$c(1)$ 164.2; (2)39,990(3) 1,376; (4) .006764; (5) 5,710.
$d(1)$ .4983; (2) .3874; (3) .3984; (4) .7487; (5) .2437.
$e(1)$ .0000007372; (2) 51.46; (3) 3.47; (4) 19.43; (5) 783; (6) .2367; (7) 5.343; (8) 87.74; (9) 1.55; (10) .09456.
$f(1)$ 2.298; (2) 11.77; (3) 24.43; (4) 33.37 (5) .4509; (6) .4725; (7) .04088; (8) .6153; (9) .0576; (10) .35367.

Paragraph 142.
a 96 square inches. b 36 square inches. c 25 square inches. d 15 square inches. e 14.422 square inches. f 5.657 square inches. g (1) Parallelogram, $A = bh$, 120 square inches; (2) Triangle, $A = \dfrac{bh}{2}$ 4.025 square inches; (3) Circle, $A = \pi r^2$, 314 square centimeters; $C = \pi D$, 62.8 centimeters; (4) Trapezoid, $A = \dfrac{B+b}{2}$ h, A = 60 square inches. $h(1)$ 3 inches; (2) 4$\frac{1}{2}$ inches; (3) 8.8 inches; (4) 5 inches. i 78.5 square inches. j 100 feet. k 82.5 square feet. l 48.496 inches.

Paragraph 153.
$a(1)$ c = 8.603. (2) a = 6.08. (3) b = 39.5. (4) $c = b\sqrt{10}$. (5) $b = m^2 - 1$.
$b(1)$ $\sin A = \dfrac{4}{7}$, $\cos A = \dfrac{\sqrt{33}}{7}$, $\tan A = \dfrac{4}{\sqrt{33}}$, $\cot A = \dfrac{\sqrt{33}}{4}$, $\sec A = \dfrac{7}{33}\sqrt{33}$, $\csc A = \dfrac{7}{4}$.
(2) $\sin A = \dfrac{2}{13}\sqrt{13}$, $\cos A = \dfrac{3}{13}\sqrt{13}$, $\tan A = \dfrac{2}{3}$, $\cot A = \dfrac{3}{2}$, $\sec A = \dfrac{\sqrt{13}}{3}$, $\csc A = \dfrac{\sqrt{13}}{2}$
(3) $\sin A = \dfrac{1}{2}$, $\cos A = \dfrac{\sqrt{3}}{2}$, $\tan A = \dfrac{\sqrt{3}}{3}$, $\cot A = \sqrt{3}$, $\sec A = \dfrac{2}{3}\sqrt{3}$, $\csc A = 2$.
(4) $\sin A = \dfrac{1}{2.4}$, $\cos A = \dfrac{1.09}{1.2}$, $\tan A = \dfrac{1.2}{1.09}$, $\csc A = \dfrac{1}{2.18}$, $\cot A = 2.18$, $\sec A = 2.18$, 2.4.
(5) $\sin A = y\dfrac{\sqrt{y^2+1}}{y^2+1}$, $\cos A = \dfrac{\sqrt{y^2+1}}{y^2+1}$, $\tan A = y$, $\cot A = \dfrac{1}{y}$, $\sec A = \sqrt{y^2+1}$, $\csc A = \dfrac{\sqrt{y^2+1}}{y}$.

(6) $\sin A = \dfrac{\sqrt{55}}{8}$, $\cos A = \dfrac{3}{8}$, $\tan A = \dfrac{\sqrt{55}}{3}$, $\cot A = \dfrac{3\sqrt{55}}{55}$, $\sec A = 2\frac{2}{3}$, $\csc A = \dfrac{8\sqrt{55}}{55}$ $A = \dfrac{8\sqrt{55}}{55}$

$c(1)$ a = 17, b = 29.4, c = 34. (2) a = 9, b = 12, c = 15. (3) a = 12, b = 16, c = 20. (4) a = 17.5, b = 10$\sqrt{11}$, c = 37.5. (5) a = 10, b = 6, c = 2$\sqrt{34}$. (6) a = 37.08, b = 18.4, c = 41.4.
$d(1)$ b = 10$\sqrt{3}$, c = 20. (2) a = 7, c = 7$\sqrt{2}$. (3) a = 4$\sqrt{3}$, b = 4. (4) b = 3$\sqrt{3}$, c = 6$\sqrt{3}$. (5) a = 12.5, b = 12.5$\sqrt{3}$.

Paragraph 164.
$a(1)$ .02618, .99966, .02619, 38.1885. (2) .26584, .96402, .27576, 3.62636. (3) .53238, .84650, .62892, 1.59002. (4) .59693, .80230, .74402, 1.34405. (5) .70690, .70731, .99942, 1.00058. (6) .70706, .70716, .99986, 1.00014. (7) .57649, .81710, .70553, 1.41737. (8) .81370, .58129, 1.39982, .71438. (9) .74811, .66357, 1.12740, .88700. (10) .92429, .38169, 2.42158, .41295.
$b(1)$ 14° 54' 51''; (2) 66° 35' 51''; (3) 19° 56' 54''; (4) 25° 17' 5''; (5) 40° 23' 35''; (6) 68° 45' 2''; (7) 22° 11' 47''; (8) 34° 5' 19''; (9) 52° 13' 2''; (10) 51° 29' 49''.
$c(1)$ 44° 43' 29''; (2) 10.29; (3)32.5(4) 19.76; (5) 12.4; (6) 54° 18' 52.5''; (7) 33.69; (8) 16.5; (9) 36° 28' 9''; (10) 128.3; (11)30.9(12) 29° 3' 15''.
$d(1)$ 52.28 feet; (2) 80.027 feet; (3) 47.63 feet, 8.69 feet high; (4) 3,149 feet; (5) 11.734 feet; (6) 91.77 feet; (7) 206 feet; (8) 3,578 feet; (9) 16,647 feet (3.153 miles); (10) 82.12 feet; (11) 1.414 inches each; (12) side opposite 60° ∠5.196 inches, side opposite 30° ∠ 3 inches.

Paragraph 173.
a C = 62° 16' 38'', a = 14.59. b B = 69° 58'. c A = 23° 33' 22'', B = 45° 16' 31'', C = 111° 10' 7''. d A = 81° 31' 41'', B = 41° 7' 29''. e 240 square inches. f 97.880 square feet. g 55.424 square inches. h A = 32° 33' 45'', B = 84° 36' 15'', c = 15.95 inches.

Paragraph 176.
$a(1)$ .4 radian; (2) 4 radians; (3) 8 radians; (4) 2.78 radians.
$b(1)$ 35 inches; (2) 17.6 feet; (3) 18.9 miles; (4) .00198 inch.
$c(1)$ .52 radian; (2) 4.6 radians; (3) 2.77 radians, (4) 5.89 radians.
$d(1)$ 45° 50' 11.8''; (2) 1432° 23' 40.2''; (3) 197° 40' 13.44''; (4) 540°.
$e(1)$ $\pi/6$; (2) $\pi/3$; (3) $5\pi/4$; (4) 4π.

FORMULAS IN TRIGONOMETRY

1. $S = R\theta$, where S = arc length, R = radius, and θ = central angle in radians

2. $A = \frac{1}{2}R^2\theta$, where A = area of a sector, R = radius, and θ = central angle in radians

3. Linear speed = (radius)(angular speed)
   Angular speed = radians per unit time

4. In any right triangle, $a^2+b^2 = c^2$, where c = hypotenuse.

5. $\text{Cotangent}^2\theta + 1 = \text{Cosecant}^2\theta$

6. $\text{Sine}^2\theta + \text{Cosine}^2\theta = 1$

7. $\text{Tangent}(\alpha+\beta) = \dfrac{(\text{tangent}\,\alpha + \text{tangent}\,\beta)}{1 - (\text{tangent}\,\alpha)(\text{tangent}\,\beta)}$

8. $\text{Cosine}(\alpha+\beta) = (\text{Cosine}\,\alpha)(\text{Cosine}\,\beta) - (\text{Sine}\,\alpha)(\text{Sine}\,\beta)$

9. $\text{Cosine } 2\theta = 2\text{cosine}^2\theta - 1$.

10. $\text{Tangent}^2\dfrac{\alpha}{2} = (\dfrac{1-\text{Cosine}\,\alpha}{1+\text{Cosine}\,\alpha})$

11. In any triangle, $\dfrac{\text{sine } \alpha}{\text{side opposite } \alpha} = \dfrac{\text{sine } \beta}{\text{side opposite } \beta}$

12. In any triangle with sides a,b,c, $c^2 = a^2+b^2 - 2ab \text{ cosine } \angle c$

13. In any triangle with sides a,b,c, the area of the triangle = $\sqrt{s(s-a)(s-b)(s-c)}$, where $s = \frac{1}{2}(a+b+c)$.

ANSWER SHEET

TEST NO. _____ PART _____ TITLE OF POSITION _____

(AS GIVEN IN EXAMINATION ANNOUNCEMENT - INCLUDE OPTION, IF ANY)

PLACE OF EXAMINATION _____ DATE ____ _____

(CITY OR TOWN) (STATE)

RATING

USE THE SPECIAL PENCIL. MAKE GLOSSY BLACK MARKS.

	A	B	C	D	E			A	B	C	D	E			A	B	C	D	E			A	B	C	D	E			A	B	C	D	E
1						26							51							76							101						
2						27							52							77							102						
3						28							53							78							103						
4						29							54							79							104						
5						30							55							80							105						
6						31							56							81							106						
7						32							57							82							107						
8						33							58							83							108						
9						34							59							84							109						
10						35							60							85							110						

Make only ONE mark for each answer.   Additional and stray marks may be
counted as mistakes.   In making corrections, erase errors COMPLETELY.

	A	B	C	D	E			A	B	C	D	E			A	B	C	D	E			A	B	C	D	E			A	B	C	D	E
11						36							61							86							111						
12						37							62							87							112						
13						38							63							88							113						
14						39							64							89							114						
15						40							65							90							115						
16						41							66							91							116						
17						42							67							92							117						
18						43							68							93							118						
19						44							69							94							119						
20						45							70							95							120						
21						46							71							96							121						
22						47							72							97							122						
23						48							73							98							123						
24						49							74							99							124						
25						50							75							100							125						

ANSWER SHEET

TEST NO. _____ PART _____ TITLE OF POSITION _____

(AS GIVEN IN EXAMINATION ANNOUNCEMENT - INCLUDE OPTION, IF ANY)

PLACE OF EXAMINATION _____ DATE_____

(CITY OR TOWN)   (STATE)

RATING

USE THE SPECIAL PENCIL. MAKE GLOSSY BLACK MARKS.

	A B C D E		A B C D E		A B C D E		A B C D E		A B C D E
1	⫶⫶⫶⫶⫶	26	⫶⫶⫶⫶⫶	51	⫶⫶⫶⫶⫶	76	⫶⫶⫶⫶⫶	101	⫶⫶⫶⫶⫶
2	⫶⫶⫶⫶⫶	27	⫶⫶⫶⫶⫶	52	⫶⫶⫶⫶⫶	77	⫶⫶⫶⫶⫶	102	⫶⫶⫶⫶⫶
3	⫶⫶⫶⫶⫶	28	⫶⫶⫶⫶⫶	53	⫶⫶⫶⫶⫶	78	⫶⫶⫶⫶⫶	103	⫶⫶⫶⫶⫶
4	⫶⫶⫶⫶⫶	29	⫶⫶⫶⫶⫶	54	⫶⫶⫶⫶⫶	79	⫶⫶⫶⫶⫶	104	⫶⫶⫶⫶⫶
5	⫶⫶⫶⫶⫶	30	⫶⫶⫶⫶⫶	55	⫶⫶⫶⫶⫶	80	⫶⫶⫶⫶⫶	105	⫶⫶⫶⫶⫶
6	⫶⫶⫶⫶⫶	31	⫶⫶⫶⫶⫶	56	⫶⫶⫶⫶⫶	81	⫶⫶⫶⫶⫶	106	⫶⫶⫶⫶⫶
7	⫶⫶⫶⫶⫶	32	⫶⫶⫶⫶⫶	57	⫶⫶⫶⫶⫶	82	⫶⫶⫶⫶⫶	107	⫶⫶⫶⫶⫶
8	⫶⫶⫶⫶⫶	33	⫶⫶⫶⫶⫶	58	⫶⫶⫶⫶⫶	83	⫶⫶⫶⫶⫶	108	⫶⫶⫶⫶⫶
9	⫶⫶⫶⫶⫶	34	⫶⫶⫶⫶⫶	59	⫶⫶⫶⫶⫶	84	⫶⫶⫶⫶⫶	109	⫶⫶⫶⫶⫶
10	⫶⫶⫶⫶⫶	35	⫶⫶⫶⫶⫶	60	⫶⫶⫶⫶⫶	85	⫶⫶⫶⫶⫶	110	⫶⫶⫶⫶⫶

Make only ONE mark for each answer. Additional and stray marks may be counted as mistakes. In making corrections, erase errors COMPLETELY.

	A B C D E		A B C D E		A B C D E		A B C D E		A B C D E
11	⫶⫶⫶⫶⫶	36	⫶⫶⫶⫶⫶	61	⫶⫶⫶⫶⫶	86	⫶⫶⫶⫶⫶	111	⫶⫶⫶⫶⫶
12	⫶⫶⫶⫶⫶	37	⫶⫶⫶⫶⫶	62	⫶⫶⫶⫶⫶	87	⫶⫶⫶⫶⫶	112	⫶⫶⫶⫶⫶
13	⫶⫶⫶⫶⫶	38	⫶⫶⫶⫶⫶	63	⫶⫶⫶⫶⫶	88	⫶⫶⫶⫶⫶	113	⫶⫶⫶⫶⫶
14	⫶⫶⫶⫶⫶	39	⫶⫶⫶⫶⫶	64	⫶⫶⫶⫶⫶	89	⫶⫶⫶⫶⫶	114	⫶⫶⫶⫶⫶
15	⫶⫶⫶⫶⫶	40	⫶⫶⫶⫶⫶	65	⫶⫶⫶⫶⫶	90	⫶⫶⫶⫶⫶	115	⫶⫶⫶⫶⫶
16	⫶⫶⫶⫶⫶	41	⫶⫶⫶⫶⫶	66	⫶⫶⫶⫶⫶	91	⫶⫶⫶⫶⫶	116	⫶⫶⫶⫶⫶
17	⫶⫶⫶⫶⫶	42	⫶⫶⫶⫶⫶	67	⫶⫶⫶⫶⫶	92	⫶⫶⫶⫶⫶	117	⫶⫶⫶⫶⫶
18	⫶⫶⫶⫶⫶	43	⫶⫶⫶⫶⫶	68	⫶⫶⫶⫶⫶	93	⫶⫶⫶⫶⫶	118	⫶⫶⫶⫶⫶
19	⫶⫶⫶⫶⫶	44	⫶⫶⫶⫶⫶	69	⫶⫶⫶⫶⫶	94	⫶⫶⫶⫶⫶	119	⫶⫶⫶⫶⫶
20	⫶⫶⫶⫶⫶	45	⫶⫶⫶⫶⫶	70	⫶⫶⫶⫶⫶	95	⫶⫶⫶⫶⫶	120	⫶⫶⫶⫶⫶
21	⫶⫶⫶⫶⫶	46	⫶⫶⫶⫶⫶	71	⫶⫶⫶⫶⫶	96	⫶⫶⫶⫶⫶	121	⫶⫶⫶⫶⫶
22	⫶⫶⫶⫶⫶	47	⫶⫶⫶⫶⫶	72	⫶⫶⫶⫶⫶	97	⫶⫶⫶⫶⫶	122	⫶⫶⫶⫶⫶
23	⫶⫶⫶⫶⫶	48	⫶⫶⫶⫶⫶	73	⫶⫶⫶⫶⫶	98	⫶⫶⫶⫶⫶	123	⫶⫶⫶⫶⫶
24	⫶⫶⫶⫶⫶	49	⫶⫶⫶⫶⫶	74	⫶⫶⫶⫶⫶	99	⫶⫶⫶⫶⫶	124	⫶⫶⫶⫶⫶
25	⫶⫶⫶⫶⫶	50	⫶⫶⫶⫶⫶	75	⫶⫶⫶⫶⫶	100	⫶⫶⫶⫶⫶	125	⫶⫶⫶⫶⫶